ED HOWE: Country Town Philosopher

THE UNIVERSITY PRESS OF KANSAS
Lawrence and London

ED HOWE:

Country Town Philosopher

by Calder M. Pickett

Library of Congress Card Catalog Number: 68-25821
Printed in the U.S.A.

To NOLA, CAROLYN, and KATHY,
who never seemed to resent the fact that for five years an old Kansas editor had been the fifth member of our family

PREFACE

This is a kind of biography of the Atchison, Kansas, editor, Edgar Watson Howe. "Kind of biography" because I found early in my research into the man's life that the conventional data—letters, manuscripts, and the like—were not in great quantity. About this I complain frequently, I am afraid, but this proved to be a real problem. So, without the little things that provide intimate details about a person's life I learned to lean on something else–the man's writings. And I read about as much as anyone could physically and psychologically manage—his newspaper, his monthly, his books, his diatribes.

I got started on Ed Howe when I realized that no standard biography of him had been written, just the charming but frustrating autobiography that he called *Plain People*. I also got started not liking him much, regarding him as a weird curiosity. I wound up with a considerable affection for him, even knowing that were he living today our votes would cancel each other out here in Kansas. And in my years with Ed Howe I wound up a terrible bore, to my family, my colleagues, my students, people who must have come to think that I could tell an Ed Howe story to cover all occasions. My students, especially, have had to suffer by getting an overdose of Howe in History of American Journalism and some of them having to read *The Story of a Country Town* in the senior seminar in American Studies.

So I thank my students, and I thank my

colleagues, for putting up with me and Ed Howe. I especially thank my wife, Nola, who read my manuscript and helped me catch several blunders that would have looked pretty silly in print.

And there are other people, too, that I want to mention:

The late Miss Adelaide Howe, a lovely little woman who was Ed Howe's niece and housekeeper and lived in the family home in Atchison and dug into her recollections to help me tell about "Uncle Ed."

Other members of the Howe family, notably James Howe of Walnut Creek, California, Howe's only surviving child.

Paul Allingham and the staff of *The Atchison Globe,* who must have tired of seeing me arrive Thursday mornings in 1964 to read *The Globe* files on microfilm.

Nyle Miller, secretary of the Kansas State Historical Society, who read my manuscript carefully and critically and made many marginal notations and who also gave me help and advice in my research.

Others of the staff of the Historical Society, friendly and helpful people who work in one of the remarkable historical institutions of the land.

The library staff of the University of Kansas, especially the people in Special Collections, who turned over books and files and scrapbooks, and the library directors, who gave me a study where I could read and write and type in telephone-free seclusion.

Professor George Anderson, chairman of the University of Kansas Department of History, who let me use his files of *The Globe* (you could have tracked me across the campus by following the trail of crumbling bits of 1890s-vintage newsprint falling from the files I packed from his study in Hoch Auditorium to my office in Flint Hall).

Professor Philip Mangelsdorf of the University of Arizona, a former Atchison resident who has written extensively on Ed Howe and who read my manuscript and made many suggestions—a good many of which I considered carefully.

Professor S. J. Sackett of Fort Hays Kansas State College, who gave me assistance.

Robert Rollins and William McCorkle, both of the *Kansas City Star,* who were doing research on the *Star* and sent me notations they found about Howe and *The Globe.*

Robert Harwi, a former resident of Atchison and an ex-*Star* man, too, who let me use a paper he had written on *The Globe.*

William McReynolds of the University of Texas, whose thesis on Gene Howe was helpful.

William J. Argersinger, associate dean of faculties for research at the University of Kansas, who gave me encouragement and help in obtaining financial assistance, paved the way for the generous research grant awarded by the

University in 1964-65, and even sat down a few times and tried to read—as he put it—*The Story of a Country Town.*

Former Dean Burton W. Marvin and Dean Warren K. Agee of the William Allen White School of Journalism, University of Kansas.

Professor Edwin Emery of the School of Journalism, University of Minnesota, my thesis adviser and friend for many years.

The late Professor Warren Price of the University of Oregon, who seemed to me one of the great historians of American journalism.

Bernard W. Bowron and Mary Turpie of the Program in American Studies, University of Minnesota, who inspired me in my student days.

The University Press of Kansas, especially John P. Dessauer, director, and Mrs. Yvonne Willingham, who was the editor of my manuscript.

Calder M. Pickett

Lawrence, Kansas
January 1968

CONTENTS

4
THE EDITOR'S VIEWS IN THE *GLOBE* YEARS

5
LAST YEARS ON *THE GLOBE*

6
E. W. HOWE'S MONTHLY

Illustrations

ED HOWE: Country Town Philosopher

1

THE HERITAGE OF AN EDITOR

Howe and Irwin

His name was Edgar Watson Howe, a name quite impressive in the nineteenth century, when great writers bore ostentatious names like Ralph Waldo Emerson or Henry Wadsworth Longfellow or William Dean Howells. Yet he was really just Ed Howe, editor of a small-town newspaper in Kansas; Ed Howe, homely philosopher labeled "The Sage of Potato Hill."

Not the kind of man whose editorial trumpetings set men to marching, or altered the courses of political campaigns, or stimulated governmental executives to change policies. Not an imposing person—thin, somewhat bony, pale blue eyes, not unhandsome but quiet, generally unimpressive in appearance. Ascetic, to fit the Spartan manner of life he followed—and advocated—most of his days; a man who looked as though he had never eaten well. Sometimes taciturn, a kind of Calvin Coolidge, glum and with little to say, except on his editorial page. Yet charming sometimes, too, and talkative, and gallant to the women he was believed to loathe.

Ed Howe revealed much about himself as a man, more than many men reveal, but what he was like as a boy comes through only skimpily in his writings, and there are no photographs from the early years. As boy and man, he was marked, if not marred, by his father, and unfortunately he had some of his father's least lovable characteristics—an intolerance on some subjects and a puritanical approach to the behavior of other people. In his moods he went from high to low and back again, and in so doing he terrified his family, especially his wife, and some of his employees. He also drew from the other heritage in his family, for there was a kindliness in him that probably came from his mother. And for Ed Howe, more than for certain other celebrated editors, the family, the simple relationships of family life, remained paramount throughout his life. Right from the beginning it was family, and family ties—frequently painful ones—that marked this boy Edgar Watson Howe.

Other newspaper editors of Ed Howe's time concerned themselves with politics, with national affairs, with local crusading, but Ed Howe always found people, and their contrary behavior, most important and most interesting. He was influenced first, and most, by his father; then by his beloved half-brother, Jim. He wrote cynical and bitter words about the women he knew, but many women obviously influenced him—his browbeaten mother, his own wife.

He never knew much about his parents, or his relatives, and what he did know was vague. He kept practically no records, no diary, few letters, no family documents to speak of. He *thought* he knew things; he *thought* he remembered things. He "recollected" that a certain event occurred at a certain time, but it would take the most genealogically dedicated scholar to construct family tables for the Howe family.

He didn't know for sure where his father, Henry Howe, was born, though he thought it was Pennsylvania or Ohio. He knew that his father had brothers in Ohio, and he believed that that was where the family originated. He remembered that his father often talked "Dutch" to amuse the neighbors. Whatever the father's background, it was a plain one. The Howe people were farmers, and the father was a farmer. He was also a school teacher and a Methodist circuit rider. Mid-nineteenth century years were drifting years for many Americans, and Henry Howe, early in his life, moved to Indiana, where he married a woman named Roby (and who, Ed Howe thought, may have been a widow with one child). She died six or seven years later (there is always such vagueness in the Howe reminiscences), and he then married Elizabeth Irwin, who had two children from an earlier marriage—Jim and Sarah Jane.[1]

Religion colored his parents' lives, even though Elizabeth Irwin did not come from a religious family: her father, Charles Irwin, remembered as a tall, good-looking man, was known to Ed Howe only as a shingle maker. Henry Howe was deeply, if not fanatically, religious, a member, possibly the head, of the "Holiness Association" in Indiana—a "shouting" kind of religion.

There was gossip about Henry Howe's second marriage: an old Methodist preacher in Fairview, Missouri, had told the story that Henry's second marriage came within a few months of the death of the first wife. Such gossip disturbed young Ed Howe. There were also stories of Henry's sister, Susan, who worked in a bureau in Washington, and of another relative reported to be a coachman. There were no addresses of relatives among family records. There were no keepsakes, no heirlooms.

When Edgar Watson Howe died in 1937, newspaper reports said he was born May 3, 1854, in Treaty, Indiana, at a farm site, at least, called Treaty. Not until late in life did Howe learn that he really was born in 1853. The proof was in a family Bible shown to him by his brother Bruce—this one time he believed something he found in the Bible. Ed believed that the "Watson" in his name came from *Watson's Commentaries,* an exposition of the Bible that the Howes kept in their home. He didn't know where the "Edgar" came from, but he concluded that if one must go through life as "Ed" it was better that the "Ed" be from "Edgar" than from "Edward" or "Edwin." Besides the older half-brother and half-sister there were a younger sister, Minnie, and three younger brothers, Bruce, Charley, and one whose name Ed Howe never recorded.

Treaty, Indiana, was near Wabash, and in 1901, while traveling by train to Buffalo, Ed Howe passed near Wabash. That caused him to reflect on how his father had ruined his health while clearing his Indiana farm of timber. The elder Howe was a hard worker, and he hated the coming of night, because it meant he would have to go into the house, and just loiter. He was a wanderer himself, yet he had no use for a man who couldn't stay in one place. When Ed was small his father took him to a phrenologist, who felt the bumps on the boy's head and concluded that he would never remain long in one place.

That must have been after the family settled in Missouri, though as usual Howe provided no dates. He did know that when he was three years old (the biographies say 1857, but it may have been 1856) the family journeyed by wagon from Indiana to Harrison County, Missouri, in the northwest corner of the state. He later conjectured that the trip was over the same route he traveled by rail in one night, and he was sure the wagons crossed the Mississippi River at Hannibal. He had no memories of the family talking about the trip, but he remembered looking out the window of the Indiana farmhouse and seeing a covered wagon standing in the yard. There were loose horses and cattle to drive, and Howe remembered that one of the horses on the family wagon was known as old Sam, a big sorrel, a "free horse," one that was willing to work himself to death. Sam's mate, Dollie, unfortunately was the kind willing to let Sam do just that. One day the wagon train encountered a railroad train, and Howe remembered all the menfolk in the party hanging on to the frightened Sam, who was trying to run away.

That was one story, then, that Ed Howe recalled. He wrote about the trip west in 1901, and his recollections were skimpy—the skitterish horse, the train. By the early twenties, when he wrote about the trip for the *Saturday Evening Post,* his memories—or his imagination—had improved. There was a camp at the home of one Aaron Fair, who then joined the party. There were many other people heading west. There were the river and the steamboat at the Mississippi crossing, where the horse Sam acted up again, and where young Ed, according to his father's later account, was delighted at the steam ferry and jumped up and down. There were prayer meetings every night, almost revivals, at which the women did most of the shouting. Howe "remembered" one of their songs:

> Our camp's in the wilderness a few days,
> And then we're going home,
> And we'll hail our Saviour there,
> When we arrive at home.
> Oh, won't that be delightful,
> When we arrive at home?

In the evenings, when the singing was over, the women sat around and smoked their clay pipes, which the children were told helped relieve neuralgia. Young Ed (a likely story) smoked his aunt's pipe, and his father gave him what became routine in his boyhood—a whaling. Whippings were common in the camp; Ed remembered how a boy named Joe Adams fought back when his father tried to whip him, and how the camp gossiped about it. In the party there was a man named Old Lee, a good hunter, who one Sunday brought four turkeys back to camp. Ed had been Old Lee's hunting companion, and someone told Henry Howe, who then made Ed eat side pork while the rest of camp ate turkey.

All this happened to a boy of three or four. This boy also saw a party of Indians nearby; and he had occasion to go into a saloon, which he didn't like. And there was a camp scandal: a man named Lang ran off with a woman named Mrs. Burt, and when the two were brought back to camp, someone struck Lang. It may have been Henry Howe; that was Ed's belief. There was a light-fingered boy named Nate Benton in the party, who visited stores in the towns and came back with various loot. (Ed Howe said that Benton called on him forty years afterward in a hotel where he was staying, and when Benton left, a handkerchief was missing.) Ed remembered the food on the trip, mainly pork in some form, cured in Indiana, and the corn bread. It was the vanishing frontier through which he traveled, with rolling country and woods at the end of the trip. And when Howe wrote about it in the twenties he said: "A strong impression in my mind as I write is the change in the world since the middle 50's. I have seen wild pigeons and buffalo. . . . There is no such thing in 1924 as I saw when traveling to the West in a covered wagon, with miles and miles of good land along the way, and only an occasional cabin."[2]

The Farm and the Country Town

Harrison County, Missouri, is near the Iowa border. Its county seat is, and was in Howe's youth, Bethany, but it was at a settlement called Fairview—a barren, treeless area, a church and the other farms—that the Howes made their home. And there most of Howe's recollections began. Henry Howe built a church-school near the home, and there he preached without charge, serving as the only pastor the church ever had. He also preached on the circuit, Ed climbing onto the horse and riding behind his father as he went forth to spread the gospel through the countryside. This meant leaving home Saturday night and being gone all day Sunday, returning in time for the week's work on Monday. It was no life for a boy like young Ed Howe. He and his father had to stay in homes while riding the circuit, and he would watch the women cook in their fireplaces with hanging pots called "spiders." The Howes had to undress in the presence of the family, "and my first recollection of politeness is of parents and children steadily gazing into the fireplace while we were exposed."[3]

There were camp meetings, which attracted large crowds, men gathering on the fringes to fight and argue and use rough language and sell beer and whiskey. The camp meetings and the meeting-house routine, rather than inspiring Ed, kept him from the church. He never joined, even though other children became members when quite young. Nor was he invited to; he was puzzled about this, but he laid the matter to his being an unbeliever from boyhood. Ed liked to mock the rather primitive religion. He remembered that his brother Jim, after joining the church, moaned in bed that night, because of his sins, and that he joked him about it. Soon the boys were fighting, and fortunately Henry Howe was out of the house, for only Mrs. Howe was there to catch Ed at his sacrilege. She laughed, and soon Jim laughed, and the matter was forgotten. Howe said that many years afterward Jim said that if he went "to the bad place, I would be responsible, as he once started right, and that I made such fun of him that he again became a sinner." Ed mocked not only Jim: he watched people at his father's services, people acting "queer," in his opinion, and he imitated them in private, to the amusement of his mother, brothers and sisters, and other children, but never his father, who would have given Ed a beating had he caught him making fun of the godly.

One of Howe's reminiscences provides a vivid picture of camp meeting life in the days before the Civil War. In 1859 he went with his father into Iowa, and he remembered hearing that when you crossed the line into Iowa you would know it because the farms would be better kept and the land worth more. On the way he saw a flock of wild turkeys, and prairie chickens and quail, and when he and his father arrived it was dark and the evening service was already in session. It was the biggest crowd he had ever seen. The grounds were lighted by platforms five feet high and five feet square, each platform raised by means of four forked posts, and on each a floor of sticks, covered with dirt and with fires maintained in the dirt. A large stand had been built for the preachers, and people were seated in front, on benches made by laying planks across strings of logs. An aisle led to the pulpit, men on the right, women on the left, sinners on the fringes—"doubters, scoffers, free thinkers, who seem to have existed in that day as in this." Iowa was comfortable country for the elder Howe: he was known both as a preacher and as a man who had been arrested because he said the Bible did not sanction slavery. So he was given a seat on the platform and assisted in the preaching and singing, for Henry Howe had a good voice and frequently used his talent in church services at home and on the circuit. Ed also had a good singing voice, and that may be why Henry took his son with him. Ed thought his companionship meant little to his father, but that his father thought the two singing together could help to move congregations. "My father was not a shouter," said Howe, "but he knew how to make others shout."[4]

Even though Henry Howe was a prosperous and important man in the neighborhood, with much wild land and extensive farming operations, he was a man of independent thought, an abolitionist and a Methodist who preached both doctrines at the county courthouse. Both doctrines were unpopular in Bethany, which was largely Democratic and Campbellite, a town whose people loved to sit about questioning doctrine by the hour. At one time Henry Howe was arrested on a charge of "inciting slaves to rebellion," and his trial became one of the most celebrated in the history of Harrison County.

Henry Howe also spoke his mind in his sermons, arguing that slavery was inconsistent with divine law, and his arguments led to numerous rows. So controversial was the subject of abolition in the neighborhood that the boy Ed thought maybe the Battle of Bull Run had begun in his neighborhood after Henry Howe had offered an anti-slavery prayer. Ed himself became so involved in the arguments that he came to believe the war was being fought to decide whether the Bible favored slavery. Abolitionism, slavery, and war talk were common in the Missouri countryside; at one celebration a young man dressed as Lincoln split rails for the crowd. When war came Ed and Jim helped the War Widows, women whose husbands were in the army. Ed's father organized a company of Union soldiers and served as their captain, but he became ill and came home after a year. He then bought a "rebel newspaper" in Bethany so that he could carry out his abolitionist principles in print. News of the war was commonly discussed in the Howe neighborhood. Battle reports came in to Bethany by stage from Chillicothe, and the fighting at Pittsburg Landing was of special interest, because a company from Fairview was in the action. Howe remembered the soldiers coming home, especially one called "Cap," who had been shot through the chest but not, apparently, severely injured. He also remembered a party of three soldiers, with a prisoner, being fed by his mother at their home, and he heard an oration at the Campbellite church after the assassination of the President.

Dominating his boyhood was his stern father. Often in later years Ed Howe would reflect on the meaning of his father in his life: "I have long had a feeling that my recollections of father may be unfair; that I can have no dependable opinion now as to what sort of man he was more than sixty years ago," he would write in 1929. Life meant the circuit, on which young Ed sometimes fell asleep during the sermons, and even through the shouting, so that his father would have to awaken him to assist with the singing. Henry Howe was popular in the Fairview community, but Bethany had no use for him. As for Ed, he had no affection for his father, only respect, because of his father's capabilities and his leadership ability.

In those days most fathers dominated their families, and Henry Howe brought up Ed like a "bound-boy." He showed no affection. He drove Ed constantly, and he berated him because he was not producing enough for the family: "One of my recollections is of his saying that I had been an expense to him until I was seven years old." The Howe boys worked long hours in the fields, driving the horses, threshing wheat, cutting it with old-fashioned cradles, carrying water to the workers, stripping sorghum in the field and boiling it into molasses, husking corn, helping their mother make tallow candles, helping kill hogs in "long killing" in the fall and "short killing" in the spring. Whippings were common until Ed was about 13, by which time he was working on his own as a printer. Whippings were bad, "but conscience-whipping was worse: I was saved from ruin not by a switch laid on by an angry, unreasonable father, but by conscience-whipping. Let those I have wronged know I have been punished." Ed learned how to make the whippings easier on him: he'd drop to the ground at the first stroke, scream, and cause his father to stop. But his brother Jim was made of tougher stuff: he was stubborn and would never cry. One whipping came when Ed and Jim took a visiting friend to a plum patch on Sunday; Henry Howe beat all three of them. The father was unnecessarily harsh. He once knocked out Edgar's tooth, which was aching, with a cold chisel and hammer. "It was an efficient way, but nearly killed me, and he whipped me for crying."

Howe's childhood recollections were vivid; he was especially influenced by his father's views on marriage. Henry Howe often referred to the "ownership" of husbands by wives as the worst thing man meets in life, and years later his son was somewhat startled to find similar views in two books by an English writer, *Man, an Indictment,* and *Woman, a Vindication.*

Life on the Missouri farm was bleak. Ed had few friends, one of them a boy in a family he identifies as the "Meeks," but he did not remember whether the friend was Henry, Pascal, or Abram. There was school in the church in winter, taught by a man dimly remembered as Hayworth, and by a woman who taught in a log schoolhouse before the church was built. Ed said he learned nothing at school, and that he quit at an early age. "I never studied grammar at all, and common fractions so discouraged me I could not get the faintest glimmer of their meaning." He learned to read at home before he was sent to school, wondering what the books in the house were for, and learning how, by himself, to make out the words. Real education came when he started to work in the printing office when he was 11 or 12. A typesetter had to know how to spell, and Ed learned, getting a whipping from his father, now a printer as well as preacher and farmer, if he made too many errors in the proof galleys. He also learned sentence construction. Howe thus developed his contempt for formal education, coming to believe that the best men have not been formally educated and that college can only ruin a boy.

Life was primitive, almost raw. Ed never had a bathroom in a house until he had a family of his own. He was taught to wash his face and hands, but he did not recall Saturday night baths. He did not recall hearing about Christmas while living at Fairview, and there were few luxuries except for taffy made from sorghum molasses. His joy was being able to parch corn, grind it in a coffee mill, and eat it with cream. He also enjoyed cracklings from the rendering of lard. The family diet conditioned his tastes throughout life. Salads he never got, and he never cared for them later. He was raised on meat, gravy, bread, potatoes, milk, butter, and pie, with green corn, watermelons, wild blackberries, and plums in the summer. There were trips into the woods for nuts, but there were no fruit-bearing trees on the farm. Gardens were uncommon; the family never raised vegetables, in either Fairview or Bethany.

So the golden glow of pioneer life that marks sentimental novels was not part of the Howe family life, nor of that of their neighbors. There were no purely social affairs. A big event was that of a child being able to stay all night with a friend. Young men once gave a play in the church, and he remembered his parents visiting a neighbor's house one evening, and his father whipping him when he returned home. "I doubt if there is in the world to-day a neighborhood as melancholy as ours was about the time of the beginning of the Civil War," he wrote.

Henry Howe moved his family into the county seat of Bethany when Ed was still a little boy—again the family vagueness about details—and life became a bit brighter. The family home was small, one-story, and brick, but the real home was the printing office, which Ed found full of wonder. He was the devil, as low as a boy can be in a printing office, but he gradually learned the trade in those primitive days of handset type and tiny newspapers that were mainly partisan organs. Bethany itself was just a little place—a few hundred people, a courthouse, a jail, a schoolhouse, and several stores. But there was magic in the newspaper office, and Ed was particularly delighted with a printer named E. R. Martin, who slept in the place and played a guitar—Ed's first look at a musical instrument, his first knowledge that there was such a thing in the world. Martin was the best all-round country printer Howe ever knew, and there was another printer friend named Humphrey Ramer, a cripple who had to use crutches and who taught the boys the way of life in a country town. Ramer pretended he knew where the local women went swimming in the creek, and he took a group of excited boys there, but there were never any women; Ed later learned the women had no favorite swimming hole. Soon the printer friends were gone, for Henry Howe let them go and made his family do the work. Aunt Lu, the widow of Howe's Uncle George, set type. Edgar and Jim had a key to the office and frequently slept there. During the day they had to defend themselves against the town boys, who were contemptuous of the country lads in the printing office, and made faces at them through the windows. Ed had to fight them to gain acceptance, and there was a long series of battles with one boy which finally ended in a truce.

Ed's work for the paper included delivering copies to the town's subscribers. Martin had printed a "carrier's address" for the boys to deliver at the new year, and the practice was that the carriers would sell the addresses for what they could get: "for a half dollar or quarter, if we could persuade subscribers to such extravagance, but to take a dime, or five cents, if we could do no better." Jim told the subscribers just that, and he got five cents from most people, but Edgar received more, and Martin ruled that he should keep it, even though Jim thought the grand total should be divided.

It was mainly hard work in the printing office, the boys being allowed to go to school only on occasion. They worked in the office until school time, then came back, worked until supper and again in the evening. They worked all day Saturday, from seven in the morning until six at night, with an hour off for dinner. In the winter Ed and Jim started work before daylight and finished by lamplight.

Then the newspaper was sold, and the family engaged in storekeeping in the same building, Edgar working in the store but also for the owner of the newspaper. Henry Howe collected the boy's wages, and Ed rarely had money, except for five dollars which he remembered giving to a woman who was going to teach him to paint with oils.

There had been diversions, despite the stern morality of the father. Life in the village was to be brightened by the arrival of the Miles Orton circus in 1864, and Henry Howe announced that he would not "pollute his columns with a circus advertisement, as circuses were immoral." He said he would use his influence to see that few attended, and so his anti-circus campaign was launched. Many times in later life Ed told his story about going to the forbidden circus, at which there was a routine between a drunk and the clown. It started when the clown asked: "What has become of that old Howe who used to teach the school?" "Why, hadn't you heard?" the man answered, "He is running a paper here in Bethany about the size of a postage stamp, and is so good he won't print a circus advertisement." And then the crowd went wild, and Jim and he joined in. They knew they were to get a whipping after the show, and thought they should get all the enjoyment possible.

Henry Howe learned, of course, that his boys had gone to the circus, and when he asked them about it Edgar said the circus was not very good (though he had loved it). He told his father that the clown's joke did not go over very well, that the townspeople told the clown and the drunk that Henry Howe was Bethany's leading citizen and that they did not approve of such abuse. The white lie mollified Henry Howe, and Ed, for a change, escaped a whipping.

The Tramp Printer

Reminiscences of the adult Ed Howe were always a mixture of fact and anecdote. Seldom could he put his finger on the exact date when something happened; almost everything was impression; names would be omitted; descriptions would be few.

Perhaps the bitterness of his life had marked some events so that they became difficult to remember in detail. But there was one important exception, the shock he received when Henry Howe ran away from home and abandoned his wife and children. This was the moralistic Henry Howe, the preacher who had beaten his son for being ungodly (though Ed had long observed that Henry had been friendly with certain women in his congregation, some of whom he invited to the home). Ed was 14 when the incident occurred that clearly marked his attitudes toward both marriage and religion. Henry Howe called a family council in the living room and there informed the family that he was going to leave, that there had been family talk, and that he didn't like it. The talk, he said, was about him and Aunt Lu, who had been helping him with Methodist matters, and who had marched with him out in front in a church parade, singing with him out of the same hymnal. The family then had a row, and Ed's older half-sister, Sarah Jane, who was a school teacher, argued with her father, who told her "she had always been an impudent, unmanageable child, and that if she didn't change her ways, he would 'take it out of her,' even if she was grown, and a school teacher."

Sitting quietly by in all the fuss was Ed's much put-upon

mother. Henry finally left, and a day or two later he told Edgar to take his mother to visit her parents. A few days passed, and then the children saw a new covered wagon with matched horses pull up in the yard at Bethany, and watched their father leave. Ed soon learned that the congregation had "churched" his father in disgrace because of the affair with Aunt Lu. Henry Howe had arranged for family support and had given them the name of a lawyer they could consult if necessary.

The episode brought to an end Ed's life at home. Life in the country town soon gave way to life on the road, the kind of life lived by many printers in the late nineteenth century. The slim youth, already hardened by life, began to move from job to job. He was an accredited journeyman, and his first outside work was in Gallatin, Missouri, where his brother Jim had gone to work on the *North Missourian*. Ed was only fifteen; his wages were five dollars a week and board. The Gallatin printing office was in the courthouse, and there were two proprietors, one named Kost, the other Day. Ed began to board at the Kost home, but Mrs. Kost thought him too noisy, so he went to a house kept by a Mrs. Ewing. Jim left town to work on a paper owned by Kost and Day in a nearby community, but Ed stayed on, forming a friendship with a printer named Charley Post.

One can only guess at what Edgar Watson Howe was like at this time. He pictures himself as a rather dashing type, and he must have been a young man not at all hard to look at—the dour years were ahead. In the year that he spent in Gallatin he either had a gay time or later remembered it so: he was young and lively and developed a reputation of being quite the young lover. In Bethany he had a brief romance with a girl named Fair. In Gallatin there were at least four women: Libby Sayles, who was twenty-two; Libby's friend Maidie; a milliner named Miss Belle; and a forty-year-old named Miss Hattie. Ed professed love easily and openly, most of all for Libby Sayles: "I thank her memory with a whole heart, for the women I have known since have not been so considerate." Sixty years later he wrote of Libby: "Possibly she had had lovers before, and knew, but I am certain they were as harmless as she found me; for how that girl could take care of herself!"

He must have done a good deal of his courting in the countryside, for he ran a sizable bill at the livery stable. He was rescued from matrimony (if there had ever been much danger of that for the fifteen-year-old) when Kost and Day sent him to another town, Maysville. There he was soon in love with the sister of the wife of the hotel proprietor. This was a short-lived affair, for the girl had too many gentlemen friends for Howe. "I have never been able to take much interest in a divided affection," said Howe. "There are so many hearts that I have always believed there should be a whole one for everybody."[5]

He was meanwhile forming those philosophies that would dominate so much of his later writing. He came to understand small town and business attitudes as he talked with the salesmen in the hotel lobby. He listened more than he talked, and he absorbed country-town doctrine. While at Maysville he received word that his mother was ill back in Bethany, and he left to go home. On the way home word came that she was improved, so he changed his plans and went to St. Joseph, the big town on the Missouri River which had been the eastern terminal for the Pony Express years before. There he worked on the *Herald,* serving as what printers called a "sub," or extra man. In St. Joseph he had to stay in the printers' boarding house, and he concluded that poor people in a town the size of St. Joe got along worse than in a town the size of Gallatin or Maysville. He also found that in St. Joe he could know the principal people only by sight, while in Maysville he knew the merchants, bankers, county officials, and the judge as speaking acquaintances, and was able to attend parties with the best people in town.

He remembered little of his days in St. Joseph, though he recalled seeing a play called *The Pearl of Savoy* and making a trip home to see his ailing mother. He had a flirtation with a woman who ran the home where he lived; he pretended to be a Democrat (he did not know a Democrat from a Republican at the time) to get along with her. When his mother died, he returned home for her funeral. Then his father returned and collected his family together, taking them to St. Joe and on a river steamer to Council Bluffs, Iowa, where he had established a place for them to live. Sarah Jane, whom Ed had never liked, did not go with the family, nor did Jim.

Ed Howe's days in Council Bluffs were brief. He worked for an editor named Chapman on the *Nonpareil,* a newspaper printed on an old-time Washington hand press like those Howe had known in Bethany, Gallatin, and Maysville. Soon he quit in anger at the new foreman and went to Chicago, where he had heard there were good wages for printers. But the big city was not for the Missouri country boy, even though he did sneak in through the back stairway to take a look at the office of the *Tribune*. Then he went to Omaha.

Ed remembered working for a time on the *Omaha Republican*. His memories consisted of living in a frame hotel with a beer garden attached, and meeting a remarkable printer named Joe Franklin, a musician and hard drinker, who became a long-time associate of the drifting boy. Life proved dull in Omaha for both Howe and Franklin, and they decided to try the West. It must have been an enjoyable journey across the prairies, Franklin teaching singing along the way, and Howe singing with him on village streets to draw crowds. They sang a song called the "Larboard Watch," and they sold an Indian remedy that they represented as coming from herbs and tree barks. For a time the two were in Cheyenne, Wyoming, the roughest town Howe had ever seen, a town of expensive board and room, with the cronies forced to live in a shack of boards and canvas. One can envision the wild winds of Wyoming blowing through the fragile shanty, and encouraging the two to head further west. Soon they were in the booming Mormon community of Salt Lake City, which was the most fascinating town Howe had yet seen.

He had never joined his father's church, but religion remained a powerful influence on him, and he was absorbed with the Mormon experiment. He heard the preachers and listened to the choir, and he could not see how the services differed from what he had known as a boy, except that the sermons were more doctrinal and stressed such matters as polygamy. Howe worked for the *Deseret News,* the church paper run by Brigham Young, and he sometimes called at the home of a church apostle and came to know one of his three wives, whom he called Aunt Rachel. His boyhood imitations of the shouting Missouri Methodists came in handy for him, as he amused both the apostle and Aunt Rachel. The *News* was just like other papers so far as he could tell, and he later wrote that he had "never enjoyed life anywhere more than I did in Salt Lake City." It was a community of some cultural pretensions, and Howe liked the theater and the music, which were thriving attractions. He frequently saw Brigham Young, sometimes in the company of two or three women.

But soon he was on the road again, going east and visiting in Omaha and Council Bluffs, where he saw his family. In St. Joseph he learned that the editor of the *Nemaha Valley Journal* at Falls City, Nebraska, a man named W. S. Stretch, needed a printer. Stretch offered him twelve dollars a week, but Howe argued the salary up to eighteen dollars, and soon he was earning twenty, a good salary at that time.

In Falls City he began to develop a contempt for the alcoholic and the intemperate. For a time, on his way to dinner, he would stop at a saloon every day for a drink, but he soon quit the practice: "Whisky was always a mistake: an old, foolish notion modern man should have long ago abandoned." He had tried drinking in St. Joseph, getting drunk one time with a friend named John Devers, and being caught and humiliated. "I have been a tiresome preacher of temperance ever since. I have never been able to see any sense in intoxicants; if I want to play the fool, I can find a dozen things more promising than whisky." Unlike Omaha and Salt Lake City, the little community of Falls City offered few of the musical or theatrical advantages that Howe would so love all his life. There were church services, and there were socials, and Howe began to sing in the choir and to play the organ. He had not gone to church in the other towns where he had worked, but the church was about all there was in Falls City, a community center with an interesting and well-liked pastor. "I do not recall any of the religious discussions at Falls City that had distinguished Bethany, but everyone went to church on the ringing of the bell, as they went to their meals, and said little about it." He also played in a band, even though he could not read music, and performed in a dramatic society, which produced, among other things, *The Rivals*.

Howe's Falls City days were probably the happiest he knew in his youth. He had friends, he had responsibilities. The owner of the newspaper took a wife and left Howe in charge of the paper for two weeks, and Howe said that many told him the paper improved under his management. "There was even talk of raising money and starting another paper with me in charge, but there is always talk of this kind in a one-paper town, and means nothing." An important influence on him was a man named Charley Morden, who came to Falls City from a position as manager of the *Oregonian* in Portland. The advice and example of Morden were more valued by Howe than what he read in books and magazines and heard from the lips of statesmen or preachers. Late in life Howe would quote another man who had known him in Falls City: "His industry was remarked upon favorably, and I never heard of his taking a day off or doing any act the people found fault with. At our bank it was agreed his note was good, but he never let us have it."[6] Another man who knew him recalled that Howe had been foreman, pressman, and local editor of the *Nemaha Valley Journal.* "Ed was my ideal young man of the town. He was splendidly built, erect, strong of arm, witty, and a lover of music. . . . I never heard him speak a scandal, tell a smutty story, or utter a disrespectful word about any girl or woman. . . . I do not remember hearing him use an oath, nor did I ever see any signs of his drinking . . . ."[7]

As a sharp young man-about-town earning twenty dollars a week, Ed Howe was able to move with a good set. And he met a girl named Clara Frank, "the object of my special affection," who had just come back from the East and an education in a girls' boarding school. She was "as fine a woman, I thought, as Mrs. Kost, of Gallatin, must have been as a girl—and here she was 'going with me,' appreciating me beyond my deserts, giving me music lessons on a melodeon, and other agreeable attentions when I visited her almost every evening of the week. It was the first fine thing in my life impressively presented." But his stay in Falls City was interrupted by some kind of disagreement with the owner of the paper, a dispute probably due in part to Howe's "latent disposition." "I left my heart there, and doubted I would ever be able to get it back," he later said, doubtless referring not only to Clara Frank but to the good life he had known in the Nebraska town. He then went west again, met his old friend Joe Franklin in Denver, worked briefly as a sub on the *Rocky Mountain News,* and then went to Golden, a town twenty miles away, in the foothills of the Rockies. Golden was a booming village, with a railroad, smelting works, paper mill, coal mine, school of mining education, and, in Howe's opinion, many pleasant citizens. He and Franklin worked and struggled to get together enough money to buy the *Golden Eagle,* the opposition paper in the town. Then, for two years, 1873-75, Ed Howe was associated with the paper (referred to in some writings as the *Golden Globe*), but they were not his best years.[8]

One problem was Joe Franklin, who was drinking too much and was drifting into Denver and loafing around the area. The two finally parted company after an encounter on a country road when Howe was returning to Golden after visiting a nearby town to inquire about another newspaper. But Howe retained his affection for Joe throughout his life. "Somewhere in my inner self now I have a feeling that Joe Franklin was the best friend I ever had. He hadn't a bad habit, so far as I knew, except drinking, and this did not debase him as much as it does others." The second problem was that Ed Howe was trying to be a humorist when he should have been covering the news of the town. So ashamed was he of the paper that in later years he looked over the bound files and quietly burned them so that his sons could not see them.

But he was attracting attention to himself as a writer. Stanley G. Fowler of the *Denver Mirror* praised Howe's work and reprinted extracts from the Golden paper. Howe may have become overly modest, but he did not believe his paper was a good one. "When I say there was not a line I wrote for the *Golden Eagle* that had sense in it, I am not trying to be over-modest; I am only telling the truth as it is illuminated with fifty years of later experience in writing. I did not have sufficient judgment to devote my time to local happenings, as I should have done, but attempted to be witty when I had no wit."

In the newspaper he boosted the city, which was being touted for great things. On April 19, 1873, he wrote an editorial entitled "GOLDEN. What the City Is and Why." He set forth the assets of the town, observing that "Every Golden man is proud of the town, her achievements and her institutions, and they can't be blamed for the inclination to blow over outstretched rivals. . . ." He observed that thirty trains entered and left daily, that there were ores, coal, lumber, grain, groceries, provisions, and flour to keep up the flow of business. This was the kind of small-town boosting for which Howe would later become well known.

In the midst of the Golden venture he went back to Falls City to marry Clara Frank. A clipping from an unidentified newspaper told, in heavy-handed humor, about the marriage, though someone had confused the bride with her sister: "Ed. W. Howe, formerly of this place, but now of Golden, Col., was married at Falls

City, Neb., on the 18th inst., to Miss America Frank. To be 'frank,' Ed. always was popular with the girls. May he and his 'America'-n Girl live to celebrate their 'Golden' wedding."

The wedding was too elaborate for Ed's simple tastes. It was on a grand scale, he said, in accord with the bride's management of the affair throughout:

"There was in it a simulation of the grandeur of palaces, courts and cathedrals, although it occurred in a story-and-a-half house in a country town. There were bridesmaids, old schoolgirl friends who had come on from a distance, and a wedding march played on a melodeon. The bride threw her bouquet; there was a wedding dress and veil; two officiating pastors; the curtains were drawn (it was in the afternoon), and the lamps lighted. No detail was neglected that a romantic woman might hear of."

Howe gave her a ring—"a poor one, but I had a hard time getting even that"—on which he had had engraved, at her request, the word "Mizpah," which she thought meant "The Lord watch between thee and me." Years later, Howe said, he read that the word had a Phallic origin, and he was amused at what he learned when the word "Phallic" sent him to the dictionary.

The young couple spent their nuptial night, as Howe put it, in Atchison, Kansas. Then they went to Golden to live, at first staying in a hotel, then buying a house on credit, because Howe had been told a married man should have a home. In Golden, in the summer of 1874, their first child, Bessie, was born, "the daintiest creature I had ever known. I stole a poem to celebrate the event, and my admirer on the *Denver Mirror* caught me at it, and was never the same afterward. As a result, I have since been careful to give credit."

Howe's Golden newspaper finally folded, even though the editor sent a message to his brother Jim to come and help rescue him. Howe had become overextended in everything. He had heavy debts, which he had accepted on the promise that subscribers would pay when their crops were harvested the following summer. He had a series of partners who did not help matters. The depression of 1873 caught him in its backwash, and he lost some support because of his stubborn propensity to talk about women, religion, and politics.

Yet recognition was coming to him, the kind that would come again in the 1880s and 1890s. His style was a bit cumbersome, but it made its points, and his comments were picked up by newspapers in thirteen states. In his own section of the country the *Douglas County News* wrote of his paper: "It's newsy, spicy, bold and fearless. Howe says just what he thinks." The *Denver Mirror* called the paper the best in the territory. But there also was the *Central Coach,* which said of it: "Run by a scavenger." And the Denver *News*: "Not crazy, but worse." News in the Golden paper ran to this kind of report:

> A Minister's wife up town tried to mend her husband's coat with the thread of one of his discourses. It scarcely held till she got over the threshold. . . .
>
> Arrived, on Monday afternoon, at the house of the editor of this paper, a naked baby. Sex, female; Religion, Methodist; Politics, Republican. We make the statement on the authority of its estimable mother that it can recite the Lord's Prayer from a to izzard from memory, and that it could talk if it wanted to. It's a noticeable fact, however, that it hasn't wanted to so far. . . .
>
> It's one of the inexplicable things of this life that so many book agents live to a ripe old age.[9]

Howe finally sold out to a young man for cash, and returned for a second venture in Falls City. There, in the winter of 1876, a son, Ned, was born to the Howes. Ed had an opportunity to go to Philadelphia to the great Centennial Exposition, and there he ran across his father, who had an exhibit, "a contrivance that year to revolutionize the steam engine." His father had "resumed his old Fairview temper," and the meeting was not a pleasant one. Howe also visited New York, but he preferred Philadelphia, even though he enjoyed Madison Square Garden and Pat Gilmore's Concert Band.

He also learned a lesson in humility in his last years in Falls City, after printing an item about a stuttering man. Howe had heard a funny stuttering story, and attributed it to the man, who was deeply offended. The two had a fight on the street, were arrested by a constable, and taken before a justice of the peace. Howe's lawyer was regarded as the best in town, and the opposing lawyer also was a good one. The two "performed as grandly as though delegates to a World Peace Congress, greatly to the delight of a large crowd that speedily gathered, including many women." The attorney for the stuttering man abused Howe, and he was greatly humiliated. Then his attorney spoke, in beautiful and eloquent words that moved Howe to tears, or so he later wrote. Another citizen spoke in Howe's behalf; then one denounced him. Finally the young editor realized that it had all been a town joke developed at his expense.

2

THE ATCHISON GLOBE: FIRST YEARS

Town on the Missouri

Atchison is a city in northeastern Kansas, seated on the bluffs of the Missouri River, distinctly agricultural in setting, with farming the occupation of many in the vicinity, possessing a rich soil and climate as favorable as any in frequently sultry—or frigid—Kansas. It was something of a boom town when Ed Howe reached there in 1877, and even though he often said he did not know why he chose Atchison, it is likely that he knew much about the city. He had honeymooned there, and it was relatively close to Falls City, in the southeastern corner of Nebraska, and to Omaha, Council Bluffs, and St. Joseph. (In his autobiographical *Plain People* he later said he did not know why he had chosen Atchison, but in a special edition of *The Globe* two years earlier an article had said: "Atchison was selected because of the acquaintance of the Howe brothers with J. E. Utt, then general passenger agent of the old Atchison & Nebraska. They knew no one else there."[1]

The first permanent settler of the Atchison region was a Frenchman named Paschal Pensoneau, who went there about 1839 and in about 1844 settled on the bank of Stranger Creek. The first to locate on the later townsite of Atchison was a man named George Million, in 1841. In 1850 a military road was laid out from Fort Leavenworth, about twenty-four miles south of Atchison, to Fort Laramie. Many had traveled over this road, a branch of the Oregon Trail. Then in the 1850s came intensive emigration following passage of the Kansas-Nebraska Act of 1854. Many settlers came into Atchison, particularly Missourians, some of whom were trying to hold the Kansas territory for slave-state sympathizers under the squatter sovereignty terms of the law. Abolitionist-slave state warfare followed, though most settlers were more interested in building their homes and getting ready for the winter than in voting in the territorial elections. On November 29, 1854, voters in Missouri began to cross into Kansas and to take possession of the polls. Battles over the free-state Topeka and slave-state Lecompton constitutions followed, and in the disputes the town of Atchison became the stronghold of the Law and Order party, pledged to establish slavery in the territory, as was Senator David R. Atchison of Missouri, president pro-tempore of the Senate after the death of Vice President King. It was Atchison for whom both town and county were named.

Early in the fighting there came the pro-slavery *Squatter Sovereign* and the establishment of journalism in the county. And after border warfare that was frequently bloody, Kansas entered the union January 29, 1861.

Atchison County was one of thirty-three original counties created by the first territorial legislature, and except for Doniphan County it was the extreme northeastern county of the state. The site of the city was selected because of its geographical location on the Missouri, which bent inland at that point. Senator Atchison thought the town would be of commercial advantage, and it was established July 4, 1854. For years its boosters, including Edgar Watson Howe, saw it as the natural gateway to the West. It was incorporated as a town August 30, 1855, and as a city February 12, 1858. Much of its early success may have been due to vigorous promotion by the *Squatter Sovereign,* which advertised its business houses, its warehouses, its newspaper, its hotels, its blacksmith shops, wagon makers and carpenter shops, its ferries, its brickyards and lime kilns, and the other matters that induce settlement. The city directory of 1884 told of the city's origins in terms glowing even for that romantic time in American history:

> The city of Atchison owes its origin, partly to that universal tendency to expansion which animates the average American breast, but principally to the fact that those who first reached this favored spot did not care to go anywhere else. . . .
>
> It is said that the city was quite small at first, but there was a "right-smart" piece of rolling prairie for it to grow in, and it grew. . . . [Historians] all recount in glowing periods how the original inhabitants swept down from the heights into the valley of "Old White Clay," while the fresh arrivals that were constantly coming in, ascended the hills that bound that classic

> stream, until to-day the landscape-loving traveler, who surmounts the eminence on which is located the grandest reservoirs of the temperance element in the state, sees spread out beneath him a multitude of beautiful dwellings embowered in green, row upon row of magnificent warehouses of commerce, and the smoke of innumerable manufactories ascending to heaven, and tinging with the sign of unlimited prosperity the azure sky above us—verily inscribing upon the clouds that Atchison is the abode of peace and progressive industry.

Even before the storied Atchison, Topeka & Santa Fe came to town the community had its noted visitors. Ben Holladay of stage line fame was often there. Horace Greeley and Artemus Ward had been through; Civil War reporter Albert D. Richardson had lived there. Such celebrated Kansans as Samuel C. Pomeroy (a citizen of the town) and Jim Lane were well known in Atchison in their time. These names Ed Howe mentioned late in life, and he probably knew about them before he went to the town himself. John J. Ingalls, whose political fortunes Howe would be promoting in the 1880s and 1890s, had been in the territory since 1858. The celebrated "Santa Fe" was organized in Atchison in 1859 as the "Atchison and Topeka." There were many rail lines in the town in its optimistic boom days. Freighting was the big business in the years before the railroads; Atchison had been headquarters for Holladay's stage line, and early trails to California, Colorado, and Montana reached Atchison. As a Missouri River port the city was an outfitting point for Salt Lake freighters. It had one of the best landings on the river, and during the overland freighting era, it was said, more trains left from Atchison than from any place on the Missouri. Some of these factors led Ed Howe to see the town as "an interesting, promising place with history and 'characters,' including a gang of the most noted three-card monte men in the West."[2]

Railroad booms marked the city's early history. In 1860, eight years before the last stage left, the city claimed connection across the river with the Hannibal & St. Joseph from St. Joe. Several other lines followed: advertisements showed that in the 1890s there were 96 train departures and arrivals daily at the depot.

Despite all this early prosperity and development, one still wonders what drew this editor to the town in the mid-1870s, for it was a time when disillusioned settlers were leaving Kansas and weary people who had tried the plains country were dragging themselves back to what they viewed as civilization. To Ed Howe, Atchison resembled Missouri, Illinois, and Iowa; he saw his part of Kansas as "no more like western Kansas than it is like Arizona."[3] But life in Atchison was barren for many, even in those growing years of the trans-Mississippi prairie. A historian of the sod-house era has described a prairie town that easily could have been Atchison:

> . . . the wild lonely spirit of the prairie was reflected in the somber architecture and in the absence of houses distinguished in form and color. There was a deplorable lack of the esthetic. The rows of plain houses were scrambled along the streets in a manner that suggested a clash between the various edifices. . . . The interiors of the business places were not designed to welcome or please. They were dirty and cluttered with large cuspidors or a dirty floor that was uninviting to the woman who in that day wore a cumbrous train which mopped up the filth.[4]

Many settlers were homesteaders, fighting the virgin land, trying to accustom themselves to a country whose mood seemed unfriendly much of the time in those years when disillusioned farmers were beginning to organize. There were floods in the spring, menacing cabin or dugout, and drought and searing winds that withered the crops in the summer. There were insects that took what was left, and sometimes in the fall there were prairie fires that took everything in their path, and in the winter there were blizzards and below-zero temperatures that claimed man and beast.

But in selecting Atchison Ed Howe had chosen an essentially lovely city, with steep hills and trees and a creek running through town, and the Big Muddy, which dominated the region, and grasslands and hard maple trees. Once a farm boy himself, he was attracted, in all likelihood, by the black soil, the coarse wheat stubble, the heavy growth of prairie grass. And the railroads and local governments were actively propagandizing for Atchison and for other communities. It was a fairly substantial city to which he came, only then fearing that it would lose out to nearby Kansas City in the competition for regional importance. A foundry company had been established in 1871, a seed company in 1875, and later mills and groceries. It is likely that the tramp printer had been exposed to publicity from Atchison, such as a pamphlet called "Atchison, the Railroad Centre of Kansas." The *Daily*

Champion had printed that one in 1874, spelling out the advantages of launching a business in the growing town.

Founding of The Globe

Ed Howe had chosen a city where he would have to fight hard to survive. Kansas was newspaper country. There were newspapers in Kansas before there were sufficient settlers to support them. There was a press in Atchison before there were schools and churches, the town company donating four hundred dollars to Robert Kelley and Dr. J. H. Stringfellow to start the *Squatter Sovereign* early in 1855. That journal passed into the hands of the New England Emigrant Aid Society in the fall of 1857, and soon was sold to one O. F. Short. It then was purchased in 1858 by John A. Martin, who called it *Freedom's Champion* and made it an alert proponent of the free-state view. It was leased in the fall of 1863 to John J. Ingalls and Robert H. Horton, and when Martin came back from the war in 1865 he took over again, consolidating the *Champion* with the *Atchison Free Press,* under the name of *Champion and Press.* He was sole owner and editor of the paper until his death October 2, 1889, and he also was governor in the mid-1880s. The other major paper with which Ed Howe had to compete was the *Patriot,* which had been established by Nelson Abbott October 25, 1867. Abbott was largely in control of the *Patriot* until 1875; H. Clay Park and E. W. Beall had the paper at the time Howe came to Atchison, and Park himself ran it from 1877 for the next twenty-five years. The more powerful of the two papers was undoubtedly the *Champion,* then the newspaper leader in northern Kansas, and the field did not look too promising for the young man from Nebraska and points west. But the paper Ed Howe was about to establish would be quite different from the existing competition, and not much like any other newspaper then in existence.

He had looked over the Kansas-Missouri area before choosing Atchison, and had even given thought to Kansas City, which would be invaded three years hence by a man from Indiana named William Rockhill Nelson. But big cities had not been to Howe's taste; Kansas City was too much like the overwhelming Chicago.

So for him it became Atchison, and it remained Atchison for sixty years, until his death. He was a small-town man, he understood small-town life, and he was satisfied with the rewards one could find in the little river and prairie villages of the Midwest.

His start was not auspicious. There were the *Champion* and the *Patriot* to buck, and he had a record of semi-failures. He had a wife and baby and maybe two hundred dollars capital. He had to borrow money to buy a Gordon job press, and he brought a font of brevier with him from Falls City. With this, and with the assistance of his brother Jim, he started on December 8, 1877, a newspaper of one sheet, 10½ by 15, with two pages only: "the queerest daily paper ever seen in the United States, I have no doubt."

He had left his family in Falls City, and for weeks he and Jim did all the work and also the job printing. He slept in the office, and worked all day and part of the night. Howe once recalled that he had written James A. Loper, the business manager of the *Champion,* for a job as reporter, and that part of his reason for coming to Atchison stemmed from Loper's refusal. Loper also refused to do the press work for the Howes; so they started a daily instead of a weekly, to give the *Champion* some competition. The *Champion* being unwilling to help, they turned to the *Patriot,* whose owners did the printing for three days, then said they no longer could do it. So the brothers suspended publication for five days, until a press could arrive from St. Louis (money to buy the press was borrowed from unidentified sources at Falls City). After the press arrived, they added job printing, and their first job was five hundred letterheads for a local butcher named B. F. Tomlinson.

There was no time for the brothers to write their copy. Ed would come in from the street, which he had been tramping for news and advertising, and place his notebook on the type case and set type directly. Jim frequently set up news stories from "verbal skeletons" provided by Ed. "If I had an advertisement, I put it in type, and placed it in the forms where it belonged. If I brought an order for job work, I kept it in my pocket, and that night we got it ready for delivery next morning."[5] The two learned that there might be a profit of a dollar and a quarter in five hundred bill heads, and they went to work to try to please their customers, who fortunately were not used to the most professional work.

Success of *The Globe* was not instantaneous, but the Howe brothers did fairly well. Howe had wit and a certain amount of charm and he liked people, and hard work made it possible for the paper to pay its expenses after two weeks and for the proprietors to have money to pay for board and room. They gave away copies of *The Globe* for two weeks; then they told the delivery boy to collect ten cents a week. The boy reportedly returned with his pockets bulging with money.

The office of *The Atchison Globe* was in a room over the furniture store of Theodore Intfent; it later was moved to a room over another business house. The Gordon press was able to accommodate only two pages, but the Howes soon were able to print four pages by running each sheet through the press twice. Bigger and faster presses followed: a drum-cylinder model, turned by hand power at first, and then by a water motor; a two-revolution model, run by a steam engine; and finally a Goss perfecting press.

The boarding house where Ed and Jim lived was the old Otis house, which became the Byram. The town was primitive—not a block of street paving, no waterworks, no electric lights. There was a gas works, however, and there was a theater (at which Howe saw and heard Joseph Jefferson, Mary Anderson, Henry Ward Beecher, Oscar Wilde, and Theodore Tilton).

The little paper must have been a joke to some of its readers. One Harry Orr looked it over for a few issues and then said: "I like your sample; bring on your paper."[6] In the tradition of the American journalist, Ed Howe issued what he termed his "Salutatory":

> The first thought of the average Atchisonian respecting the little GLOBE, if he is so good as to think of it at all, will be that it is very small. We frankly admit it—it is the smallest paper we have ever seen, but may it not occur to you that it will, therefore, have abundant room to grow? . . .
>
> We shall confine ourselves almost exclusively to the small affairs of humanity not ordinarily noticed by newspapers. While, perhaps, only one man in twenty will read an article on the expansion or contraction of the currency, every man, woman and child, will read of the new baby, or the new preacher, of a party, social event, or other item not confined solely to great men and lunatics. . . .
>
> We came to Atchison because the thrift, prosperity, and the apparent intelligence of her people, led us to believe that they

> read newspapers. We do not expect to revolutionize the business, or do anything remarkable, and have no expectation that will [printing unclear] the town to fulfill. . . .

Howe acknowledged cheerfully anything the *Champion* and *Patriot* might say about *The Globe.* He promised temperance, morality, virtue, order, sobriety, truth, reform, and "paid locals." He told his readers that he had planned to publish a Sunday morning paper, but that the *Champion* refused to do the press work. So he was printing a small daily and would start the Sunday paper as soon as possible.

"Atchison must be a rich field for printers, judging from the fact that our neighbors are doing such a slashing business. A rich field is what we are after. We are partial to rich fields. This is our apology for starting here. We desire to make money, and where there is so much work we can certainly get our share of it." The subscription terms: ten cents a week, or forty cents a month. Advertising rates would be made known by the solicitor, who would be calling soon (Dec. 8, 1877).

The content of the first issue included a little story about a drunken man, some editorial paragraphs (the mainstay of *The Globe* through its many years), brief items from the telegraph, undoubtedly borrowed from elsewhere, a poem called "The Little Globe" that described the woes of the world, and a series of brief items of local interest, mainly "A. & N. Notes," for the Howes leaned on their acquaintances with employees of the Atchison & Nebraska Railroad to fill the space. The second issue was largely "sketches," a communication from someone labeled "The Autocrat," an essay by one "Johnny Crab" which owed its inspiration to the literary comedians then popular with American readers: "The cow is a nubul bruit. Their is severial kinds of cows—the short horn cow, the long horn cow, the muley cow and the cowcatcher—but the lowin' kine is good enough for me. (This is a goak.)" (Dec. 10, 1877).

Fortunately there was little of this kind of thing. Edgar Watson Howe early established as the virtual trademark of *The Globe* the brief, pointed commentary which has been an inspiration to journalism in Kansas ever since. These were in the first issue:

"Go to church tomorrow, you miserable sinner.

"Remember the poor with your cold buckwheat cakes.

"Mon dieu is French for the devil you say.

"Over in Missouri they hang a man for dealing himself five aces" (Dec. 8, 1877).

And these in the second:

"When a young man is able to lick soup out of his moustache, he has every reason to feel encouraged.

"The Adventists have positively announced the millenium for the day after Christmas, and no postponement on account of the weather, either" (Dec. 10, 1877).

What may have been Howe's first "editorial," so far as later editors of *The Globe* knew, appeared in the first issue as well:

> We have often noticed that one of the first requisites to become distinguished is to be a gentleman. All the men of prominence we have ever known were distinguished equally for their gentleness and politeness. There is no loud braggadocio or supercilious self praise from a man who has won the confidence and the esteem of the people. Such a man is chary of sickening flattery. It is not his stock in trade. But he does not hesitate to pay a merited compliment. He is always polite and agreeable to every one. We warrant the assertion that among the leading men of Atchison will be found those most considerate to strangers; the men most gentlemanly in their everyday intercourse with their fellows; the men who lift their hats to ladies; the men who are never rude. The same principle applies with equal force to the great men of the nation, and if ever you are so fortunate as to gain an audience with the president, you will find him as gentle and polite as the pastor of your church. The young clerk who politely opens the door for the old countrywoman, and overlooks all of her blunders, is in training for the position his employer now occupies, for the people are determined that their representative men shall be gentlemen. [Dec. 8, 1877]

And Ed Howe was writing from personal philosophy, for throughout his life, despite his moods and despite his occasional gloom, he was known for his courtliness and manners. In the second issue he philosophized on dreams, providing the kind of country humor so marked in *The Globe:* "If you dream that the Atchison bridge stands in a perpendicular position, the cars laboring up one side and rushing down the other and never getting across the sluggish channel, it is a sign that the blonde girl has gone back on you, but that you can get the brunette by asking. It is also a good sign that you were drinking beer and eating bologna before retiring" (Dec. 10, 1877).

It was just *The Globe* in those days, not yet *The Atchison Globe.* Under the page one nameplate appeared a heading familiar for years to readers of the paper: "A Daily Evening Poster Devoted to Gab and Gossip, and Paid Locals." The paid locals became part of the success formula; a man could advertise and get his item in among what appeared to be the news, but it cost him. Howe gradually got rid of the job shop, but he persuaded farmers to advertise their sales in the paper and he encouraged politicians to run display advertisements. The latter may have been an innovation in advertising practice; Ed Howe so claimed throughout the years he ran the paper.

Of the brothers, Ed was the more outgoing, so he solicited the advertising, Jim not caring to work on the streets. Ed also solicited job work and subscriptions and served as business manager. Howe later said: "I was not only business manager, editorial writer, managing editor, paragrapher, advertising solicitor, circulation manager, and type-setter occasionally, but wrote the society news." That put him in a class with most country editors. He was successful on the streets because he knew everybody in town, even though he had a difficult time with names. He had known one farmer for years but could never remember the man's name when he paid his subscription. He would describe the man to a hardware store worker named Perry Hayes who knew everybody, but sometimes even this did not work out, and the wrong man would be credited for paying the subscription money.

Early Causes, Issues, and News

Separating truth from fiction in a country paper like *The Globe* is no easy task, for Howe, like many other editors, had to improvise. Howe pretended to receive letters from readers, and he invented controversies. There was a series of letters from an imaginary hired girl: her ambitions, her troubles, her employer. These were written by Jim. There was another controversy started by a man: "Why Does Not God Kill the Devil?" Howe thought this pretty perceptive, but later learned that Friday asked the same question in *Robinson Crusoe.* He attacked the mighty *Champion* and *Patriot,* from his locally insignificant position, especially lampooning their political affectations. He printed imaginary interviews, the most famous being with the actress Mary Anderson, in town to play "Ingomar." Howe's interview had the interviewer doing all the talking, about Atchison people and incidents, and he heard later that the story delighted the actress. There also were fake interviews with Joseph Jefferson, the star of *Rip Van Winkle,* and with Henry Ward Beecher.

Ed Howe modestly deprecated the success of *The Globe,* but this became a familiar pose from this man who protested almost too much that he was of the plain people. "I am sure that for four or five years *The Atchison Globe* was of little consequence, but somehow it was received kindly: I am certain that within a few weeks hundreds of citizens were patting me on the back, and enjoying our 'jokes' on the other papers, both edited by strong men."[7]

In the 1920s, while preparing his autobiography, Howe told about scanning the files since 1877. He found a story about a burly character who stepped up to him on the street, pistol in hand, and announced his plan to kill him. The man had been offended because Howe's paper had mentioned his name in connection with a runaway accident. Another citizen charged that *The Globe* had persecuted an important local institution into moving to Kansas City; Howe proved that he had supported the "institution," which reportedly had been paid $150,000 by the Kansas City Stockyards Company to move to the bigger city.

Childhood memories of camp meetings and circuit riding provided what became the most controversial of all *Globe* attitudes: Ed Howe's attacks on religion. He did this in a time of intense national piety, and in a section of America often regarded (and so referring to itself) as the Bible belt. His comments on religion seem, in retrospect, tame, calm, and reasoned, and, considering his lack of formal education, reasonably intellectual. In the fourth issue of *The Globe* appeared a commentary that apparently launched the anti-religious career of the paper:

FOR HELL, 41; AGAINST HELL, 55;
ANTI-HELL MAJORITY, 14.

That's the way it is footed up in the *Chicago Tribune*. Out of ninety-six congregational ministers in Western Massachusetts, fifty-five do not believe that endless, conscious suffering

> awaits the impenitent. By a majority of fourteen, we are told that the sinner need have no fear of the wrath of God.
>
> Now, such unsound orthodoxy as this puts us out of patience with the Congregational clergy of Western Massachusetts. A religion without a hell is no religion at all. Christianity takes the New Testament as the guide book to heaven. They accept it as the divine and inspired truth. They all unite in saying that, with the exception of a few figurative passages, it means just what it says. They all believe that Christ was born, that he died to save sinners, and that he arose on the third day. They have faith in all his glorious promises of salvation, but they cannot believe in his threats of vengeance on the unbeliever. In short, they believe just so much of the Divine Law as happens to suit their fancy, and reject the balance. Now what is this but a mild form of infidelity? . . . [Dec. 22, 1877]

He had no religion of his own, but he was sincere in his comments about those who tried to remove fear of the devil from their own. If there was a heaven, there had to be a hell. As 1878 began (cold weather and a lack of local copy might have pushed him into the religious controversy even more), he wrote further about what he called "the hell question," one day allowing most of the front page to be consumed by the matter. If there's a hell, he said, it should be a bad one, so that our enemies may not get off soft in the next world.

Howe wrote a story—no names included—of two local gentlemen who were engaged in a discussion of religion, one of them telling about a man who was struck dead by lightning, on a clear day, for uttering blasphemy. The other scorned the idea and said that he was willing to—and would—defy the Lord. "At that moment he was struck with a peculiar sensation at his heart and was barely able to totter to his bed. Although previously one of the rankest infidels, he now renounces it, and cannot be induced under any circumstances to hold to his old doctrine" (Feb. 9, 1878). Two days later the testimony itself was published in *The Globe,* in an article signed "Former Infidel." The gentleman in question said that, after reading a lecture by Robert Ingersoll in *The Globe,* he told his friends that "all the wealth in the world wouldn't induce me to defy God Almighty" (Feb. 11, 1878). And shortly afterward the stricken sensation left him.

But Ed Howe, despite his demonstrated irreligion, was not yet ready to announce anything as controversial as atheism to his readers. Tongue in cheek, he informed them that he was far from being an unbeliever. "Were it not for the fact that Christians have to put on a clean shirt every Sunday morning, we have an idea we would be a very good one. Whatever our example may have been, human nature being weak, we have always been on the side of religion" (Feb. 16, 1878). He could regard the Sabbath lightly, and turn off the question of Sunday laws with a joke: "A farmer called at this office in great indignation to-day to protest against church members going out to his farm on the Sabbath to shoot quail and chickens. He says they come out with lean and hungry dogs to chase his sheep, and endanger the life of his stock by careless shooting. We suggest with considerable sternness that this practice be stopped. Hereafter go to Missouri to shoot on Sunday, where the people are neither religious nor particular" (Oct. 16, 1878).

Supernaturalism also met his scorn. And there was the matter of dreams and marriage and talking in one's sleep. One Arabella (probably Howe) wrote frequently to *The Globe,* commenting on the wonders of her marriage and about her husband's talking at night. She was puzzled by a monologue such as this: "I rise ye one, Go you two better, Two blind, I see you, Four kings, O, hell, I'm busted" (Jan. 11, 1878). References to marriage and women were frequent in the early issues. Howe told about a North Atchison woman who got up in the middle of the night to go into the kitchen and when she returned to bed said: "There! I knew something was out of kelter. Somebody has left the broom standing on the brush end" (Dec. 24, 1877).

There were other foreshadowings of future *Globe* attitudes. The editor spoke of the likelihood of a temperance movement starting in the city, noting particularly the woman at the Methodist church who condemned "the practice of putting brandy in mince pies, or anything else for that matter, except the gutter" (Jan. 15, 1878). He spoke for personal temperance, too, condemning the practice of sowing wild oats: "We therefore feel at liberty to denounce the whole system of seed time and harvest in one's morals as disgusting nonsense and outlandish idiocy. The young men ought to begin to realize that to even make a common living is no child's play, but a man's work" (June 25, 1878). There was a lighthearted comment about a "long-nosed maid" who regarded the waltz as "inelegant, ill-bred and immodest." Howe observed that for such reasons a law would have to be passed either to regulate or abolish the abomination. And on one of his indignant (or amused; one never knows for sure) days he suggested that a law be passed to curb the extravagance of women, who were spending their money on wasteful clothing. "Let us pass a law forever prohibiting the manufacture or sale of lace, silk, and other useless and high priced stuffs" (Mar. 20, 1882).

The two-man task of putting out a paper, even a little one like *The Globe,* was a hard one, but Edgar Watson Howe believed in the Puritan ethic, even though he did not accept many of the trappings of Puritanism. He announced to his readers his intention of getting out a small daily every day at four, "the Lord willing." He vowed to accomplish the result by working fifteen hours a day if necessary. He had been told that the *Champion* was "an awful big institution to buck." That was not his purpose; all he wanted was to be left alone to do the job: "We may be the spirit of Horace Greeley for all you know, though it must be confessed we have as yet evinced none of the symptoms" (Dec. 24, 1877). The bright little items continued to take up more space than anything in the paper: A call for two more carriers, because "we have another subscriber." A comment that if Shakespeare himself should come to town to play *Macbeth,* "there would still be somebody to say it was a one-horse show" (Jan. 3, 1878). A letter to the editor from a woman thankful she didn't have a drunken husband like her neighbor. A reprint from the *St. Louis Globe-Democrat* (country editors must have been grateful for the big city papers to lift from) on the behavior of the President. Paid locals; wedding items; comments on marriage; comments on religion; an invitation for letters and commentaries regarding society news, fashions, and the like; and a call to the women: "If the men have faults you want to abuse, sail in" (Jan. 9, 1878). The comments came in. News and editorial, in the journalistic fashion of the day, were seldom separate, even in society news:

"A. J. Harwi and Miss Lizzie Whitehead will be joined in the holy bonds of wedlock at the Congregational church this evening, at 8 o'clock. If there is a more genial gentleman in Atchison than A. J. Harwi, or a pleasanter lady than Miss Whitehead, a great many persons have failed to find it out, ourself among the number, and the LITTLE GLOBE offers its congratulations in advance" (Jan. 8, 1878).

Up and down the streets, in and out of business houses, the editor roamed, pencil and paper in hand. He knew a milkman named Doc Morrison who gave him news tips: if the man delivered extra milk or cream he suggested to Howe that a party or company somewhere was likely. Farmers were trained to bring in news; Howe gave them notebooks and pencils. There was no telegraph news in *The Globe* at first; Jesse James was shot and killed only twenty miles away and a rival paper scooped *The Globe.* So Howe had to work to make local news interesting, training the reporters who came along to emphasize the Atchison scene and ignore politics and reform in favor of ordinary affairs of the people. Or so Howe always said. The record tells a slightly different story about the editor and politics and reform. He made an early declaration about politics, when he refused a request of local politicians to make *The Globe* an organ of the Democratic party. Aside from the obvious fact that he was no Democrat, Howe gave these reasons for refusing the offer:

"1. Because we don't believe the Democracy would support an organ if they had one; 2. There is no need of a Democratic paper in Atchison; 3. We don't believe in party organs; 4. THE GLOBE and Champion, the two papers already here, are sufficient for all needs of this people" (Dec. 29, 1877).

One of his most-quoted early editorials was one that listed his resolutions for 1878. First of all, he wished a happy new year to his readers and told them he hoped they were not among that number who ridicule a man's good intentions. "We admire a man that does it, and if he only keeps one good resolution, he becomes a better man for it. If he discards one bad habit every year, in course of time he will become a decent sort of fellow, and be more apt to reform the next year." His resolutions for the year to come included the following:

> I won't smoke. If I can help it.
>
> I won't chaw plug tobacco.
>
> I won't drink whisky, beer, gin, ale, or other spiritous or malt liquors except on the written advice of twelve disinterested and competent physicians.
>
> I won't abuse the world or my employer for not recognizing my ability, but do all I can to merit it. . . .
>
> I won't fight unless a man maliciously tramps on my corns just before a snow storm. . . .
>
> I won't run for President or discuss religion. . . .
>
> I won't abuse the town I live in, for the same unfavorable circumstances that prevail at home, prevail elsewhere. [Dec. 29, 1877]

The paper was scarcely a month old when Howe included a series of "endorsements" from his readers:

> COL. HOWE, Dear Sir: I would rather peruse your sparkling paper than my favorite family journal, the *New York Sun*. Send me three copies.
>
> Yours lovingly, R. B. HAYES.
>
> REV. HOWE: Send your paper to me regularly. Its unadulterated orthodoxy is truly refreshing. BEECHER.
>
> BRO. HOWE: Enclosed find five dollars for LITTLE GLOBE. I derive much religious consolation from its columns.
>
> Yours in Christ, TALMAGE. [Jan. 2, 1878]

The news was usually bright and sometimes exciting, reflecting the essentially rural interests of the small town. Cheerfully *The Globe* reported on "the most terrific and calamatous runaway it has ever been our pleasure to witness":

> A fiery mule team from Missouri with a load of split wood suddenly elevated their tails and struck out for the head of Commercial street tearing out Frank's corner as they went and running over Major Ben Gale and McPike of the drug store opposite the postoffice and turning at Cradish's lumber yard they came back down Commercial street midst the most tremendous excitement killing several men on the way and jumping over the Otis House into the river from whence they darted up Second street down Third up Fourth down Fifth up Sixth and thus see-sawed through the entire town until they reached the Central Branch depot which was wiped from the face of the earth in a minute whereupon they ran over Peabody and Farnsworth and made for the Missouri Pacific freight house killing all the clerks and chasing the switch engine over the bridge into Missouri and when they were caught the mules were so mixed up with each other that Halsey took them out to his elevator and run them through the seperator. [Jan. 30, 1878]

Someone from *The Globe* went to Leavenworth to describe how the "sports of Atchison" took in a cockfight, a "refined entertainment" that they watched in a cellar. The news report ended with an opinion: "A man who was present informs us that it ought to be made a penitentiary offense to fight chickens, and that every man who attends should be sent to the lunatic asylum without unnecessary delay" (Feb. 1, 1878).

Ed Howe might give notice to a cockfight; he was more cautious about traveling shows. He was a business man, and he intended to charge for items about concerts; other editors could work for nothing, he said, but not he: ". . . our space has a certain commercial value, and we intend to have it or fill it up with news" (Mar. 26, 1881). Other "Western papers" might be afraid to tell the truth about the commercial outfits coming to town, but not Ed Howe: "No forty-year-old grandmother will do for a blushing maiden at this office. Broomsticks will not answer for legs. Nor will emotions heaved from bosoms of cotton be accepted as legal tender. When the funny man is an idiot, we'll say so, and when a meek-voiced milk-sop comes out representing a villain, his only recommendation being a long knife, we shall not give the world to understand that he was 'up in his part,' or that he was a favorite with the audience."

He was less reluctant to inform his readers about certain other attractions, for, a good showman himself, he knew where his readers' interests really lay: "Barnum in all his glory and strength will arrive in Atchison to-morrow morning" (Sept. 29, 1884). Those boyhood days when he escaped the miseries of Bethany town life to go to the circus must have come back, even in recollections of circus lemonade, which had "a certain sloppy taste and general-debility twange about [it] that is obtainable in no other form. . . . We have died three or four deaths from it" (May 29, 1878). Often he retold the story of going to the circus in Bethany, and to fill his columns he wrote about his father in the Missouri days, the family miseries, the religious and abolitionist disputes. He was never one to refrain from parading family matters before his readers.

What he preferred to promote over the traveling attractions was whatever the town of Atchison could offer. His competitor Noble Prentis drew *Globe* praise: a home institution, a man of brains, and just as funny and as good a lecturer as anyone the city of Boston could provide (Mar. 13, 1878). Band concerts—good or bad—Howe loved. "Show your appreciation of the new organization by helping it along" (Dec. 4, 1878), he wrote about the local band. The Hutchinson Family Singers drew exclamation marks, even though they were not Atchison products: "Like a zealous but not worldly Methodist at a camp meeting, we can only shout 'Glory!' . . . This afternoon they gave a matinee, and to-night they will give another concert. Go, and if you don't come away a better man, you are a hard-hearted old villain" (Feb. 22, 1879).

Editors meeting in Atchison could read a front-page story

about the delights of the river town—its papers, its railroads, its pretty girls, happy wives, good husbands, and big liars. He invited the editors to come to his humble little newspaper plant. "We have no carpeted editorial rooms or reclining chairs, but we have a welcome for the entire brave two hundred; we have no fat city or county printing contracts, but we have the pith and vinegar to make a living out of legitimate business, you can bet on that" (June 11, 1878). When Henry Ward Beecher came to town Howe told his readers that the famous preacher, who had been involved in one of the most celebrated scandals of the decade, might not be a virtuous man but that Howe didn't care, for "he has more brains than any man that ever came to Atchison, by a large majority" (Mar. 26, 1878). He attended the Beecher lecture (which *The Globe* did not report) on "The Wastes and Burdens of Society," and found it the notable intellectual event of his life. "Beecher wore a shiny black coat, and looked rather tired and seedy, but I soon forgot criticisms, as he delivered the best public address I have ever heard." To Howe, Beecher's possible sins were minor alongside his power, human nature and popularity. But Beecher's return lecture in Atchison the following year brought a harsh comment that editor Howe had forgotten when he praised Beecher in *Plain People* in the 1920s:

"Henry Ward Beecher, in his sermon last Sunday night, severely criticised the newspapers, referring to them as obstacles to the progress of Christianity. Mr. Beecher should know, and undoubtedly does, that he himself has been a greater obstacle to the progress of Christianity than all the newspapers put together" (May 23, 1879).

Howe also gave a newspaper plug to the lectures by one Professor Palmer, phrenologist and physiologist. "His agent has done a splendid job of advertising, and his course of lectures ought to be well attended" (Sept. 18, 1878). But the editor backed off from helping Atchison churches, and here he ran into much local indignation and abuse. He was given a small advertisement for a church show and sent a bill, at half rate, only to find himself, for his commercial crassness, in the middle of a "terrible fuss." Why should a newspaper give away its space any more than the gas company its gas, or a merchant his coal oil or groceries, "for the glory of the Lord," he asked. A newspaper apparently was "expected to live on wind or patriotism" (Apr. 24, 1878). And all of this was in accord with his developing beliefs about religion. He knew that death led only to oblivion, he kept writing; this was knowledge, not merely belief. As Howe wrote about churches and religion he found *The Globe* in the middle of a protest by the many denominations in the town. Advertisers and subscribers boycotted *The Globe* as others had boycotted James Gordon Bennett in the New York "moral war" of the 1840s. Howe's son Gene later wrote: "But father never backed up an inch. There were periods when he would subside, but he never retracted or apologized, and when he had accumulated fresh energy and hopes he would resume the combat." Friends suggested that Howe selected religion as the biggest and strongest opponent against which he could wage battle, and his courage brought him at least reluctant admiration. Nor was the battle easy on Howe. "No person could have been more sensitive. He cringed at every blow that was struck back."[8] There were tirades, cancellations, threats and actual fights, editorials in church papers, and rebuffs in many forms, all of which led to more difficulties and more editorials.

Howe's paper always seemed happiest when it could print a juicy scandal, even one that carried no names. If the scandal happened to be connected with religion it was even better. Attacks on Howe for his impiety undoubtedly came from such stories in *The Globe* as one headlined "A RURAL SCANDAL":

> People at all conversant with the facts will agree that the community in the neighborhood of Mt. Pleasant, this county, is a very religious one, and will therefore be surprised that a scandal has developed there. The people boast two substantial and well patronized churches, of the Methodist and Baptist denominations, and the religious feeling has been so broad that there has been little of the petty jealousy and rivalry usual in such cases. . . . Among the members of the Methodist flock was one Deacon Longprayer, a thrifty farmer and good citizen, who enjoyed a large measure of the public confidence. He had been religious from his youth up, and we remember that he once called at this office to ask the editor to repent and be saved. . . . He lived on a long lane shaded by trees, and just across from his place lived Sister Classmeeting, a lady known far and near for her beautiful speeches at Thursday evening class, and for her general Christian hospitality. . . .
>
> About two weeks ago Brother Longprayer went to his pastor, and made a confession to him of this tenor: He had loved Sister C. in secret for two years! When he felt the feeling

> coming over him, he went to the woods and prayed for strength to overcome it, but he rapidly grew worse, and the devil so planned it that when he made his usual neighborly visits to Sister C.'s house, Mr. C. was in Atchison, and the children at school. The devil also conspired with his angels in such a manner that Sister C. was similarly affected, and although they kneeled down together on the kitchen floor and prayed for deliverance, the aid was for some reason denied them. So they sinned, and have kept it up at intervals since. . . . He therefore considered it his duty to advise with his pastor.
>
> The good shepherd immediately went to Sister Classmeeting, and told her of Brother Longprayer's confession. She denied it entirely, with this exception: Brother L. once came to her house in the absence of her husband and children, and made love to her, while she was preserving blackberries. She hit him a vigorous lick across the face with the preserving spoon, and he then left the house. (Several of the neighbors now remember that about that time Brother Longprayer had a scar on the bridge of his nose.) He came again shortly, and said he was certain the people knew about it, for they looked at him as they would look at an elephant in a menagerie. [May 24, 1880]

Howe also commented on "a certain divine" of the vicinity, known as a dissenter, who "lately electrified and horrified his congregation by openly justifying adultery" (Jan. 21, 1880). He predicted that the man likely would be turned out of his church. Another news item recalled the shock Howe had felt in his own boyhood: "Rev. E. W. Howell, pastor of the Methodist church at Baxter Springs, has left his sheep at the mercy of the wolves, and fled with the wife of one of his elders, with whom he has long been criminally enamored and intimate. He leaves a wife and seven children behind in poverty, having sold everything he possessed before leaving" (Jan. 31, 1880).

Ed Howe knew that he was angering the community, and he quoted Sol Miller, who edited the *Kansas Chief* in nearby Troy, as saying that the newspaper was "very disreputable." It was that, said Miller, because it told the truth about the wickedness of good people. And when the high and mighty committed crimes and indiscretions, and tried to get the facts suppressed, *The Globe* was just as willing to trumpet such news to the world as news about the lowly, so that "those papers which are devoted to upholding the law and defending the holy, [must] get out their whitewash brushes, and go to spreading a coat of it upon the accused, hinting of blackmail, blood money, dirty slander, et settery" (July 17,

1885). *The Globe* was drawing criticism at the same time for the views it was expressing about women. Howe seemed to be suggesting that women were ruining and demoralizing men, but as many of his later writings indicate, he was placing clearly as much blame on the man, especially in those boy-girl relationships before marriage that often resulted in a scandal for the town to chew over.

So Ed Howe was busy making enemies, and friends, too, as he bluntly recorded life as he saw it. In an opposition paper a man wrote that Howe was insane, possibly because Howe had denied that the fellow had a cure for consumption. Another said Howe had hounded him for years; Howe thought the man was angry because he had never mentioned him in his paper. He once refused to keep news of a suicide out of *The Globe,* and he was sure that two persons disliked him because he mentioned "very briefly and respectfully their shot gun marriage; they wanted a lot of details about bridesmaids and floral decorations when there was no such elaboration."[9] Another time he wrote: "A couple who were only married about two months ago, were made parents last night by special dispensation of providence. Up to noon to-day, fifteen persons had called at this office for a copy of the paper containing their marriage notice" (Aug. 7, 1879). Still another anonymous report was this story, the kind that reaches few society pages: "An interesting sensation is circulating about the streets to the effect that a certain young widow was deserted by her affianced on the very eve of their marriage, last Wednesday. The cake was on the table, the guests invited and the bride in her robes; in fact, everything was ready for the ceremony, but up to the present the perfidious groom has not been heard of" (Oct. 31, 1879).

This was the kind of story that was characterizing the small-town *Globe,* as similar stories were common in Dana's *Sun* and soon in the rejuvenated *World* under Pulitzer. Howe described a tearful tale about two girls who arrived in Atchison from "somewhere up the Atchison and Nebraska road," and were promptly victimized by local rowdies—prominent business men, at that—who, hearing the girls were interested in the location of the variety theater, proceeded to obtain a tape line and to measure the girls for tights, then to dismiss them because they did not meet qualifications. Young girls coming to Atchison were creating numerous scandals, *The Globe* wrote, by not realizing that in the city one must pull down the shades when making one's toilet. "An awful case occurred on .... street last night" (Dec. 5, 1879). Now all this anonymity in the press made even the editor realize that he needed to offer proof now and then; he did so at one time by informing his readers that there were thirty divorce cases pending in district court (Nov. 28, 1879). Howe answered his critics on another occasion by telling them that although *The Globe* had been accused of levity and ridicule it had not been accused of untruthfulness and wilful lying: ". . . in matters of news the GLOBE never lies," he said (May 9, 1881). He must have felt the problem of suppression, too, for he commented that he had never seen a city where there was more news in circulation, "but the people are so respectable that the papers are not allowed to say anything about it until three weeks old" (May 11, 1880).

Portrait of a Small-Town Paper

Practically no sophistication, no erudition could be found in *The Atchison Globe* of the late 1870s and early 1880s. Except for changing type faces, as the editor experimented, and a gradually enlarging format the paper looked the same from year to year. In the fashion of the time advertising was placed on the front page, usually advertising from the same people. "Watering-place notes" called attention to society doings in the East for the land-bound residents of Atchison: "The young man who does not dance is frowned upon by the ladies at Cape May. Barnegat has a novelty in the shape of a floating hotel for sportsmen and their families" (Aug. 1, 1879). (This must have been lifted from the exchanges.) Subject matter of the brief news reports and the paid locals was not calculated to interest the big-city dweller, except for the humorous twists Ed Howe frequently provided. Commentaries were about the big dance at Mrs. Mahn's gardens, the beginning of operations at Trimmer's grain dumps, the sexes being "equally divided in the police court this morning" (Aug. 12, 1879), items from the almanacs, news from East Atchison, a pantomime artist coming to the Corinthian Hall, certificates of warranty, sentimental poetry, "The Little Globe" page of news and comment (for in the early years it was on that page that most of the crisp observations of the editor appeared). There were fires, one that consumed a saloon, and Howe was inclined to pin the blame on a "swaggering, half drunken fellow" who lost money at the place and boasted "that he would get even with the d-n whelp yet—he'd never win another three dollar pot in that house again" (Jan. 3, 1880). There was a jeweler who had discovered the meanest man on earth, a bridegroom who refused to pay for his engagement ring. There was news of a party of Atchison dwellers, including Howe, who went to "Old Joe" to see Haverly's Mastodon Minstrels, "but really to infuse into that sluggish city a little Atchison boom." Howe's paper said of another city: "Kansas City is probably the most disagreeable town on this continent." He noted the way in which the Negro was becoming an issue in American politics, and in local affairs, too: "All the black folks, accompanied by their nephews, grandchildren and nieces, went to Leavenworth to-day to celebrate" (Aug. 1, 1879). With some pride, he told how he had helped to defeat a local mayor:

"I noted one day that a great number of Negro women were registering, and that all declared they intended voting for the Republican. Every day thereafter until the registration closed, I printed the number of colored women who registered, and said they went to the trouble that they might vote for the Republican. The result was that the white women registered and voted, and as they greatly outnumbered the blacks, the Democrat [whom Howe favored] was elected."[10]

Atchison was a country town with saloons, gambling, houses of prostitution, and scandals. The "joints" were frequently in the news, and as the issue of prohibition became critical in Kansas the saloons received even more attention. Howe had a brush with a lawyer who was appointed assistant attorney general and who made it known that he believed Howe was responsible for exploding a bomb on the back porch of his home. Howe succeeded in clearing himself and in suggesting that the gentleman probably exploded the bomb himself, to call attention to the work he was doing to enforce the prohibitory law. Lawyers and doctors were frequently the object of attacks by the editor—the lawyers for their high fees and faulty administration of justice, the doctors for their high fees: "We know men who could not command a dollar and a half a day in any other walk of life who easily earn three or four hundred dollars a month with physic" (Dec. 8, 1879).

Every day, for many months, prominently on the front page, there appeared a picture of a long-haired gentleman, one Dr. Lameroux of Chicago, who had opened his office over O'Donnell's store, where he could be consulted on all chronic disease, he being a curer of cancer, consumption, spermatorrhoea, liver complaint, rheumatism, catarrh, neuralgia, and "all diseases peculiar to women" (May 14, 1878). And yet in the column next to this display, Howe could write as follows: "A medical journal asks, 'Shall doctors advertise?' We answer in the negative. When they get their diploma, which has cost them so much time, money and study, they should hang out a shingle, retire to some secluded attic, and wait patiently for patients. The quacks alone should be allowed to advertise and make all the money" (May 18, 1878).

The interests of the editor were bounded by transportation and communication in those days, *The Globe* at first focusing its attention on its own city but also on nearby communities. As the 1880s progressed there came to be more news and commentaries from Emporia, Lawrence, and Wichita, and still more from Kansas City, which commanded the Kansas-Missouri area. Circulation of the little paper was increasing: Howe frequently printed boasts of his gains—436 papers early in 1878 ("We can't lie. Our little weekly was to-day mailed to something less than one hundred subscribers"; it would be foolish to "talk about our legion of readers"); 837 in early 1880; city circulation of 1,000 in October of that year, and Howe challenging any doubters to call at the office to verify the figures. He was scornful of those who felt that a newspaper had to perjure itself about its circulation in order to succeed, and in late 1883 (Dec. 29) he was claiming that *The Globe* circulated three times more dailies in the city than its competitors combined ("If the *Champion* had 800 and the *Patriot* 600, then *The Globe* has 4,200"). Atchison meanwhile was growing. *The Globe* headlined a story of the town's new union depot and its display of decorated engines. At that time the town had three breweries (which were closed by prohibition the following year), two flour mills, railroad shops, and packing houses. The town historian wrote, "Log houses have given way to fine commodious houses, steam heated and electric lighted; great barns shelter the stock, and house the grain."[11] The city's growth and the popularity of *The Globe* were causing the advertising lineage to increase—four-column display ads and classified and small business ads usually dominating the front page; more advertising on the other pages. And the paid locals were interspersed with news and editorial matter: "Whatever you may believe with reference to politics, or as to the guilt of Mrs. Tilton, please don't forget that H. B. Stout & Co. run the boss boot and shoe store of Atchison" (Apr. 22, 1878).

At about this time, as the 1880s were bringing success to Ed Howe and farmers' complaints were beginning to become an issue in American politics, Howe was spending his evenings at home working on a book that would be regarded by critics as a dour complaint against the miseries of rural and small-town life. Yet if Howe was a critic of small towns his editorials of the period fail to prove it. From him might come a Will Rogers-ish comment: "A country town don't amount to much nowadays unless they have a telephone and the best brass band in the State" (July 27, 1878), or a disgusted call for somebody to clean up the streets, "a disgrace to a village of Hottentots," with choked-up sewers, mud and water on the pavements, crossings accessible only to experienced swimmers (Jan. 27, 1879). But generally Howe was as big a boomer as some of the people he laughed at in his novels.

"Atchison can offer better inducements for a glucose factory than any point on the Missouri river between Omaha and Kansas City," he said. There was corn in unlimited quantities and at good prices, and there were fine facilities for transportation. "No manufacturing establishment could be more worthy a bonus from Atchison than a first class woollen mill," he wrote. Such an institution would have many skilled workmen and pay good wages, and Atchison had the best location, "as it can command the growing wool trade of Kansas." Boom the woolen trade, "and work it for all it is worth" (June 9, 1887). Booster editorials were published to shake up the people who had gone to sleep:

> If you want your town to improve, improve it. If you want to make your town lively, make it. Don't go to sleep, but get up and work for it. Push. Advertise it. Talk about it, and talk favorably. If you have any property, improve it. Paint your houses; clean up your back yard. Make your surroundings pleasant, and you will feel better and your property will be worth more dollars in the market. If you are doing reasonably well, advise your far away friends to come and invest near you. Work steadily for your home place and home interests. Trade at home; help your home dealers. Keep your money at home as

> much as possible, and it is likely to help you in return. The successful towns of Kansas have been made successful by the property owners pulling together. Public improvement is an investment that pays. Don't waste your time over some dirty neighborhood quarrel, and hold back your aid from some good object through spite, but work for some good, and you will find yourself benefitted. [Mar. 2, 1887]

Bad times were generally a myth to Howe, who hated the growlers and the malcontents then beginning to agitate in his state. He looked about him—or talked with travelers—and saw the beauty of the Kansas wheat fields, and he predicted abundant harvests: ". . . with the prospect of a large yield of grain, our farmers feel jubilant" (Feb. 29, 1878). Grasshoppers had not made a point of lighting down yet in Atchison, but they would come, he told the gloomy: "It will perhaps be remembered that the prophets of evil have been expecting this, in connection with dry weather, for several seasons" (Sept. 15, 1879). He could resort to the kind of complaint that is so representative of Kansans, too, and get a laugh from his readers: "During the recent high winds, a couple of gentlemen in an interior Kansas town were holding on to a hitching post and discussing the weather. Said one: 'Oh, this country would be the finest country in the world if it had a good climate and plenty of water.' Said the other: 'So would hell!' " (Apr. 19, 1880).

Most of the time he foresaw only golden days for his section of the state, predicting great growth, observing that northern Kansas lands were better than those to the south and that only a lack of concerned railroad people had prevented progress. And almost once a year this one-man Chamber of Commerce would rhapsodize about the glories of his region:

> Kansas is the garden spot of the world. Like a handsome maiden, she is rosy, smiling and beautiful. She is winning new suitors every day, and although she may jilt them occasionally by some trifling freak, they still look upon her with love and admiration. Even though some may receive disappointments, they still, like the young lover who had been rejected, look upon her with love and adoration, and envy those who are favorably treated by her. The lover returns to his "first love" at the first opportunity, and winks at her as fondly as before, and at times a little more so. Oh, there's no use talking, she's the belle of the Union, and the paradise of the earth. If you live in the muddy, gloomy, drowning east, don't hesitate a day, but sell

> out your swamp, and come to the country where your possessions will make you fifty or seventy-five per cent. richer the first year. Come along and be happy with us. [Sept. 5, 1884]

Ed Howe meanwhile appeared to be gaining community acceptance, despite his brutal frankness and his attacks on religion and womanhood. A *Globe* story told how "Major Ed. W. Howe" was publicly caned: the young editor had his twenty-fifth birthday, and his friends arranged a party at which he was presented a gold-headed cane which cost his friends, he learned, thirty-six dollars. Howe knew the affair had the ring of a lampoon, but he was proud enough of the incident to write about it in later special editions. He became cynical enough, too, to know that a man's fame is in proportion to his being alive or dead, however: "A newspaper which will persistently refuse to tell the creditable truth with reference to a living man, will lie ridiculously in praising him after he is dead" (Dec. 24, 1883).

He wrote less and less as the years went by and picked up more and more from other papers—the Kansas City press, the *Chicago Tribune,* the New York *World,* the New York *Sun.* He noted with interest the successful appearance of a new daily in the rival city down the Missouri: "The *Kansas City Star,* the new afternoon daily, is very pretty, very newsy, and well edited, but can its staff keep it up for a year—two years, or twenty? That is the test of a thorough newspaper man" (Sept. 21, 1880). And he found in the *Star* a sense of truth akin to his own standards: "The *Kansas City Star*'s society reporter knows how to draw a distinction. He does not refer to a ball recently given at the Comique as a 'brilliant reception.' On the contrary, he declares that it was a public revel of the bawds and bummers of the city, at which disgusting scenes of rioting and debauchery were witnessed; that it was a motley gathering of blacklegs, abandoned women and social scum generally, with a fair sprinkling of Metropolitan police" (Feb. 7, 1882).

The public received frequent progress reports of changes in *The Globe* and its moves to new sites. In early 1879 an item told about the new power press due to arrive the next week, and there was an invitation to come up and see "three of the prettiest machine presses that ever mashed a finger—two of Gordon's latest, and one of Campbell's complete cylinders" (Apr. 2, 1879). In early 1881 Howe announced that the "mammoth edition of the

WEEKLY GLOBE" would be printed on the single-cylinder country Campbell press: "Seats have been arranged around the room for the accommodation of the ladies" (Feb. 17, 1881). In the same year he announced that *The Globe* would have the most complete printing office of its own in Kansas; that it would be sending out a traveling correspondent into the state. So the newspaper slowly changed. It converted in early 1883 to a steam press, and a year later it had to deny reports that it had been sold and would not be issued any longer. On the contrary, said Ed Howe; "The GLOBE will be considerably enlarged and improved within a few weeks" (Feb. 22, 1884). As progress came so did attention to evolving patterns in American newspapering. It was now *The Atchison Globe.* Advertising remained on page one, but there were more display heads, news was collected under "news in brief," and it became easier for the reader to find what he was looking for. *The Globe* still provided problems for some readers, but Howe had an explanation:

> Occasionally a man with a mysterious look takes us aside, and says he noticed an amusing typographical blunder in a previous issue. If our readers could be in this office every afternoon, they would not wonder that errors creep into our columns. The editor's table stands beside a Gorden press, with two others only slightly removed. There is a constant buzz and hum of conversation; yelling about words, about copy, about job work, and about everything else. In addition to this, we are constantly surrounded by men who call on business, or to talk politics. About three o'clock the noisy carriers commence to arrive, and no power on earth can keep them still. They fight all around us over new subscribers; quarrel over the choice places to fold papers, and in the midst of this the editorial work is done. [Mar. 5, 1879]

The Globe carriers were both pride and joy. Howe wrote about the two boys who had the principal routes on the paper and the way they settled who should have both routes: ". . . they would let their little brothers fight, and the one winning should have both routes! The little roosters promptly came to the scratch, and tied their galluses around their loins with bloody intent, but some of the printers interfered, and stopped a settlement of the question" (May 17, 1878). He knocked the "distinguished citizens" who were known to bilk his carriers out of forty to ninety cents as being no better than those who "would steal coppers from a blind

THE GLOBE.

A Daily Evening Poster Devoted to Gab and Gossip, and Paid Locals

PRICE, TWO CENTS. ATCHISON, KS., APRIL 1, 1878. VOL. 1. NO. 87.

HATS AND CAPS. | FURNISHING GOODS.

CHARLEY THOMPSON ON HAND!

C. H. THOMPSON,

The Great Gentlemen's Furnisher,

Hereby gives the LITTLE GLOBE readers notice that his

NEW SPRING STOCK HAS ARRIVED!

Comprising EVERYTHING that the most fastidious and tasty gentleman can call for.

HATS AND CAPS!

The assortment is a complete as can be found in the best retail store in New York City, including every new novelty and style, at every price and to suit every taste.

His stock of **UNDERWEAR, Suspenders, Collars and Cuffs, Canes, Umbrellas, Gloves, &c., &c., IS SIMPLY IMMENSE!**

PRICES REDUCED ALL ROUND! DON'T YOU FORGET THAT!

HE GUARANTEES THE BEST STOCK AND THE LOWEST PRICES.

No trouble to show goods! Go in and see for yourself whether you want to buy or not. The great Thompson and his gentlemanly assistants will be glad to see you. They will take your lilly white hand in their'n and show you a stock of goods that catches all the boys.

HATS AND CAPS. | FURNISHING GOODS.

HETHERINGTON'S BANK, Atchison. Oldest in the city.

GILBERT & OCKER, Attorneys at Law, Fourth st.

DR. D. J. HOLLAND, Physician and Surgeon, Atchison, Kansas.

J. BEETENSHAW, the Practical Hatter, Cor. of 8th and Kansas.

WESTERN ELEVATOR Co. [illegible] Grain wanted in car load lots.

E. C. JOHNSON, The Best Shoe Store. Oldest in the city.

A. C. HAGAN, Attorney at Law. Office in Hetherington's bank building.

JOHN C. TOMLINSON, Attorney and Counsellor at Law, Atchison, Kansas. Office rooms: Hetherington's bank building.

Wm. E. Smith. H. C. Solomon.

SMITH & SOLOMON,
ATTORNEYS AT LAW,

S. E. Cor. Fourth and Com'l sts.
Will practice in all State and Federal Courts. [illegible]

MARKS' OTIS HOUSE BILLIARD SALOON. Finest in Atchison.

WASHINGTON HOUSE, 4th st., near Kas. ave. Mrs. F. Mahn, Proprietress.

W. S. GREENLEE, Attorney at Law, 425 Com'l st., up stairs.

ATLANTIC HOUSE, cor. 6th and Com'l st. Mrs. N. K. Wakefield, Proprietress.

GEO. MAYHOOD & SON, Third Street Meat Market, 3rd and Com'l sts.

PURE Kentucky Whisky, five years old. Choice Wines and Cigars at Duffy's sample room.

HAGEN & TREFZ, Bakers and Confectioners. Dealers in Cigars, Fruits, Oysters, Fancy Goods, etc. [illegible] Com'l st.

CHAS. KROESING, [illegible] Commercial st., is the man to see when you get [illegible]

FRANK E. EVEREST, STENOGRAPHER, with Everest & Waggener, Atchison.

10 POUNDS of [illegible] sugar for $1 at J. M. Edmiston's, [illegible] Com'l st.

M. MARCUS, wholesale wines, liquors and cigars. Sample room in connection.

EVEREST & WAGGENER, Attorneys & Counsellors at Law, over Hetherington & Co's Bank, Atchison, Kansas.

J. A. NORTON & SON, [illegible] Watches, Jewelry [illegible]

J. HIGBY, Practical Gas and Steam Fitter, and Dealer in Iron and Wood Pumps, Hose, Iron Pipe and Fittings, 606 Com'l st.

C. WEBER, Clothing, Furnishing Goods, etc. Suits made to order. 310 Com'l st.

D. H. SALINGER & Co., Cigars & Tobaccos. "S & K," 10c; "Vanity Fair," 5c.

DR. J. E. THATCHER, Homeopathist. Office in Burnes' block, 512 Com'l st.

FOR Cheap, Reliable Fire Insurance, call on C. A. Goodrich, 514 Com'l st.

CHAS. TERRY, Boss Music Man, Atchison. Don't fail to see him before buying.

H. BRADNER, the Merry Anheuser Man. A good man to know.

L. KIFER & SONS, Hides and Leather, 613 Commercial street, Atchison.

D. C. BRADFORD, 512 Com'l st. Best organs and pianos. BEST TERMS.

OTIS HOUSE, Atchison, Kansas. C. C. Burnes & Co., Proprietors. Leading hotel of the Missouri Valley. Every modern convenience and improvement.

T. M. PIERCE, Attorney at Law, Atchison. Office in Hetherington bank bl'k.

McPIKE & FOX, Wholesale Druggists, Atchison. Compete with anybody.

KELSEY & SIMPSON, Furniture. Largest house in the Valley.

DR. HAGAN, Photographer. Best in Atchison. Photographs $2.00 per dozen. Pictures copied and enlarged. Also, coloring in India ink and water colors. 409 Commercial st. 46

THE GLOBE JOB PRINTING OFFICE. Fine Commercial printing a specialty. Business men are invited to call and examine specimens of work.

Dr. Bowen, Atchison's leading dentist, has fitted up a splendid suit of dental rooms over Kelsey & Simpson's, where he is now prepared to receive all his old customers and friends, together with any new ones that they may see fit to bring along. 83-1m.

Robert A. Heim, the "boss" wall paper man, will open a complete stock of the above article, on or about April 5th. Look out for it. Every roll new. No old patterns. 85-tf

REPUBLICAN CITY TICKET.

For Mayor,
CLEMENT ROHR.
For Marshal,
CHAS. W. BENNING.
For City Attorney,
W. D. GILBERT.
For City Treasurer,
WM. LAMBERT.
For Treasurer of the School Board,
A. H. LANPHEAR.
For Constables,
JAS. W. TRUESDELL,
GEO. W. GRAVES.
For Councilmen,
First Ward—HENRY T. SMITH.
Second Ward—A. D. McCONAUGHY.
Third Ward—JAS. A. LOPER.
Fourth Ward—W. S. GREENLEE.
For Members of the School Board,
First Ward—H. A. COATES.
Second Ward—J. L. BLISS.
Third Ward—SAM. C. KING.
Third Ward—JOHN SEATON.

If you want to buy meats of a man that gives full weight, and gives you just what you call for, patronize Ed. Haug, corner Fourth and Commercial. 72-1m.

Robert A. Heim, the "boss" wall paper man, will open a complete stock of the above article, on or about April 5th. Look out for it. Every roll new. No old patterns. 85-tf

Carpenters! Call on A. J. Harwi and see his stock of Jennings' Bits. Also, Bailey's Iron Bench Planes.

That celebrated Anheuser always on draught at John Kaffer's Commercial.

Atlantic House, corner 6th and Commercial, by Mrs. N. K. Wakefield. $2 per day. 1m.

If you want to buy clothing cheap, see L. Frank about it.

OPERA HOUSE.

One Night Only.

Thursday, April 4th

John Dillon,

Supported by a specially selected company from McVicker's Theater, Chicago, and under the management of J. H. McVicker in W. D. Eaton's late comedy success, entitled

"All the Rage."

John Dillon as Atwood, the Cheropodist.

Popular Prices:

General Admission, 75c. Gallery, 50c.

No extra charge for reserved seats, for sale at Brown's Postoffice Book Store.

W. F. CONKLIN & CO.,

Wholesale

CARRIAGE

Manufacturers,

412 and 414 Pine Street,

ST. LOUIS, MO.

CARRIAGES, Buggies, Phaetons, side bar Road Wagons, Platform Spring Wagons, &c., at 50 per cent below any other first-class manufacturers. No shoddy or shoe fly work manufactured. Send for circulars and Price List. CORRESPONDENCE SOLICITED.

Buggies on sale in Atchison.

An early front page of *The Globe,* this graced by more advertising than was customary (Courtesy Kansas Historical Society)

Gene Howe
(Courtesy Kansas Historical Society)

Mateel Howe Farnham
(Courtesy James P. Howe)

James P. Howe
(Courtesy Associated Press)

The Howe home in Atchison, North Third Street
(Courtesy *The Atchison Globe*)

man" (Nov. 23, 1878). Howe was a sharp business man: Early in 1883, while vacationing at a mineral springs in Waukesha, Wisconsin, Howe revealed his business sense in a letter to Joseph R. Kathrens, an early-day reporter and printer's devil on *The Globe:* "During your present experience I would advise that you keep a sharp lookout all the time for advertising and printing, for they are the life of the establishment, and the more you get the more I can pay" (Jan. 28, 1883).

The Editor and His Family

Few glimpses and no portraits exist of the young Howe family or of the editor father then only in his twenties. Enigmatic comments appear; so do anecdotes and pleasant pictures like that drawn by young William Allen White when he visited Howe in Atchison in 1886. But the editor provides no dates of birth of his children, no physical description of his wife, no names of the two babies (Bessie and Ned) who died so young, probably at the very time he was trying to compose his first novel as well as edit a struggling newspaper.

Experience with families he certainly had, enough to make him critical of the newfangled approaches to child-rearing: "There is a new way of bringing up babies. Every habit practiced by the good old fashioned mothers, is discarded. If the baby cries, it is permitted to cry. If it doesn't cry, the supposition is that it is ill, and a doctor is sent for. The baby is fed only four or five times a day. We don't believe in it. We venture the assertion that the new theory was invented by a wise old maid. We say, feed a baby when it is hungry; we say that when a baby cries, there is something the matter. We say mothers know more about babies than old maids" (Apr. 28, 1902).

Always Ed Howe had the experience of having a family around, of the noise, the confusion, the problems. Get-togethers might be family reunions to some; to him they were bores. How much cynicism, how much genuine conviction lay in a comment like this? "We have noticed that in a family group photograph, each member seems ashamed of the rest of them" (Mar. 10, 1892).

How much tenderness and compassion, how much bitterness, out of his own experiences, in this?

> One of the rarest things in the world is to see a perfect friendship existing between a father and his children. You see it every hour between a mother and her sons, and a mother and her daughters, but in the distribution of family affection, the father is in most cases left out. Every woman has all the patient and tender instincts of a mother: not one man in a hundred is a success as a father. He is impatient with the children when they are young, and they remember it, and are impatient with him when he is old. In many cases the mother is innocently to blame: instead of making herself a link between the father and his children, she makes herself a barrier. She pictures him to the little ones as a bug-a-boo who will whip them when he comes home at night for all their naughtiness through the day. They are taught to regard him as a punishment for wickedness, instead of some one who loves them in his way, and who will reward them for being good. [May 12, 1892]

He must have known fairly early that his marriage was a failure. Family disaster he certainly knew in his first year on *The Globe,* when diphtheria took the lives of his two oldest children. Such tragedy probably lay behind this distraught and apologetic note: "The LITTLE GLOBE never did amount to a great deal, but it has amounted to less the last four or five weeks than we ever intended, owing to a series of misfortunes that have kept the editor-manager-collector-solicitor either at home, or so near crazy as to render him incapable of attending to his ordinary duties. In apologising for the loose manner in which the paper has been conducted during that time, it is with the direct understanding that we will make every endeavor to make it up in time to come (Aug. 27, 1878).

And it must have been callous souls who led Ed Howe, almost a decade later, to make this tortured observation in his paper: "Among the grave charges made against the editor of the GLOBE is that when he first came to Atchison, two of his children, the only ones he had, died within a week of diptheria [sic]. . . . The charge is true; there is a monument in Oak Hill cemetery to prove it" (Feb. 14, 1887).

Of the three children who survived Howe, the oldest was James, who was born February 6, 1879. Next came his beloved daughter, Mateel, a name which he also gave to the miserable heroine of *The Story of a Country Town,* and which he said he took from a Frenchwoman's pronunciation of "Mathilde." Mateel was born May 21, 1883, and Howe wrote most eloquently of her impact upon his life, when he was reviewing his life in the late 1920s: "The nearest approach to that beautiful thing, an angel, is a little girl of ten or twelve. Women of sixteen or twenty, and into the shadowy regions beyond, are of course adorable, but when my only daughter was twelve I loved her so much that frequently I took her on long trips that I might have her all to myself. We went through Yellowstone Park in the days when I believe she was the prettiest and most adorable child in the world, and I a young husband and father. Today I stood before a picture taken in that remote time, and walked away almost in tears; we have both so greatly changed."[12]

Mateel, then, was the joy of his younger days. Of the boy Jim it is fair to comment that his effect on his father was negligible, even though Jim's later success was occasion for fatherly pride. From the beginning Jim never really knew Ed Howe as a father. In *The Globe,* Howe recorded vignettes that suggest he was aware of the problems of being a father, however, such as his struggle to cut himself down to three cigars a day, a struggle being witnessed by the son, and "we believe he will never learn to smoke or chew tobacco" (Mar. 10, 1883). There was another note at Christmas time:

"If the toy makers and dealers continue to multiply, it will finally become impossible to please the children, and they will cry because they cannot get the earth. The writer of this has a son who wants a live elephant, as big as the one with Barnum's circus (which he was unfortunately taken to see), and we are certain that there will be trouble Christmas morning if we fail to procure an elephant" (Dec. 23, 1884).

It was just a little house in which the Howes lived in the early days in Atchison. But later in the 1880s the family moved to a big red brick home in a hilly yard on Third Street (there Howe's niece, Adelaide, lived after Ed Howe died). Howe had wanted a home resembling one he knew in the neighborhood, and there was little more than hazelbush on the property when the land was cleared for the house. There was more money coming into the home by then, and Howe was able to employ four servants and to keep a horse, carriage, cows, dogs, chickens, and cats when the children were still small.

His son Gene was born March 22, 1886, in the big house, the only child born there, and it is from Gene's writings that the chief insights into the family and its concerns may be obtained. But Gene was a baby in the 1880s, the storm and turbulence of the Howe family lying a decade or so in the future. Ethel Ingalls of Atchison, who knew the family intimately, wrote of Howe's love for his children, and suggested already the troubles to come:

"Outside his paper, the only objects of interest are two of his children, a boy and a girl, 7 and 9 years old. Children as a rule irritate him, but in those two mites of humanity he takes much comfort, and, though known as a cold, unresponsive man and totally indifferent to all those tender impulses that ennoble our character, these children are the joys of his life and the objects for which he works. His oldest child is a lad of 11 who fell from grace by running away from home, and his father has never forgiven him for this infantile escapade."[13]

Human Interest and News in the 1880s

What a newspaper prints provides one dimension of its place in a community. How it says it is much more important in the case of *The Atchison Globe.* And *The Globe*'s editor, Edgar Watson Howe, was becoming a celebrated figure in the Kansas of his time, largely through the vigor and style of his expression. He scoffed at the matter, but he even received a boom for governor in 1883:

> "Hon. Ed. W. Howe, of the Atchison GLOBE," says the *Lincoln Journal,* "has been favorably mentioned for Governor of Kansas by a number of his confreres of the press." In justice to ourselves we will say that we have never intimated to any one a desire to be Governor of Kansas. A short time ago we were waited upon by a number of gentlemen and urged to make the race, but we positively declined. We informed the gentlemen that our candidacy under existing circumstances was simply out of the question. They stormed and even threatened, but we were immovable. They left our office in a despairing, hopeless sort of way, but we afterwards learned that they called

> on the editor of our morning contemporary and urged him to make the race. He partially agreed to do so, but requested that nothing be said about it at present. That's all there is about our candidacy for Governor. Of course we are not without ambition, and some day we may gratify a clamoring public by consenting to serve as their chief executive. But in the meantime we shall be content to pursue our present humble calling. The brethren of the press who are now shouting for us will therefore please desist. [June 16, 1883]

If he ever sought prominence in life the fact is not revealed in the columns of *The Globe*. What he wanted was comfort, a life that would contrast with the hardship his parents had known. For him, "the sum of a contented existence is good health, a pleasant place to go to at night, an evening free to do as you please, a clean and comfortable bed to crawl into about ten o'clock, a good breakfast at seven o'clock, and enough to do during the day to keep you from lamenting over misfortunes" (Apr. 3, 1883). He was critical of the complainers, who feared the fruit had been injured by the bad weather, who foresaw a siege of dry weather, and maybe chinch bugs and grasshoppers, and a slump in business and inflation in prices, and more rheumatism and sore backs. As conditions became worse in the midlands there were more people complaining, and more people looking for work or for a handout. "The tramps are getting remarkably thick again," he wrote. "If any of them call on you for a meal, inform them that men are wanted at the packing house to clean fat off hog bowels" (Jan. 11, 1879).

He loved to look at the exchanges and observe that the big boys had blundered. The *Chicago Times,* he said, was the "exponent of western grammar, and discharges everybody who fails to say 'on yesterday.' " So for Howe it was a point of great fun for the *Times* to report that one Samuel G. Seaton was looking for one W. J. Riley, "who is understood to have did him out of $500" (Aug. 9, 1879). The *St. Louis Globe-Democrat* was in error for praising the performance of the performer Carlotta Patti, and that put the *Globe-Democrat* in a class with the "one-horse papers of the Missouri Valley" (Dec. 4, 1879).

He carried some news from the big cities—prominent deaths, politics, the suicide of Cornelius Vanderbilt, in 1882, things like that. Page sizes and type sizes changed to accommodate changing times. Area news sometimes received extensive play: the rise of the Missouri in the spring of 1881, to 23 feet 4 inches above the low water mark. Howe missed the beat on the shooting of Jesse James, but he took the occasion to comment that by all rights the outlaw should have been killed in Kansas City, which appeared to have been his headquarters, where he had relatives, where he had committed crimes, where he was chummy with the newspaper reporters. "In allowing himself to be assassinated in St. Joe he showed himself to be an ungrateful sneak, and we are not surprised that the Kansas City papers are handling him without gloves" (Apr. 4, 1882). *The Globe* editor apparently was determined not to be beaten on similar stories, for he reported the trial of Bob Ford in the murder of Jesse, carried stories from the West, and reported on town rivalries. But when Frank James surrendered October 6, 1882, *The Globe* was forced to take its details from the morning *Kansas City Times,* and the rival *Champion* once again had the scoop.

Those were the years when Dana was refining the news principle, building human interest into a newspaper standard. But human interest was always in the country town *Globe:* children, animals, humor:

> This morning, as little Ed Gilson was going up town accompanied by a large Newfoundland dog, his usual attendant, the dog ran into the street and was kicked on the head by a horse. Gilson, thinking that the dog had received his death, burst into tears, and wept pitifully. He had the dog placed on the sidewalk, and went to work like a young surgeon to help him. The dog had only been stunned, and soon got up, wagging his tail, and frisking knowingly about his young master. Said the little fellow, as he patted the animal and prepared to move away: "That dog, I love better nor anything. He took me out of the Kaw river with his teeth three years ago, and I'd fight for him." Bravely spoken words, young man. [Jan. 21, 1880]

> A green countryman from this county went to Leavenworth yesterday morning, and before night became gloriously drunk. Wandering down toward the coal mine, he crawled into an empty car to sleep, which was shortly afterwards let down into the mine. In the course of an hour or two, he woke up, and found a hundred or two of men around him digging coal, with lamps in their caps. He studied the matter over awhile, and staggering up to one of the men, said: "In hell, just as I expected. Mr. Devil, what shall I go at?" This is the story as we heard it. We don't vouch for its truthfulness, or guarantee that it is funny, but out in the community where the young man

> lives, it is thought to be a very remarkable circumstance. [Feb. 21, 1880]
>
> The average town boy will take no rough talk from anybody except a circus man. If an ordinary mortal calls him a dirty nosed little thief and orders him to clear out, he leisurly [sic] backs away, the while hurling the most bitter and insulting epithets at his accuser. But if a circus man calls him vile names, he walks away without a word, firmly believing that he has incurred the displeasure of a great and good man. [Aug. 2, 1880]

Huge ads graced the front page of *The Globe* to herald the coming of the Grand Circus Royal English Menagerie, with a picture of a snorting rhinoceros, and W. C. C. Coup's New United Monster Shows, with a picture of a chariot race. These must have taken the editor back to the occasionally happy days of his youth. The fraudulent, so much a part of the formula of human interest, appeared in *The Globe* as in other journals: "There being a dearth of editorial matter, we depart from our usual rule and publish the annual rural lie: 'On the farm of Samuel Logan, near Palmyra, last week, was born a calf with two perfect heads and necks, five legs and feet, no sex" (Jan. 6, 1881). Deaths were reported in grisly detail: "When the car struck Brown, he gave a frightened scream, and the next moment the bystanders heard the merciless wheels crushing the bones of his neck and head. One of his teeth was picked up this morning from beside the rail, and another had been crushed to powder" (Feb. 13, 1880).

Like Dana, and like the later editors of the *Denver Post* who knew the value of a good dog fight on Champa Street, Howe readily reported such things as a local fight between dogs that almost brought on a fight between their owners. Rural America could be interested, especially, in stories about animals, and if an irreverent editor could work in a religious dig so much the better: "In Missouri, the other day, a mule deliberately committed suicide. He put his head through a post-and-rail fence, slipped his neck down to a narrow place, pulled back, and choked himself. The cause of the suicide is not known. He had not been drinking, and there was no trouble with his family. It is thought by some to have been the result of religious excitement" (Feb. 1, 1883).

The colored population of Atchison afforded him both annoyance and amusement: "A colored woman called at the residence of a member of the Second ward relief society this morning, and said she wanted relief. 'Have you a husband and family?' asked the lady. 'Oh, yes,' she answered, 'me and the old man has been married for twenty-three years, and got thirteen children, but I want relief.' 'What sort of relief?' interrupted the lady. 'A divorce,' said the colored woman. 'We can't live any longer together.' The case was referred to a lawyer" (Jan. 23, 1885).

The Globe had a formula of writing and news coverage that was as anti-pretentious as that of any paper in mid-America. Howe frowned on big words: "The word 'anent' that is just now being used so extensively by country editors is a half brother of excerpt, yclept, etc., and the GLOBE will have nothing to do with it" (Jan. 26, 1881). He was proud that the paper had never used the phrase, "Wee sma' hours," and he shamefully admitted that the paper once referred to a gathering as the *creme de la creme* of society. A man who had mystified his wife about an old trunk which he thought filled with treasures but found that it held only "four bunches of cigarettes, two cigars, a lot of newspaper clippings, (mostly poetry) an old scarf, a pair of woolen mits, and three socks" (Nov. 4, 1889); or a woman trying to drive horses: "When she arrives at the end of her journey, the horse is as much surprised as she is, for it is something he never expected to live to see" (Dec. 5, 1889)—these were the homely matters with which *The Globe* entertained its readers.

Howe reserved his sharpest shafts for the great and the mighty who stopped in Atchison, either on business or to bring cultural enlightenment to the community. Jay Gould "seemed possessed of that uneasy, restless disposition that leads a man to employ himself with his eyes and ears when sitting down" (Nov. 28, 1879). Oscar Wilde was the target of the paper through many seasons. First *The Globe* reported that the celebrated writer, then on his American tour, would *not* be coming to Atchison because the town had prohibition and Wilde was a man who liked to drink a good sturdy toddy. Then Wilde arrived, and Howe deprecated both the performer and those who would go hear him, as he stood, lily in hand, and talked on the local stage: "A nation which has produced such natural curiosities as Walt Whitman, Joacquin [sic] Miller and Col. Nicholas Smith could hardly have been expected to get so much excited about Oscar Wilde as to give him $300 a night for showing his calves" (Feb. 7, 1882). Then came a veritable barrage of anti-Wildean comments in *The Globe,* notably "The Darwinian Theory Illustrated," the title of a feature article on Wilde. Two drawings appeared on the page, the upper one a monkey holding a coconut—"As he appeared when first captured"; the lower one Oscar Wilde holding a flower—"As he appears after being trained." The story:

> The Darwinian theory of evolution, which was first promulgated in 1859 by Charles R. Darwin (who, by the way, died last Thursday), was at first received with derision by the world, but gradually grew in favor, and is now accepted by most of the leading scientific men of the world, including Huxley, Tyndall, Herbert Spencer and others. The evidences in support of the evolution theory which have been adduced by naturalists and laborers in other fields of science have been sufficient to establish its truth in the minds of students and thinkers everywhere. It is now a tenet of orthodox science that man was evolved, by a process of natural selection, from the lowest animals. Another proof of this has recently come to light. There has recently arrived from England a creature who presents many of the features of the quadrumanous animal of the class mammolia, known to savants as *pithecus,* but to the vulgar as "ape." A common distinction between the monkey, baboon and ape is that the first has a long and prehensile tale, the second a short one and the third none at all. *The Globe,* which is ever laboring in the cause of science, has procured, at the expense of four dollars, express added, two pictures which are above presented, one representing the pithecus and the other the British What-is-it, which has been on exhibition in this country for some months past, and which is at this precise moment said to be secreted in a sky parlor at the Otis house, hiding from the curious gaze of the female guests of that caravansary. The external points of resemblance are so numerous and striking that it is unnecessary to enter into any detailed comparison of the habits and manners of these two peculiar specimens. The illustrations are merely presented as striking confirmations of the theory of evolution which has long been a bone of contention in the scientific and religious world.
>
> The pithecus can be seen in a tent just outside the corporation this afternoon, and those who expect to see the What-is-it should make it a point to see the pithecus first. [Apr. 22, 1882]

Howe, usually ready to tongue-lash the town when it did not avail itself of cultural offerings, was delighted with the reception it gave Oscar Wilde. The lecture in Corinthian Hall drew an audience of forty-three, including the ushers and janitor. The cash receipts were around twenty-five dollars. ". . . Atchison had the honor of snubbing Mr. Wilde more effectually than any other city in the United States," said Howe. After the performance a number of local gentlemen obtained audience with the great man: "They found him posing in a dressing room, before his valet had relieved him of the absurd toggery which he wears on the stage, and on being introduced to the gentlemen, cordially shook hands with them, very much as a Kansas lecturer would have done, and talked with them quite freely . . . . He is very tall, has a very large head with bushy hair, and long and thin legs, which were encased in velvet knee breeches, and black silk stockings, and when he talks he rests his elbow on a shelf, or against the wall, in a very gawky manner" (Apr. 24, 1882).

The Globe also reported for "insipid and absurd females" who believed Wilde lived on "broiled moonbeams and toasted sighs" the list of foods sent to his room from the Otis House: "Three pieces of tenderloin steak, trimmed with parsley, Saratoga chips, lemon and toast; stewed chicken; mutton chop; fried sausage; five varieties of cold meats, vegetables and a cup of coffee. All the plates came back beautifully polished" (Apr. 24, 1882).

It was quite different for one of the perennially popular showings of the dramatic version of *Uncle Tom's Cabin.* Howe was pleased to see the people fill the stairways and corridors and make the scene at the ticket office resemble that at a circus wagon. For a celebrated stage performer of the era he reserved his most brutal language, after going to St. Joseph to see her before the footlights:

> At exactly 8:31 last night, Sara Bernhardt made her appearance on the stage of Tootle's Opera House, walking down the centre as though she had but one joint in her body, and no knees. Her first action was to shake hands with the stage company with arms as long and wiry as the tendrils of a devil fish, which wound around them occasionally with the soft grace of a serpent. Perhaps the first thing remarked of her by the average auditor is that she is almost red-headed, and that she wears her hair in light Dutch braids. The second, that she is distressingly ugly, and that her smile is painful, because it displays a big mouth and a prominent row of butter teeth. Her nose is of the pattern referred to as a "hook," and of her figure it is enough to say that it could not possibly be worse . . . . She talks fast, and takes tremendous strides across the stage. Her arms were encased in white kid to within an inch of her shoulders, and

> whenever she pointed the villain or other disagreeable person to the door, and said, "Go!!" we saw that the color of the hair under her arms was sandy. This was our first impression of Bernhardt, and the second was that a lady so ugly and ill-shapen should not, in justice to her sex, challenge the criticism and opera glasses of the public. . . .
>
> After the play, while smoking a cigar in the Pacific House office, the writer had the pleasure of meeting Bernhardt face to face as she came up the steps from the street, on her way to her room. She was a mass of furs and wraps, and looked neither to the right or the left. [Mar. 2, 1881]

The humor and the human interest, some of it urbane and some of it country town, could not have been—nor was it—Howe's alone (nor, perhaps, the cynicism and the bitterness). Many unsung reporters must have contributed the bright vignettes of life; Howe was quite a traveler, and he did some public speaking, but even with his tremendous capacity he could not have done the job by himself. He was an admirer and frequent quoter of Eugene Field, "the wittiest writer in America," and in the 1880s, at some predictably unidentified time, Field spent a short time on *The Globe*. Another of Howe's reporters in the 1880s was a later well-known Kansan, Walt Mason, who came to Atchison one day looking for a job, and was hired. Prose poetry in *The Globe* became the hallmark of Mason's work. It was around 1885 that Mason worked for the paper, out on the streets looking for news items. "Mr. Howe set the pace, and I have always marveled at his tireless industry," wrote Mason. "I soon learned that in chasing after news it was necessary to call on people every day, not once in a while." Mason's sources included a Negro policeman named Officer Baskett, who "seemed to gather up news as a sponge absorbs water," and Officer Flannery, and the wholesale grocery of Julius Kuhn, whose staff extended themselves to find copy, and the drug store people and the court house. Said Mason of his *Globe* days: "I have worked on many newspapers since and have never seen one that pursued local news with the diligence of the *Atchison Globe*. I have tried to introduce that system on several papers, but never found reporters willing to do such marathon stunts as we used to do. In those halcyon days every reporter was anxious to make a scoop on the loathsome contemporary and no work was too hard, no discomfort too great, when there was a chance to triumph. And *The Globe* used to beat its rivals on local news every day of the week. . . . The old *Globe* system was hard on shoe leather, but it got results" (Dec. 8, 1927).

Globe reporters were all over Atchison. A tour of the local jail brought a *Globe* cry for improvement of conditions: "The foul odor which continually hovers about the general cell is sufficient to take the flesh off any man who is accustomed to decency and cleanliness. We asked the prisoners how they fared, and they could not find words to express themselves" (Oct. 20, 1884). A tour of the local packing house brought another kind of plea from Howe: "The next time a GLOBE reporter makes a tour of the packing house, please run him through the scalding tub and scraper before dismissing him. On his return to the office this morning, after visiting your guano and killing departments, our Mr. Rank had the air of a foul sewer about him" (Dec. 22, 1886).

Howe was amused by a discussion in the Kansas City papers called "Can a reporter be a gentleman?" " 'We believe he can,' he replied. 'However, he must be very sly about it, and not let his employers know it' " (Apr. 3, 1883).

It was a time for philosophizing on journalistic matters, a favorite occupation of Ed Howe's throughout his newspaper days. New processes in printing and engraving were arriving on the American scene. The little *Globe* was becoming more than a repository for local news and comments. There were feature articles, drawings, farm and garden columns, reprints, retrospective pieces on the great battles of the Civil War, fashions, and extensive coverage of such stories as the death and funeral of Ulysses S. Grant, which occurred while Howe was on one of his jaunts away from the office. Howe was issuing his *Weekly Globe,* and he carried a boast that the current issue had thirty-six illustrations, twice as many as *Harper's Weekly* of the same date.

Into the *Globe* office were coming the more and more sensational papers from the big cities; soon Howe would issue his periodic condemnations of William Randolph Hearst. He was especially provoked by what one paper did to a Kansan, or someone the newspaper chose to call a Kansan:

> The New York illustrated police papers combine every possible bad quality—untruthfulness, exaggeration, libel of everything decent, etc. In a late issue—we happened to pick it up in a barber shop—a "Kansas man" is represented as riding up and down in a hotel elevator, holding a cocked revolver in

> each hand, and declaring that he likes that room, and proposes to spend the night in it. Many ignorant people will laugh at this wretched picture, and, concluding that Kansas is made up of such men, carefully avoid it. It keeps the respectable press busy counteracting the police press, which is thoroughly unscrupulous not only in this, but in every other particular. [May 15, 1883]

Howe's own zeal for honesty, a trait that was always getting him into trouble, prevented his bending to outside pressures. He believed that a newspaper should not be blamed for publishing the news; that was its reason for existence. A newspaper, however, should be permitted slight inaccuracies on occasion, because of the difficulties of obtaining exact information. It should not be overly concerned for the people about whom it writes, for if it suppresses what the people want to know it will lose its patronage.

"The GLOBE makes its living by selling papers in which the news is printed, as a dry goods merchant makes his living by selling dry goods, and it would be as great a piece of business folly for it to refuse to print that which the people demand as it would be for a merchant to refuse to sell an article in his line which the customer stood ready to pay for. . . . The paper has no favorites to reward, or enemies to punish, and it publishes the news as near as it can be had for no other reason than that its readers expect it, and will not otherwise patronize the paper" (Aug. 24, 1883).

He also had words about censorship. The *Seneca Courier* had demanded prohibition of the *Police Gazette* and the *Day's Doings* in Kansas, and he wrote that that would just cause many young men who had never heard of the publications to rush right out and buy them.

3

THE BUILDING OF A REPUTATION

Man of Letters

In 1882, as Ed Howe's newspaper was acquiring both reputation and strength, *The Story of a Country Town* appeared. It was Howe's first, best, and most famous novel. Its success helped to make the author a national figure.

The 1880s were a significant decade in American letters, a decade that produced possibly more good novels than any similar period. Mark Twain, William Dean Howells, and Henry James were producing some of their notable works; so were George W. Cable and Henry Adams, plus such lesser figures as John Hay, Constance Fenimore Woolson, Margaret Deland, General Lew Wallace, Helen Hunt Jackson, F. Marion Crawford, and Frank R. Stockton. H. Rider Haggard's stories for boys and Tolstoy's works were obtaining readers. Literary tastes were varied. "Idea" books such as Henry George's *Progress and Poverty* and Edward Bellamy's *Looking Backward* were successful, as were books with "success" themes, such as one Ed Howe may have read, Russell Conwell's inspirational *Acres of Diamonds.*[1] There were books with utopian messages; there was inspirational fiction; there were saccharine tales by Mrs. Southworth, E. P. Roe, Augusta Evans, Frances Hodgson Burnett, Ouida, and Louisa May Alcott.[2]

Such works, popular or escapist, were not in the tradition that would claim Edgar Watson Howe's best-known book. He may have been following the writers of the local-color movement, the stress on sectional writings—books and stories by Bret Harte, Edward Eggleston, Joseph Kirkland, and of course Mark Twain. These writers indulged in some romanticism but mainly were depicting the uncompromising realities of life, the struggle for success, the fight against nature, the efforts to escape a drab existence, particularly in the sterile towns of the hinterlands.[3]

Such writings, perhaps, were sounding the death knell for the predominant myth of America, one that had marked our literature and our politics since Jefferson had written in *Notes on Virginia* of the "chosen people of God" who work in woods and fields and have the most substantial virtues of all Americans. Life *was* bleak and narrow in the country towns of Howe, Garland, and Kirkland, but, as far as Ed Howe was concerned, it was bleak everywhere. Hamlin Garland's people wanted to escape their environment; Ed Howe's people, like Howe himself, perhaps, had come west "to grow up with the country," and they were not about to leave. The presence of cheap land in the West had been a factor that conditioned many of our most pervasive attitudes and values, and helped to create both symbol and myth about the land.[4] But it greatly overstates the case to insist that each writer who wrote about the small town and the soil had rejected the Jeffersonian agrarian dream.

Or perhaps Howe had done just that. Perhaps he did not *know* what he was talking about when he wrote how he had observed farmers as a class while working at Falls City, and had never known "any like those in American fiction or cartoons." Perhaps he was only deceiving himself when he said: "The farmers I have known since have been mainly bright and capable, and ready and able to spring to arms to enforce their rights."[5] Years after he wrote *The Story of a Country Town* (and years before, for that matter), Ed Howe was a vigorous booster of small-town life and values, the kind of booster he might have laughed at in his own novels.

There was probably a legion of country editors who aspired to literary greatness in Howe's time; after all, they had seen such country boys as Howells and Twain come out of Ohio and Missouri and achieve national fame, Howells practically being anointed by James Russell Lowell as the literary king of New England. Rather than join the ranks of the realists and the local colorists (it is probable that he did not know our literature *had* such schools), Ed Howe wanted to write a novel and make some money from it. His first attempt at writing a "story" was something called "The Spirit Child," which he wrote and set directly in type. Then came those long hours at home, by the kitchen table

Charles M. Sheldon, whom Ed Howe lampooned for years in *The Globe* (Courtesy Kansas Historical Society)

A poster advertising the celebrated Carry Nation, who was not one of Ed Howe's passions (Courtesy Kansas Historical Society)

Mary Elizabeth Lease, Populist, do-gooder, hell-raiser (Courtesy Kansas Historical Society)

John J. Ingalls, U.S. senator, great man of Atchison, recipient of many *Globe* boosts (Courtesy Kansas Historical Society)

Alfred M. Landon, Republican presidential candidate in 1936, calls on the aging Howe in Atchison
(AP Wirephoto)

William Allen White, editor of the *Emporia Gazette,* "Old Bill White" to Howe
(Courtesy University of Kansas Alumni Association)

The Ed Howe home, Potato Hill, near Atchison
(Courtesy *The Atchison Globe*)

in all likelihood, as he composed *The Story of a Country Town,* after days when things had not gone too smoothly and when the family was undergoing hardship and tragedy. When else would he write the book but at night? Joseph R. Kathrens, who worked for *The Globe* at that time, said the staff knew that Howe was working at night, even though it was a secret elsewhere, and that one morning Howe announced that the story was completed and produced "an ordinary manila country store daybook, with leaves the size of a sheet of foolscap. The right hand pages were used for the text. The writing was in ink."[6] No one dared ask Howe what the story was about.

Ed Howe took his manuscript to Miss Anna Nicklaus, a schoolteacher who was his neighbor, to ask for criticism. He had intended to read the story aloud to her, but got only as far as "The Story of a Country Town." That was when, according to Howe's one account, Miss Nicklaus protested: "The title is wrong, to begin with; it should read: 'A Story of a Country Town,' so I took my manuscript, and went home; that quick, vinegary attack made me mad. But I have wrangled with her over grammar, and syntax, and history many times since. She is the best educated person I ever knew. . . ."[7]

In Howe's *other* version of what happened, he tried to read the story to his brother Jim, but Jim stopped him and said the title should be *A Story of a Country Town.* That ended the discussion.[8]

The Story of a Country Town appeared in 1882. Howe had no publisher, and he had to print the book himself, running it off four pages at a time until approximately two thousand copies had been produced. He wrote a preface for the September 4, 1883, edition of the book, and it reveals much about Howe, the novel, and its genesis in such words as those of the opening paragraph: "Should *The Story of a Country Town* find readers, it may be interesting to them to know that it was written entirely at night, after the writer had finished a hard day's work as editor and publisher of a small evening newspaper. I do not think a line of it was written while the sun was shining, but in almost every chapter there are recollections of the midnight bell."[9]

The Story of a Country Town, despite its realistic touches, is a basically romantic yet lugubrious tale into which the author pours his accumulated prejudices, particularly those relating to love and marriage. These are more important to the plot than any incidental depiction of the grim and dull life of a village, this village being in Missouri, incidentally, and not the Kansas town in which Howe was composing the novel. Autobiographical it was without a doubt; the parallels between the novel and Howe's own boyhood are many. It concerns the family of the Reverend John Westlock, who like Ed Howe himself had gone west "to grow up with the country." The family lived on a farm near the church where the father was volunteer preacher, a setting like Ed Howe's own boyhood home: "On the highest and bleakest point in the county, where the winds were plenty in winter because they were not needed, and scarce in summer for an opposite reason, the meeting-house was built in a corner of my father's field."[10]

The narrator is Ned Westlock, the son of the preacher, and he tells how the family traveled to the town of Fairview, and of the crowds that collected around his father. Fairview is a place that "remained new and unsettled after counties and States farther west had grown old." It is a village of isolation, not like the places to the west, where cheap lands and towns sprang up on credit and farms were opened up with borrowed money. Life is dismal for the boy, as grim an existence as one could imagine in a land of supposed opportunity, a place where the sun never seemed bright.

With the Reverend John Westlock for a parent life could not be much different. Ned is sure that his father "regarded children as troublesome and expensive—a practical sort of punishment for sin, sent from time to time as the case seemed to require." Westlock has only two children to burden his life, but that is enough. And he has a wife who is overpowered by her domineering husband. Another member of the household is Mrs. Westlock's younger brother, Jo Erring. Ned and Jo love to visit a nearby miller named Damon Barker, but aside from that their life is dull. There is church and there is prayer and there are singing and shouting. When Ned is eleven another minister comes to the countryside to be preacher, and Jo falls in love with his daughter, Mateel. Jo works to improve himself to earn her love, but unfortunately he learns that a lawyer named Clinton Bragg also is courting the girl. Jo still loves her, and he spells out his love for the eager ears of young Ned:

> All of my ambition is connected with her now. If I hope to become a worthy man, and well-to-do, it is that she may be

> proud of me, and feel that I have worked to please her; if I study Barker's books diligently by the light of this lantern at night, it is that I may become more intelligent, and worthy of the good opinion she has of me. I dream of nothing pleasant in which she does not have a part. If I fancy I am happy, she is beside me, and the cause of it; if I have grown rich and great in a night, I am only glad of it because it will please Mateel. Always and everywhere, when my better part is uppermost, she is in my thoughts, but never when I am contemptible in any way. There seems to be no doubt, in short, that I am desperately in love.[11]

Soon Jo goes to the Barker mill to learn the milling trade, and soon Westlock sells his farm and buys a newspaper in the nearby town of Twin Mounds. There Ned is put in the shop to learn printing; there he studies the town and its people. The town has a post office, a number of stores, a jail, and about six hundred residents, most of whom are obsessed with religious discussion. "They never discussed politics with any animation, and read but little, except in the Bible to find points to dispute; but of religion they never tired, and many of them could quote the sacred word by the page."[12] The townspeople also have drinking, gossiping, and fighting to occupy their lives, but mainly they have the fine points of religion.

Jo meanwhile stays at the home of Damon Barker, and makes such progress that his friends and neighbors help him to start a mill of his own. He also obtains the promise of Mateel to marry him. The routine of the Westlocks is shattered when the preacher father leaves home and property to Ned and Mrs. Westlock and runs away with another woman. With his son he leaves a letter that describes what has happened. The blow to the Westlocks is a great one, but the family recovers, and young Ned unquestionably feels a sense of relief. Jo Erring and Mateel Shepherd are married, and their troubles begin, as Jo begins to demonstrate a sense of disturbance and agitation. The marriage is a misfortune from the start, even though life for Ned Westlock and the rest of the people of Twin Mounds appears to be settling down. The shallowness, the smugness, the petty preoccupations of the townsfolk oppress Ned, and he prefers to talk with his only crony, Jo, even though the talk is becoming more and more a querulous monologue from the unhappy husband. One cold winter night (in this book almost nothing tragic takes place in calm, sunny weather) Jo Erring appears at the Westlock door and tells Ned that his wife had written to Clinton Bragg before her marriage and told him that she could never love another man. Jo (like Ed Howe) has peculiar ideas about love and marriage, and he reveals them: "I am convinced that a man who has loved but once makes a better husband than one who is in doubt as to whether he ever loved at all. I would as soon marry a widow with children as a woman who has been engaged, and permitted the familiarities which are common under such circumstances."[13]

"My first impressions of the subject are that I would as soon marry a widow as a girl who had been in love before. If I were the king of a country I would punish second marriage with death, and make it unlawful for a man or woman to be engaged more than once, thus preventing the marital unhappiness which I am sure always results when either the wife or husband knows the other has been in love before."[14]

This kind of philosophy almost punctuates the latter pages of the book. Ned and Jo, meanwhile, return to the mill and to Mateel, and then Clinton Bragg disappears. That winter the preacher Westlock returns and tells Ned that his life has been a mess since he left home, that the woman with whom he ran away does not love him. Ned gives his miserable father some money and his father disappears into the night. And things continue to deteriorate between Jo and Mateel. No longer is Mateel a perfect woman, and "the queen of my heart." Jo can never be the same again: "The very wheels in the mill give voice to her entreaty to Bragg to remember that she will never love me; every sound mocks me that my wife is proud of her love for another, and piteously begs that it may never be forgotten."[15] The marriage obviously is breaking apart, and so is the health of Mateel, who begs Jo to let her go her father's house, and he finally agrees. It is Bragg (who never seems to come through as a truly villainous type) who drives up to take Mateel away. And there is more trouble in the Westlock home, for Ned arrives home and finds that his mother is dead: "Let the bleak winds take up the cry of the unhappy son, and carry it across rivers and fields to the wanderer, that he need not return; that the light in the window has gone out, and that the watcher who waited so long to forgive him is dead."[16]

Then comes spring, and a cruel rainstorm in which Ned goes

to visit Jo. The mill is empty, but in a moment Jo walks in, carrying Mateel, and he tells Ned that he had waited along a road until Bragg and Mateel came along in a buggy, and that he had dragged Bragg from the buggy and murdered him as Mateel looked on. For he had thought it better to kill Bragg and to die than to live with his torment:

> I am satisfied now that I made a mistake in thinking of love as it should be, not as it really is, and I unwisely built on that foundation, but I blame no one for it; a man who is ignorant should submit to the penalties without complaint. But I shall always think that I should have been very contented had it turned out as I expected; I shall always justify myself with the belief that had Mateel brought as much enthusiasm into our marriage contract as I did, we should have been of great use to each other. I hope you will not think hard of me if I say that she had the experience which I should have had, while I had the innocence and faith in marriage which a wife should possess.[17]

Jo then is taken to jail, but he is never tried. He takes poison and dies, a letter to Ned clutched in his hand. Ned leaves Jo's burial and goes to the Shepherd home, where poor Mateel is living, her mind gone. That night she dies, and soon Ned is able to throw off all this misery and marry a lovely girl named Agnes, who has been waiting in the wings almost like Agnes Wickfield in *David Copperfield*. And the agonies of Ed Howe's story of a country town have come to an end.

That is the novel. In mood and sentiment it is like much of the trash of the 1880s. But in its realistic depiction it is far superior. There are good portraits of the people of Twin Mounds. And there also are vivid and believable descriptions of the newspaper office and of the task of the editor: "Other trades and professions are most secret, and their contemptible transactions generally hid from the public, but all my work had to be submitted to the criticism of every idle vagrant who cared to pick up the sheet."[18] There is an oafish country character called Big Adam, with a not entirely believable way of expressing himself:

> "He is always saying that," Big Adam said indignantly, "but I assure you on my honor that he never held a plough or pitched hay a day in his life. Why, he is not here a third of his time. He came home last night after an absence of four weeks; I don't know where he had been, but to some of the towns a

> long way off, probably. At ten or eleven o'clock he will breakfast, and then I shall hitch up and drive him over the place, during which time he will point out and suggest enough work to keep a dozen men busy for months; and after assuring me it ought all to be done before night, he will return to the house to lounge about. In a day or two he will go away again, and come back when he gets ready. That's the kind of a farmer Biggs is, but I must say for him that he is quiet and peaceable. I wish I could say as much for his sister, the old pelican."[19]

There is the lovely Agnes: "I have never seen a bird-of-paradise, and have no knowledge of them, except that they are very beautiful; but if their manners are as graceful as their plumage is beautiful, and it is conceded that we of Fairview were as ungainly and ugly as crows, I hope the impression made by the coming of Agnes Deming to the settlement will be understood."[20] And there is Lytle Biggs, about whom Big Adam soliloquized, a horse trader, "a lesser and sourer Josh Billings," who presents the cynical philosophy of Ed Howe as Jo Erring presents the romantic philosophy.

Howe liked to argue that the book was merely a novel, that he did not aim for accuracy, that there never was a Mateel Shepherd or Clinton Bragg or Jo Erring (though in his preface he had commented on the similarities of his characters to people he had known). He admits similarities between his father and Westlock. He says Fairview had no mill and had no tragedy, and that he never learned what his father thought of the book.[21] An acquaintance of Howe's youth, Henry Clay McDougal, wrote that he believed he recognized people from the towns of Bethany and Gallatin in the various characters, notably Jo Erring, Big Adam and The. Meek. "With the hand of a master, Howe sketched the country and the people as he and I knew them a quarter of a century ago. His pictures are at once strong, dramatic, pathetic and humorous, and, what is better, human and true."[22] Yet many years before, Jim Howe had written this in *The Globe:*

> The majority of those who have criticised *The Story of a Country Town,* seem to labor under the impression that it is the biography of the author, but the fact is that the novel is almost entirely imaginary. There was an Agnes, and she taught school at Fairview, but she taught only two terms. . . . Jo Erring was a real character, but he never rose above mediocrity. He worked on the Rev. John Westlock's farm until that austere divine moved to town to engage in the newspaper business,

> when he tramped to a southern county, bought a piece of land on credit, and married a fat and slatternly wife. He now tills the soil in summer and gets out railroad ties in winter, and is a happy man. Little does he care how many times his wife was in love before he married her. . . . The author's father was not gloomy or austere. On the contrary, he was eminently sociable, and nothing delighted him more than a house full of company. . . . The Rev. Goode Shepherd, his insipid wife and fragile daughter may have existed, but they never lived at Fairview. . . . The fact of the matter is, that *The Story of a Country Town* is not autobiographic. It is not the experience of the author. It is purely fiction, and the author should have credit for his creation. I know what I am talking about, for I am his brother. [Sept. 2, 1883]

So the controversy went. Recognition of the book was far from overnight. Howe sent copies to a number of persons, both in the eastern press and in Kansas. Fred Schrader of the *St. Joseph Gazette* praised it. John J. Ingalls commented on "the somber, graphic and impressive style prevailing throughout the book." But most important to the success of *The Story of a Country Town* was the fact that William Dean Howells liked it, and second was that Mark Twain liked it. The story—or the legend—is that Howells found a second-hand copy in a bookstall in Boston, read it, wrote about it in the *Century*,[23] and thus gave Howe the assistance he so badly needed. Howells wrote that he had been reading two books of late, the other being Edward Bellamy's *Miss Ludington's Sister,* that he was impressed with the realism of *The Story of a Country Town,* but that he was troubled by the "sentimental excess and unbalance" of the homicidal protagonist Jo, which he wrote "comes near spoiling the strong, hard-headed, clear-conscienced story." Howells said that he considered the "literary unskilfulness to be less important than his honesty and nerve in putting squarely before the reader some unpalatable truths about human nature and the Western village."[24] With obvious pleasure, Ed Howe printed in *The Globe* a letter written to him by Howells, a letter which has become widely quoted:

> I wish to thank you for the very great pleasure I have had in reading your "Story of a Country Town." Consciously or unconsciously, it is a very remarkable piece of realism and constitutes a part of the only literary movement of our time that seems to have vitality in it. I have never lived so far West as Kansas, but I have lived in your country town, and I know it

is every word true, down to the perpetual Scriptural disputes of the inhabitants. Fairview and its people are also actualities, which, even if I had never seen them—and I have—your book would persuade me of. The people in the story are excellent, both natural and sentient, except the last half of "Jo," who drops into sentimentality and wickedness wholly unworthy. "Biggs" is delightful, and all his household. "John Westlock" is a grim and most pathetic tragedy; his wife moves me less, but she is alive, too. I have no time to specify, and I don't know how to tell you of the impression of the simple, naked humaneness that the book gives me. It has faults, as any fool might say, but be sure you have written so good a book that it will be hard for you to write a better. I am afraid that you will never write another so sincere and frank. I wish I could see you; but upon your honest piece of work, I give you my hand with my heart in it. [Apr. 21, 1884]

How Ed Howe loved that letter! And he wrote to Howells in reply:

I think it is very much to your credit that you have taken an interest in my poor affair; the next time I meet a lame dog I will see if I cannot do something for him. There are so many contemptible and mean men in the world that it is a real satisfaction to meet one who is not only great, but good. I mean that very few gentlemen at the top of the ladder have heart enough to reach down, and encourage those at the bottom. I have always admired W. D. Howells and Mark Twain; I will admire them more than ever now that I know what splendid fellows they are. I have about concluded that every man who becomes great by his own efforts is a good man; if I have a hope to become a great man, it is also a hope to become a good one.

The letter and the picture came to hand, and I am very proud of both. I can only hope that in the future I may prove worthy of your good opinion. I intend to try and make the new story read so smoothly that Mr. Howells and Mr. Clemens can say when it appears: "I knew there was *something* (not much, but a little) in that fellow. I am glad I wrote to him." When I get out my writing at night now, it is with a view to satisfying Howells and Clemens rather than the public.[25]

Howells brought the book to the attention of James R. Osgood, his publisher; the Osgood imprint gave *The Story of a Country Town* wide circulation. When the Osgood firm failed, Ticknor & Co. took over, acquiring the Howe novel with other properties. (Among the companies which had declined to publish the novel were Funk & Wagnalls, Scribner's, Harper's, Houghton

Mifflin, Holt—and Osgood. Some of these published later editions of the book.)

Mark Twain's assistance to the novel was not as direct as that of Howells. His help came through a letter to Howe written February 13, 1884, and sent from Hartford, Connecticut. The first part of the letter indicated that it could be made public; the second part was clearly labeled "Private!":

> Dear Mr. Howe:
>
> I am glad the book did not come to me in manuscript; for I can tell hardly anything about a book which is written in an unfamiliar hand; and so, lest I express a lame or unjust opinion, I express none at all.
>
> People are greatly surprised that publishers often reject books which afterwards achieve high celebrity. I believe that it was this unfamiliar handwriting that made the trouble, usually.
>
> I like your book so much that I am glad of the chance to say so. Your style is so simple, sincere, direct, and at the same time so clear and so strong that I think it must have been born to you, not made. Your pictures of that arid village life and the insides and outsides of its people are vivid, and what is more, true; I know, for I have seen it all, lived it all.
>
> Your book is a history. Your scissors could have turned it into a tale—and that would have been better, maybe, for many can write a history whereas few can write a tale. You could have knocked out an obstruction here and there, and then your history would have become a story, flowing with gathering speed and uninterrupted current.
>
> By the small space which you give to Big Adam, I judge you did not perceive that you were contributing a mighty figure to the procession of originals that is marching out of the ark of American literature to possess the land. Your other characters are good, they are well done and worth the patient art you lavished upon them; but when Big Adam strides by it is Gulliver in Lilliput. You give the others big space in the book and Adam little: now then, bring him on the stage again, and reverse these proportions; so shall you deserve well of the nation. You see I can speak calmly; but when I read passages about Big Adam to George W. Cable, he forgot himself and shouted, "Superb, superb—he is colossal!"
>
> You write as a man TALKS and very few can reach that height of excellence. I think a man who possesses that gift is quite sure to write a readable book—and you have done that.

Then followed the section of Clemens' letter that was long unpublished:

PRIVATE!

All that (before) is public—to use as you please—or any part of it. But this is private and not the public's business.

You have allowed tears to plash on the floor once in the preface and thrice in the book. The figure is very striking—and jokes and striking figures should not be repeated. You might retort that Adams' corks should not be repeated, then; but not so—no time to explain why, but you know why. I'd rather hear Adam draw an imaginary cork than another man a real one—even at my thirstiest.

(You ought to write a drama at once and make Adam the central figure. Keep him on the stage all through the piece—there's dollars in it if you get the right man—a new actor—because a celebrated one would have to have the bulk of the cash. I don't know whether you care for the cash but still—well, give it away.)

Next time, I wish you'd leave out Biggs or anybody else whose diversions interrupt the story. NOTHING should ever be allowed to break the speed of a story.

Mateel carried my heart and sympathy right along and into her grave with her; but from the beginning to the end I was pretty generally down on Joe; and when Mateel made her appeal to him—oh, but damnation I cut him dead there, and then, and we have never spoken since. Usually I don't care a rap what becomes of the people in a story but I was interested in these folks.

You are like the Frenchman who said "I WILL drown, nobody SHALL help me"—which was just the reverse of what he meant. Everybody has some small grammatical infelicity or other—yours is the continuous and accurate misplacing of your "wills" and "shalls." But you won't do it any more.

There—that's all; except that you apologize in the preface; and you handicap Joe [sic] there, too—though you didn't for me, because I read the book through first. Cable and I are of one mind that the preface should have been left out.

I am talking pretty freely but I mean no harm. You may have caught the only fish there was in the pond—it's a thing that has occurred before—but I am not able to think so. And so I talk—otherwise I would be silent.

Still, it is the first time I ever DID talk. Out of the six and thirty million times I have been asked for an opinion about a book I believe this is the first time I have ever furnished one—not that I am loathsome and unsympathetic but because the books were worthless.

I wish you would come and see me. I should be very glad. You would be welcome.

Truly yours, S. L. Clemens.[26]

The letter from Mark Twain became one of Ed Howe's most prized possessions. He, unfortunately, did not follow enough of the advice of either Howells or Twain. But through *The Story of a Country Town* he was assured of a secure place in American literature. Soon the book was being reviewed by others, including an unidentified critic in the *Atlantic Monthly,* who evaluated the book along with works by Cable, S. Weir Mitchell, Charles Egbert Craddock, F. Marion Crawford, and Helen Hunt Jackson:

> He has described a community which feeds its higher life with a faith no longer held as an inspiration, but as a warning; the people, meanwhile, have been dislocated from the conditions which brought them into healthy association with the world. They are engaged in a sordid struggle for existence; they have lost their ideals, and the world seems to mock at them. A more dreary waste than the country town which Mr. Howe describes could not well be imagined. It appears to have no traditions even of beauty, and certainly no anticipations of hope. It is degraded spiritually and mentally, and nature itself seems to take on the prevailing gray hue, and to shut in upon the narrowing circle of life.
>
> The circumstances of this life are recorded with a pitiless fidelity.[27]

Interest in the novel developed, and others provided critical appraisals. H. G. Crickmore gave the book favorable notice in the influential New York *World.* Charles Dudley Warner termed it "the most remarkable novel of the year." In Howe's own state, young editor William Allen White termed it "one of the ten best novels written in America." The *Topeka Daily Capital* said it "will be a surprise and a pleasure to every reader. It is a genuine western production, strong in all its parts, original in style and interesting from first to last." The *Hiawatha World* said: "Its moral is thoroughly pagan; that human nature is contemptible; success is a failure; mankind a mistake."[28]

Within two years the book went into twenty-five editions. The author received favorable attention in the influential *Saturday Review* of London, and when he visited Europe a few years later he called on the writer of the article, even though he had expressed his annoyance in *The Globe* at the criticism given the book:

> The London *Saturday Review* of October 18th contains a two column editorial based on "The Story of a Country Town," a novel written and originally published in Atchison. It is

> headed, "Mournful America," and is an ingenious attempt to prove that the vast district lying west of the Mississippi is inhabited by a people surrounded by fatness who do not know how to appreciate prosperity. There is some truth in this criticism, for American people are all better than they seem, while the English, as a rule, pretend to more than their real worth, but so little is known in England of American geography that many absurd mistakes are made; for example, the opinion is expressed that "outside of a few Eastern States" every country community is a "Fairview," and every country town a "Twin Mounds." The *Review* pays the book itself a compliment, but uses it as an attack on America which is peculiarly English in its slyness. We are informed by the author that "The Story of a Country Town" refers to a district lying between the Mississippi and the Missouri rivers, nearer the Missouri than the Mississippi, and that he does not think it would be applicable to States west of the Missouri or east of the Mississippi. [Nov. 5, 1884]

Thus *The Story of a Country Town,* and Ed Howe's surge to literary significance. He could not know it, but never again would he create a work with its power and drive.

A Trip to Europe

Now he was a celebrity of sorts, and a man of some local, as well as national, prominence. Now the years of struggling were coming to an end, and Ed Howe was able to get out of the provinces and see the big world. And no surer indication of the early financial success of *The Globe* exists than Howe's own published reports of his travels. It perhaps was a conceit for him to assume that the public required a full description of his journeys, but in this he certainly did not differ from many editors before and after his time. Each summer *The Globe* would carry a detailed report of Howe's vacation, and in Howe there seemed to be a kind of compulsion to see all the sights at regional and national expositions.

He went to New Orleans in early 1885 to visit an exposition, sending home a long and heavily geographical report of the trip. Some of the comments are in the vein of his sharper work; some are prosaic. "A visitor to the Exposition sees very few handsome women," he reports. "Those in attendance on the booths are all ugly. At the Centennial [the Philadelphia exposition of 1876] one of the greatest features was the pretty faces. There seems to be little doubt that the handsome women of the United States live north of Mason & Dixon's line; and it is equally certain that visitors from the North and East are not numerous" (Feb. 24, 1885). On the way south he visited Hot Springs, Arkansas, and went to see the battlefield at Pilot Knob, Missouri. He also commented at some length on the condition of both Negroes and "poor whites" in the South:

> We cannot imagine that the condition of the black people in the South could be worse than it is; when the traveler sees them lounging about the stations, in company with their mules, dogs and children, he cannot help thinking that the negroes suffer by comparison with the mules, but the condition of the poor whites is said to be even worse. They want nothing better than corn bread and the greasiest kind of side meat, with the addition of rum and tobacco for the men, and snuff for the women, in the way of luxuries. We refer more particularly to the "po" whites in rural Arkansas, where the towns are built around the saw mills, and where the chief end of man is to saw logs with which to buy quinine. [Feb. 25, 1885]

The trip to Europe was more exciting (to both Howe and his readers), even though the comments were as sardonic and as bored as those about his other travels. Though he makes no reference to the book, Howe probably had become acquainted with that volume by his literary idol Mark Twain, *The Innocents Abroad,* which had been published in the late 1880s. His writings occasionally resemble some of the Mark Twain passages, and the European trip reports signaled the first of his many entertaining descriptions of days spent abroad.

With a party of friends—Charlie Shoup, Webster W. Hetherington, and Frank Everest—he sailed on the *Germanie,* a ship of the White Star Line, on July 9, 1885. "We have nine different remedies for seasickness, in addition to Florida water, brandy, steamer chairs, steamer hats, steamer caps, overcoats, umbrellas, rubber coats, soap, candles, and much other stuff which will probably be thrown overboard," he wrote (July 12, 1885). He planned to land at Queenstown, make a tour of Ireland, and visit Scotland, Switzerland, Germany, and Italy, sailing from Liverpool to return August 20 or 27. He praised the pleasant custom of sending flowers to a ship, and he soon encountered feelings familiar to most ocean travelers: "The ocean swells, like the deserving poor, have been with us always, but otherwise the sea has been unusually kind." There were four meals a day, and he became accustomed to being served oysters, game, and fish, though he found the cooking too greasy for his tastes. The only "westerns" aboard were the Kansans, all of whom ate at the captain's table. Howe saw two whales, and he noted that "porpoises are as common as hogs in Kansas." The nasty smell of the ship, and the sight of water for eight days, made the first view of the Irish coast a pleasant experience for the normally landlocked Midwesterner.

His letters home from Ireland were a combination of travel report and local commentary. Queenstown he found a pretty harbor town, Ireland a handsome country. He traveled up river to Cork, and met a guide named Fry, an auctioneer who had lived at Valley Falls, not far from Atchison. He went from Cork to the Killarney lakes and the Kerry Mountains, which seemed to him similar to the Rocky Mountains, though not so high and having no snow cap. The Irish country roads were better than the streets of Atchison, and he was interested in the people begging and selling "Mountain Dew and goat's milk."

Dublin was like an American city; when you're there it's easy to imagine being in St. Louis or New Orleans, he said. The trip from Dublin to Glasgow on the ship *Duke of Argyle* convinced him that man belongs on land (he made such an observation on almost every voyage). Glasgow also seemed like an American city, and he marveled at the many monuments and tributes to Scott and Burns: the public house where Tam O'Shanter got started on his monumental ride was "a noisy and dirty saloon." He found, generally speaking, that Scotland was more like the United States than was Ireland. Next he went to Edinburgh, took a steamer ride on Loch Lomond, and went to Loch Katrine by stage. He wondered at the lack of kilts: he had seen more kilts in Barnum's circus than in Scotland. Already he was tiring of sights, and the fact that Loch Katrine was the scene of *The Lady of the Lake* interested him scarcely at all. Too many battlefields, castles and abbeys, monuments and ruins; Howe was winning bets by his predictions that monuments would be in honor of Scott. There came a local touch so that the folks back home would know he had not become a traveling snob: "When I return home I shall refer to Mud Lake as Loch Mud, and to the Sixth street bridge as Brig White Clay; a lake is always a loch here, and a bridge always a brig" (Aug. 7, 1885).

From Scotland the Kansans went to London, which seemed even more like American cities. "There were at least a thousand tourists in Westminster abbey when I visited it to-day, and they chattered away in the livliest [sic] fashion in spite of printed requests to the contrary" (Aug. 10, 1885). Two days was all he required to see the sights: Westminster Abbey especially impressed him. He liked the channel crossing from Dover to Calais: no seasickness. He also observed that France was even more like the United States than the other places he had visited, for the energy and pushing way of the French appealed to him, and so did the fact that there were not many ruins to look at. He was weary of the whole trip: "I am thoroughly tired of traveling, and now regret that I was not restrained when I talked of coming. Although there are wonderful sights to see, you soon become indifferent, and finally feel like the man who sat down to his thirtieth quail" (Aug. 11, 1885). He and his friend Hetherington were about ready to leave August 13 instead of a week later.

An interlude in Howe's sight-seeing was provided by his decision to pay his respects to the critic who had given *The Story of a Country Town* the encouraging notice in the *Saturday Review*. Howe sent his card and by return mail received a letter inviting him to meet a gathering of his English admirers. The westerner—raw and uneasy in the European setting—anticipated meeting a literary woman and a gathering of Bohemians. Instead he was taken to a great house in the fashionable part of the city, where two servants in livery ushered him in. "To his great chagrin, he discovered when too late, that he had been betrayed into the society of a fashionable literary set who were waiting to celebrate him as a lion." It was too late to retreat, so he met with the gathering, people quite unlike those he knew in Atchison. He was in his traveling clothes, and "His eccentricity of dress—for the occasion—was probably excused on the ground that he was an American from the woolly West, and himself in a sense as much an anomaly as Buffalo Bill would have been, or at least Joaquin Miller."[29] Howe was kindly treated, and had the honor of escorting a woman in to dinner who turned out to be (he solicited the information later) Lady Colin Campbell.

Readers of *The Globe* were finding such accounts in articles headed "A Gray Abroad." The American tourist was showing his American traits, advising people to stay away from restaurants where bad French was used in the bill of fare, because the food would be no good, adopting the mucker pose to observe that the French pronounce the name of their famous museum "Louver," though traveled Americans call it the "Louv." He could not see why the originals of great paintings were any better than some of the copies he saw being made, and even the copies "were usually being painted by the oldest and ugliest lot of men and women I ever saw." He visited Versailles, and he found the Notre Dame cathedral a disappointment after Westminster Abbey. His guide, whom he referred to as Napoleon (another affectation he perhaps borrowed from Mark Twain), got drunk at the Hippodrome and went to sleep on the way home. A further letter told about a French sleeping car; Lake Geneva, which was the scene of the painting on the drop curtain in Price's Opera House in Atchison; and Mont Blanc, which looked nice to him and which he vowed to admire from a distance. The letters to *The Globe* then ended; the reader next encountered him on the way home: ". . . when I went on deck after a restless night, I saw the fairest sight I have ever seen: America; land; home. Every American is a better American after seeing New York harbor from the sea, and he will love his flag more than ever after seeing it flying from the forts, on Staten and Long Islands from the deck of an English steamship" (Sept. 2, 1885).

The final footnote to the trip came in comments about the music he had heard abroad. There had been the Strauss band in Vienna, and the band of the Coldstream Guards, which he liked best. There had been orchestras in Baden-Baden, Lucerne, Frankfort-on-the-Main, Brussels, Cologne, and Interlaken, and the Royal Siamese Band he heard in Albert Memorial Hall: "The music was only a step in advance of that heard at Indian war dances, and all the performers played 'by ear' " (Sept. 3, 1885).

The Later—and Lesser—Writings

It is difficult to conceive of a time in the 1880s when the Atchison editor was not bent over a desk, working, writing. Even on his travels he was busy. Though he was acquiring a good staff on *The Globe* he still was preparing much of the copy for the newspaper; this is evident from both style and content.

But Edgar Watson Howe had literary fever. He had tasted recognition, and for much of his life he would be composing fiction from time to time: novels in the 1880s, short stories, and brief sketches later. A practical as well as creative man, he advertised his work constantly in *The Globe,* making *The Story of a Country Town* available to the people of Atchison and to readers elsewhere, impressing upon these good souls the fact that they had a novelist in their midst.

Not a very good novelist, unfortunately, but still a novelist. Howe did not follow Mark Twain's advice not to rush into print too soon. Years later when the celebrated Clemens died, Howe wrote in *The Globe:* "The advice was from the best possible source, but the Atchison man did exactly what he was advised by Mark Twain not to do: he didn't appreciate the importance of the good advice" (Apr. 22, 1910). But he was impelled to write. And he had enough confidence in himself to believe he could duplicate the success of *The Story of a Country Town.*

The realistic elements of that work, which tended as time went by to obscure the romanticism and the melodrama, were a minor part of the later novels. This suggests that E. W. Howe did not see himself seriously as a writer of realism. Or, probably, that he was unaware of the meaning of specific literary modes. He was mistaken in believing that his later books would be on the level of the first novel, and one critic maintains that he "never quite got over, consciously or unconsciously, blaming himself for those eager days when his imagination moved through spacious, rebellious regions of romance and tragedy."[30]

Few readers today are aware of the novels that followed *The Story of a Country Town.* The first of these was *The Mystery of the Locks* (1885), which is a curious combination of sentiment and literary naturalism. The novel begins in a Gothic setting of melodrama and mystery:

> Davy's Bend—a river town, a failing town, and an old town, on a dark night, with a misty rain falling, and the stars hiding from the dangerous streets and walks of the failing town down by the sluggish river which seems to be hurrying away from it, too, like its institutions and its people, and as the light of the wretched day that has just closed hurried away from it a few hours since.
>
> The darkness is so intense that the people who look out of their windows are oppressed from staring at nothing, for the shadows are obliterated, and for all they know there may be great caverns in the streets, filled with water from the rising river, and vagabond debris on their front steps. It occurs to one of them who opens the blind to his window a moment, and looks out (and who notices incidentally that the rays from his lamp seem afraid to venture far from the casement) that a hard crust will form somewhere above the town, up where there is light for the living, and turn the people of Davy's Bend into rocks as solid as those thousands of feet below, which thought affects him so much that he closes his blinds and shutters tighter than before, determined that his rooms shall become caves.[31]

Davy's Bend, a hick town quite like many Ed Howe had known, a town existing in eternal inferiority because of the proximity of Ben's City, a town that somehow became successful while Davy's Bend languished. Into Davy's Bend comes a mysterious stranger, Allan Dorris, arriving on a dark night, talking with the hotel clerk, Silas Davy, and learning about an old mansion called The Locks (because of the many keys required to open its many doors), and finally electing to buy the place. The Locks is a place of wild and weird portents, with a wooded tract, a heavy iron gate, neglected trees, and rank undergrowth.

His housekeeper is a kindly and talkative old character named Mrs. Wedge, who wonders that Allan Dorris has selected Davy's Bend: ". . . they all agree that you do not amount to much, else you would have gone to Ben's City, instead of coming here." No one comes to Davy's Bend who has any successful pretensions. The people of the town despise each other because none of them moves to Ben's City, "and we live very much as I imagine the prisoners in a jail do, in cursing our home, in lounging, in idle talk, and in expecting that each one of us will finally be fortunate, while the condition of the others will grow worse."[32] A town like Twin Mounds, then, with comparable townspeople. The reader is introduced to the people as a whole and one at a time. The town paper is "a ribald folio appearing once a week." The poorest of the merchants is called "a merchant prince." "Puffery" and boosting are common among the townspeople.

Among the residents of Davy's Bend is Tug Whittle, the village drunk who is proud of his bad reputation, who is estranged from his do-gooding wife, and who has a sweet little son right out of *Uncle Tom's Cabin* who has been farmed out to work in another town. Another is the somewhat self-righteous Thompson Benton, merchant and town leader, whose lovely daughter, Annie, plays the organ in the church and with whom Allan Dorris falls in love. And about the mystery in the title: there is a ghost—or something—that prowls about The Locks, and a wild woman who spies on Dorris and a shadowy figure that seems to be accompanying her.

Another resident of the town is John Bill, editor of the *Davy's Bend Triumph,* who "found his time taken up in earning his bread by writing palatable falsehoods." Bill is given to printing anything and everything submitted by the people of the town, and much of this appears as the opinion of the editor; this means that one week he is taking one stand and the next week the opposite. About as unlikable a character is Mrs. Tug Whittle, who can say little that is good about anyone, who minds other people's affairs and lets her little boy Ben run about "sick, distressed, ragged, and dirty."

His village portraits out of the way, Howe gets into the story, showing how Allan Dorris has fallen in love with Annie Benton. But because of his past (as yet undivulged) and because he loves Annie too much, he decides he must leave:

> "Then I think I will refuse," he said, "though I would give twenty years of my life to grant your request. What a request it is! It appeals to me with such force that I feel a weakness in my eyes because of the warmth in my heart, and the hot blood never ran races through my veins before as it is doing now. You have complete possession of my heart, and I am a better man than I was before, for you are pure and good; if I have a soul, it has forgotten its immortality in loving this earthy being in my arms. But it is the proudest boast of a loyal wife that no lips save those of her husband ever touched hers, and my regard for you is such that I do not wish to detract from the peace of your future. If I have made an idol of you, let me go away without discovering my mistake; grant me the privilege of remembering you as the realization of all my

> dreaming. In a year from now you will only remember me to thank me for this refusal of your request."[33]

Is the author condemning Annie for having had a previous affair? No, not this time; something else is being suggested in this heavily sentimental interlude. Despite such a scene, and such a statement, Dorris stays in the town, for the power of this good woman is too great. And he and Annie are married. He tells her that "the most bitter hatreds in the world are those between married people who do not get along." He believes there are thousands of good husbands but that deep down in all their hearts "not one in ten would say he was glad he had married." So once again Ed Howe is treating his readers—even in this romantic novel—to his pessimistic views about marriage. Nor can Allan Dorris match his wife in religious piety: ". . . while I hope that there will be a resurrection, I know that those who have gone away on the journey which begins with death send back no messenger, and that nothing is known of heaven except the declaration of pious people that they believe in it." He hears the laughter of children, but that does not tell him that the world is a place that excites laughter and that there are no tears.

Storms, blizzards, lightning—all find a place in the climactic scenes of Ed Howe's novels. In *The Mystery of the Locks* it is a flood, which has been devastating the up-country and finally sweeps down on the little village of Davy's Bend. Allan Dorris goes out heroically to do rescue work, but he fails to return, and this is the anticlimactic scene of the novel, one that can only leave the reader flat:

> In the bottom of the boat, lying easily on his back, the rowers found Allan Dorris, dead; his eyes closed as if in disturbed sleep, and his face upturned to the heavens. His right hand was gripped on the side of the boat, as if his last wish had been to pull himself into a sitting posture, and look toward the town where his faithful wife was watching for his return. The flash of the torches made the face look ghastly and white, and there was a stain of blood on his lips. Those who looked upon the face saw in it an expression of regret to die, which remained with them as long as they lived; they spoke of it tenderly to their children, who grew up and gave their own children descriptions of Allan Dorris's pitiful face as he lay dead in his boat on the night when the waters of the great flood began to recede. It is said that the face of a sorrowing man looks peaceful in death; it may be equally true that death

> stamps unmistakable regret on the face of its victim who is not ready.
>
> O, pitiless Death, you might have spared this man, who was just beginning, and taken one of the mourning thousands who watch for you through the night, and are sad because of your long delay. This man desired so much to live that his white face seems to say now: "I cannot die; I dread it—Oh, how terrible it would be to die now!" And his eyes are wet with tears; a touching monument of his dread of thee![34]

But even this is not the end. Literary naturalism has had its moment (along with some awful Victorian sentiment), but there must come the melodrama of retribution: Tug Whittle, town outcast, thinks he knows who was responsible for Allan's death, and he pursues the murderer to a town some distance away, where he kills the man and brings back an ear, to prove that the man is dead. The villain was known as "The Wolf," and Tug reveals that the woman who had been spying on Dorris had once been his wife, that she is demented, and that the murderer of Dorris was her brother. All of this gives the reader a lushly sentimental ending. The drunk Tug Whittle has been redeemed, and everyone is happy except for the beautiful Annie, whose life has been devastated by the death of her young husband.

Such is Edgar Watson Howe's *The Mystery of the Locks.* Trash by present standards, but, though bound by the conventions of romantic fiction, it has some good touches. In the death of young doctor Dorris there seems to be a kind of pessimistic determinism at work: Dorris must suffer for the sin of his earlier marriage. His past, the small town, the power of the flood—all seem to have conspired to bring his doom. In the portraits of the venal and unlovely people of the town Howe reveals ability, and also in what one modern critic calls a "picture of a decaying river town, whence all the ambitious have departed, where there remain only the human flotsam and jetsam, the spiritual mud left by the great flood that swept over the Midland."[35] There was little critical recognition of *The Mystery of the Locks,* and the modern reader can see why, even though many books that were not much better were surviving in those sentimenal years.

In *A Moonlight Boy,* which came the next year, Howe made perhaps a slight improvement, though it is difficult to understand his intentions in writing such a tale. Again the tone is one of extreme sentiment; again there are good touches of small town life, and also of life in the big city. In this book it is quite obvious that Ed Howe believed there were no inherent virtues in people anywhere, but also that the country town offered greater opportunities for happiness than the city. *A Moonlight Boy* might have been pointed toward younger readers; it resembles the Sunday school literature of the time, and the portrait of the young hero might have been inspired by Tom Sawyer or Huckleberry Finn.

This hero is a boy known as "King Cole," who lives in the town of Three Rivers with Tibby Cole, a band leader and music store operator, and his wife. The boy is puzzled because he is called a "moonlight boy"; he had been left on the Cole's doorstep in a basket twelve years before the story begins, and there is some question about his heritage and background, and especially about an identifying "T.C." medallion that was with the baby's clothes. Comes a snooping stranger (Howe's books have several), who tries to steal King and does succeed in taking him to the nearby town of Warburton, where the boy escapes. Out goes the posse to search for the abductor, but the search fails. Then comes a series of small town vignettes and characterizations (a customary pause in Howe's writings), notably that of Pidg Behee, a friend of King Cole.

The story, slow and dull and ordinary for the most part, picks up a bit when the boy King, who plays for Tibby at various musical events, sees the kidnaper. And comes a letter from New York, suggesting that his parents have been found, so off goes King Cole to the city, a country lad overwhelmed by the noise and the excitement.

So, with all its Victorian touches, the story unfolds. It develops that King Cole is the lost child of wealthy parents, who, though they are somewhat dubious about his possible claim, are impressed by (1) a scar and (2) the medallion. So they turn King Cole into Tom Courtland, even though they continue to call him King, and believe that he is their son who had been stolen from his room when a baby. As for King, he has his problems with New York and society life, such as his experience in trying to eat a lobster: "when I went to digging around under the shell after the meat, I could not help comparing the proceeding to cleaning my finger nails, and concluded that lobster was not what it had been represented."[36] He is sent to a commercial school and also works on a paper, *The Night Watch,* which prints mainly religious news and is run by a man named Barton. Soon Tibby Cole and his wife come to town from Three Rivers, and Barton finds the friendly Coles a refuge from his bitchy wife.

King Cole, meanwhile, is trying to become adjusted to his new parents. He likes his father, but not his mother, he is embarrassed by the various relatives, and he finds a kind of escape in telling wild stories about life in the rugged West—Indian lore, for example, though he knows almost nothing about Indians. He finds life at *The Night Watch* more interesting than life at home, even though the paper's religious views are almost too much even for a relatively young boy: "The paper edited by Mr. Gruff was a profitable one, and had a large circulation among a class of people who believed that they and *The Night Watch* were in favor of good morals in opposition to all the rest of the world, and I believe to this day that our subscribers did not take other papers because they occasionally read in them references to their own follies. We never found fault with anything save Sin and Intemperance, and perhaps this was one reason we did such a profitable business; for there are so many ways of doing wrong that perhaps it is not surprising that a charitable paper like *The Night Watch* had many ardent admirers."[37]

The climax of *A Moonlight Boy* has all the complications familiar to persons watching melodrama (or Gilbert and Sullivan) in those years. A villain named Gruff, the man who had kidnaped King Cole, is forced to reveal the truth: that Aunt Caroline, the sister of the boy's newly found mother, had accidentally killed the woman's baby, and buried it, and that the medallion had been left with the clothes on the doorstep of the Coles, with a basket containing another baby. That was the mixup; thus the story is resolved. Then all go back to Three Rivers, and King Cole, grown up, marries a girl he had met in New York.

The story of *A Moonlight Boy* is incredibly involved, and the only important points of view presented by Ed Howe are those residing in his portrait of Tibby Cole, a decent man who is placed in contrast to those about him ("His disposition was so amiable that his first thought was to do that which was manly and honorable"; "Tibby was a man of unusual qualities who was content to live a modest and blameless life")[38] and in the obvious distinction between the goodness and kindness of Three Rivers and the cheapness and materialism of New York.

Howells, whose praise had helped to make Edgar Watson Howe's name one of some importance in American literature, was silent about *A Moonlight Boy,* as he had been silent about *The Mystery of the Locks* and would be about the later books. But Hamlin Garland, who was then writing his literary creed into *Crumbling Idols,* asked himself, "Where is the representative for the great mid-West?" and considered Ed Howe as that likely person. For the prairie West had had no novelist until Howe came along with *The Story of a Country Town,* "a singularly gloomy, real yet unreal, narrative written in the tone of weary and hopeless age." And after *A Moonlight Boy* appeared Garland wrote to Howe, in July, 1886:

> DEAR SIR:
>
> I have just finished reading the "Moonlight Boy," and after careful attention to your first works, I want to say that I like your stories. Your delineation of the monotonous and provincial life of the rural West compels my admiration, though it grieves me to think how unavoidable the most of that life is. You speak of these people not as one who coldly looks on them as "picturesque" but in an earnest, sincere tone as *from among them.* Your work has an *indigenous* quality which appeals to me very strongly, perhaps more strongly than to most critics. I can value your strong, idiomatic, Western prose, I think, better than one who had not heard it spoken. . . . Among representative names standing for "local scene and character painting," in which category you stand alone in representing the great West (myself your only rival, not having published yet). In the midst of my press of study and writing upon critical lines, I am myself striving to express some of the unuttered thought of the Western prairies.
>
> Pray do not think I ask for a biography or anything approaching it, but if you see fit to give me some sketches of your boyhood residence, schooling, etc., I could at the least give you a column in the *Transcript,* which would be something. I shall have some hand in the review of the "Moonlight Boy," which, by the way, is puzzling Eastern readers—myself included. "All the conventional novelist would have done he has avoided," is one of the notes I sent in when I returned the book to Mr. Hurd of the *Transcript.*
>
> It is not so tragic, so powerful, of course, as the other two, but it has a charm of its own. I like it for its faithful treatment of homely, prosaic people in their restricted lives.[39]

Howe replied to Garland, giving him biographical information, telling him that the original of Davy's Bend of *The Mys-*

tery of the Locks was Brownsville, Nebraska, a town which he had once visited. He told Garland that he had written *A Moonlight Boy* in five months, working at night, as with the other books. "When I quit the newspaper I will write my best book," he said, "but I am successful at newspaper work and am afraid to give it up." (It is of some interest that Garland later felt, despite his kind words about *A Moonlight Boy,* that Howe had "shot his bolt" in *The Story of a Country Town,*[40] that none of the later stories equaled it in significance and that he lost the representative position he had gained.)

The fourth of the novels, and the one which revealed much about Ed Howe's primary concern with the relationship between man and woman, was *A Man Story* (1888). This curious title, or variants of it, appears from time to time in little editorials in the pages of *The Globe;* here it appears over a story told by a boy named Chance who is growing up in the town of Fog Lake. Chance tells the story of his family: his father, a storekeeper, an aggressive town promoter known as The Boomer; his two grandfathers, the first known as Number One, whom the boy dislikes, the second Number Two, who goes on big benders in which he has imaginary reunions with his buddies of Civil War days; and Aunt Florence, usually referred to as Mrs. Tom.

Chance's father reads like a combination of the town boosters so prevalent in Howe's day, and a little like Howe himself: "Whenever he found an account of a fire in a newspaper, he at once wrote and invited the man to rebuild in Fog Lake, at the same time offering a lot for the purpose, and as many merchants and manufacturers thus written to had politely replied acknowledging his kindness, and saying they would 'think of it,' the Boomer believed he was sowing seed in very good ground, and worked early and late. Indeed, he thought his plan of watching the newspapers for accounts of fires was a particularly good one, and we were requested to keep it very quiet, as my father feared that the Boomers in other towns would adopt the same course."[41]

The boy's observations about his father and grandfathers are side excursions from the main business at hand: the marriage of Mrs. Tom and Uncle Tom Saulsbury. Uncle Tom lives in "The City" and comes frequently to stay with the family and tell about his work as a traveling salesman for Barnaby & Co. Whenever he comes he engages in long, loquacious soliloquies in which he tells

Mrs. Tom how much he loves her, and how much greater is his love for her than the love of Barnaby for his wife. The reader early begins to wonder whether Uncle Tom is protesting too much: "I was never in earnest in my life until I fell in love with you; you are oftener in my thoughts than religion, business, and patriotism combined, and I cannot feel flattered when I reflect that this one enthusiasm of my life is liable to be forgotten in a year. I regret that love is not like the true religion,—something that you can be constant to all your life, and find a comfort when death itself comes; but it isn't; every man who has deserted his wife has probably felt love as keenly as I do, and expressed it in almost exactly the same words."[42]

What is the man getting at in such an excessively private commentary that should be for his wife's ears only but is given to the entire family? When will something happen in this curious novel? Well, something finally happens. The young hero runs away to The City after Number One grandfather goes into a tirade about the boy not being out in the world making a living. He goes to Barnaby & Co. to look up his Uncle Tom—and finds that Uncle Tom *is* Barnaby & Co. He is shocked to find his uncle so different, so short-tempered and businesslike, not a superfluous word escaping his lips, his employees jumping to attention when he is around. He also learns that there is another woman, a "Mrs. Barnaby," a shrew who once was married to Tom and berates him endlessly, making his life in The City so miserable that he becomes another person when he returns to Fog Lake. And while Chance is away from home his uncle goes to Fog Lake for a visit, and Mrs. Tom writes to the boy that her husband is acting strangely.

All has gone, then, too smoothly in this quiet book. Then, in one of his rows with Mrs. Barnaby, Tom finally strikes back, and he vows to take her to Fog Lake for a confrontation, so that the whole business will be off his conscience. His plan unfortunately does not succeed; despite his great faith in and love for her, Mrs. Tom refuses to see him and he has no opportunity to tell his story. So he leaves, and disappears, and Chance goes back home, where he finds Mrs. Tom repentant: her story now is that she had been too stricken to come to Tom to forgive him. And Tom (like other characters in the Howe novels) returns for a short, surprise visit, meets the boy and Mrs. Tom in the woods, and leaves again, for the great West, ostensibly lost for all time.

So the wild tale continues. From the postmark on a letter, Chance guesses where his uncle is living, and he goes to the bustling town of Hooper, where Tom has become an important business figure. And Mrs. Tom comes to visit him, and listens to his story: that he had kept his first marriage a secret, that Mrs. Barnaby had returned from a trip and said she never heard of the divorce proceedings. But despite Tom's love for his wife he tells her he cannot return, for she had not had the necessary faith in him.

Tom is a man who expects nice little courtesies from his women. He is a strange character in a book that is throughout a combination of Gilded Age hogwash and realistic comment. As the climax approaches, Uncle Tom becomes ill, goes into a collapse, and seems to be dying, issuing his "ante-mortem statement." "I acknowledge before all men, as I shall acknowledge before my Creator, that my conduct toward you was often wrong, and often monstrous in its wicked stubbornness, but I declare now as my last declaration that I could not help it; your half of the blame was conducted in a manner so distasteful to me that I could not help acting as I did. When I asked for bread, you gave me worse than a stone,— a blow, and so cunningly directed that it reached my tenderest part."[43]

The agony seems to be almost over, but Chance sends for the dying man's wife, who comes to the bedside, saves Tom, is reunited with him, and soon (though not *too* soon) presents him with that unfailing device to rescue all literary marriages: "There was great excitement at our house one day, and, after an absence of several hours, Uncle Tom came into the room where I was at work, and said he had a Rival; a roaring boy, who looked like his father, it turned out to be . . . ."[44] Tom and Mrs. Tom become solid citizens of their community, Mrs. Barnaby repents, and everyone lives happily ever after. In fact, these could have been the words to conclude this novel.

As with the other books since *The Story of a Country Town* there was little critical attention. One person made an observation: William Allen White, who soon would be obtaining some literary attention himself, thought the book better than *A Moon-*

light Boy, more rational than *The Mystery of the Locks,* and that its best passages were devoted to the minor characters.[45]

Two more books remained to be written before the initial literary surge of Edgar Watson Howe would be exhausted. Neither could be called a novel, though each was cast, to a certain extent, in a fictional mold. Their year of publication was 1891.

The Confession of John Whitlock, Late Preacher of the Gospel, was the first; *An Ante-Mortem Statement* was second. The first was a long diatribe against religion, containing those themes and points of view which Howe had been drilling into his readers. The reader is introduced to a former minister who tells the whole awful story of why he has rejected the gospel and refuses to teach it any longer. In his church, he says, the belief is in experimental religion, "that the faithful are permitted to know by the experience of years that they are acceptable to the Master, and that they are drawing nearer day by day to the throne for which they started." Despite his ministry, such knowledge has never been presented to him—no message, no sign. "An old, white-haired man, I am no nearer the Master than the repentant rebel, though I have always been a faithful soldier of the cross."[46] His service in the "Army of Calvary" has brought no sign to him from the Commander.

So he asks himself, "Why did I profess for forty years a faith in which I did not believe?" He did it to encourage others, he concludes, thinking the spirit some time would come to him. He was forced to accept the belief of others that they had received answers to their prayers, even though no answers came to his own. He had found nothing to give him faith in doctrine, in prayer, in growth in grace. "I have served a master who would not admit me to his confidence, although our doctrine teaches that I am entitled to this mark of favor; that the faithful always have it."[47]

He had found no solace in the Bible or in the religious commentaries. Others might find it, but not he. "I still believe that there are great sacred truths, but from some cause, I know not what, I have not read them aright. . . . I cannot believe that there is a divine intention that the people should so ruthlessly neglect the truth . . . ."[48] And he thinks that the hypocrite who says he has faith but does not have it will find it more difficult to achieve salvation than the man who has lived an honest life without faith. "The world is full of hypocrites who try to deceive God with long prayers and attendance on church, although they pretend to believe that not a sparrow falleth to the ground without the knowledge of God."[49]

Yet Whitlock is sure there are good people, more of them than other kinds, and he believes there was a beginning and that a man named Jesus existed and was a valuable teacher. He cannot speak to the question of the divinity of Christ, but he does know that following His teachings can benefit any man. And he knows the church itself has failed: "The world would be better off if the cross should be banished as a symbol of the atonement, and a whip put in its place. Men who cannot understand the doctrine of future punishment, can understand the doctrine of present punishment. The police can regulate where the church fails."[50]

Where is morality in the world? the despairing man asks. Not in the churches, for if emergency struck your community you would find that not ten of the fifty best men in town would be pious, or those who prayed in church, or earnest supporters of doctrine, or possessors of faith in prayer, or professors of conversion and experience. Only in rationalism is their hope, in a religion that teaches that every kind of wrong brings punishment here and now. "I do not mean punished hereafter (for none of us believe in hell any more), but punished here on earth, as certainly as we all must die."[51] Dogmas, finally, must be shunned; reason must triumph. There was never a more monstrous dogma than Calvin's teaching of the elect. The Reformation did not reform religion; it merely adopted a new set of dogmas to take the place of the old, and the world today sees no difference between the dogmas of Catholicism and the dogmas of Protestantism.

Though this was strong stuff for the readers of his time it was Ed Howe at his best, in a way, writing clearly, giving what he called his "sinner sermons" of a later day, calling for beliefs like those of Tom Paine and Voltaire in preference to the Fundamentalist notions that he thought characterized his day. *An Ante-Mortem Statement* was quite another matter; though it may not be, as one writer has suggested, "187 pages of raving by an abnormal mentality,"[52] it is still the old Howe complaints against women, complaints placed within a long and frequently tedious monologue.

This story begins in melodramatic fashion—a screaming woman, a dead judge, "an ante-mortem statement" left by him. It was a case of suicide that directly followed a marriage, a man who found that his first wife had had vast experience in love. "There will probably be great interest in me to-morrow, for the day people hear a man is dead is the day he is the most popular," the judge writes.[53] He tells the reader that he is about to take what he believes to be the full right of a man—the step called suicide.

There comes a wild and labored disquisition on love and marriage. Nothing is worse in the judge's eyes than a dissatisfied husband; both past and future are distasteful to him. ". . . he is married, yet he has no wife; he has no home, though compelled to pay the expense of an establishment."[54] And for the judge, the "tiger in me was released" when his wife told him that all her other lovers had tired of her. All her other lovers! She should have had none! This was humiliation, that he should be wed to someone who had loved and had been rejected. "My castle in the air came tumbling down to earth, and with the rubbish obstructing my way, I could no longer find excuse for my life affair. I felt like a man who had been robbed, and then compelled to make a partner of the robber; her confession staggered me like a blow."[55]

He justifies his position, knowing that to most women and to some men he will be believed unreasonably jealous. But "It is not in the power of any man who loves his wife to be undisturbed when he thinks of her old lovers."[56] Like Jo, in *The Story of a Country Town,* he feels that a woman who has loved before is like used goods. People will not use a napkin or towel after it has been used by another. "Are people more particular in the matter of napkins and towels than they are in the matter of love?" The words "I love you" are a confession of the most important relation between man and wife, and any sensible man will admit that he would prefer a wife who had not been in love before. Women may say differently, but they are mistaken.

The roles of men and women are different. Girls in the old stories might wed princes out of their class, but princesses never select a poor plowman from the field. "The world has always judged men by one standard, and women by another." And a wife may disgrace her family, with no hope of regaining her reputation, while a husband may commit many indiscretions without injury to the social standing of his wife or his family. This may not be just, but it is the way the world is. Women may say that the man should have forgiven the woman, but that to him would be like forgiving a hunchback for his deformity. And "Precisely as a hunchback never goes on the streets that he does not meet a stranger that looks curiously at him, a man whose wife has had lovers before him never goes into a crowd that he does not hear names like theirs."

The judge's marriage had become a mockery within hours. Already he was set to reflecting on the horrors of the domestic relationship. Why do not American mothers warn their daughters that familiarity with men can lead only to contempt? Why do they not control their daughters' relationships? Young people are left alone together, girls of sixteen and eighteen, and the system of courtship is so entrenched in our social system that it cannot be repaired. Young men are allowed to call on young women and to be left alone with them. They go for drives together, unsupervised; they are left in parlors together, unsupervised. Dangerous familiarities are permitted within engagements, and sometimes the lovers go beyond the bounds permitted by society. There can be no excuse for a custom that sanctions unguarded relationships, for these lead only to conflict and unhappiness.

For, he says, at the very time controls are needed, youth is permitted almost complete freedom. How could the Devil, "commissioned to lure a man from chastity," best do his work? Simply by giving man the opportunity to sin. To lure a woman from chastity he need only "bait the hook with a pleasant and apparently honest young man." Set up a love affair, then an engagement period, then the familiarities our society permits. Then bring about a quarrel and a separation, causing the young woman to lose faith in love; then place an older man on the scene, a sympathetic and kindly man, an honorable man. Then the procedure might repeat itself, leading to marriage. But is he objecting to engagements? Not at all. "I only insist that during these engagements the men keep their hands off."[57] Nor is he saying that our women are not the most virtuous on earth. They are virtuous, but they should be protected from temptation.

He has been a judge, and he has heard divorce quarrels. ". . . were divorces as easily obtained as marriage licenses, it might be better."[58] He knows that his statement reads only like an attack upon the follies of women, and he replies to this that "the men are as wicked as the devil desires them to be, but this is no excuse for the folly of women." After all, "a dangerous enemy should inspire caution; to admit that there is drunkenness does not mean that any one can drink to excess without suffering the consequences of his debauch."[59] And there can be, finally, no forgiveness. A man may suggest forgiveness, but he is like the man who suggests that other men should be of good cheer during hard times. "They may be compared to idle rich men who say that the greatest peace is found in poverty and toil."[60]

Howe composed *An Ante-Mortem Statement,* he said, out of the madness of his character Jo Erring (he probably was impressed, also, by Tolstoy's *The Kreutzer Sonata*). The book died a quiet death, and then twenty years later a New York newsman sent the book to Edward Bok of the *Ladies' Home Journal,* who offered Howe five hundred dollars to print it as a serial.[61] The last of Howe's early fictional works, then, had a kind of resurrection, appearing in the years when he was writing his essays on success as a leading writer for the Curtis magazines and editing his *Monthly*.

Competitive Days in Atchison

The excursions—geographical and literary—were only interludes. Mainly Edgar Watson Howe was trying to make a living and compete with the other newspaper editors of his city. And newspaper work, in his opinion, was not easy: "If you are engaged to be married, and want time to fly, get a position on an evening paper. From noon until half-past three does not seem like fifteen minutes. We have known the long hand on the clock to travel half way round while a printer laid down his stick to find his tobacco" (Jan. 20, 1888).

He took occasion to remark on the sameness of news—the suicides, murders, fires, and rapes; the good and mean men; the prejudices; the ridiculous claims and foolish comment. "We often become very tired of newspapers" (Jan. 11, 1889). He looked at other papers and concluded that it would be relatively simple to write editorials for most of them, with their circulation claims and their announcements of things to be printed the next day. Life was a rut, and the man who had found his comfortable rut would be wise to stay in it. "Time your life by the clock, and do the same things at the same time to-day you did at the same time yesterday. It may not be an ambitious life to live, but it will be a contented one" (May 26, 1891).

The Globe, the *Champion*—which Howe often called "The Old Reliable"—and the *Patriot* went on in Atchison while others tried and failed. The years recorded newspapers there called the *Atchison Church Visitor,* the *Midland,* the *Abbey Student,* the *Kansas Churchman,* the *Sunday Morning Call,* the *Atchison Blade* —short-term, church-owned, slanted toward Negroes, slanted toward immigrants. There were fights to obtain official status, which could mean the financial benefit of county legal notices and official printing. Howe often wrote about how he disliked the prevalent system of taxpayers bolstering up a newspaper business against their will. "A newspaper that cannot make a living without aid from the city and county, does not deserve to live. . . . we ask the city and county to give their patronage to the lowest bidder" (Apr. 24, 1880). In the early years it was generally *The Globe* that did not receive the county printing; on one occasion Howe cheerfully admitted that the *Champion* would do the printing instead of the *Patriot,* and that after all it was the best paper—including *The Globe*—for the job.

There were early struggles to obtain readership; in 1878 he commented wryly that editions of *The Globe* were "not exhausted at five o'clock in the evening, and there is no mob in front of our office to gulp down palatable doctrines fresh from the press" (July 12, 1878). The *Champion* had declared that *The Globe* was not recognized by the press of the state, but in reply Howe copied what the *Seneca Courier* had written: "We are in receipt of the *Atchison Daily Globe*—the newsiest, sauciest, and most readable paper we have seen in Kansas" (Oct. 26, 1878). He continued to challenge the opposition, saying that circulation of *The Globe* was the highest in the community. He announced that *The Globe* would not publish proceedings of meetings after they had been made public in the *Champion*; let the opposition print the stale news.

That was the age when newspaper editors all across the land assumed that their readers were interested in bickerings back and forth between rivals. Howe was as adept a sniper as any in his state: "If the long tobacco chewer of the *Champion* persists in referring to us as the cruel King of Athens who imprisoned Plato, we hope he will spell our name right. We hope he will call us Dionysius instead of Dionysas. Nothing makes a monarch so mad as the misspelling of his name" (Apr. 30, 1881). He recommended that the *Champion* and the "Old Soldier" consolidate: "The town ought to support one newspaper and a little local sheet like the GLOBE very comfortably" (Feb. 9, 1882). Atchison owed *The Globe* nothing; Howe contended that the larger the town became the richer *The Globe* would become. "We do not ask the merchants of this town to donate us anything because we blow for the place" (Feb. 18, 1882). But it hurt him that his boosting brought in so little financial support: "a great many business men of the city who freely give the other papers (including the weekly and foreign publications) advertisements, have nothing but good advice for the GLOBE" (Mar. 23, 1882). And the advertising policies of *The Globe* were on a higher plane than those of the competition: "The GLOBE publishes a good many pictures of prominent men, but it does not print the pictures of men who have been cured of loathsome diseases by patent medicines, as the *Champion* is doing. The line must be drawn somewhere" (Jan. 27, 1886).

In the competitive battles of Atchison in the 1880s a sordid episode was that concerning Howe's row with an evangelist named John N. Reynolds. On his return from the trip to Europe, Ed Howe learned that his brother Jim and Walt Mason had been criticizing Reynolds, a former convict in the Iowa penitentiary, who was holding revival meetings in a country schoolhouse near the town. Reynolds called on Howe, according to the editor, and told him that what had been said about him was true but that he had reformed and was trying to do better. Howe believed him, was favorably impressed, and the two became friends, Reynolds consulting Howe from time to time and then announcing plans to start a livestock insurance company, which Howe advised him against. Reynolds later started a bank, and he began to alarm the townspeople, who went to Howe in concern, causing the editor to criticize Reynolds. All of this was the stimulus for another publication, the *Atchison Daily Times,* started by Reynolds February 3, 1887.

The *Times* was unquestionably a fly-by-night operation, launched out of malice, lasting for a short time only, existing as a daily and then a weekly and then a daily again. Howe did not handle Reynolds gracefully, and apparently the people of Atchison, or some of them at least, were quite willing to join in an attack on the editor of *The Globe*. The gist of the Howe-Reynolds dispute was Reynolds' management of the insurance company and his failure to pay his advertising bill with *The Globe*.

"John N. Reynolds accuses the GLOBE of being a 'blackmailing' sheet, and for this reason: We contracted with him to do certain advertising at the same price charged for similar work to such firms as A. B. Symns & Co., McPike & Fox, Bowman & Kellogg, Chicago Lumber Co., Howell, Jewett & Co., Lukens & North, etc., and he (Reynolds) beat us out of the amount, $56.10. A notorious thief refuses to pay his bill, and then claims to have been 'blackmailed;' these are the facts, which we will establish to the satisfaction of any reputable man" (Jan. 22, 1887).

The *Times* used its columns to attack Howe, and Howe replied in kind, not realizing, as he later wrote, that he should not have responded at all: ". . . I was young, peppery and foolish, and did what I thought was my best, but which I now realize was my worst."[62]

Particularly humiliating to Ed Howe was the knowledge that many Atchison people greeted the Reynolds abuse with delight:

> Men I had never injured in any way, and with whom I was friendly, became violent partisans of Reynolds, and assisted him substantially with money. He imported rough newsboys from Kansas City, and these sold his paper on the streets with vile cries about me. I pretended I didn't care, but did care enormously. This Reynolds incident was a part of my education; it taught me many things I could have learned in no other way. After Reynolds was dead and gone, you may be sure I was a more careful, a more useful editor. I cannot learn from a suggestion in a book: I must learn from experience and humiliation. Young people believe they are admired because of their youth and promise, but I began to realize, after the Reynolds affair, that young as well as old must earn respect if they have it. There are scars on my heart now because of humiliations in my early years that were unnecessary.[63]

Apparently the entire community sobered up from the Reynolds affair. The *Times* succumbed August 6, 1887, and Reynolds finally went to the state penitentiary. A later historian of the town commented that Reynolds "was looked upon by many as an irresponsible demagogue, and it was supposed that he ran his paper for blackmailing purposes."[64] And Howe realized that the townspeople, like him, had learned from the dispute. "If they at first enjoyed four papers engaged in a fierce row, and a gutter weekly appearing anonymously, they soon tired of it, and have not longed for it since."[65] For it was *The Globe* that emerged, in later years, as the lone newspaper of the city.

The year of the Reynolds affair also was the year of bigger issues of *The Globe,* some of them six pages, of seven columns each. Telegraphic news was appearing (Howe had been fighting through much of the time to obtain telegraphic service from the Associated Press, which he termed the "Associated Ring"). A reader could find news of Congress, women's fashions, and details of politics, as in the summer of 1888, when the Democratic national convention was being held in St. Louis, and *The Globe* was describing in some detail the renomination of Grover Cleveland. Plans to establish papers to beat out *The Globe* led to an editorial blast, Howe writing that the gentlemen with such intentions "will think they have encountered Banquo's ghost before the final collapse occurs." Two other papers had tried for years to put him out of business and had not succeeded, he said.

For the area press, too, Ed Howe had his comments to make, and his little digs. The strong temperance leanings of the *Topeka Daily Capital* prompted him to tell about the young man in Montrose, Iowa—a temperance town—who got drunk, started home, went in the wrong house, and was mistaken for a burglar and killed (May 1, 1880). The *Capital* had accused *The Globe* of being "a small literary pirate," and Howe encouraged the editors of the *Capital* to scan the third page and note that a sketch about the First Arkansas Regiment appeared originally in *The Globe.* "There should be honor among pirates as well as honor among thieves" (Nov. 4, 1880). The editor of the *Hiawatha Herald* was labeled an "old fanatical Methodist" for becoming angry on hearing that prohibition could not be enforced in Atchison. The Kansas City "circulation liars" were surpassed only by their "cyclone liars." Colonel D. R. Anthony, editor of the *Leavenworth Times,* got the Howe needle for his observation that the Republican party would elect the next president. "This declaration, coming as it did from the leading Republican editor of the State, may be considered very significant. Republican editors never predict party success unless they know what they are talking about"

(July 16, 1883). And there was this summary description of much of the press of the state:

> The character of a community can be gauged truly by the character of the local newspaper. Now there is the *Troy Chief*. Every man in Troy has a fund of dirty stories to relate. When you meet a man from Troy, you can safely calculate on hearing the latest man story with all its dirty details. The *Paola Spirit* runs to poetry, and as a natural consequence every man from Paola can recite poetry by the yard. The *Holton Recorder* is fanatical, and of course every man you meet from Holton is a rampant, argumentative fanatic. The *Wichita Times* is a blatant infidel paper, and the Wichita people are accordingly always howling against God and scoffing at the devil and hell. The *Hiawatha Dispatch* is a hypocritical Methodist paper, and the Hiawatha people are accordingly always making loud prayers in public places. The *Beloit Courier* runs to military matters, and we are informed that every man in Beloit carries a sword and goes arrayed in full uniform. The *Kingman Mercury* is a fool paper, and of course every man in Kingman is more or less foolish. A newspaper actually molds the sentiment of the community in which it is published. The *Champion*, of Atchison, is a strong Republican paper, and the town is accordingly Republican—or would be if the Democrats and independents had decency enough to abstrain [sic] from voting. A newspaper is a great institution. If we had capital sufficient we would publish one. [Jan. 9, 1882]

The Globe *in the 1890s*

The once-little paper was evolving into the pattern that would characterize its last twenty years under the editorship of Edgar Watson Howe. "Paid locals"—advertising inserted within the editorial matter—were becoming standard, "written in a sparkling style, containing volumes of genius, worth 15 cents a line, at only 5 cents per line" (June 15, 1888). You paid to get certain news about yourself in *The Globe*: "There is one class of announcements that THE GLOBE will print free of charge; announcements of surprise parties" (May 4, 1889). Sheet music—words and music of the sentimental ballads of the day—was common in the paper. Extensive and detailed features appeared: plans for the centennial of the nation, with recollections of the homesteads of 1879, the opening of the West, a recitation of the nation's history. A six-column New York *World* interview with John J. Ingalls was printed, and *The Globe* commented that Ingalls had introduced a bill for a world's fair, but that the measure did not locate the mighty event at Atchison. As in papers everywhere there was interest in the coming fair, and the plans being made in Chicago. Howe observed that "Since 1892 makes everything popular connected with Columbus, Ferdinand and Isabella, it will probably cause a boom in Castile soap" (Mar. 12, 1890).

Howe's city had a population of 17,000 in 1890; fifty-six acres of parks; sixty-seven public electric lights and two private. The editor was publishing a large supplement in early 1891, but the basic formula of *Globe* success remained this kind of thing:

> S. Guerrier has a Bible nearly 300 years old.
>
> A South Atchison girl supports the entire family.
>
> At Omaha the ice on the river is eighteen inches thick.
>
> The Prosser extension of the Central Branch was snowed up yesterday.
>
> The women have no trouble in keeping their husbands home at night this kind of weather.
>
> The Hampton stock will be sold in bulk to-morrow, and will undoubtedly be reopened at once.
>
> The ladies of the Christian church gave the distressed Robins family some bedclothes yesterday.
>
> An infant child of W. J. McSorley ran a stick through its soft palate Sunday, causing a painful injury. [Jan. 19, 1892]

It was a real newspaper being printed in the 1890s, not just a little sheet about which the editor pretended to be ashamed. Illustrations, national and international news, humor, much advertising; many comments on marriage, women, success, engagements, parties, the basic subject matter of country town journalism. The editor was still a man of deep and instinctive prejudices, which revealed themselves in commentaries on affairs of the day, but *The Globe* was looking like the papers that were setting the tone for American journalism as it entered its big business age.

Howe admired the New York press, finding metropolitan papers "devilish and interesting," but finding cause also to rejoice that his home was in the country and not in the wicked city: ". . . what a contempt they have for what they call a 'gray,' meaning an honest and pure minded man from the country!" (Dec. 7, 1895). Chicago drew his attention in 1893, after the Columbian

Exposition opened, *The Globe* giving special coverage in a two-page supplement that spread forth the majestic white city for the underprivileged folks in the small town. And of course Howe went to the fair, sending back notes on how he met an Atchison woman to whom he never spoke at home, how the fair surpassed even circuses, how he had heard there were nudes at the fair but that he did not know where, how he had seen no people there making love in public. The year 1893 also was the time for changes on *The Globe*: sale of the old press and purchase of a Goss perfecting press, which the editor announced and described in the paper. An all-capital headline was carried across the top of page one: "THIS IS THE FIRST PAPER EVER PRINTED IN ATCHISON ON A PERFECTING PRESS." And the page was adopting a format more in keeping with bigger journals (even though the familiar ad for Climax baking powder could be found at the bottom of the page). On another day a large headline read: "YOU CAN SEE THE GLOBE'S NEW PRESS RUNNING AT 4:30 NEXT MONDAY AFTERNOON." The paper even carried a full-page feature on the press, complete with a diagram and drawings (Oct. 28, 1893).

With installation of the new press, an overline head—a banner line of 24-point type placed under the nameplate, usually making a humorous comment on events of the day—began to appear each day, and made itself a standard feature of the paper. In 1894 came a huge historical edition of *The Globe,* a many-page affair, with articles about the city and the state. *Printer's Ink* wrote that the edition was unusual, with its many half-tone illustrations, and "the mothers of the carriers assisted in its delivery, with the aid of family horses and buggies."[66]

He had made a brief venture out of Atchison, when he sank $8,000 into the *Kansas City Mail* in 1893. It was but a brief venture, and he failed to record in his memoirs even the year in which he tried to rescue what he called a "failing paper" in the big city down the Missouri. Nothing came of it, "owing to the failure of a bank and trust company which was custodian of funds I intended to use in financing the venture." He was glad, in a way—he concluded that he could not have been successful in Kansas City, as he certainly was becoming in Atchison.[67] Like another Kansas editor of his time—William Allen White—who soon would be going to Emporia, he was deciding that the small town was his niche.

"Globe Sights" and National Fame

Few country editors acquire national recognition and lasting fame. Howe's fellow Kansan, William Allen White, was one who did, when "What's the Matter with Kansas?" was circulated nationally in 1896. Edgar Watson Howe was another. In his time he acquired fame through two routes: one his book, *The Story of a Country Town,* the other the universally quotable "paragraphs" that he wrote for *The Globe.*

Such paragraphs he had been writing as early as the Golden, Colorado, days. They were a mainstay throughout the early years on the Atchison paper, much of the time being interspersed with straight news. Sometimes they were the concluding sentence of the news story. There were longer editorials, many of which bore the by then traditional form developed by Bennett and Bryant and Greeley and the other masters. But for the most part Ed Howe became known for the short commentary, frequently consisting of only one sentence:

"There are two ways of raising boys; but judging from the men turned out, both ways are wrong.

"If you go slow others will overtake you; if you go fast, you will exhaust your strength and die young.

"Business is one thing, and pleasure is another; if you can combine the two, you are a very remarkable person" (June 22, 1889).

Howe, like the more famous Charles A. Dana, knew "that the newspaper must be founded upon human nature." Howe knew that entertainment was an important part of the total package of the paper, too, and his paragraphs entertained the reader as they made him nod his head in appreciation or shake his head in annoyance. And mostly the paragraphs dealt with the immediately identifiable person, thing, or situation. "Every paragraph in a newspaper ought to have some reference to the public," Howe said. "No paragraph in a newspaper should reflect the prejudice of one of its writers. THE GLOBE is sometimes guilty of both mistakes, but it is trying to improve" (Aug. 21, 1889).

"Globe Sights" became standard and popular in *The Globe* because it was part of the editor's formula, and because paragraphing for him was no chore. Howe regarded "Globe Sights," rightly or wrongly, as the first true newspaper column, and the idea to group his saying as "Globe Sights" came when he learned that he was being quoted so widely. The sayings were developed as part of his reporting, as he worked day and night, tramping streets and countryside, sending his staff out to do likewise, coming to know almost everyone in city and country, writing about people and their neighbors, learning to doubt the truth of much of what he was told: "For more than fifty years I have been a newspaper reporter; every day I have gone on the street looking for news. One man I met, when asked if there was anything new, invariably answered: 'Nothing for sure.' That is, the air was full of gossip, most of it unreliable, mean or mischievous; but nothing for sure. Somehow this man's answer impressed me. Nine-tenths of conversation and print is unreliable; you instinctively know it is prejudiced, wholly or partially untrue. But frequently there comes out of the babbling something of value."[68]

A Kansas editor wrote that "Carl 'Snort' Brown, who worked for *The Globe* for many years, once said that Howe was an unparalleled reporter because 'he dug jokes, jests, useful information and cold facts, figures and fiction out of farmers, merchants, bankers, railroad men, preachers, peddlers, gamblers, hack drivers, janitors, doctors, dentists and blooming idiots.' "[69]

Howe was well aware that "Globe Sights," and the column's predecessors, had made his newspaper so extensively quoted. He claimed the familiar "Better be safe than sorry," and he said he once saw the advice repeated in big lights at a San Francisco exposition. He also said most of his paragraphs were insignificant, that in compiling *Country Town Sayings* he must have rejected ninety-nine out of a hundred items.

"If I have been able to write an occasional good paragraph I am entitled to no credit: they come into my mind almost complete; if they do not, I can not write them. When I am compelled to 'dig' to fill a page, I fail. In the old days on *The Atchison Globe,* I wrote all day: sometimes more than a hundred different pieces of copy, long and short. Fortunately for me, some of these were liked. A record was once kept in the *Globe* office without my knowledge, and it developed that I really supplied a lot of copy; one day, seven ordinary newspaper columns."[70]

"Globe Sights" began to appear as a column October 27, 1893, and from then on it was a standard. Generally speaking it consisted of paragraphs containing a universality of thought that gave them both immediate acceptance and lasting value. The specifically slanted editorial observations, based on news of the day, appeared in the column to the left. Almost any of the "Globe Sights" would demonstrate Howe's method; this column is as representative as any:

> No man ever loved a woman he was afraid of.
>
> William Randolph Hearst and God still reign.
>
> Remember this: a man doesn't have to look the part.
>
> The weather is pretty fair, but the Octopus is as bad as ever.
>
> A young woman seems to get as much comfort out of a love letter as an older woman finds in a cup of tea.
>
> An Atchison girl has such a good time single, that no one can explain why she intends to get married.
>
> Today, for the first time in the history of THE GLOBE, rooms for rent are advertised with ladies preferred as tenants.
>
> If there is anything in this "blot upon the escutcheon," and you have one, don't you suppose it looks like a boy's copy book?
>
> An Atchison girl who has never been fifty miles from home, tries to create the impression that she has been to England by calling an elevator a "lift."
>
> Five minutes after a man starts for his room to retire, the noise is heard all over the house of his shoes dropping, and that means that he is all in for twelve hours.
>
> "I wouldn't mind getting a new job," said a man today. "I believe that I would light on my feet, but I am afraid the flight through the air might be painful."
>
> This Freedom you hear so much about; there's mighty little of it in this country. Think it over: how much Freedom have you? Isn't there some one standing over you with a club night and day?
>
> It is related that when an Atchison woman found a hair on her husband's coat, he became indignant because she cared, stating that if she were as bald as he, she wouldn't care where the hairs came from, so that she had them.
>
> A description of the ideal modern wife in a woman's magazine says that "when the children get sick, she must pack them off to the hospital, and not worry over them, and lose her good looks." There seems to be a domestic anarchist who has re-

> ceived so much encouragement that she is expounding dangerous theories.
>
> Lillian DeTalente, the girl who married Olin Castle, is described as follows in the telegraph: "A slim girl of medium height, with gold hued hair worn pompadour, light blue eyes, and big, frank freckles." We suppose by "frank freckles" is meant that she used no face powder to conceal them. Are your freckles "frank" ones? [Apr. 25, 1903]

Other observations delighted his readers because of their humor and down-to-earth quality. "Girls named Fanny should never visit on a farm," he said. "There are one or more cows on every farm named Fanny, and it always makes the visiting girl mad" (Nov. 10, 1898). A person would read such a comment and believe it, even though he had never heard of a cow named Fanny. "It is said of an Atchison woman that her heart is so cold that it will finally freeze, and kill her" (Oct. 30, 1882). One was topical: "When it is announced that a Kansas girl will give a party, one doesn't know whether he is expected to take his dancing pumps, or study up arguments on suffrage" (July 5, 1894). "When a man has a great big moustache, it's a sign that he has but two things in the world: a homely mouth, and an ambition to cover it" (Feb. 14, 1890). "The little serious-faced girl who thinks the world too serious to laugh at, and who thinks there is nothing but trouble, trouble, in store for her, grows up to be a big, fat woman whose laugh can be heard a block away" (Mar. 13, 1890). And one that would be understood by almost any parent: "The average girl knows but two adjectives, and they are 'horrid' and 'cute,' which she uses on every occasion from describing Shakespeare to the appearance of a corpse" (Feb. 4, 1893).

Some of the paragraphing formula of Ed Howe lay in his ascribing observations of the day to either "Parson Twine" or "Drake Watson," creations who presumably could bear the brunt for him. Howe later said Parson Twine was a Negro who had a bright comment to make every time he met him. "I quoted him so frequently that he became famous locally: sometimes I credited him with bold things I did not care to father myself. He liked it so well that for years he devoted his spare time to thinking up what he hoped were wise sayings." These words were attributed to Parson Twine in *The Globe:*

"A letter bearing the Oklahoma postmark, and the word

'Personal,' scares me; I know that some unfortunate friend wants a loan" (June 10, 1889).

"If I never tried to reform the world, it was because of the knowledge that the people laugh at a reformer oftener than they listen to him" (Feb. 27, 1890).

"I am beginning to realize how much of a nuisance I was in my youth. My son is learning to play the piano by ear, and he just about sets me crazy. But other people were patient with me, and I have decided to be patient with him. But it is awful" (Apr. 14, 1894).

Ed Howe was busy picking up news and editorial comment from other papers, in his own locality and elsewhere, and it is obvious that other editors were becoming aware of views in *The Globe* that might entertain their readers. Atchison people were getting used to Howe's iconoclastic views and becoming proud of the growing reputation of the editor; they were proud to have the best-known small-town editor in America, and their town became "Ed Howe's town." His son Gene later said he did not believe that any town was ever so dominated by one man, that the early-day dislike or hatred became love or affection.[71]

He was branching out into other fields, too, giving lectures in his dry, laconic way, a talk "on boys" for the people of Hiawatha that he announced in *The Globe* and even listed the times the excursion train would leave and return (Feb. 17, 1894). He received a little boom for Congress in late 1903, possibly more serious than the sometimes joking efforts to promote him for the governorship of Kansas. He looked with gloom sometimes on his own local situation, even though the people of the town gave him "a repeating gold watch" in 1900, worth $500 (he inquired around to learn the cost),[72] and he could compare himself and his fortunes with another "E. W." well known in Kansas:

> Every time we realize that Atchison people like to give us a "dig"—and we realize this pretty often—we turn for comfort to the fact that E. W. Hoch, in his recent candidacy for governor of Kansas, did not carry his own county.
>
> No one doubts that E. W. Hoch is a Good Man, however patent the fact may be that the editor of *The Globe* does not enjoy this distinction. An anonymous correspondent, whose missive is printed to-day, says of the editor of *The Globe,* "You ain't no angel, and everybody knows it." . . .
>
> So when trials beset us, and the sun shines darkly, we turn

> for comfort to the fact that E. W. Hoch, a really and truly Good Man, did not carry his own county when he ran for governor, and when it was known the wolves were chasing him pretty hard. [Nov. 16, 1906]

The Ed Howe voice was beginning to carry far. Howe was known in the eastern capitals; a cherished family heirloom for many years was a marked copy of the *Boston Globe,* containing fifty-eight paragraphs clipped from *The Atchison Globe.* He became known to the young Will White, who during the Christmas holidays of 1886 made his "first literary pilgrimage." A friend had given White a copy of *The Story of a Country Town,* and White was learning of Howe's fame: ". . . he was a notable figure in our part of the world. He was running the *Atchison Globe,* a local paper, and I can remember that I spent an hour in *The Globe* office with his star reporter, Joe Rank, talking of Mr. Howe and preparing myself for the visit." White also went to the Howe home. "Possibly he was used to visitors bringing the frankincense and myrrh of flattery, and maybe he liked it, for he was more than kind, and we talked much longer than I should have stayed. I came back to Lawrence walking in the clouds, for I had seen my first literary hero."[73]

Ed Howe also was receiving small attentions in published works. Walt Mason, once of his staff, wrote about him for the *American* magazine: "Others may adopt his style and mannerisms, but they can't borrow the strange, original intelligence that eternally ignores the obvious and seizes upon the bizarre, showing how much of the bizarre there is in every-day commonplace life."[74]

And Sheffield Ingalls, a Kansas historian, published a contemporary view: "The personality of Mr. Howe as described by those who know him best, is that of a quiet, courteous gentleman, amiable and kind to all. His patience in teaching the young reporter and his indulgent ignoring of the mistakes of his office force, have been frequently remarked upon. It is said that he never discharged anyone, but always assisted them to make good. To those who have been associated with him he is a greater man than he is to those who only know him through the printed page, and the longer and closer the acquaintance, the more remarkable seems his genius."[75]

Another Kansan, Noble Prentis, whom Howe once had praised as a leading figure of Atchison, described the editor in his

History of Kansas (1889) as one of several writers who had been attracting attention, grouping Howe with such persons as Charles M. Harger, Albert Bigelow Paine, Will White, and Charles M. Sheldon.[76] *The National Cyclopaedia of American Biography* gave brief mention to Howe in 1900, touching mainly on his newspaper work and the literary praise accorded *The Story of a Country Town.* The mighty *Encyclopædia Britannica* mentioned his paper: "*The Atchison Daily Globe* established in 1877 is one of the best known of Western papers" (Dec. 8, 1927). And a volume called *Eminent Men of the State of Kansas* mentioned Howe in 1901, a writer, H. S. Canfield of the *Chicago Times-Herald,* being quoted as saying *The Story of a Country Town* was the best American novel since Hawthorne.[77]

It is likely that recognition from the unimportant of the land pleased the editor as much as the praise from the famous that he was coming to acquire, even though Ed Howe by no stretch of the imagination was a blushing violet of journalism. When a letter in commendation of *The Globe* came to the office it would be mentioned in print: "A. R. Miller, editor of the *Democrat,* at Washington, Iowa, writes THE GLOBE: 'I send money herewith for two yearly subscriptions to the WEEKLY GLOBE. It is better than any magazine we receive, and more eagerly read when it arrives.' A very pretty compliment for a little old country paper. Have we a right to reprint it? Is it modest? So much fault is found with THE GLOBE that we confess to liking a compliment for the paper" (Feb. 17, 1902).

A subscriber, a Christian Scientist, writes THE GLOBE: "I read your paper religiously. I find much in it that pleases me; it frequently benefits me. But occasionally you say things that make me mad. They make me mad because they prevent THE GLOBE reaching a hundred thousand circulation, and doing much good. Why do you thus needlessly injure your own cause? I object to your flings only because they injure THE GLOBE; I would like to see some of its ideas spread over the earth" (Mar. 24, 1904).

"A young newspaper man, in a recent reference to THE GLOBE, says it is 'the best newspaper in the west.' While we are grateful to the young man for his good opinion, we know THE GLOBE isn't the best newspaper in the west. One of the impossibilities is to print the best paper in the west at Atchison. If Joe Medill, Horace Greeley, James Gordon Bennett, and a dozen others in their class, should come back to earth, and work on a paper in Atchison, they couldn't make it the best in the west. That would be out of the question. Kansas City, Topeka and St. Joe are too strong to permit of the best paper in the west being printed at Atchison" (Apr. 9, 1904).

It was in those years of growing national recognition that Edgar Watson Howe experienced the two personal losses that removed from him a substantial part of his past. In late December, 1891, he returned to the office from being out on the street, and when he saw the girl at the counter crying he knew instinctively that his brother Jim was dead. Jim had been living in New Mexico; the telegram said he died peacefully and unexpectedly, with his sister Sarah Jane at his home.[78] Howe poured forth into a front-page *Globe* editorial his affection for Jim and the loss he felt:

> My earliest recollection of my brother Jim is of people gently saying of him when he did not hear: "Poor fellow, he has the consumption." Although he was five years older, I cannot remember the time when I was not the stronger of the two, but he always had the tender regard for me that must have distinguished him when he was teaching me to walk.
>
> . . . Whatever Jim said settled all childish disputes in our family; whatever he said was accepted by mother as the truth, although she was sometimes compelled to decide against her own children, and all of us were proud when we heard him praised as the best boy in our neighborhood. . . .
>
> I was not more than nine years old when we removed to town, and began work in our father's printing office. In two years I was compelled to set two columns of brevier every day, or receive a whipping at night, but it was never necessary to give tasks to Jim; he did his best, anyway. . . .
>
> I was an equally good printer, but in other respects I could not equal him, and I never hope to. I learned his industry in time, but I never could learn his wonderful patience, his unselfishness, or his sturdy manhood, and I never knew any other man who equaled him in either of these virtues.
>
> We were in the mountains together, always the same steadfast friends we had been as boys; in all our lives we never had a cross word. Finally, fourteen years ago this month, we came to Atchison together, and started THE GLOBE. . . .
>
> As the business grew, he tried to go on the streets to solicit news and business, but he disliked to meet strangers, and always came back asking to remain in the office. Several times he tried editing and reporting, but he never liked either. . . . Frequently

> he wrote paragraphs that were simply faultless in conception and style, and most readers of the paper recognized his hand; for years his occasional contributions were famous. . . .
>
> I believe I never told him, face to face, how much I thought of him, but after he went south the first time, I wrote a letter in which I confessed what I believe he always knew. Indeed, that was his answer; he had always known it. . . .
>
> He died at one o'clock Saturday morning. I had been wakeful that night, and tossed about thinking of him. I came to the conclusion that he was better; at about the hour he died I was thinking he was better, and that I would receive a cheerful letter in the morning. My greatest regret is that I was not with him, but I feel sure he understood it. [Dec. 29, 1891]

A year and a half later came the second loss, the death of Ed Howe's father, who had been divorced from his last wife, as he had been from two others, and who had made the run into Oklahoma, living on a claim in a house his son Ed built for him. The father had cirrhosis of the liver; he had wandered around much in the past few years, and at one time Ed sent him to Hot Springs, Arkansas, for his health, and later brought him home to Atchison, where he died. This was the obituary his son printed in *The Globe:*

> Henry Howe, father of C. F. and E. W. Howe, died at the residence of the latter yesterday afternoon, aged 71 years. Interment took place at 4 p.m. to-day, at Mt. Vernon. The deceased had been a resident of Oklahoma during the past four years, entering that country at the opening, and securing a claim on the border of Oklahoma City, which attracted a large number of contests because of its value. About a year ago he was taken sick, which resulted in cirrhosis of the liver. A few weeks ago he went to Hot Springs, but failing to improve, he came to Atchison a week ago yesterday. Fifty years of his life he was a frontier Methodist preacher. In his younger days he was a circuit rider in Indiana, at the same time opening a farm in the woods near the present town of Treaty. In 1857 he removed to Harrison County, Missouri, where he was active as an abolitionist. In 1859 he had a public debate with a southern Methodist on the question of slavery, and was arrested by the state, charged with exciting the slaves to rebellion. When the trial came on, the Iowa men came over the border, and openly defied the court, and the war put an end to the matter. Later he established a Republican paper, which he edited with a great deal of vigor. Although he suffered intensely, his mind was clear to the last moment, and almost with his last words he reaffirmed his devotion to his religion. [June 19, 1893]

To the last Henry Howe was involved in controversy. His Oklahoma land claim was the subject of lawsuits, one of which was taken to a federal circuit judge, and was finally carried to the U.S. Supreme Court. Out of the case two Oklahoma lawyers were disbarred, and Henry Howe's land suit won. Ed Howe gave his interest in the suit to his brothers and sisters.[79]

Hard Times, Big Crops, Corn Carnival

Over the years Ed Howe wavered in thinking about the crop and financial conditions in his state that would lead to agrarian discontent and culminate in the historic election of 1896. He was a compassionate man, even though he generally believed people were meant to solve their own problems with help from neither their government nor a divine providence. Thanksgiving time in 1880 had led him to comment that "a hard-hearted President will ask the people on the frontier of Kansas to thank God for famine, hot winds, and hungry children" (Oct. 21, 1880). The Kansas settlers would be unable to observe Thanksgiving with either full hearts or full stomachs, he said. In the same year his "Little Globe" column led off one day with the comment, "By the way, we need some rain" (Nov. 23, 1880).

Yet he was cynical about drought times, too. It must have been of slight amusement to some readers when he commented that a damp and rainy season would have brought more fevers along the Missouri, that "we might have raised splendid crops, but there wouldn't have been enough well people to gather them in" (Aug. 13, 1881). He saw a general improvement in 1882 in the counties of western Kansas, "a general stiffening of the vertebrae column," and he believed that prosperity soon would shine on scenes of hardship and affliction, that crops would be good and that the mild winter would help the settlers make it through the year. These comments were generally reserved, perhaps, for times when conditions were critical elsewhere. Drought times in Atchison brought words like these: "To the Lord, greeting: Of course You know it, but we hope You will not take offense if we mention that it is very dry. The dust on Main street this morning was two inches thick, and if the Lord will vouchsafe a little rain, it will be very kind in Him" (Aug. 19, 1882).

Times seemed bad all over the country. Kansans knew that thousands of people, drought or not, were coming into the state, and that the eastern states were full of people whose ambition was to come to Kansas. The grasshoppers were making their headquarters in Indiana, and "A train load of provisions from fat Kansas to the sufferers in Indiana will be about the right thing this fall" (June 21, 1888). Dakota territory had its problems, and the town of Wichita was going to send a carload of corn to help out: "Out of our plenty we can well afford to help the starving settlers of the northwest, and at the same time advertise the advantages of a country where destitution such as exists in Dakota is unknown" (Nov. 1, 1889). Howe applauded the good people of Atchison who demanded that the owner of the prairie schooner which bore the words, "For Kansas or Bust. Busted, by G-d," either rub out the offensive legend or get out of town" (July 17, 1888).

Not for Ed Howe were the cries of the Populists, or the injunction by the lady reformer Mary Elizabeth Lease to raise less corn and more hell. Perhaps his dream of the Corn Carnival was being born in these years of protest; Howe annually encouraged positive thinking about crops and farming. "Enormous crops of wheat and oats have already been harvested, and everything is all right," he said in June, 1888. "If the farmers of Kansas get another big crop, we don't know what will become of them," he said in 1890. "The bigger the crop, the greater their troubles" (Mar. 17, 1890). And there continued to come the near-ecstatic little editorials praising the glories of his adopted state:

> Added to the corn and wheat possibilities of the state, we have the most delightful climate on earth. The nights are cool and delightful, and the days pleasant, while in every other state in the union the sun is hot enough to hatch out chickens during the day, and hot enough to boil eggs at night. [July 6, 1891]
>
> Have you been out in the woods and seen the new Easter bonnet Mother Nature is getting ready? It will be of a delicate green, with a light fringe of dainty crocuses, a crown of violets, and rosettes of pretty kitten-breeches, with streamers of pretty grass. Her milliners, the Sun and Rain, have the crocuses ready, and the violets will be ready by Easter. Every one is invited to attend her spring opening, the rich and the poor alike.

> Especially are the poor invited. Instead of loading your hearts with envy and your pocket book with debts attending artificial openings, go out and enjoy her spring delights. The closer you live to Nature, the longer you will live, and the more you will enjoy life. Take your children with you. She is the only landlady in the world who loves them. [Apr. 5, 1892]

The miserably hot city dweller, the impoverished farmer may have wondered what Ed Howe was talking about (and generally speaking he was not a man who dwelled on the beauties of nature). Could this be Kansas? More representative would have been those news reports in *The Globe* in 1893, about days of national panic, about days when all the wheat in northern Kansas was damaged by the drought, much of it dead; when hundreds of acres were to be plowed up and planted in corn. Or the news of grasshopper invasions, more drought, petty stealing, tramps coming into town to beg. "Cyclones, Grasshoppers and Populists Have Existed to Prove That Kansas Cannot be Ruined," read an overline (Nov. 22, 1893). "When Reports Come in of Ruined Wheat, Remember That Kansas Has Been Slandered Before." Or a lighter note: "The town cow has commenced looking around to see who is going to put in gardens" (Mar. 19, 1895).

Even in stricken 1893 Howe advocated that his readers drive out into the country to see the corn, one of the best area crops yet, a crop planted when drought hit the wheat in the spring. A year later he was trying to lift spirits with this sardonic overline: "The Case of Asiatic Cholera Comes in Handy: People Were Looking for Something to Worry Over" (Sept. 6, 1894).

Think positively and times will improve, he said. Wet years follow dry, and even though the drought succeeds in depopulating western Kansas and Nebraska, the following years will be wet, and people will forget the past, and rush in, and it will be like moving onto virgin soil. The year of the Corn Carnival was at hand, an event that would be a culmination of Ed Howe's belief that drought and hardship can be eliminated by hard work and enterprise, the end result of the boosterism that so belies the literary myth of Ed Howe as our chief critic of country town values.

In late summer of 1895 *The Globe* was getting the city ready for its first Corn Carnival. A streamer early in the summer had read: "Kansas Has the Best Corn Prospect in Its History; Some Even Say That Wheat and Oats are All Right" (June 4, 1895).

Another: "Indications Are That Corn Will be King in Kansas Again, and Will Get Rid of the Mortgage on Its Crown (June 6, 1895). In August: "Kansas This Year Raises One-Third More Corn Than in 1891, Heretofore Known as 'The Great Corn Year' " (Aug. 10, 1895).

The Corn Carnival which *The Globe* sponsored brought entertainment to the people of town and countryside and a kind of international reputation to Atchison. It was community booming of the first magnitude—with calls to the city to promote the affair, to make it a kind of Thanksgiving day in September. And then a grandiose editorial from Howe:

> The Indians, the earliest Americans, had a habit of celebrating a good corn crop. This is the basis of the Corn Carnival to be held in Atchison: a celebration of a big corn crop, which happens this year to be the largest in the history of Kansas.
>
> It is not proposed to have a parade, and keep the people waiting for hours: the people themselves are invited to take part, and be as merry as possible in celebrating the return of prosperity to Kansas. Everyone is expected to do whatever is amusing, original, good natured and noisy.
>
> It is expected that the excursion trains will arrive about noon; it is thought best to start the trains from Falls City, Hiawatha, Greenleaf, Topeka, Leavenworth, etc., from 8 to 10 o'clock in the morning, so that excursionists will arrive fresh and good natured. The trains will leave for the return not later than 10 or 11 in the evening, as all night rides are exceedingly disagreeable.
>
> From noon until 10 o'clock at night the fun will be fast and furious, but always innocent and good natured. Hundreds of people are expected to mask their faces, and wear ridiculous costumes; and everybody will blow a horn.
>
> In some of the great carnivals of the old world, the people pelt each other with confectionery. At the Corn Carnival in Atchison, the people will pelt each other with shelled corn and sunflowers. And every man who does not smoke a cob pipe will be a special object of attack.
>
> Every building will be decorated with corn stalks, corn leaves, corn tassles, shocks of corn. Some of the maskers will represent stalks of corn; others ear of corn. Others will have corn blades sewed to their clothing. Corn will be the predominating idea.
>
> There will be a bogus police force; a bogus fire department. Open summer cars brilliantly lighted will run up and down Commercial street filled with all sorts of spectacles. One

summer car will be loaded with a hundred pretty little girls wearing white dresses and blue sashes.

A great many of the principal features will be kept secret, but the general idea is for everybody to take part, without waiting for a committee of arrangements. If a citizen has a feature, he can bring it on the streets whenever he is ready, and have it pelted with corn. Novelties are wanted; no difference what they are.

One crowd of young fellows will appear as New Women, wearing enormous sleeves, bloomers and bustles. Another crowd has organized a bogus brass band. A society of young people will build an arch across Commercial street. Other societies will get up similar features, and the girls will be as active as the boys. There will be no spectators: everybody will take part. If you cannot do anything else, you can blow a horn, and pelt people with corn.

This should be remembered particularly: The people must be good natured and do nothing that annoys others. Amuse the people on the streets, but do not annoy them. [Aug. 27, 1895]

It was a stunt, even in its naïveté and provincialism, to make small town Chambers of Commerce of the twentieth century envious. A *Globe* editorial declared that there would be no speaker (one almost senses that the carnival was Howe's personal property), but that prominent visitors likely would come to Atchison—editors like Charley Finch of Lawrence, Will White of Emporia, Joe Hudson of Topeka, "and a lot of that gang" (Aug. 28, 1895). September 26, 1895, was to be the date. Already newspapers as far away as the *Chicago Inter-Ocean* were writing to commend the event.

In *The Globe* there was a three-column display advertisement (Sept. 5, 1895):

"Kansas People Should Raise
More Hell, and Less Corn."
—Mary Ellen Lease.[80]

They have Raised too much Corn again, and
will raise some of the other at the Corn
Carnival in Atchison September 26.

Thousands of Features.

The carnival presented an opportunity for a little enterprise by *The Globe,* whose editor wrote that every visitor to town would be entitled to a free copy of the newspaper. The government was predicting fair and cooler weather, with westerly winds. "Hurrah," said *The Globe.* Then came the celebration itself, just as Ed Howe had outlined it, with much local advertising, features, poetry, and a sketch of *The Globe* press to depict newspaper coverage of the day. Howe advocated annual observance of the carnival, which lasted three days. And it did become—for a time —an annual affair. William Allen White copied the idea with a three-day street fair in Emporia. The *Strand Magazine* of London heard about it and gave the attraction fourteen pages in 1897. The *Kansas City Times,* in 1905, called the event "the perfect art of the moving spectacle, the harmony of the color scheme." The magazine *Judge* said the carnival was over "but its glory is shining still like the mellow afterglow of a gorgeous sunset."[81] The Santa Fe Railroad's passenger department issued a pamphlet containing a poem, "Walls of Corn," written about the glories of the state's crop, and the railroad put the poem on sale at its booth at the 1899 carnival. Edward Bok, whose *Ladies' Home Journal* was riding high in national circulation, wrote Howe a letter of praise and announced plans to print an article and pictures about the event. And the people of Atchison gave Howe a solid silver water set, worth about $800, for promoting the affair. In 1896 Howe wrote that Mary Elizabeth Lease, who in a way had inspired the carnival, wanted to come to town: "We have raised the corn, and do not need any assistance from girl orators in raising the other thing" (Sept. 9, 1896).

4

THE EDITOR'S VIEWS IN THE GLOBE YEARS

Reformers and Politicians

Somewhere, sometime, in those early years, as he moved from job to job, as he reflected on the miseries of his boyhood and the tragedy of his parents' marriage, Edgar Watson Howe was forming those philosophies of life that would dominate his novels, his paragraphs and editorials in *The Globe,* his later observation in *The Monthly.*

Village life undoubtedly contributed to his bitter pessimism, his scorn for reform and reformers, his contempt for politics and politicians. A frequently—but not always—rational mind helped to shape his ideas on religion. Personal tragedy gave him rabid views about women. As he grew older, certain philosophers provided revelations, but he was not well educated and he read few philosophers in the busy years on *The Globe.* He was too hard at work, too concerned with providing for a family to spend much time with the Nietzsche and Schopenhauer that he later said he admired.

It was a damned human race to him, as it was to his literary idol Mark Twain. The American people love abuse, he believed. Yet coupled with the evil of the race was an essential civilizing influence that he saw; there was an Age of Progress to Ed Howe as there was to most Americans of his time. The age was *not* a selfish one, he wrote, despite what the preachers told people from their pulpits:

"The world was never so good as now; men were never so philanthropic and sympathetic as they are now. How they plundered each other; how they butchered each other; how they hated, and cursed, and persecuted each other in the famous old times of history. What accumulation of tortures—what endless inquisition of cruelty! To-day men are comparatively peaceful; the lion lies down with the lamb, and to use a homely expression everything is lovely. The fact is, the world grows better as it grows older and becomes more civilized, despite the croakings of would-be reformers, who can only be of any benefit to the world by reforming themselves" (Oct. 27, 1881).

And if there was no sense in reformers there also was no sense in studying a thing like public opinion. If someone polled the town of Atchison to ask about Mayor King's administration he would find that half the voters thought it abominable and the other half admirable. And if that is the way the public thinks, why trust the public? Trivialities dominate the interests of the world, he said. The next hero of the American people probably would be D. Frank Ingram, who was engaged to marry Nellie Bly, that trouble-making reporter on the New York *World.* People care more about a man who jumps off the Brooklyn Bridge, a principal in a murder case, a man who eats a thousand hard-boiled eggs in a thousand hours, or a woman who does something that a man should not do. And it has probably always been that way. Human nature is unchanging.

The world will not advance, then; yet less than a decade earlier (perhaps on a sunnier day) he had declared for the progress of mankind. On one gloomy day Ed Howe carried a page one overline: "At Some Time in His Life, Every Man Sympathizes With Vanderbilt, Who Said: 'The Public Be D....d' " (May 6, 1897). On another day "Globe Sights" provided this advice: "Don't slander the dead: if you do justice to the living you will be kept busy" (Oct. 12, 1899).

These were well-thought-out philosophies, in a way, ideas to which he had devoted time and thought, as representative as anything Ed Howe ever wrote. He was almost always the debunker, the iconoclast, the foe of phonies: Daniel Webster's last words were not, "I still live." They were really "Give me some brandy." Great men do not say things like "I will meet you beyond" or "Don't give up the ship." They more likely say "I am sick at my stomach" (Jan. 13, 1893). Washington was not the founder of his country; he was merely one of a number of wise and patriotic men living at that time. (That was the message of *The Globe* on the birthday in 1902 of the father of our country.) Forget the past: Mark Twain, probing the ashes of his boyhood, "scraping the moss off his memory," was doomed only to disappointment. Trying to turn backward brings "only a great shaking up of stiff limbs and illusions" (June 2, 1902).

Political observations in *The Atchison Globe* were a combination of such cynical views and Howe's boomer attitudes. A common belief about Ed Howe, one fostered by his own writings and by his son Gene, is that he had no interest in politics and government. This is nonsense. The files of both *Globe* and *Monthly* point to the falseness of such an idea. Ed Howe did *not* participate in the political arena like his contemporary, William Allen White, but there was scarcely a day when *The Globe* did not discuss politics. And on some days politics dominated both news and editorials.

Yet Ed Howe did believe that politics was a fraud. He said newspapers that would not allow any advertising on the editorial page would turn over columns to "the praise of some two-cent candidate." To him "the name of a shop where you can get a good beefsteak at a low price, is of more vital importance to the average man than the fifty-line announcement that John Smith, Esq., has consented to enter the race for the office of Hickmuckamuck" (Apr. 21, 1892). Politics was a fickle and futile pursuit. "One year the quiet man wins, but the next year the man with the largest mouth is elected. It is certain that occasionally the voice of the people is not the voice of God" (Apr. 8, 1891). Howe's views of the politician—and of other local types—could be found in a broad satire like that which he called "The Globe Primer" (and which leaned heavily on other newspaper humor appearing in those days):

> This is a candidate. The man he is shaking hands with is a voter. He is asking the voter about his health. He will go into a wicked place called a saloon presently, and invite the people to drink. The people will accept. After he has gone away they will call him a gray, and watch for his opponent. In private the candidate refers to the people as "cattle." A number of cows collected together are called cattle. He will be very busy to-morrow. To-morrow is election day, and he will fill his pockets with half dollars and quarters to convince the people that he is the best man.
>
> Behold the Greenbacker! He has no money, for he spends

> it in hiring orators to tell him how he is being robbed. He is crazy; he does not know who robs him, but he has an idea it is the government. You inquire, Tommy, what he believes. We don't know. Nobody knows. He does not know himself. Always treat a Greenbacker kindly. You may be unfortunate some day yourself. Get your mother to pray for the Greenbackers. It is said that they have souls. If so, we ought to try and save them.
>
> Here we have a lawyer. His business is to quarrel for other people. You notice he is well dressed. He has just closed up a clothing store, and is wearing his fees. The ambition of a lawyer is to become fat and dull, and be elevated to the bench, where he can be avenged on his associates who have not treated him well. After he becomes a judge, he spends his time in wondering how the people can have so much respect for his learning, and know him so well. He does not talk much, for fear of giving himself away. Some of these days he will retire from the bench, and then the people will find him out. It is unfortunate, children, that judges are selected from among the lawyers, for they usually believe that the judiciary was instituted for the benefit of the bar rather than for the benefit of your fathers, who are called the people. [Nov. 7, 1881]

Politicians and their activities were standard fare in *The Globe*. Ed Howe was usually a Republican, but he enjoyed applying the whip to the Republicans as well as to the Democrats. His earliest political promotion in *The Globe* was an effort, lasting over several years, to obtain a third term for Ulysses S. Grant. Howe made an early announcement for Grant, out of his conviction that the Republicans were sure to win in 1880. Then he added a name to the ticket: "How would Grant and Ingersoll for 1880 strike you?" Grant's nomination depended, he was sure, on the good sense of the American people, whose good sense, in this case, surely would jibe with that of an editor on a little newspaper in Atchison, Kansas. Then came a formal declaration, early in 1880, "*The Globe* for Grant."

The third term argument, which was being used against the Grant candidacy, was nonsense to Ed Howe, who wrote that human progress was due to men who had scoffed at precedent: ". . . what would this world have amounted to if it had been governed entirely by precedent? . . . If Christ had followed the precedents laid down by the Jews, we would all be Jews to-day. If the early Christian church had followed precedents, we would all be idol worshippers to-day. If Martin Luther had followed precedents, we would all be Catholics to-day. If John Calvin had followed precedents there would not have been a Presbyterian church in the land to-day. If Tom Payne [sic] had not dissented from the orthodoxy of Christianity in general there would have been comparatively little infidelity in the land to-day" (Feb. 24, 1880).

But as the campaign went into the critical year of 1880 Ed Howe began to see that the chances for his hero were slim, that too many newspapers were supporting him, for example, and that the unanimous backing of the press meant defeat. Howe was bracing himself for defeat, and getting ready for the years of rationalization. The nomination of Garfield gave him occasion to observe that Garfield's nomination of Sherman was forgotten until lightning struck Garfield himself. "Now it is being published in full by every Republican paper, and pronounced the most masterly oratorical effort ever made by an American statesman" (June 10, 1880). There was a touch of sour grapes in the post-defeat editorial on Grant, which laid the general's failure to his ambition and consequent amassing of enmities over the years. Howe was laughing editorially at the many acquaintances of Garfield back in Ohio, who knew of "Jim" Garfield's genius, of his days on the canal, his hardship working in the fields, his Lincolnish studying at night by candlelight. All very well, said Howe, but not quite the truth: "Mr. Garfield was given a college education by a rich old farmer who took a fancy to him, and he lives to-day to realize that his money was not spent in vain. In this age of free schools and cheap newspapers, it is not necessarily creditable that a man fit for President should have educated himself" (June 12, 1880).

Ed Howe had an extraordinary capacity for forgetting what he had written just a few days before, and throughout the campaign of 1880—and those that followed—he frequently would be found praising a man he had criticized early in the year. He was in Garfield country, of course; Kansas editors could be expected to cheer the nomination of any Republican. His words about the Democrats were almost always of the "bloody shirt" variety: "'Let us forget the past,' says the Democrat. We re-echo the sentiment. Let us forget the revolutionary war. Let us burn the Declaration of Independence, and forget that it ever existed. Let us forget to celebrate the Fourth of July. Let us forget the war of

1812. Let us forget the Mexican war. Let us forget the war of 1861. In short, let us lose our memory entirely, and become a nation of imbeciles. It is easy enough to propose forgetfulness, but memory is not treacherous enough. Memory cannot help recalling the scenes and issues of twenty years ago. The human mind feeds upon reminiscences of the past. Let a man forget the past and he is a fit subject for the mad house" (July 2, 1880).

The Atchison editor was back in memory in those Bethany days when his abolitionist father was doing battle with the slave state sympathizers. The bloody shirt had been buried too soon, he wrote when Winfield Scott Hancock was nominated. "The Democrats have the soldier and we have the statesman and our bloody shirt is under the ground, and if we are beaten we can blame nobody but ourselves" (July 6, 1880).

Yet Howe, with that essential honesty so bound up in his confusions and contrariness, and his feeling for fair play, also could turn his indignation on the Republicans when necessary. He was critical, for example, of the Republican effort to injure Hancock by telling the tale that "Hancock once brutally insulted Company C, Fourth Ohio Volunteers, by calling them G-d d-n s-s of b-s" (Aug. 7, 1880). A lie, he said, but a lie that undoubtedly would be met by a similar one from the Democrats.

On July 2, 1881, James A. Garfield was shot down by an assassin, and every newspaper in the land expressed its shock. The earliest comment that came from Ed Howe was to the effect that Arthur should not be permitted to become president; that was the editor's chief response to the tragedy. "Even though he is innocent of any complicity in the shooting, the people will always have their suspicions .... He was a corrupt politician, and was elected simply because the people had no fears of his succeeding Garfield. The idea of his being President never occurred to the general public" (July 2, 1881). Such political naïveté from Howe could be laid, perhaps, to his thin background in history; he had read relatively few books. But he had harsh words for those persons who seemed glad about the assassination, persons who were "no better that Gitteau [sic]" (July 5, 1881).

When Garfield died, Howe placed the blame where he thought it belonged, on press and politicians. He also wrote that *The Globe* had not respected Garfield at first, because it had been prejudiced by the Democratic press, but that its respect had grown. The newspaper had admired Garfield's family ties, and the proof of his heroism, and it was ready to do justice to Garfield's successor. Howe hoped the Democratic press would do as much, but he did not think it likely. His old love for Grant was disappearing, and in late 1881 Howe declared that his paper no longer would support a third term candidacy, for the former president had turned "into a wire-pulling, gabby politician," a man trying to push into office all his old cronies who had been shunned by the Garfield people. By 1912 Howe had forgotten that he had *ever* favored Grant: "Grant was president eight years, and presided over scandal and villainy blacker than the country had thus far witnessed. In spite of this record, he weakly tried for a third term, and being refused it, became the victim of a Wall street gambler; his name was used to further a brazen game of thievery."[1]

Arthur met much criticism from *The Globe,* especially for being what Howe termed a spoils politician. The bosses must be defeated or the Republican party would not survive, he wrote. Perhaps it was time, too, to bury that perennial argument, the Civil War, especially on the part of the Republicans, who were using it on every possible occasion:

> The Republican party reminds us of the Catholic church. Periodically it holds a soldiers' reunion, or political high mass, as it were. Some general, colonel or major, acting as a sort of political high priest, appears among the multitude, mounts the platform, and after conducting appropriate services, proceeds, amid a solemn hush, to open the box and produce the Republican Host. This is a small wax figure of Abraham Lincoln as he appeared just after the assassination. The soldiers look at it and prostrate themselves on their faces while "John Brown's Body" is being chanted by a choir of ex-drummer boys. When the ex-soldiers resume a standing position, the Relics of the party are produced. First comes an army musket, then a haversack, then a canteen, and so on down the list until the flag—the battle-torn, powder-begrimed flag—is reached. Again the ex-soldiers prostrate themselves, and the choir of ex-drummer boys chant "The Flag Is Still There," and the political high priests retire, congratulating themselves that the country is safe. It has been suggested that a confessional be established for the benefit of those old soldiers who have strayed away from the party and insulted the flag by voting an independent ticket. [Feb. 14, 1883]

As the campaign year of 1884 neared, Ed Howe continued his satires and began to express an interest in the gubernatorial prospects of a Civil War figure who had caught his fancy: ". . . we would like to see Ben Butler re-elected Governor of Massachusetts by a crushing majority. We like the cock-eyed old spoon thief." Yet early in 1884 *The Globe* announced its support of James G. Blaine for the Republican nomination, and it provided extensive coverage of the party's convention early that summer.

Though illustrations were uncommon in *The Globe* of the 1880s, the newspaper did provide drawings of both Blaine and Cleveland in the convention summer of 1884. It forecast the nomination of Cleveland (whom it did not like)—and the Republican convention had just barely adjourned. It also informed its readers that there would be no interviews with leading citizens on who would be the best man, because the Republicans would favor the Republican and the Democrats the Democrat. That could be known without interviews.

Ed Howe, who scorned the prohibition movement, was interested in another political campaign in 1884, that being waged by the Prohibition party, which *The Globe* reported had met and nominated that well-known Kansan, Colonel John P. St. John, governor of Kansas from 1879 to 1883, as its presidential candidate.

The scurrilous campaign of 1884 drew some criticism from Howe, even though he obviously hoped Grover Cleveland would never enter the White House. Scandals had been linked to all candidates. There had been scandals about Grant and Hayes, and Garfield and Arthur, and now they had touched the candidacy of Cleveland. Howe also was dubious about the qualifications of one famous American as the investigator of charges that Grover Cleveland was the father of an illegitimate child: "It is claimed that Henry Ward Beecher had 'investigated the charges against Grover Cleveland's private character, and finds that Cleveland acted honorably,' since he agreed to support the child. It is barely possible that Mr. Beecher would conduct an 'investigation' of a matter of this kind with a great deal of charity; Mr. Beecher has been the victim of unholy love himself" (Aug. 11, 1884).

Howe continued to abuse the Democrats for being concerned about those who waved the bloody shirt. After all that shirt had come from Gettysburg, from Appomattox, from Vicksburg Landing, from Richmond and from Antietam, and "it was dyed in the blood of their fathers and brothers" (Oct. 31, 1884).

The results of the 1884 election, undecided for several days, became obvious fairly soon to the Kansas Republican, and he appeared ready to accept with grace the defeat of Blaine (who, incidentally, had received comparatively little attention in *The Globe* concerning those financial perfidies other newspapers were outlining in detail). Howe also was not surprised when the Democrats showed little eagerness to promote Civil Service reform, despite their "howlers" before the election. "To the victors belong the spoils" could be a slogan applying to either party, he concluded (July 3, 1885).

The family of Grover Cleveland felt the sharpness of Ed Howe's attacks like no other White House family until the coming of Theodore Roosevelt. He was amused on hearing that the sister of the President had said she would be ashamed to wear a low-necked dress. "Inasmuch as Miss Cleveland is rough-skinned and scrawny, and has an ironing-board bust, we don't blame her" (Mar. 19, 1886). Cleveland's girth was a constant object of Howe's derision: "If the President should die, would Mrs. Cleveland be inconsolable? The President is old and fat, and no doubt snores horribly at night, and there is some reason to believe that his young wife would find it difficult to mourn as much as propriety requires. Not that she is heartless, but no one mourns much for an old fat man, or for one who snores" (Jan. 1, 1887).

Most of Howe's political observations in the 1880s were either disavowels of an interest in politics or laughing criticisms of the institution. He offered his ticket in 1886: "After a good deal of serious consideration the GLOBE has concluded to hoist the straight Republican ticket, as follows: For Associate Justice, An Old Grandmother; for Governor, A Great Big Grunt; for Lieutenant Governor, A Cord of Wood on Subscription; for Secretary of State, A Played Out Doctor; for Treasurer, A War Reminiscence; for Auditor, A Whisky Bottle With Water in It; for Attorney General, The South End of a Horse Going North; for Superintendent of Public Instruction, Mr. Who" (July 14, 1886).

When Cleveland was renominated in 1888, Howe wrote:

> No. The GLOBE is not a Democratic paper, assertions of contemporaries to the contrary notwithstanding. Were the

GLOBE a Democratic paper, it would come out with the following brilliant editorials today:

Whoopla!
Victory is assured!
Don your white tile! [sic]
The man of Destiny!
Get out your bandana!
The noblest Roman of them all!
Cleveland and Thurman and Victory! [June 8, 1888]

As America moved into the late 1880s the issues dominating political life more and more came to be connected with reform. Ed Howe, so cynical about so many issues, was an advocate of one such new reform—the Australian ballot: he saw it as one way to eliminate corruption and intimidation. But, as a proponent of rural interests, he consistently fought that one celebrated Republican plan of the day, the high tariff, a somewhat contrary position for such a man. There was no manufacturing in the West, he said, because the Republicans had protected the manufacturers so long that they could form trusts strong enough to curb any industrial activity elsewhere. And he saw Republican revolt on the question of the tariff as a likelihood, for storm signals already were being raised in the prairie lands. These storm signals largely were connected with rural and not urban revolt, and had been festering in the plains country and in the South since the 1870s. Ed Howe had made numerous comments on the activities and attitudes of the malcontents, most of whom did not fit his notions of successful people. Reformers and members of Granges were unfair in the things they said about the railroads, he wrote, for railroad men by and large were a credit to their communities and the more of them we had the better off we would be.

Socialism was spreading throughout America along with ideas of Grange and Greenbacker, but perhaps it would pay to listen to the grumblings of these rabble-rousers, he said: "The corruption that has been rampant for years is now bearing its legitimate fruits, in dissatisfaction and murmurings, and if the proper remedy is not applied, it will result as did the murmuring and dissatisfaction of the French people before the commune" (June 11, 1879). Greenbackers were "well-to-do vagrants," no better for Kansas than grasshoppers.

Kansas to Ed Howe was a kind of chosen land. Troublemakers were out of keeping with the good land and the good people Ed Howe remembered from his traveling days and his years on *The Globe*—hopeful and cheerful people, who could keep their humor to the fore and laugh at hard times.[2] For he had selected Kansas, and he had selected Atchison, and Atchison deserved his work and devotion. His paper's platform was "Peace and Decency," and he had contempt for malcontents and busybodies. He placed in his newspaper sketches of the town's manufacturing and producing enterprises, for the city "should make every effort to fasten her grip upon the attention of the country" (Aug. 14, 1878). He pushed for new homes so that the people sure to come to growing Atchison would have a good place to raise their families. "If we can't wake up the old fogies to a realizing sense of their duty, we will advocate that an outraged public hang a few of them" (Sept. 5, 1878).

Patronize home merchants, and let the tramp peddlers get jobs sawing wood. Look at the example of the electric light company, which invested thousands of dollars in the town when it was a dull place in need of promotion. Look at the Atchison, Topeka & Santa Fe, the coming railroad of the land, "and it won't be many years until the commerce of the world will pay tribute to Atchison" (Dec. 11, 1878). Look to plans for the Southwest railroad project, and let Atchison be the town that issues the invitation to provide facilities. Look even to the University of Kansas, where courses in civil, mechanical, and electrical engineering were being taught: "striking evidence of the young state's belief in fostering whatever is helpful in its onward march toward the highest civilization" (Aug. 8, 1890). And where could one find a place more worthy of settling down, or locating an industry, than the thriving city on the bluffs of the Missouri?

The small town was the repository of the best values of civilization, Ed Howe was saying. "The great crimes and scandals come from the big cities. The best people in the world live in the small towns and rural communities. Not one great man in a hundred was 'raised' in a city. Nearly all the useful and distinguished men were trained in homes in the country, or in homes in small towns" (May 28, 1904). This was his creed, and he preached it, and modifications of it, through a long career. The reformers of the Grange and the Greenbackers and the Farmers' Alliance believed in rural values, too, but they wanted changes made. Ed Howe and the agrarian reformers parted company on the question of change. As early as 1881 Howe was charging that the Farmers' Alliance was itself responsible for a swindle being perpetrated upon the farmers of southern Kansas, who had bought seed for "mammoth corn" that had been advertised in the newspapers of the alliance. The growth of the alliance worried him; its 70,000 membership in 1889 and growth of two thousand members a month could mean havoc for the Republicans in 1890, he feared. The Democrats, quite naturally, were flocking around the alliance, and that could mean real trouble.

The Farmers' Alliance won in 1890, and agrarian revolt was on the move in Kansas and in much of the nation. The cries of Mrs. Lease were being heard, and the alliance newspapers were calling on "this scolding old woman"—as Ed Howe described her—to stump for their interests. Howe heard that "Colonel Lease" would lecture before the state agricultural college at Manhattan, and he observed that "A woman whose idea of agriculture is to raise less corn and more hell is an odd person to select to address a crowd of youngsters" (Nov. 25, 1893).

Occasionally he could go along with some of the things the agitators were screaming about. When he noted that people were not crowding into Kansas, but were becoming more numerous in Nebraska, he blamed it on the coming of prohibition. Four years before William Allen White issued his famous editorial on the ills of Kansas, Howe was writing in this vein:

> Business is never good, but it is as good now in Kansas as it ever is. Men are always waiting for good times, and they should take notice that they have arrived; that is, they are as good as they ever will be. A man who is not doing well in business now, might as well quit. Kansas is the centre of prosperity now, and other sections that have lately been prosperous, are very dull. Good times travel about. Texas lately had it, and Kansas was suffering from hard times. Now the case is reversed. The Pacific coast lately had everything pleasant, but it is now suffering from general depression. . . . The people should also take notice that times will finally be hard in Kansas, and arrange their affairs accordingly. Good times are always followed by hard times, and when times are hard, remember that good times are traveling your way, and will reach you if you are patient. [June 23, 1892]

Mainly the paper was concerned with farmer politics and growing revolt in the years leading up to 1896—much about Populism in the summer of 1894, comments about the mad old women who called themselves suffragists and the Populists who favored giving the vote to such harridans. Everybody was telling everybody else—but notably the farmers—how to be saved, and even children were doing it in Kansas, taking their example from Mrs. Lease, finding "boy preachers" who would go out and "tell gray bearded old men their duty" (June 26, 1894). When the Populists suffered defeat in the 1894 election Howe viewed the matter with equanimity, and gave the repudiated some advice, advice also for the rest of the good folks of the state:

> To the honest Populists: Your defeat yesterday will prove a good thing for Kansas. Your representatives at Topeka conducted themselves in such a way that the good of the state demanded their repudiation. The honest men in the Populist party intended reform, but their representatives refused to carry it out. . . .
>
> The defeat of equal suffrage in Kansas yesterday was in no sense a rebuke to the women. The great majority of good women have no desire to vote, and never asked for suffrage. Had the better class of women made such a request, the men would have cheerfully granted it at the polls. . . .
>
> Now let the people of Kansas take the necessary steps to get rid of prohibition. Kansas people seem to have their usual good sense again, and should lose no time in ridding the state of prohibition, because it is injurious, and is not an effective temperance measure. Nine states of the union have tried prohibition, and discarded it. Kansas should be next on the list. [Nov. 7, 1894]

Other matters were stirring up the Atchison conservative in the early 1890s. Too many tramps, for one thing, an average of three showing up at the police station every night for lodging, stopping at homes and telling sad stories and getting a meal from sentimental housewives. "The tramps generally say they are 'victims of circumstance' " (Jan. 18, 1893). Ed Howe knew better; they were lazy men who could be successful if they wanted. Then came Coxey's army and its march on Washington, at first a joke, then a serious matter—"The Only Difference Between a Coxey and a Congressman is That a Congressman Gets a Salary," one overline read (Apr. 28, 1894). The woods and the fields—and now the highways—were full of reformers, and "The demands of these lazy, useless people are as impossible of accomplishment as would be a demand to have daylight all the time, to the end that there would be no darkness to aid evil doers" (May 8, 1894).

General Coxey's revelation that men in his army had left destitute families at home really roused the ire of *The Globe* editor:

"We can think of nothing more contemptible than a man leaving a destitute family to march to Washington on a fool's errand like Coxey's. A man with a spark of manhood would remain with his family, and try to provide something for them to eat. Although times are hard, there would be more prospect of accomplishing something at home than on the dusty road to Washington" (May 8, 1894).

It was a year for gloomy observations:

> We suppose the Fourth of July orators will wave the eagle in the usual extravagant fashion this year, and tell how every man is an intellectual giant, and a patriot, and a kind father and indulgent husband, but as a matter of fact, that sort of nonsense is becoming a little tiresome. Americans have flattered each other so much that many of them are becoming unbearable in their conceit and nonsense. Liberty has been carried so far that many people believe we have too much of it. The striking coal miners who refuse to work, or to permit others to take their places, are one result of too much liberty. Coxey is another result. America is overburdened with nonsense, and the next set of Fourth of July orators ought to tell the exact facts, and give the eagle a rest. Out of our abundance we have made as sad a mess as people of other countries have made of their poverty. We need a good talking to; we are all Coal Oil Johnnies who have spent money too recklessly, and are howling because more money cannot be gathered from bushes and birds' tails. [May 25, 1894]

Then came the great Pullman strike by the American Railway Union. Howe ran a series of editorials, some of them at least a little sympathetic to the strikers: "The strikers are mean during an occasional strike, but the railroad officials are mean all the time" (July 3, 1894). He warned the union that violence would bring only sympathy for the side of management, and he suggested that all the foolish sympathy being talked of only injured the cause of the union, that the Pullman officials might have been wiser had there been "a good raking" to bring them—as well as the union—to their senses. There were too many do-gooders abroad in the land, in the opinion of Ed Howe, too many associations "for the Advancement of Human Welfare" announcing that they needed money. Too many preachers: Mrs. Lease had gone to preaching and even St. John was filling a pulpit, charging twenty-five cents admission to "hear a lecturer advocate that every man, woman and child in this country receive a ten dollar gold piece every Thursday morning" (Feb. 18, 1896). Too many politicians, as a matter of fact: "As soon as a man becomes so depraved that he is willing to live by politics, he should be arrested, and put in some kind of a reformatory, for such a man is a public enemy; he is willing to make it his business to rob the people by means of unnecessary appropriations, and the creation of unnecessary offices" (Mar. 24, 1896).

The Election of 1896

The "non-political" *Atchison Globe* showed perhaps its greatest news enterprise when the Republicans met in St. Louis to nominate a presidential candidate in the summer of 1896. Ed Howe had been laying it on the Democrats and the Populists for almost two decades; their current cries about "free silver" had roused his impatience even more. This year, for the first and only time in his career, he attended a national political convention and sent back reports to his newspaper. Already he was quite aware of the front-runner in the party, William McKinley of Ohio, whose pro-tariff speeches had been making Howe angry for some years. Now he would see McKinley nominated, but he would be on the scene as a detached observer, not as one of those worrisome political editors who were more concerned with running the affairs of the nation than making a living on their own newspapers.

When the convention opened, Howe was there to file a dispatch for *The Globe:*

> Special to THE GLOBE.
>
> ST. LOUIS, MO., June 16.—The thing that impresses me most is the respectability of the crowd. I have never seen a finer looking lot of men together. I interpret this to mean that the best men in the country want McKinley and protection, and have turned out to the convention.

> The weather is fine to-day, and, the crowd having become located, everything is more orderly. I have not interviewed any leaders, but it seems to be in the air that the platform will be a mild one; a compromise between two extremes. This would be the sensible course, and McKinley's manager is a sensible man. . . .
>
> There is nothing whatever in the story sent out from Wichita that Marsh Murdock will bolt the convention, and become a candidate for governor of Kansas on a silver platform. . . .
>
> At noon, the galleries were not more than half filled, but were rapidly filling up. The first proceeding was a march by the brass band, followed by cheering and waving of flags. On the entrance of a noted man, every other man in the press gallery stood up, and the others cried "sit down." There is as much confusion in the convention hall as on the streets. The brass band, playing in one of the upper galleries, sounds blocks away.
>
> At 12:25 p.m., another cheer went up. I do not know what it was about; no one around me knew. There was so much confusion that I made a tour down towards the speaker's stand to see if the convention had opened. I found the same confusion around the speaker's stand that is prevailing elsewhere. . . .
>
> At 12:35, there is a great confusion. I hear an aye vote and cheering. The temporary chairman is speaking, but I cannot hear what he says. Occasionally there is a cheer, or hand clapping. This will probably continue some time.[3]

Most of *The Globe*'s actual coverage of the convention came in Associated Press dispatches, but an article by Howe led off the convention coverage the next day. The editor was sure that the party had gotten up enough momentum to elect McKinley, and that the Democrats were making a strategic error in placing so much faith in free silver. Howe's personal notes, not surprisingly, were much more interesting than his news accounts. He spent much time with William Allen White, who later recalled ranging about town with Howe, "who, being an old stager, knew the good places to eat. We discovered Tony Faust's restaurant, then famous all over the Midwest, and went to a comic opera in an outdoor beer garden. I remember I saw 'The Bohemian Girl' for the first time. . . . Ed Howe was ten years older than I, but we roamed the city together, good comrades."[4] Howe's own account was carried in *The Globe* under the heading of "THE ST. LOUIS CONVENTION":

> I arrived at St. Louis Monday morning, in a rain storm. I found a room on the corner opposite the Union station, and

spent the first part of the day in watching the crowds. My room is in the second story, and as double track trolley roads cross at this corner, the Roar reminded me of the first time I visited New York.

It is the best looking crowd I have even seen, and the largest. At the ordinary lodge convention, or church convention, you find a large number of ridiculous looking people, but the men who are attending this convention average very high in appearance. I never before saw men who could wear badges without looking ridiculous.

The car in which I came to the city was full, but not crowded. There were five Pullman sleepers, and I understood that every berth was taken. Two delegates from Wyoming asked permission to sit in my section, explaining that a woman had taken their seats, and they did not know how to get her out. "We are going to St. Louis to right the wrongs of the country," one of them said, "but we are unable to get our own rights in this car." In every section there were three or four men, but every woman in the car was occupying more space than she was entitled to. Women always have the best of it in a crowd.

Two of the Murdocks, the Father and Holy Ghost, are here. The Son is at Wichita, looking after the Eagle. The Holy Ghost is making the fight of his life for two tickets; one for himself, and another for a friend.

I saw a funny thing last evening: a lot of fellows had a friend who looked like Mark Hanna, and they were introducing him to everybody. One stranger took the bogus boss off to one side, and tried to "fix" something. I didn't know what the stranger wanted, but Mark kept saying he couldn't possibly do it. I followed the bogus Mark Hanna around an hour; he was an Indiana man, and was having an awfully good time.

I was eating dinner with Bill White to-day, and the waiter was somewhat slow in serving us. "Here Oscar," Mr. White said to him; "hurry up a little. We're McKinley and Reed, and have got to go to the convention in a few minutes." Mr. White does not take the convention at all seriously, and says it is no more interesting than a protracted meeting. Many a man is spending borrowed money liberally in St. Louis this week. [June 17, 1896]

On the day the Associated Press reported the nomination of McKinley, *The Globe* gave the candidate attention with a page one picture. Howe's account of the nomination was a perceptive —and funny—analysis of the political process at work:

> This is the way the national Republican convention actually appears to nineteen out of twenty spectators: it is the way it actually appeared to me:
>
> I went in a half hour before the proceedings were advertised to begin, and watched the crowd assemble. Members of the managing committee were rushing about, carrying little badges of office that looked like miniature May poles. There were hundreds of petty officials, appointed from the different states. There was a good deal of quarreling among members of the managing committee, and suppressed swearing. Most of the members of the managing committee lived in St. Louis.
>
> If the convention was advertised to "take up" at 10 o'clock, it was called to order a half hour later. I could hear the speaker's gavel, otherwise I would not have known when the sessions began. When there was an adjournment, I could see the crowds break for the doors. . . .
>
> Proceedings in detail: A lot of men standing on the speaker's platform. The speaker apparently introduces a man, who turns out to be a colored bishop. All the people present stand up. Could not hear the bishop. "Yesterday," a man near me said, "they had a Jewish rabbi.". . .
>
> A man gets up on the floor, and reads something. I can hear a voice, but cannot hear what is said. The speaker arouses a great deal of enthusiasm, and there is a great waving of fans and flags. . . .
>
> I came home not because the crowds scared me, but to hear the news of the convention. Associated Press reporters have seats adjoining the speaker's stand. They hear everything, and the officers of the convention take pains to tell them everything. [June 18, 1896]

The Democrats still had not met, but *The Globe,* in the predictable practice of much of the American press, made its choice. Free silver was a step toward barbarism: ". . . we might as well talk about giving up type writers and steel pens, and return to goose quills, as to talk about free silver." It has been tried and abandoned, Howe said; adopting it would be like giving up our great railways and steamships and returning to canoes and stagecoaches. The gold standard was to be equated with "patriotism, progress and honesty," free silver with repudiation. Honest money men were being called "gold bugs," but they were the men who believed in paying off their debts and in keeping the nation sound (June 20, 1896).

As the Democrats met for their convention (an event of small importance to *The Atchison Globe*), Howe was sounding off against a man he deeply disliked, John P. Altgeld—a foreigner, a millionaire, an anarchist, a liar, a traducer, an owner of a big office building, and a proponent of free silver. The next day's *Globe* brought the first of a long line of editorials about a gentleman named William Jennings Bryan, a line that would stretch down to 1925. There also was a small picture, and there was a brief story about the candidate of the Democrats:

"We have no objection to W. J. Bryan further than that he is referred to as the 'Boy Orator of the Platte.' Boy orators, like boy evangelists, are very tiresome prodigies. If Mr. Bryan is so young he can still be called a boy, he is too young to be president. 'Boy orator' savors too much of such declamations as 'The boy stood on the burning deck,' and 'You would scarce expect one of my age,' to take the fancy of a people in need of a guide through the wilderness" (July 10, 1896).

Bryan was speaking such rot, said Ed Howe, as the fact that he had had no desire to enter the White House, that his chief aim in life was to retire and practice law and give his children "a tender father's care." Howe felt sure that the voters would "see that his wish is gratified next November: No one so bound up in a sweet home life should be rudely torn from it to accommodate an ungrateful public" (July 11, 1896). And there was Bryan's apparent belief that he would be assassinated. "Who would do it?" asked Ed Howe. "The anarchists and crazy people are all on his side" (Aug. 24, 1896).

The brutal campaign of 1896 was off and running in Kansas, a pivotal state that election year. William Allen White was writing an editorial called "What's the Matter with Kansas?"—an entertaining and vicious piece of name-calling that would help make him a national figure. Ed Howe was reprinting it in *The Globe* (and probably every other editor in the state was rushing the thing into print). Howe was listening to the cries about hard times and giving a philosophical reply that revealed much about both himself and the times in which he lived:

"We are not sorry when times are hard. The women then cook noodles with the chicken, to make the chicken go round; make good gravy to save the meat; serve apple pie oftener than plum pudding; do away with servant girls who can't cook, and display their own skill; stay at home more with their children, because they have no fine clothes to wear gadding; try their hands at nice old fashioned ginger bread, instead of angel's food; the general health is better, and people who would otherwise come and visit a month, stay at home. There is nothing so terrible about hard times, if a real clever woman manages the home" (Oct. 12, 1896).

He was making his own comments on what was the matter with Kansas: "So many Kansas people spent money in Kansas City at the carnival that Kansas City merchants have been compelled to lay in a second stock of winter clothing. That is one thing that is the matter with Kansas that the women could help, if they would" (Oct. 23, 1896). He was advising his readers that times might be bad but that at least the people knew how things were under present financial policies, and that free silver might bring a disastrous panic. For panic had come in 1893, and it had come under a Democratic administration. Kansas must—and should—go Republican, to bring good times and to help remove the stigma being attached to the state, the stigma like that coming from, one may presume, the editorial by his friend White.

The weeks preceding the election brought some of the least memorable journalism in the nation's history, and not just in the hinterlands, like Kansas. There were outcries like the Populist protest at a Republican display of the Stars and Stripes: "Nine-tenths of the old soldiers are for McKinley," said Howe; "therefore, why shouldn't the McKinley people make a display of the American flag on the 31st, or any other day?" (Oct. 22, 1896). Came the editorial attacks on Bryan, like those in which Ed Howe said the Democratic candidate had used every method, fair and foul, that he was at the end of the political road, that "he will not live long enough to be voted a great man by Americans" (Oct. 31, 1896). Much of this reads today like desperation, in view of the outcome of the election. But there were desperate politicians and editors. Yet soon Ed Howe, like other editors (Republican and those who, like him, were Republican but denied it), was able to issue the triumphant headline: "McKINLEY SAFELY ELECTED." In *The Globe* there was a secondary headline: "BRYAN HAS LOST THE ELECTION, BUT HE STILL HAS HIS COLOSSAL NERVE." Kansas had gone Democratic, however, and Howe printed an overline: "It Looks as Though Kansas

People Saw an Opportunity to Make Geese of Themselves, and Accepted It." His editorial was in more contented mood:

"McKinley was elected president yesterday by such a landslide that it is foolish for the opposition to talk about Mark Hanna's money controlling the result. The result is so emphatic that it will be accepted without question. It was intended that the majority in this country should control, and in this case the majority is so large that even the Bryan men are accepting the result good naturedly. . . .

"THE GLOBE is proud of the result of yesterday, because it demonstrates that the people of this country are capable of self government (Nov. 4, 1896).

Though the election was over, *The Globe* continued to give the defeated man editorial lumps, even in a headline: "THE BOY ORATOR SHOWS HIS USUAL LACK OF SENSE BY HANGING ON." That was a bit rough, even from Ed Howe, especially because it was printed over a story filed by the Associated Press which was extremely objective. Howe felt disgraced that Kansas had not been in the company of Pennsylvania and New York, with their pluralities of 280,000 each for McKinley, instead of being with "Texas, Arkansas, Georgia, Mississippi, and that gang!" But Atchison had done *its* duty—a plurality of nearly nine hundred against the Populist candidate for governor.

A year later, William Jennings Bryan came to Ed Howe's town, and Howe wrote an editorial on Bryan that bore the headline: "Long Live the Fool Killer." It was a pity, he said, that so gifted a man could not talk sense instead of nonsense. Bryan had no business charging for his foolish talks, in which he recommended panaceas to the people when he knew they would not work. Repercussions continued from William Allen White's celebrated editorial, which was widely reprinted and may have been of some importance in the 1896 election. Ed Howe reported that "What's the Matter with Kansas?" was one of the leading subjects of discussion in the East, and he suggested that the editorial had done Kansas more harm than anything else. But he had some fun with the Emporia editor: "Will White is in North Dakota getting material for a big wheat farm story for *Scribner's* magazine. What's the Matter with Kansas?" (Nov. 7, 1897). Generally his feeling for White was that of affection, and when White had local troubles Ed Howe took time to reflect on the Emporia editor,

Emporia itself, and the problems of publishing a newspaper:

> They are "laughing" at W. A. White down at Emporia, because an excitable old man struck him from behind with a cane. After the fight, a young fellow "laughed" at White, and White knocked him down.
>
> Men dearly love to "laugh" at each other.
>
> THE GLOBE has no disposition to join in the merriment over White's fight. We admire White, and if he has been humiliated, we are sorry. We suppose half the people of Emporia hate White, as is true of most newspaper men. If Emporia had another institution that attracted as much attention to Emporia, as White, it would point to it with pride. White causes the word "Emporia" to be printed oftener than all the other institutions in the town put together, including Sunny Slope Farm and the suicide and bank failure that went with it.
>
> No man can run a newspaper without being unjustly criticised: everyone who runs a newspaper must accept this fact as a part of the business. As soon as everybody in a town hates a newspaper, it is a sign that that newspaper is becoming useful. When the people of a town fail to appreciate a paper that tries to be fair and useful, and really has some success along these lines, the people of that town cannot be very highly commended. For it is a fact that when the vicious assail an honest newspaper, the honest people should stand by it as unfailingly as they stand by an honest bank, an honest woman or an honest man. [Apr. 7, 1899]

Ed Howe knew that Kansas, which even in the 1890s was developing its characteristic inferiority complex, could bounce back from abuse and difficulties. He believed that people who live west of a given point are as honest as those who live east of it, and that Kansas people are honest people. He knew that Kansans could abuse their own state but also could point to it with pride, as they had reason to do, in his opinion. For, in the years after the hate-filled election campaign of 1896 was over, this was the Kansas—presumably a Populist-free Kansas—that he saw on a lovely summer's day:

"This is the people's year. How cool and bracing the summer; how timely the rains! The rain of Sunday morning was so gentle that not a drop got away: there was no wash in the corn fields. It came down so straight and orderly that it was not necessary to close open windows. The day following was warm, and the corn sprang up to meet the sunlight. If heaven is as good as Kansas this year, we shall be satisfied.

"Why not have Thanksgiving day earlier?" (June 16, 1902).

But there was the other Kansas, too, the one that creates the typically Kansas mood of self-deprecation, the one that Kansas residents know best in the heat of July or August: "In order to thoroughly appreciate the beauty of this season in Kansas, a man should leave the state and read poetry about the sunflowers in bloom while in the mountains, or at the seashore" (Aug. 25, 1898). There was the more practical side he saw, too, which he was describing in a *Forum* magazine article in 1892, that side which concerned the boomers of Kansas: "I wonder that a great poet does not come out of the West. The confidence of the Western man that his town lot will finally make him rich, somehow reminds one of the bard who longs so ardently for ambrosia and nectar, although about all he ever gets is cornbread and creek water."

Kansas Politics

Newspapers were founded in Kansas for political reasons, in towns like Atchison to support the Southern cause, in towns like Lawrence to back the Free State movement. The editors of the state have always been politicians in their own right, in a sense, men who have exerted influence over state policies and who occasionally have even run for office, sometimes successfully.

With Edgar Watson Howe and *The Atchison Globe* comments on politics in Kansas always read like a side excursion from the main events. Of course Howe had to comment on state politics; it was an editorial obligation. But his commentaries often seemed perfunctory; there seemed no studied philosophy, or plan, in his approach, and national affairs always seemed to stir him up more.

There was one exception—the celebrated Atchisonian named John J. Ingalls. Ingalls was perhaps the dominant figure in Kansas politics in the late nineteenth century, a man who created an unforgettable picture in the U.S. Senate: ". . . a tall, gaunt figure with a ramrod-straight backbone that supported an elongated, scrawny neck with a head of dark thatch that was parted in the middle. Triple-lens spectacles above the mustache and goatee added to the appearance of inscrutability. Clad in a long-skirted Prince Albert, sporting a scarlet cravat, a towering silk hat, and wrapped altogether in a checkerboard ulster, Ingalls was, despite vigorous competition from his colleagues, a distinctive figure. Common people stared at him in awe."[6]

Ingalls was a New Englander, born in Massachusetts in 1833, educated at Williams College, coming to Kansas in 1858, serving in the Wyandotte constitutional convention in 1859. He was in the U.S. Senate for eighteen years, and there he became known as a "master of sarcasm and satire, as well as of eulogistic oratory."[7] He wrote a famous poem called "Opportunity" and an essay on Kansas that starts with the arresting sentence: "Kansas is the navel of the Nation." Ingalls fell before the Populist surge of 1891, but prior to that time he had been the pride of Kansas and the special pride of his home town of Atchison. And particularly of Ed Howe, who seized upon Ingalls as a kind of political symbol and was promoting Ingalls and his career in government from 1878 on. This early editorial, for example, was published in Howe's first year on *The Globe:*

"Influential newspapers all over the country, from Maine to Frisco, are saying complimentary things of our distinguished citizen, Senator John J. Ingalls, intimating that if the people of Kansas know on which side their bread is buttered, they will return him to Washington. All these things only go to prove our assertion that Mr. Ingalls is a man of National renown, and that every time his distinguished presence rises up in the halls of Congress, it is an excellent advertising medium for Kansas and Atchison"[8] (Sept. 25, 1878).

Whenever Ingalls came to town *The Globe* sent an editor or reporter to interview him, that person likely being Ed Howe himself ("Mr. Neversweat, a very careful and cautious reporter"). Of Ingalls, *The Globe* wrote: "His head was drawn down, his eyes were fixed intently on the ground, and a dark frown was gathered on his noble countenance. . . . I might have stood there all day gazing at him had he not broken the spell that bound me by making a lunge and letting fly a huge volley of oaths at the family dog which happened to cross his path" (Aug. 4, 1879). The newspaper also praised a big civic reception held for Ingalls in 1880, one that featured seven hundred dollars worth of fireworks for one city park alone.

Ingall's speeches always received considerable attention, like one delivered in early 1891 on free coinage. When Ingalls spoke in Topeka in the 1880s Howe commented: "The brainy Atchison man is on horseback, and galloping toward greatness" (Apr. 13, 1887). Much of this was boasting about a local man who had made good, yet there seemed to be sincerity, and there was certainly consistency, in Ed Howe's editorials about Ingalls. Most typical were the editorials recommending Ingalls for a cabinet position, or higher:

"There is but one man in Kansas of whom it may be said without laughter that he is entitled to a cabinet position. That man is Ingalls, but the conditions are such that it will not be offered to him" (Nov. 8, 1888).

"If Senator Ingalls lived in New York instead of Atchison, his nomination for the Presidency would be one of the possibilities. There is no doubt that he is one of the famous men of the country, and his aggressive policy has won him many admirers" (Feb. 2, 1897).

After the defeat of Ingalls in 1891 *The Globe* issued declarations calling for his return to the Senate, particularly in view of his long and successful record there. Ed Howe campaigned especially in January, 1895, for the naming of Ingalls by the State Legislature, but the campaign failed. Howe also singled out Ingalls as the greatest Kansan when area newspapers were doing some speculating on the subject in the spring of 1896:

> The *Topeka Mail* recently invited a large number of Kansas men to express an opinion as to the greatest Kansas man, living or dead. Preston B. Plumb, John Brown, Jim Lane, D. W. Wilder, Chas. Robinson, C. K. Holliday, Chancellor Snow, S. J. Crawford, A. H. Horton, J. W. Gleed, Dudley C. Haskell, and John A. Martin received votes. John J. Ingalls, the only great man the state ever produced, is not mentioned at all.
>
> John Brown and Jim Lane were never creditable to Kansas, and were adventurers of the worst sort. Some of the others mentioned are of no importance whatever. Ingalls is more widely known, in a creditable sense, than any other Kansan. He is the greatest statesman Kansas ever produced. He is the greatest orator Kansas ever produced. He is the greatest scholar Kansas ever produced. It is a little peculiar, therefore, that Ingalls did not receive a single vote. Possibly the explanation is that every man who sent in a vote knew that it should have

been for Ingalls. Ingalls will not be a Kansas hero until he is dead. Every man who amounts to anything is hated while he is alive. [Apr. 11, 1896]

While Ingalls was the hero of *The Globe,* no politician in the early Howe days received more editorial lumps from the newspaper than the unfortunate John P. St. John, whose years in politics were characterized most by his adherence to the issues of temperance and prohibition. In the 1880 campaign *The Globe* carried as its masthead slogan, "The Globe Ticket for Governor, Anybody to Beat John P. St. John" (Oct. 7, 1880). The slogan was repeated in 1882, Howe adding, "But as there is no prospect that J. B. Johnson can do it, we are NOT IN FAVOR OF HIM" (May 18, 1882). Howe declared against St. John in 1880 because, among other reasons, the candidate had "colonized a lot of Negroes from North Topeka to vote for him in the primary," an action which Howe considered both illegal and indecent (Sept. 2, 1880). A physical lampoon of the governor was one of the more striking examples of Ed Howe's attacks on the man:

"The hugeness of St. John's moustache has excited a great deal of bitterness among young politicians with hairless lips. We ourselves confess that the secret of some of our opposition to the Governor was on account of that great and enviable hursute [sic] appendage. Had he let it grow wild and natural we would not have envied it so much, but every day he waxed, painted and scented it, thus adding artificial attractions to what was naturally magnificent" (Apr. 3, 1882).

Howe also published a threat against St. John—and the beloved Ingalls: "If Senator Ingalls stumps the State in favor of St. John, he will wish in years to come he hadn't. That's all we have to say" (Oct. 6, 1882). That year George W. Glick defeated John St. John for the Kansas governorship, and *The Globe* saw the defeat as proof that the voters were tired of the St. John-backed experiment of prohibition: "Whisky is sold in more places to-day in Kansas than before the law was adopted, and St. John was rebuked because it was for the best interest of Kansas" (Nov. 8, 1882). Ed Howe then was free to move against St. John on the national stage, as the Kansan entered the ranks of the Prohibition party. "Prohibition was his measure, and the Republicans have once suffered defeat by following his crazy lead." Resubmit prohibition to the voters and see how quickly it is repudiated, *The*

Globe suggested (Nov. 7, 1884). Howe had another Kansan to comment on—that well-known politician John A. Martin, his newspaper competitor whom he favored for the governorship as early as 1880 and who achieved that position in the next decade.

In state politics Ed Howe was as doggedly Republican as he was nationally. Yet scandals and corruption outraged his Puritan senses in Kansas as much as they did elsewhere. In his annoyance he sat back and groused: "In all seriousness we ask what consistent claim has the Republican party in Kansas for any further support and confidence on the part of the people. There has not been a State administration for years, if ever, that has not been tainted with scandals, corruption and jobbery" (July 22, 1886).

Sometimes satire suited his purposes better, as in the prayer he recommended for a Republican politician in Kansas: "Our father who art in Topeka, Bradford be thy name; thy kingdom come, thy will be done, in Atchison and Leavenworth as it is done in Manhattan and other drug store towns. Give us this day our daily injunction, and forgive us our meddlesomeness as we forgive those who attend strictly to their own business. Lead us not into court as witnesses, but deliver us from the open saloon (until after the campaign, at least) and thine be the power, and the glory, until the end of thy term. Amen" (Sept. 6, 1886).

He continued to be convinced that all politicians were crooks. Convening of the Kansas Legislature meant merely inaction, or worse, all leading to "genuine distrust on the part of the people." Legislatures begin with a promise, but soon it is apparent that promises are designed to lull the voters, and soon we see that every member is out to further his own cause, or sell his vote, or vote for something worthless. He would not go to Topeka to observe all this taking place, for he could sit in *The Globe* office and *know* that it was taking place.

Occasionally he saw a face appearing on the political scene that looked fresh and interesting—Henry J. Allen, a spellbinder in whose honor a torchlight parade was being arranged; Charles Curtis, "the champion of the Wronged Indian," whose activities were reported off and on in both *Globe* and *Monthly* for thirty years. The interference of his friend William Allen White in politics bothered him; so did the activities of the editors and politicians who got together each January for the Kansas Day Club banquet (their elocution struck him as being much less interesting than the matter of where, in dead of winter, they managed to find fresh corn on the cob). And as a country printer who had had to fight against the handing of county printing to the opposition, he had especially harsh words for the system of electing state printers, whose income, Howe suggested, suddenly would rise from around a thousand a year to fifty thousand. "This princely income for the state printer is, of course, paid by means of taxes wrung from the people" (Jan. 15, 1903).

For ultimately, with Ed Howe, politics and politicians came down to the practical matter of what the people were getting for their money. He opposed expansion and he opposed the tariff; and he thought the American people should worry instead about such things as reducing county, city, and township expenses, especially when those expenses were salaries for fat and idle officials. And every political crowd that invaded the statehouse was as bad as the one that had preceded it—all bent on taking money from the honest taxpayer and passing a lot of stupid bills that were not worth the paper they were printed on.

The Futility of Reform

In none of his travels had Ed Howe seen much to suggest to him that the human race was worth saving. True, he could speak of progress and commercial development, but these had nothing to do with his ingrained belief that reformers, busybodies, and socialist troublemakers had no hope of solving the problems of the world. The tragedies in his childhood, the marriage that was not working out, the frequent slumps into despair—all combined to fill him with disgust for the meddlers. And yet, in a sense, *he* was a meddler, a reformer, though not at all in the twentieth-century meaning of the word. The conditions he wanted to change were those stemming from marriage and relations between the sexes, from religion, and from the idea of success, because he believed man could choose success over failure, and plot his life accordingly.

Howe's span on *The Atchison Globe* paralleled one of America's greatest eras in reform. The optimism of an earlier time, when reformers thought all problems could be solved, had given way to a more realistic reform, but there were still optimists in America, even as buccaneers were seizing land and building up vast fortunes. Labor agitators, free thinkers, prohibitionists, woman's righters, agrarians, preachers of the Social Gospel—all were busy on the scene in Ed Howe's day. And he believed such people were wasteful, malicious, and in some cases downright evil. They were out to change the world; why not work to improve the individual? Busybodies were collecting money to send to the heathens in foreign lands when right in Atchison one could see Negro boys in need of attention: "The urchins are poorly clothed, and are compelled to make their own living by blacking boots. Most of the boys have drunken fathers whose names are familiar on the police court docket" (Jan. 6, 1892). Busybodies were pointing out the ills of others, but the real reform that was needed was in themselves. They were like the man whose business failed because he was so concerned with others' follies. "He had never accomplished any good, but he might have done something for himself had he given up the business of bothering about other people" (Mar. 9, 1888).

Especially pointless to Ed Howe was the attempt to reform poverty. Poverty was basically a matter of individual choice, and writing about it in newspapers did not help matters. Once he had traveled to western Kansas, and "In driving about, I saw real poverty for the first time in my life. I wrote something about it, and the people out there growled at me for years, saying I had made their condition worse than it was, and that they were 'getting along.' " He was sure that if a person had habits of thrift that he would survive:

"Poor people are poor because they do not appreciate the value of money; the man who holds on to his nickels and dimes, and carefully invests them in the shape of dollars, is the one who leaves money for his children to quarrel over. A blind beggar has been playing an accordeon [sic] on the streets to-day, and most of his contributions have been from extremely poor people, who can appreciate his miserable condition, though they have no appreciation of the value of money. Economy carefully practiced during a life time usually insures a competency" (May 4, 1883).

Howe's philosophy was not a heartless one, however; the poor for whom he had no use were "the professional poor," and the Howe newspaper frequently made its calls during harsh winters to assist old people, widows, and children with food and fuel. This was a paradoxical man, really, one opposed to poverty reformers but urging aid to the poor in severe weather, harping on a professional philanthropist like Andrew Carnegie, who gave no aid to the workingmen but sank his wealth in libraries. Though he became a great admirer of Carnegie in later days, he frequently wrote of Carnegie's folly in giving money to libraries, money that might have been used for homes for the aged—or for a brass band of seventy men who would give two free concerts every day in some part of the country. This dislike of Carnegie and the libraries had other roots in Ed Howe: his abiding anti-intellectualism and his disgust for what he considered trashy literature.

His views about the shiftless in society were part of his growing admiration for the successful business man. As he talked with friends in Atchison he came to believe that business was the cement of a good society. He sincerely believed that competent and trustworthy assistants in a business firm were hard to find, that it was the carelessness of employees that created financial hardships for employers. His fixed preference for the employer, his unswerving belief in the essential goodness of business (for the anti-religious Ed Howe was actually a deep believer in the Puritan ethic) made him have little use for the labor movement that was on the rise in America in the late century. It was the violence of labor that he mainly deplored, however, not the organization of unions—though he got to that later, too. Rather than standing dogmatically on the side of management in any labor dispute *The Globe* usually weighed the issues (which it did not always do in other matters) and considered the question of general good. In a policy statement early in its history the paper said it was "everybody's friend and well-wisher," that it did not favor strikes or lawlessness, that it favored "giving the workingman all he can earn, according to his aptness and ability" (May 4, 1881). A local strike on the Missouri Pacific Railroad brought frequent pleas from *The Globe* for settlement, and hopes that management would meet the strikers halfway. For Ed Howe could look about him and see the effect of a severe strike on the fortunes of the city where his career was being furthered.

As for those economic agitators whose origins were too exotic for the prairie editor, they should go back where they came from, he seemed to say in an editorial the day after the Haymarket bombing in Chicago:

> In the old country, where the Communist originates, he is shot down by soldiers when he does not behave himself, therefore his presence in this free country, where he is at liberty to raise the devil without interference. It is a matter of wonder to us that these gentlemen of lip do not appreciate freedom, and go to work, instead of going to work to induce industrious mechanics to disgrace the best government in the world. It will finally become apparent that the Communist does not want Work, but Trouble, and we have an idea that he will get all he wants of it. The people of this country are patient, but under certain circumstances they are not to be trifled with. [May 5, 1886]

Howe's position on the accused anarchists was similar to that taken by many editors: ". . . the jig is up with them; they have thrown their last bomb, unless they resume their avocation in sheol, which will be their next stopping place" (Aug. 7, 1886).

As Howe became older and more successful himself (at least in a material sense), his convictions about success and failure became even more fixed, and they reached a peak in the teen years of the twentieth century. He believed that if someone advertised for a "good man" that all the worthless men in town would apply for the job, because no man thinks he is anything other than a good man. Without stating it in so many words he subscribed to the Horatio Alger theme: "Boys who have to start out to care for themselves always amount to more than the petted curley haired sissy boys. The boy with holes in his clothes, an unwashed face, and stone bruises on his feet, may not be as pretty as the boy in dresses and curls, but you bet in twenty years he will amount to more" (May 7, 1892). He suggested that, to accompany the law compelling children to go to school, one be passed compelling able-bodied men to go to work. "Why put all the energy of the law into going after school children?" he asked (Jan. 5, 1904).

The Globe *and Demon Rum*

In March of 1856 John Brown, Jr., presented a prohibition memorial to the Topeka legislature of the free-state movement, the year after the first attempt had been made to regulate the sale of liquor in Kansas, and although no action was taken there were other efforts in the years that followed. All were in harmony with the national movement for what was being called "temperance." The growing years of Ed Howe, during which the young editor came to have little use for alcohol, were also the years of continued efforts to bring prohibition to Kansas. From 1871 to 1881 there was agitation in the state, and the Republican party in 1874 declared itself against drunkenness. The Prohibition party held its first state convention in 1876, and its gubernatorial candidate, John Paulson, received 393 of more than 12,000 ballots cast. In the early fall of 1878 the National Temperance Camp-meeting took place at Bismarck Grove, and when in that year John St. John was elected Governor the temperance people took heart. It was in St. John's administration that liquor control came into being in Kansas—a constitutional amendment that passed in the general election of 1880 and enabling legislation that passed the legislature in 1881.[9]

Thus prohibition came to Kansas, and it became so fixed that the state became almost a symbol of the national temperance movement. Prohibition became a central subject of concern in *The Atchison Globe,* and Ed Howe was still discussing the question of liquor as late as 1933.

One of his first commentaries on the movement bore the kind of satire that marked almost all his utterances on the subject:

> A young man tells us that nothing so cheers him after a night of dissipation as the perusal of a fierce temperance paper. It comforts him to read how the rum-seller lives and flourishes for a while, and then dies in great agony, surrounded by ten thousand devils and as many ghosts of men that he has sent to hell. His soul revels in the story of the man who has never touched liquor in his life, and as a consequence is rich and prosperous and benevolent. . . . Our young friend reads all this, and then arises in all his manhood and registers a vow by the heavens above and the earth below never to drink any more rum. He then goes out and orders a whisky cocktail, good and strong, to brace up on, and instructs the barkeeper to put no rum in it if he values his life. [Dec. 23, 1878]

Ed Howe in those days did not believe that, man being such an imperfect creature, prohibition could ever work, and his belief colored what he wrote. He thought that the moralists who had crusaded against pleasant home amusements—parties, singing, dancing, card playing, and light drinking of alcohol—had brought about the saloon, as a refuge for the man who had to flee his own house. He was sure that to tell a man he may not do something is to assure his doing it; there is a basic cussedness in the animal, like "the cow wearing a bell, who insists upon eating weeds in front of your house at night instead of seeking the rich grasses on the river bottom" (June 9, 1880). Howe quoted with approval the Kentucky editor, Henry Watterson, who was scarcely averse to taking a nip himself but who said he "would walk seven miles barefooted over a turnpike to the funeral of a fool who would try to make a corkscrew out of a mule's tail, but he never could shed a tear for the idiot who had no better sense than to kill himself drinking whisky" (Aug. 24, 1880). Temperance was what Howe really advocated; perhaps he was advocating temperance in *all* human actions.

He shook his head in wonder at his fellow citizens who could eat cheap cheese and rye bread and wash it down with beer in preference to going home for a good cooked meal. Saloons and their daily inhabitants gave him many an opportunity for an editorial-page joke:

"A Dying Temperance Agitator, loath to exchange the hardships of this wicked world for the Unknown Beatitude of Heaven, asked his Parson (who claimed exclusive knowledge on the point) if there would be any saloon keepers there. 'No, no,' replied the Parson soothingly. 'No Dutchmen?' anxiously inquired the Prohibitionist. 'None,' responded the other. 'No outlaws at all?' questioned the Dying Saint, with intense anxiety. 'Not one,' answered the clergyman. 'Alas! How can I be happy there?' gasped the Dying Man, as his spirit passed away" (Dec. 10, 1883).

But Ed Howe was a practical man about liquor, too. As long as there was drinking in the world it might as well fit into the success formula of *The Globe,* the paid local: "So long as people continue to drink beer in the face of law and advice to the contrary, we will advise them to drink the best. This is believed to be the Anheuser article sold by Henry Brandner, whose size would indicate that it is fattening, if nothing else" (July 1, 1882). *The Globe's* policy on both temperance and prohibition (they were always separate matters to Ed Howe) was, through the years, essentially as he had set it down in 1884:

> The *Champion's* statement that Atchison will not be completely ruined if the saloons are closed, is true, but that it will be seriously crippled no one will pretend to question, unless he has a retreating forehead. The GLOBE believes in temperance, and has always practiced and preached it, but it does not believe in prohibition. On the same platform will be found many of the most intelligent as well as pious divines of the country, and the history of the past has been that prohibition is not an effective temperance measure. The GLOBE does not believe in death, but death, like truth, is mighty, and will prevail, whether men approve of it or not. The same is true of intemperance. We believe that God Himself is responsible for intemperance, precisely as He is responsible for thousands of other human weaknesses, in order that those who are brave and strong may lead decent lives, and be rewarded; we believe that it is His intention that prohibition shall not prohibit, and that the people shall always be surrounded by temptation, and we believe that we might as well attempt to effectually close the graveyard as to effectually close the bottle. The saloons may be closed temporarily, but whisky will still be manufactured, and prevail, and the very fact of prohibition will cause many men to drink it who would otherwise let it alone. [Jan. 19, 1884]

He contended that of all the cities in Kansas, Atchison had the best attitude toward prohibition, maintaining its "joints" in better condition, shunning the agitations of people like Frances E. Willard, president of the Women's Christian Temperance Union, who came to town to talk and spoke before empty benches, Atchison thereby setting an example for its sister cities. Atchison licensed a few "joints" and regulated them; Leavenworth was wide open: therefore the prevalence of lawlessness in the rival community. "Atchison is so well behaved that other towns could adopt the Atchison policy with profit" (July 30, 1901). He constantly called on Kansans to look at what was happening in other states. The experiences of Maine and Massachusetts in ridding themselves of drunkenness had not been reassuring, and "if people in those steady New England States would and did get drunk notwithstanding the nominal absence of liquor, what wonderful achievements in this line may we not expect from the rugged and heterogeneous population of a western border State?" (Nov. 13, 1880). Prohibition "drives out bloated capitalists, raises the price of whisky, increases taxation and drunkenness, and plays the devil generally" (Dec. 22, 1880).

The problems of drinking men from Missouri coming into

Kansas (or of drinking men from Kansas going into Missouri) gave him cause for editorial laughter:

> A man from Missouri came to this realm of prohibition last night, and while on the depot platform was seized with the delirium tremens. He ran into the depot, howling, and jerking his boots off, and declared that the father of all snakes was chasing him. He was taken to the police station, where he enjoyed the jim-jams all night. [Feb. 27, 1886]

> Thirsty individual to Kansas City man on Sunday: "Can't you put me onto a place where I can get a drink?" Kansas City man: "Saloons are all closed in Kansas City; you'll have to go across the State line, into Kansas, if you want anything stronger than lemonade." [May 21, 1888]

> Law works by contraries. There is a statute against gambling in Missouri, and men go from Kansas to Kansas City when they want to get into a good game of poker. In exchange for these, Missouri men come over to Kansas on Sunday when they want to get drunk. [July 17, 1889]

Frequently he blamed prohibition for the "downfall' of Kansas, for the decline in population, for Omaha having more people than Kansas City. He saw prohibition as the greatest fraud in Kansas history, editorializing that Kansas might be a temperate state but that with its prohibitory law it bought nearly as many liquor licenses from the government as Alabama, Arkansas, Florida, and Mississippi combined. Iowa should have learned its lesson, too. "In trying to account for her loss in population Iowa wonders if her fanatical laws haven't driven people away. Lord bless you, no. If that were true Texas would be depopulated and Kansas a cattle range" (Dec. 7, 1910).

As prohibition became a national issue Ed Howe had even more cause for comment. Now he was able to strike at the "religious lobby" that was trying to bring about legislation comparable to the "anti-canteen law," which Howe felt had been highly injurious to the armed forces (Nov. 20, 1902). Now he could write about John L. Sullivan, the mighty fighter who had become a temperance reformer and was lecturing on the evils of drink and tobacco. "Sticking to something he knows about is better than groping in the darkness of the dramatic art" (Jan. 25, 1905). Each new generation of readers was able to read a restatement of the old position of *The Globe*.

The emergence on the Kansas and national scene of that celebrated temperance reformer, Mrs. Carry Nation of Medicine Lodge, gave Ed Howe a handy target for several years. One of the earliest *Globe* editorials on the celebrated "Smasher" came early in the century, when the paper reported that Mrs. Nation was in jail in Wichita for wrecking bar fixtures. Howe expected that the Good Citizens' Committee of Topeka would welcome her with a band, but not Atchison. "Mrs. Nation is 60 years old, very fat, and very ugly. . . . we blush for Wichita, and Leavenworth and Atchison will have to draw up closer, and leave Wichita out" (Dec. 28, 1900). This woman was the very acme of troublemakers, a woman who actually had the gall to walk up to men on city streets and pull cigars out of their mouths. If she were not a woman she would be lynched for her terrorizing of Kansas towns, her destruction of property, her whipping a sheriff, her slapping a policeman in the face. *The Globe* itself had no reservations about what it recommended for this reformer:

> We point with pride to the fact that we lack some of the "finer feelings" which many people exhibit. We would like to see Mrs. Carrie Nation whipped, and rolled in the dirt, and her clothes torn off.
>
> We despise the Mrs. Nation sort of woman: that sort of woman is a pest, and does more harm in a community than a saloon.
>
> Mrs. Nation is a coward. She has no hesitancy in striking a man, knowing that a man dare not return the blow, but in Enterprise, Kansas, yesterday, when Mrs. Schilling smashed her in the face twice, Mrs. Nation tried to run away. If Mrs. Schilling is not deluged with letters and testimonials, common sense people will neglect a very important duty. [Jan. 24, 1901]

Day after day in early 1901 the editor carried editorial quips as well as longer editorials about Carry Nation. Her lawlessness was spreading—a woman had been murdered; Topeka had been in the hands of a mob; another mob was chasing a school teacher in southern Kansas; citizens were arming—all on account of Carry Nation, "A crazy old woman who is not endorsed by one respectable person in fifty" (Feb. 21, 1901). He was sure the woman was insane; for proof *The Globe* offered Mrs. Nation's opinion that editing a newspaper was pleasing work. Yet Ed Howe, despite his belief that Mrs. Nation should be put away before doing any more harm, encouraged the people of Atchison to refrain from violence and attack when she came to town:

> Mrs. Carrie Nation is coming to Atchison this evening to "save" the people. Yet the people of Atchison have better manners than Mrs. Nation, better sense, and are fairer and better in every way. THE GLOBE will always point with pride to the manner in which Atchison people will treat this meddlesome, foolish old woman. The key-note will be indifference. Not the slightest indignity will be offered her: Atchison people care nothing about her. They do not regard her as a teacher, or a reformer, or as a useful woman. Not a single Atchison church will permit her to speak from its pulpit, and there are good church people here, and ministers who are worthy, respected and useful. Atchison, in short, will show the world how Mrs. Nation should be treated. . . . A few Topekaites have insisted on Mrs. Nation visiting Atchison, as a joke; Atchison will now furnish Topeka with an object lesson. [Mar. 23, 1901]

Unfortunately the "silly old woman" got a bit of roughhousing from local hoodlums when she came to Atchison. Howe lamented this, but criticized her for passing herself off as a temperance worker (for that should rile the worthy temperance people) and for invading the smoking car on the way to the city and demanding that men quit smoking. "If Mrs. Nation is not insane, she is the most ill-mannered woman in the state. If a child should act as rude as Mrs. Nation acts, it would be whipped" (Mar. 25, 1901).

A Variety of Opinions and Prejudices

What was the pattern of Ed Howe's discontents, or was there a pattern? What made this small-town editor such a moralist? Was it the sternly moralizing father who had run off with another woman? Was it his own success, obtained in the conventional hard-working way? Was it just a disposition—common to newspaper editors—to pontificate from on high, to lash out at the sordidness of human beings?

It could be almost a game, this guessing how Howe would react to questions from day to day:

Prize fights—A waste of time. Why do men enjoy them?

"We wouldn't accept a free ticket; we couldn't enjoy seeing men punish each other" (Mar. 11, 1902).

Smoking—It is futile to pass laws against tobacco. But this does not mean that smoking is to be condoned. It is a stupid habit (Jan. 21, 1909).

Whipping children—"No man ever made a child love him with a whip; a great many have incurred the hatred of their children by the same means" (Dec. 1, 1908).

Hanging—The "most rude, bungling and barbarous of all modes of taking life." *The Globe* prefers "the Mormon way, to give the man who has to die the choice of methods" (Nov. 26, 1879).

Capital punishment—Why should there be a painless lawful execution? "Murderers make no such attempt in treating their victims" (July 3, 1897).

Execution of women—Women who commit capital crimes are as guilty as men; the "sacredness of Womanhood" has nothing to do with it (Jan. 10, 1905).

Prisons—Convicts have committed vile crimes and they must be punished (Apr. 9, 1906). Should criminals be permitted to do as they please at the penitentiary?

Lynchings—Bleeding hearts complain about lynchings in the South but say nothing against the crimes that cause the lynchings. "Americans are always Truly Good, in a newspaper interview" (Apr. 26, 1899).

Indians—The murderous outlaws of the West are being treated in Washington like princely potentates. "They eat after the true Indian fashion, first eating all the bread, then all the meat, then all the pepper; next all the butter, and when they come to horse-radish, they send up such a savage howl that Secretary Evarts has to run over from the State department and quiet them with a fresh treaty and a jug of rum" (Jan. 22, 1880).

Negroes—Swaggerers who proclaim their intention "to vote as they dam please, untrammeled by party ties. Which means that they will vote for the candidate who sets up the most beer" (Nov. 4, 1878). Superstitious thieves: a Georgian knowing of Negro fears of the ground where a hanging has taken place will make such a site a watermelon patch (Dec. 9, 1879). Loafers: "lazy mokes, who blink and bake themselves on the sun-warmed corners of our streets" (Jan. 26, 1880). Criminals: "The citizens of Atchison are entitled to great credit for the promptness with which they secured a stout rope, and surrounded the jail, and had Snead [accused Negro rapist] been found, his dirty carcass would have speedily dangled from some convenient tree" (Sept. 23, 1880). A race doomed to separation from the whites: The Supreme Court decision (Plessy *v.* Ferguson) must be accepted as the law of the land; separation of the races is inevitable, and whites and blacks will not mix, no matter what the fourteenth amendment may have said (May 25, 1896). An inherently lazy bunch: the impression prevails that emancipation from slavery and emancipation from the need to work for a living took place at the same time. Colored workers quit work on pay day and do not return to work until their pay is gone (June 11, 1901). "Many of them are better off working for the whites than they would be working for themselves, which may explain why Liberia is on the verge of ruin, and Hayti and San Domingo amount to so little" (Feb. 25, 1909).

Ed Howe can be excused for certain of his prejudices because of the times in which he lived and the attitudes that then prevailed. He was quite in step with his age in professing admiration for that "good colored man," Booker T. Washington; he modified his country town prejudices as he became older and more sophisticated. But they were prejudices, many of them amusing because there was relatively little danger in them, and his readers probably chuckled more than they were influenced to action.

The Atchison editor had an instinctive disbelief in certain inventions and social attitudes. Flying machines were a joke, even more so in later years. He published an amusing comment on the inventor of a "crosseyed" opera glass, by means of which one could stare at anyone in the audience while appearing to be looking elsewhere; its inventor was "a bigger man than Edison" (Apr. 20, 1878). Doctors were a definite menace to society:

> A hot lemonade at night is good for almost every ill, from cold, headaches and grip, to rheumatism. The people should quit trotting after doctors, and devote more time to lemons. [Jan. 4, 1899]

> The people should get together and form an anti-operating society: It is a rare edition of *The Globe* that does not contain mention of some one who has been cut into by the doctors, and we venture the assertion that recovery would have been possible without it in the majority of cases, or death more easy. [Apr. 6, 1905]

> Proper care in the selection of food, and the general physical condition, will lessen the chances of becoming an operation victim, whether it be fad or necessity. [Jan. 19, 1910]

There was a host of editorials in *The Atchison Globe* over the years denouncing the woman suffrage movement; this was a tired horse that Ed Howe never quit riding. Woman's place was in the home, as it was believed to be by many other men, but he suggested that if women wanted to enter politics they had better brace themselves for abuse along with praise, and be ready to be called knaves, demagogues, and shysters. Good women did not want suffrage; it was the Carry Nations—"the women from whom you want to run"—who wanted the vote (Oct. 11, 1904). The issue arose constantly, and Ed Howe kept telling his readers to vote against suffrage. He was encouraged to see that women *were* getting their equal rights: in the previous year as many women had been hanged as in the previous ten years. And in one of his most poignant editorials he considered what the equal rights movement had meant for one of its most famous proponents:

> From the time Susan B. Anthony was a young woman, till the day of her death, at 86, she devoted all her life and energy to the cause of suffrage for women. Leaving out the question of the good she has accomplished, which affords argument on both sides, has she missed or gained of the joys of life?
>
> She never had a love affair serious enough to make moonlight look any different to her than high noon; she missed the engagement showers, the excitement of preparing for a wedding, the delight of having her husband and her own home, and she never knew what it was to love and care for one's own baby, something said to be entirely different from caring and loving for a baby belonging to some one else.
>
> On the other hand, she never worried over a man's promise of love. A man in her eyes, had no more individuality than a stumbling block on the way to the polls, and perhaps not as much. She never cried herself to sleep because her lover smiled at another girl; she knew nothing of the harrowing preparations of getting a wedding outfit ready with an ambition for fine clothes that did not correspond with the father's purse. She never knew what it was to have a husband come home and scold; she was never up nights with a sick child, and never had her heart torn by a child's ingratitude; or by the fickleness of man, though undoubtedly she talked on that subject a great deal.
>
> Summing it up: Was Susan B. Anthony a gainer or a loser? [Mar. 13, 1906]

The Misogynist

Into the tortured ravings of *The Story of a Country Town* and *An Ante-Mortem Statement* he had poured his developing beliefs about the conflict between the sexes. He was able to debate with himself editorially whether or not Susan B. Anthony had gained or lost by devoting herself to the cause of woman's rights, but Ed Howe undoubtedly felt she had been better off, in the long run, by remaining single.

His own marriage was beginning to fall apart in the 1890s. Bitterness was developing within the family. Never to be forgotten were the days in Fairview and Bethany, when Henry Howe had left his family. But it was Henry Howe who left, not Elizabeth. Why the animosity toward women? Was Edgar Watson Howe the woman-hater he has been painted by his son, by literary critics, by the historians who rewrite each other year after year?

Well, only in part. He blamed the man, too, in the continuing drama of tragic romantic relationships. But the society of Ed Howe's time had double standards, and it was the responsibility of the girl to fend off the men. Of this his son Gene wrote:

"He expended a tremendous amount of his energy trying to convince men that they were being led to ruin and demoralization by their womenfolks. The development of man was such that men and women had become enemies, he believed; women had become spoiled and extravagant and so impossible that the very foundations of our civilization were threatened. He actually talked of a countrywide revolt of the men against the women, and believed it might be brought about."[10]

Nor could his son understand such a philosophy. Howe had preached in *The Story of a Country Town* his sermon that a girl should have one engagement and one marriage, no more; that a girl had been tainted if the engagement did not result in marriage. There was too much that went on between young people that should not be permitted. Especially too much kissing. Too many love affairs. Too many opportunities for boys and girls to be alone together. He could not comprehend how anyone could marry a widow. "I cannot understand it; he must be crazy," Gene once heard his father say.[11]

In selecting woman as a running target in *The Globe* (almost never relating the "evils of women" to specific events in the news), Ed Howe showed daring for his time. Woman did not have the vote, but she was in charge. Arthur Schlesinger has written of her growing importance in the 1880s and 1890s, of her reputation and renown as mistress of the home, a role in which she inspired visitors from abroad.[12] The concept of chivalry precluded attacks from most men on the sanctity of womanhood, of marriage, of motherhood, but it did not stop Howe. Out of his imagination or out of his observation he constructed editorial paragraphs that were disturbing but also entertaining. "There are three brothers in Atchison who were formerly distinguished for their good humor," he wrote. "One of them was married recently, and he is now as cross and ugly as a she bear, while his brothers, who are unmarried, are as amiable as possible" (Nov. 23, 1885). "An Atchison man who has a mother, two sisters, an aunt, a wife and three grown daughters living with him, takes eight different kinds of medicine every day of his life" (Feb. 28, 1891). "You see a great deal in sensational newspapers about gambling and drinking and women. These stories are largely inventions. The real faults of women are not gambling and drinking" (May 1, 1901).

In the first year of *The Atchison Globe* readers must have been amused when they read Ed Howe on how men are disposed to slander women; that was "one of their most noticeable and distinguished sins." He said he could "imagine of no circumstances wherein a man is justified in speaking lightly of a woman" (Aug. 10, 1878). This was chivalry in operation, but a limited chivalry, one that opposed the mistreatment of a particular woman, not the whole sex. It was woman—the sex itself—that Howe criticized. He was convinced that the country was full of women trying to ruin married men—"Gentlemen of experience inform us that there was never such a season of lust as this" (May 15, 1879).

Love and marriage was a theme as common to him as that of woman being the bane of man's existence. Affinity, he felt, was the chief thing behind marriage; young people being thrown together was far more important than intercession by the angels, who are not "in the match-making business" (Nov. 8, 1898). Someone who *was* in the matchmaking business was the object of a delightfully written comment from the sour editor late in his years on the paper:

"We want to knock hard on Cupid. Is it any wonder that

love affairs go wrong when entrusted to a little boy, so young he hasn't enough sense to put his clothes on? If there must be a Cupid to arrange such serious matters, let the part be taken by a grizzled old man who knows how love tastes when the bottom of the cup is reached, or let it be an old woman who has grown sad and wise learning about it. But a little naked boy! Why, people wouldn't trust their pin buying to one so young and ignorant" (Sept. 26, 1904).

Disillusionment was in store for anyone undertaking matrimony. Howe could understand why a woman with "a certain thing to look forward to" could contemplate suicide (June 16, 1905). "If you are thinking of getting married, make up your mind to meet a great many troubles and disappointments. It is this making a hero of a plain plug man, and an angel of an ordinary woman, that is the cause of so much disappointment and divorce" (June 4, 1891). For married life is pretty dull, if not downright miserable. The average married couple living together twenty years would eat 21,900 meals together, he wrote, and he recommended that the romantically inclined think of it that way.

To him a man was "led as a lamb to the slaughter." Men knew little about life, yet found themselves in the toils of adventuresses with almost no prearrangement on their part. Few men are gay dogs, he said. Romance palls rapidly.

"The love stories give examples of a maiden who looked into a spring at midnight and the face of a Prince appeared over her shoulder, and she married him. But how is Daughter to find her Prince in real life, when there isn't a spring on the place, and one can't see the reflection of a Prince's face in the hydrant?" (Oct. 31, 1907).

Why does love run down so fast? Why does a woman in love want to injure the man she loves? Why is a man in love so equally bloodthirsty? Howe kept asking these questions, as he read about and wrote about broken marriages and runaway husbands and runaway wives and wronged girls and murders and suicide pacts. "Why should affection between a man and woman turn into hate, and desire to injure and destroy?" (Jan. 9, 1909).

Divorce he was coming to favor, and he quoted with praise the opinion of Elbert Hubbard, in *The Philistine,* on marriage and divorce, Hubbard recommending that it should be more difficult to marry than to divorce. Howe's own divorce was not far away then. He was finding views to support those he had long entertained; he frequently mentioned *The Kreutzer Sonata,* a book that had impressed him for many years, even though he did not care for many other ideas of its author, Tolstoy.[13]

Not for Ed Howe was the fine little husband who helped out around the house, cooking, caring for the children: ". . . a man of this kind seldom amounts to anything else" (Jan. 17, 1892). Woman had a job to do and she could spend more time doing it, like cooking three meals on Sunday. To Howe there was too much religion and not enough to eat on the Sabbath: "one of the crying evils of the day" (Jan. 20, 1879). How he hated the busybody Atchison woman who formed a society to bring about a constitutional amendment requiring their husbands to be home at night and calling for arrests of men found out after dark unless they had on their persons a certificate from wife, mother, or sister attesting to illness in the family and a real need to be out on the streets. (The whole thing rings of one of Howe's comic fantasies.) He had no use for the woman who spent her time and her husband's money making plaques, learning the banjo or mandolin, foolishly trying to write books. The equal rights movement annoyed him because he believed that women were already in the best of all possible worlds: "No wonder Liberty is a goddess instead of a god. If there is such a thing as liberty, the women have it" (Nov. 28, 1906).

Take your mottoes down from the wall, wives—those mottoes that are meant for husbands to read in the hope that their dispositions will be improved. And put up one for the women, that will make life more pleasant for all: "Quit Henpecking" (Dec. 15, 1906). Once and for all, Howe wanted to make clear, in a policy editorial, how he stood on the subject of women. His editorial was entitled "WHY THE GLOBE HATES WOMEN":

> Because it is misrepresented by unfair critics. It does not hate women, and there has never been anything in its columns to indicate that it does.
>
> "THE ATCHISON GLOBE," says the *Kansas City Star,* "objects to the advancement of women." THE GLOBE never objected to the advancement of women. It never said anything that could be construed into objection to the advancement of women. It has objected to the actions of foolish women, as having a tendency to discredit their sex, and harm humanity in general, but it has never said an ill-natured word against worthy

> women, and never will. . . . we challenge the *Star,* or any other paper or person, to find anything in THE GLOBE sneering at, criticising, or speaking lightly, of modest, worthy womanhood. It never did anything of the kind, and every honest reader of the paper knows it.
>
> THE GLOBE contends that women who neglect their families, and their work, to prepare and read foolish papers before foolish clubs, on foolish topics, are fair objects of criticism, because they are accomplishing nothing beyond wasting their time. THE GLOBE does not admire the Mrs. Jack Gardner's, or the Mrs. Potter Palmer's, or the Mrs. Leslie M. Shaw's, whose names appear in the papers constantly, and cause women to be sneered at, and their worth discredited, but it has never said a word against the women who are useful, modest and worthy, as most of them are. Because THE GLOBE laughs at foolish women, it is unfair to charge that it hates women. [Feb. 13, 1902]

This was the editor of *The Globe* speaking, the man who had made so many critical comments over so many years. Was he unaware of the impact his words about women had had on his readers for more than twenty years in Atchison?

The Lay Preacher

An editor in the Kansas of the 1880s and 1890s was either crazy or courageous in selecting religion as a target. Ed Howe may have been both.

His scattergun attacks on organized religion, churches, and ministers had begun in the early years of *The Globe.* From then on there was a barrage of comments that made him the best-known newspaper critic of religion in America. It was an at least nominally religious America, too—72,459 church congregations in 1870, almost a decade before Howe reached Atchison.[14] Sunday in America was the absolute day of rest—no open theaters, no liquor sales, no open businesses, and not many open drug stores. Despite such prohibitions Ed Howe was one of those Americans who were striking out for the right of working men to have a day of relaxation on the "day of rest."

And Howe's part of America was more religious than many others. Some self-conscious Midwesterners already were using the term "Bible belt" to refer to their states and communities. The middle border was a place of revivals, like those that had led the boy Ed to mimic the serious-minded souls of Iowa and Missouri. He remembered the talk of hellfire and damnation, and he was oppressed by it, yet he also made religion a subject for jocular comment—when he was not disturbed by the grimness of some preachers and their sermons. "These are times that try newspaper men's souls," he wrote. "The inauguration is a thing of the past, the Legislative boobies have adjourned, the snow blockade is at an end, and there is positively nothing to write about except religion" (Mar. 9, 1881).

Not since his Falls City days had he been a churchgoing man himself. So his was the task of detached critic. He hooted at the ministers who complained of members of their flock leaving in the middle of the sermon; these pious gentlemen had not let the thought cross their minds that long and dull sermons could drive people out, tired or disgusted. He criticized those who called for intercession from God, for if God is all-knowing and does nothing wrong then there can be no question of man's problems being solved. The actions of good Christians in calling upon God to save the life of the stricken President Garfield made him sick. "To beg him to save the President implies a doubt that he does not know what is good for us, and doubt is despicable in the eyes of the Lord" (Aug. 29, 1881).

Church bickerings and quarreling annoyed him, and when he learned of such doings he speedily put the stories in his paper. He commented on the ease with which congregations changed denomination, for Presbyterians had once been Methodists and Methodists had once been Congregationalists and a quarrel among the Baptists had added memberships to the Congregationalists. "Religion is a matter of inheritance, to begin with, and a matter of quarreling to end with," he said (Apr. 11, 1899). And he offered a typical Ed Howe solution for a woman who had religious ailments:

> An Atchison woman is suffering with nervous prostration, as a result of trouble in her church. The last two pastors were unsatisfactory, and the quarreling over them unnerved her. One of them was half crazy, according to his own people, and she says that the other members gave him good letters, in order to get rid of him. This she didn't believe was right, and worried about that a good deal. She was also on several committees

> to raise money, and managed festivals, and has had so much church trouble that she is now sick in bed. Still, she is of as much use to her husband now as she was during the church quarreling over the pastors, for she had no time then to give her husband or her home. For ten cents, we will tell her how to avoid such worry in the future; how she may at the same time become useful as a wife and mother, and be respected in the community. Indeed, we will tell her for nothing: When going to church means nothing more than worry over the pastor, or the pastor's salary, or a new roof, or a new carpet, or a new parsonage, or a new church, quit going. [Nov. 20, 1899]

Of the extent of piety in the world he had his doubts, feeling that down deep most people believed as he did but did not have the gumption to come out and say it. His readers could act shocked but secretly smile at a paragraph from "Globe Sights" like this one: "When there isn't a high chair for a visiting child, the family Bible is brought out and put on a chair, and though everything else in the house is neat, the discovery is made that the Bible needs dusting" (May 25, 1906).

For him the most important religious reform would have been in the direction of free thinking. He deeply admired Robert Ingersoll, but knew that the old iconoclast held audiences because of his oratorical ability and not the views he put forth. When Ingersoll died, Howe wrote one of his most probing editorials on religion:

> The death of Robert G. Ingersoll removes one of America's greatest citizens. It is not popular to admire Ingersoll, but his brilliancy, his integrity and patriotism cannot be doubted. Had not Ingersoll been frank enough to express his opinions on religion, he would have been president of the United States. Hypocrisy in religion pays. Only one-quarter of the people are connected with the churches, but they run the country. Tom Paine made the same mistake. Benjamin Franklin believed as Paine did, but was too wise to discuss religion. As a result, Franklin is venerated, while Paine is cursed and despised. Intellectually, Franklin was not the equal of Paine. He was not his equal as a patriot, nor was Franklin more honest than Paine. But Ingersoll will not be execrated as Paine was, owing to the gradual change in public sentiment. Ingersoll will be openly admired by millions, and his punishment was never as severe as Paine's. There will come a time when public men may speak their honest convictions on religion, without being maligned by the ignorant and superstitious, but not yet. [July 21, 1899]

He had written a comparison of Paine and Franklin in earlier editorials; Tom Paine, that radical revolutionary, remained one of Ed Howe's heroes, and he wrote often of his admiration for *The Age of Reason.* And as Darwinian thought began to become old hat in an increasingly sophisticated America, Howe stood up for the rebels, even though he wondered what they were doing in organized churches. In one editorial he told of Dr. Lyman Abbott, pastor of the Plymouth Church in Boston, who had stated his belief in evolution and had drawn a laugh from his congregation by observing that the world evidently was made in the fall, because apples were then in season. "The Bible and evolution cannot be reconciled; fiat and science have nothing in common," Ed Howe wrote. "But the churches will finally be forced to accept the doctrines of learned men, in which event they will represent clock cases with the works removed" (Mar. 5, 1896).

He was conventional enough, however, to be able both to agree with and criticize the professor in a Methodist theological institution who had declared himself against faith in miracles. Methodists believe in miracles, said Howe, and a Methodist employee has no right to take such a stand. Thus he could avoid offending his Methodist readers and honor his convictions at the same time. Men are supposed to be free, he said, but they are not, for influences of their homes and society dominate them, and they dare not express their opinions. He commented that Lincoln had started public life as an agnostic, but religious organizations worked against him and "he soon discovered that a public man could not afford to freely express his opinions, and, after his election to the presidency, seldom made a public speech or statement that he did not endeavor to please the religious voter by some reference to divinity" (Aug. 5, 1903).

Some of his best barbs he reserved for Unitarianism, especially for Dr. J. E. Roberts of Kansas City. The Unitarian Church was no church in Ed Howe's view. He thought Roberts and his congregation should quit singing hymns and preaching sermons, but knew that they could not do so, because the Kansas City Unitarians were like those in Boston (and none of them had a chance of going to heaven). "A Unitarian is a man who has the church going habit in his blood, and can't give it up. He wouldn't stand for Calvanism [sic], so he organized a 'church' of his own" (June 1, 1903).

And how he loved to print stories about the peccadilloes of gentlemen in the ministry! The Methodists have "never believed it was right for a brother to fresco a sister's lips with a kiss," he wrote, and here was news of the Rev. J. H. Beale of Willingford, Connecticut, charged with kissing female members of the congregation (Apr. 19, 1879). In Hoboken, New Jersey, there was another kissing minister, "an osculatory gymnast that smacked his approval of a pretty cook so loud that his congregation heard it" (Jan. 26, 1880). These men were minor offenders; Howe could point to the Rev. W. M. Sapp of Andrew County, Missouri, who had been county treasurer and had fled with four thousand dollars, and had been inspired by a woman in his commission of the deed. (This must have been a kind of double triumph for Ed Howe.)

The news frequently offered a preacher's son as an offender: one who shot a young man at Leavenworth, another who shot a man near Ellsworth. Lacking stories near home to comment on he always had, in the 1880s, Henry Ward Beecher, "applauded, feted, admired, honored, and enriching himself nightly," while the woman with whom he had collaborated in sin was an outcast, a "poor, heartbroken victim," and homage the fate of Beecher. "But that's the way of this unjust world" (July 28, 1886).

For churchmen, in his mind, were reformers, and they were always telling the people of America how they should behave. The editor despised the churchgoer who was busy telling others how to live their lives, or giving to "good" causes and then backsliding. He was sure that genuine conversions to goodness are not accompanied by loud protestations of piety, that men who quit drinking do not advertise the fact throughout their neighborhoods. His idea of Christianity was a good bit different from that subscribed to by most Christians he knew. He told about the religious people of New York who had been hounding authorities to improve the tenement districts, and how a commission investigated and learned that the worst tenement houses were owned by Trinity Church, the richest congregation in the city. The tenement buildings had floors covered by filth from overflown sinks and bathrooms, halls so dark it was impossible to see, and broken stairways. "We dismiss the subject with the hope that the rector of Trinity will quit preaching charity, pawn some of his costly vestments, and apply the proceeds toward putting his tenement houses in a habitable condition" (Jan. 12, 1886).

He thus could forget his economic conservatism when the opportunity came to harpoon the church. The ministry was engaging in reform activities that generally gave Howe cause to complain: raiding the "joints" of Atchison, for example, and there was no better town morally in the state. He chortled at the discussion going on about the use of wine in the sacrament, and suggested that the Baptists who were about to administer fermented wine at communion would "now be denounced by the fanatics as a drunkard manufactory," a label already being applied to the Episcopal Church (Apr. 11, 1881). His summing-up of religious reformers was an observation that prohibitionists and pulpit-pounders calling for law enforcement should not talk too loudly about either John Brown or the Savior, "both of whom were executed as law-breakers. Certainly we would never hold them up as examples of law-abiding citizens, for history would not sustain us" (Sept. 2, 1882).

Evangelism was always a subject for him to attack. The Salvation Army "engaging the enemy" at the city of Lawrence amused him; he would prefer not to turn over his hard-earned cash to such people. A meeting at the Coliseum led him to suggest that a bit of singing would be more influential to the frequenters of the place than "the dry word of God" (Feb. 14, 1881). In reporting on a meeting at the Shiloh Baptist Church he was quite literal: ". . . the preacher described how a person 'got religion,' several women screamed, and when the preacher asked those who wanted to be prayed for to stand up, about a hundred persons arose" (Oct. 19, 1893). And there was the appearance of "The Sin Killer" in Atchison, who converted three sinners, "all of whom will probably be backsliders within a few weeks" (Nov. 23, 1898). Ed Howe thought the Sin Killer's revival was as much fun as a skating rink. Such blunt writing was not calculated to build the circulation of *The Globe.*

Not for Edgar Watson Howe was the Sabbath. He had had enough of that in his rough boyhood. He suggested to his readers that some local Christians would have been better occupied one December Sunday morning by staying home and cleaning the snow off their sidewalks. An organized movement to halt the conducting of funerals on Sunday met with editorial blasts: "Perhaps these inspired idiots can name a more holy or sacred office, or one more fitted to the Sabbath, than the burial of the dead" (Jan. 27, 1881). If a funeral must be conducted at all, he wrote, keep it as quiet and unostentatious as possible, with no processions and tolling bells and looking at the corpse in the coffin. The Sabbath was frequently violated in the communities of the middle border by entertainment and sports, and this seemed quite all right to the Atchison editor. His conclusion about the perennial dispute over the Sabbath was embodied in a front page overline: "It Is Better to Save the Wheat on Sunday Than to Loaf Around Church Talking About Saving Soals [sic]" (July 1, 1897).

But despite his invective he was a conventional man about religion, and he was most annoyed (annoyance was the typical mood for Ed Howe) by those fringe groups that regularly declared it was time to pack up and get ready for the end of the world. One such organization had set aside the 19th of June, 1881, for the dire date, and he had words of advice for his readers:

> Attend church to-morrow. You will never have another chance, for the world is coming to an end to-morrow. When Gabriel blows his trump [sic] you ought to be prepared for the worst. You ought to devote one day, particularly the last day of your life, to devotion. Help crowd the churches. The contribution boxes will probably not be passed. But if they are, do not hesitate to contribute liberally. You cannot take your money with you. Read your bibles tonight, indulge in pious meditation, arise early in the morning, take a good bath, put on your cleanest and best linen, and for once in your life deport yourself as a Christian. Remember that to-morrow is the 19th of June. [June 18, 1881]

For spiritualism Howe's contempt was deepest of all. He believed religion and spiritualism to be about the same thing, the people in the churches who contended that mysterious spirits heard their entreaties being not greatly different from those sitting around a table in a dark room waiting for the tapping to begin. He was willing to attack both ideas in an editorial like this one:

> A letter addressed to "The Doubting Thomas of THE GLOBE," has been received at this office.
>
> The writer asks: "Can you explain this: Dr. Funk, one of the noted preachers of New York, recently talked with the spirit of Henry Ward Beecher, and saw him, as he appeared in life. Mr. Beecher told Dr. Funk of the existence of certain

coins, long since lost, the whereabouts of which were unknown to any living person."

The explanation is easy: NO SUCH THING EVER HAPPENED.

If Dr. Funk is not telling a falsehood, his mind is weak, and he has been deceived by a hallucination. As men grow old, they have a natural tendency to turn to childish things, and to believe in ghosts and spirits. It is a very rare man who does not believe strange things in old age.

Don't become as big a fool as the person who tells and believes a marvelous tale. [Apr. 14, 1903]

There were warnings in *The Globe* against hypnotists and phrenologists (whose advertising he accepted), against "mythology or foolology, generally" (Apr. 13, 1910). There were warnings against believing that photographs had been made of ghosts: "There are so many real truths to learn that it is strange men spend time chasing phantoms" (July 3, 1909). Christmas was a fraud; he annually advised against going on with it any longer: all it was good for was to remind us that we were a year older. "For every promise of redemption through Christ's birth, there are a dozen promises equally well attested of damnation" (Dec. 23, 1879). He wanted no gifts. "Don't give us any Christmas presents; don't risk your immortal soul for the sake of giving us an embroidered handkerchief or a necktie" (Nov. 13, 1897).

In the late 1890s an episode began in which Ed Howe was able to pour forth his views on religion and obtain a state forum at the same time. This followed a proposal (not made by Howe) that the Rev. Charles M. Sheldon of Topeka should undertake the publication of a "Christian newspaper." The proposal ultimately turned into Sheldon's one-week experiment with the *Topeka Daily Capital,* during which he edited the newspaper as "Christ would have done it."

This curious and entertaining episode had its beginnings when Sheldon, a Congregational minister and a dedicated man who subscribed to the Social Gospel movement, published in 1898 a book called *In His Steps.* In that book Sheldon posed, as his solution for all social ills of the time, the question: "What would Jesus do?" In the novel a revolution was effected in the lives of the parishioners of Sheldon's hero, Henry Maxwell, all of whom made a promise to ask themselves that question when personal crises struck their lives during a trial year. Because of a faulty copyright, *In His Steps* was published by many firms in both America and Europe, and it became one of the best-selling books of the late century. It also led to the suggestion that Sheldon produce a newspaper that would follow the precepts of the successful book. *The Atchison Globe* recorded the news that the Topeka minister had been in Chicago trying to raise a million dollars with which to launch "a Christian paper," and Howe remarked: "Hundreds of men have advertised themselves by this scheme, and never started a paper" (July 10, 1899).

No such paper evolved, but Sheldon did make an arrangement with Frederick O. Popenoe, the principal owner of the *Topeka Daily Capital,* to run the *Capital* for a few days. The experiment was to begin Tuesday, March 13, 1900, and end Saturday, March 17. It was a plan that led to consternation in the office of J. K. Hudson, editor-in-chief of the *Capital,* delight among the state's (and the nation's) journalists, and glee in such irreverent newspaper offices as that of *The Atchison Globe.*

The Topeka minister had been the subject of quips for some time by the editor of *The Globe.* Howe had ridiculed his excessive piety (in Detroit in 1899 Sheldon had walked six miles to and from church because he believed it wicked to ride on the Sabbath). And much of the time prior to the beginning of the Sheldon experiment Howe was having editorial fun with the matter. He asked whether Sheldon would have the women of the church selling his paper, *The Daily War Cry,* on the streets as the Salvation Army sold its *Weekly War Cry.* "Were it not for the women, Rev. Chas. M. Sheldon would be compelled to go to work" (Jan. 25, 1900). Other editors also were having their laughs: William Allen White suggested in the *Emporia Gazette* that "Parson Sheldon" should "Christianize his readers and the newspaper will establish itself without aid from the outside" (July 12, 1899). The editor of Howe's competitor, the *Champion,* announced that he would run the *Champion* for one week as only the devil could. White said of this: "The *Champion* has been a h - - of a paper for some time and that week will probably show no material change" (Feb. 28, 1900). Ed Howe entertained himself by publishing these little satires in *The Globe:*

> Rev. Charles M. Sheldon will conduct the *Topeka Capital* for a week in March, on lines laid down in his book: "What Would Jesus Do?"

Of course this is an advertising scheme: even if Sheldon had an intelligent idea to work on, he could accomplish nothing in a week, except to bring the usual discredit on sincere religion that always follows advertising.

We imagine that Sheldon's local columns will read something like this:

Sister Rachael Smith went to Kansas City to-day, on No. 11, to attend a missionary meeting.

The Lord blessed Brother Emanuel Jones last night with a girl baby. Blessed be the name of the Lord. (Mark, 32: xx-2.)

Don't fail to attend preaching on the Lord's day, and all the services.

Pay your subscription to the various church funds. Remember, brethren, the Lord loves a cheerful giver. (Acts, 33:2 –8.)

Brother Samuel Kent, of New York City, is visiting his uncle, Brother Joseph Thompson. Brother Kent reports the Lord's work progressing nobly in New York. Amen! God grant that this may continue.

A package of garden seeds was received to-day from Brother Chas. Curtis, who is now in Washington, attending to his duties as congressman. May the Lord send the rain and sunshine to make them prove fertile. [Jan. 23, 1900]

Editorial paragraphs in course of preparation by Rev. Charles M. Sheldon:

Behold, it came to pass that Corbett and Jeffries did even meet in the ring yesterday.

And lo, Jeffries girded up his loins, and encompassed Corbett around about, and smote him with great potency.

And Corbett lifted up his voice and cried: "Why sluggest thou me?"

And behold, Jeffries grew exceedingly wrath, and smote his antagonist hip and thigh, that it might be fulfilled which was spoken of by the prophet: "Ye the boiler maker shall even give the pompadour some dizzy pokes."

And it came to pass that the centurian [sic] rang the bell, and the sluggers returned to their corners, and were refreshed with locusts and wild honey.

And behold, there was much uproar in the galleries, caused by the scribes, Pharisees and hypocrites, who had put up their sheckels on Jeffries.

And it was even so. [Feb. 12, 1900]

But Ed Howe was getting disgusted, too, and a mite angry. Sheldon's obvious opinion that newspapers had too little religion drew the suggestion from Howe that there was not much common sense or ability in the average sermon but that editors did not become preachers for a week. What really drew Howe into the Sheldon stunt was Howe's suggestion that J. K. Hudson of the *Capital* serve as pastor of the First Congregational Church of Topeka for a week, or, Hudson not being willing, that he himself write a sermon to be read in the pulpit while Sheldon was out showing newspapermen how to put out newspapers. Or, that not being acceptable, that "sermons" from *The Globe* editor be printed daily in the *Topeka State Journal,* the competing newspaper in the capital city of Kansas.

Soon he announced in a long statement that a plan had been effected in late January for him to write a daily sermon for the *Journal,* not "ribald criticism of the church or the clergy," but a "truthful comparison of the church and the newspapers . . . ." He was confident that Sheldon's stunt would draw abuse from the clergy as well as the press, said that the stunt was largely a sharp advertising scheme for the *Capital,* and suggested that Christian newspapers could be published by the following standards:

> The great and successful newspapers are the useful, honest newspapers. The vicious newspapers do not live long: when you find a successful newspaper, you may depend upon it that it is an honest and useful newspaper. There are no exceptions to this rule.
>
> The rules enforced in most newspaper offices, if they could be known to the general public, would excite admiration. Be fair, be truthful; be honest; help the people, rather than injure them; help your town; be progressive, helpful, intelligent—these rules are dinned into assistants over and over by every editor of a useful and honest newspaper, and very few of the other class can live or do live. Editors, like other men, have different ideas of reaching results, but it is a fact that the modern newspaper's success is measured by its persistence in usefulness, fairness, and in moral tone. [Jan. 29, 1900]

The day the Sheldon edition of the *Capital* started, Howe gave it this attention, in a front-page headline (Mar. 12, 1900):

JESUS IN HARNESS.

Rev. C. M. Sheldon, Who Represents Him, Takes
Charge of the Topeka Capital.

An editorial in *The Globe* on the second day said Sheldon believed Christ would have printed the most important news on the front page, and accordingly printed a morning prayer and four stories: a famine in India and the need for Christians to give assistance; "Militaryism," an article by a Baltimore physician on the evil of war; a symposium on the prohibition law; and a plea to Sheldon to aid consumptives in Denver. Said Howe: "These four articles he regards as more vital than England's warning to other powers to keep hands off; greater than the situation in Kentucky; the discovery of more cases of bubonic plague in San Francisco; the day in the Senate, etc. On the editorial page Mr. Sheldon defines the policy he will pursue, and it can be guessed at by the first page. It will be to fight for prohibition, to preach against the war, etc." (Mar. 13, 1900).

Not too surprisingly, the Sheldon edition brought incidental attractions to Topeka. "The fact that Jesus is supposed to be running things in the *Capital,* and that, therefore, there would be no charge for advertising religious meetings, has resulted in a Chicago woman arriving in Topeka who will lecture for a week on the anti-cigarette line," said Howe. A man would talk against smoking; another would give lectures on temperance. A woman had attempted to kidnap her daughter from a Topeka school, but this was not news in the *Capital,* "proving that Jesus doesn't know a good local item when he sees it." And a side benefit from the Sheldon editorship: "There is only one commendable feature about the *Capital* as Jesus would run it: the reader is not reminded that he has weak kidneys, that every other man needs an electric belt, or that his pimples may be cancers. We will endorse Jesus on this platform" (Mar. 13, 1900).

Another side show was originating in Atchison: Edgar Watson Howe writing "Lay Sermons" for the *Topeka State Journal.* These, unfortunately, were not up to religious utterances he had been making for a generation. But they still were perhaps his most significant religious comments, and they gave him statewide publicity. The sermons began in the *Journal* on March 13, headlines noting that they were the first of a "remarkable series of plain spoken views," and Howe copyrighted them.

His ideas, he said, were not from "infidel books" but were his own thoughts, which had occurred to him in daily life. His personal philosophy told him that a person should do no wrong, "the essence of philosophy and experience," "the one universal truth." Good conduct is a human necessity. Honesty is not only the best policy but is the more comfortable way to live. He discussed the subject of a redeemer, offering the argument that every man is his own redeemer, his savior being with him. His opinion of organized religion had not altered in the slightest: "baseless from top to bottom; . . . no foundation in reason; . . . no foundation in history or probability." He told his probably scandalized readers that if they visited China they would be shocked at temples and idols, but that our churches are as shot full of relics and superstitions and our homes as filled with pictures of the Virgin and of Christ, with crosses and the like. He said the story of the Immaculate Conception and the ascent of Christ were taken bodily from Buddhism, and that doubting readers could find this fact in the American Cyclopedia, surely a truer book than the Bible. And, in what some must have thought a blasphemous blast:

"I do not believe that Christ was the son of God; I do not believe the history of Christ found in the Bible, but admitting that he brought a message to the world, we do not know what that message was, and never can know. . . . It is positively known that men wrote every line of the New Testament without any assistance from Christ or from God."[15]

Each of Howe's "sermons" was long and labored, oppressively displayed, by today's standards, in the dull typography of 1900. He commented in the second sermon on ministers, who know they are looked on with contempt by society, as being nonproducers (a prime offense in his mind), and outside the active world. And religious principles: the Ten Commandments had existed more than twenty centuries among the Egyptians before Moses ever came upon the scene, he said, and added that if a person knows the Bible he knows nothing of real value. He denied the stories of the fall of man, the flood, Moses as authority, the Immaculate Conception, the resurrection, doctrines of every church, supernaturalism, miracles and prophecies, significance of Sunday as the holy day, original sin, redemption through Christ, existence of an orthodox God, and existence after death. This was quite a body of denials, even for Ed Howe.

So the sermons continued. The poor people have taken quite a bit of abuse from the pulpit, he wrote, and they do quite well considering what they have to go through in life. His father, he was sure, would have been a more useful man had he not been so religious—and a happier man, too. The Sunday schools, like the one over which his father had presided, are no more meaningful than the Arabian Nights, and religion gives no help to those who truly need it: wretched criminals, children, people pursued by gossip or scandal. In a personal note that must have hurt he told about how his son had gone to church and heard the minister say no one could be honest unless a member of the church, and that the boy had asked him if this were true. What could he reply? Did he have a right to defend himself?

The fourth sermon spoke of the evil ministers, the "black sheep." "I have known many bad ministers, men who were notoriously bad, but when driven out of one community, they were accepted in another." That was his reply to the contention that preachers could provide a good example to editors. Church membership does nothing for the individual; a man must account to the world for his conduct, because people judge other men on their merits and not whether they are members of a church. Get rid of the meeting-houses, and put in their places buildings where lectures on the problems of life might be heard, where great orchestras and choruses "and not quarreling choirs" might perform, where talks by men of marked ability might be offered.

Sheldon himself was the object of one attack, Howe saying the minister was not by any stretch of the imagination the equal of most newspaper men he knew. And he asked how the twentieth century could learn from man of twenty centuries ago: "How would Jesus run a daily newspaper? Jesus never heard of a newspaper. He never heard of the art of printing. The age in which he lived was ignorant and superstitious. The magnificent discoveries and inventions of modern men were then unknown. The people were slaves, and treated like cattle. They did not know the merest rudiments of natural laws."

Let people of today stand there, holding their breaths, waiting to see what Sheldon will show them about how a carpenter of Nazareth would run a newspaper. What an absurdity! No one knows and no one should care how he would do it. Christ would say: "I do not know anything about a newspaper; I never heard of such a thing, but of this much I am certain: every man to his trade: let Mr. Sheldon return to his church, and let Joe Hudson take his newspaper, whatever it is." What would the public say if some editor announced he would run his paper as Marcus Aurelius would, or if McKinley announced he would conduct his administration in Washington as Nero would? One thing was sure, Howe said: Sheldon was the best advertiser the decade had produced, and he admired good advertisers.

Ed Howe hit some high spots in that sermon, but he was running down. He next talked about his response to a man who had said to him, "If I did not believe in the Christian religion, I would defy all social and moral laws, and have a good time." What utter nonsense! The principles of law and order would be more believable on a desert island than anywhere else. What has saved mankind is not the Christian belief but the principle of selfishness: It pays to behave yourself, because good conduct is more profitable than bad conduct. The great moral forces of the world were not in the churches, he said. The great men of a community, the kind of men who would be needed in an emergency, were not churchgoers. The greatest men of all time were those who rejected orthodoxy. And his conclusion:

> From the limitless sea where rocks the cradle of birth, there is a well defined highway leading to the grave. So many have traveled the road leading across the Continent of Life, that no one need go astray; there are sign posts at every step, and living witnesses to testify that there is danger away from the beaten track. The best road from the cradle to the grave has its hills and difficulties, but every temptation to stray from the highway has been yielded to by innumerable men and women, and every one of them has died leaving this warning: "Keep in the road." For every one of the millions who have wandered away from the beaten track, there has been a cry in the wilderness. Some of the venturesome wanderers have been recovered, and their scars have borne eloquent testimony to the dangers away from the only safe road mapped out by the experience of ages.
>
> If I had the attention of the world, and knew that every living man and woman would read what I have to say, it would be that every form of wrong doing, from murder to the smallest incivility in life, is man's greatest enemy. This is the gospel that should be thundered from the pulpit by men of energy and sense: the droning sermons heard Sunday after Sunday concerning impossible faith and foolish doctrine, should be changed to warning such as a wise old man might give his children.[16]

So ended the fantastic experiment. In the midst of it, Howe wrote that Barney Sheridan of the *Paola* (Kansas) *Spirit* had offered his paper to Brigham H. Roberts of Salt Lake City (a man constantly in the news because of the polygamy question) to be run a month as the Mormons would do it. The Atchison editor's comments on Sheldon, which amounted almost to persecution at times, did not cease. A year later he gleefully reported on the servant problem in the Sheldon household, one that occurred when the hired girl set a place for herself at the table and Mrs. Sheldon protested:

" 'But your husband says in a book that hired girls should be treated like the family,' said the girl.

" 'His books don't go around here,' said Mrs. Sheldon, and the girl got up and left" (May 31, 1901).

A manufactured anecdote, no doubt. And in a kind of footnote to the whole episode, another little item appeared in *The Globe* five years later:

"The Rev. Dr. Roberts, pastor of the Church of This World, Kansas City, will tell the Kansas Editorial association at its meeting in Topeka, January 16: 'What a Newspaper Should Be.' Perhaps he knows, but he doesn't know what a preacher should be. This is generally conceded by every preacher in the country who has ever heard of Dr. Roberts" (Jan. 5, 1905).

Education, the Press, and the Arts

Ed Howe doubtless considered that *The Globe* had as one of its tasks the education of the public. Comic strips and cheap features had not come to dominate the American press, and *The Globe* was relatively staid, interesting itself in problems and ideas rather than in trash and trivia. Its editor envisioned himself as a man whose mission was to pull the people of Atchison, and readers everywhere, out of the muck of ignorance. And in both *Globe* and *Monthly* he spelled out his belief that the only education of much value was the kind that provided practical training. For too much stress on Latin and poetry and literature he blamed the teachers, never the "people." Upon the teacher he also placed blame for stressing the high schools rather than the elementary grades, where money should be spent, he contended, on a practical start for children.

Most of his criticism was leveled at the colleges. He was surprised to read about a talk by a university president that actually made sense, when President Hadley of Yale said in Kansas City that the purpose of a college education was to receive the equipment to make a living. For him education was a democratic matter, and there was too much stupid talk about "educating children above their station." "Station" simply meant the place a person could make for himself, and then maintain. "We must never lose sight of the fact that a hod carrier's children have as good a right to a college training as the sons and daughters of the millionaire, if they can get it." He was angered by women critics and ministers "who seem to have forgotten that Christ was the son of a carpenter and his disciples were common fishermen" (May 21, 1897). (So again Ed Howe utilized religious teaching to prove a point.)

He was a man who had made his own way in the world and was a success, and his own example was good enough for him. He had risen from a lowly background, and his education had been mighty skimpy, and such an education should serve for other people. Even as the idea of obtaining a college degree was becoming common among Americans Ed Howe spoke against education for everyone. Choose between practical instruction and higher education, he wrote, for many a boy would do better if he stuck to blacksmithing and many a girl if she went into millinery. College does not necessarily redeem lives; it sometimes ruins them. "It is much better to be a successful laborer than a tenth rate minister, a fifteenth rate lawyer or a petty school teacher" (Feb. 27, 1903).

His views on the subject matter offered in American schools were decided ones. Latin was taught because ages ago somebody decided it should be taught. "There is no more excuse for teaching Latin than there is for teaching fortune telling. . . . it is a useless relic that should have been disposed of years ago" (June 6, 1899). The course in practical banking at the state university sounded good, but all it would do, in all likelihood, would be to provide useless training, and teach nothing about saving "the old man's money." Military instruction at the state agricultural college made even less sense. " . . . it would be interesting to know where military tactics come in. Chasing pigs out of a yard requires strategy; but war books don't teach that kind" (Sept. 12, 1902). Rich old men were endowing colleges, but their money was going to no good purpose, for "people continue to eat soggy bread, potatoes with the water left on them, peas that taste as if they were cooked in the cook's tears, etc. If some rich man will undertake to educate the people in doing plain cooking, it will be worth more to humanity than so many colleges" (June 20, 1901). His fixation about what young women should be learning in colleges was a favorite theme:

> When a girl is making good wholesome bread, digestible pies and cake, and keeping a house homelike and comfortable for her father, mother and brothers, it is said she is missing the "higher education" necessary to a woman's life. This "higher education" is one of the mushrooms that grow in the brain of poets, spiritualists, theosophists and fools. It means that her father, mother and brothers should be content to eat soggy bread, and grow dyspeptic on canned goods, while she sits on the bank of a stream and reflects about a lot of things that do her harm. Every good and useful woman avoids what is popularly known as the "higher life," the literal meaning of which is the higher foolishness. [Jan. 6, 1894]

Throughout the American educational system money was being wasted on nonsensical things—free baths, for example, along with free lunches, in some public schools. He recommended that someone figure out a way to teach a student how to pound sand in a rat hole; that would be progress. He wondered how a course in geometry fitted a girl to make bread and pies for her husband. Why all the fuss about educating boys to become preachers, lawyers, or doctors, when in Topeka work on public buildings had been delayed because of a lack of stone masons? Was there a preacher receiving $4.50 for an eight-hour day? "What the country needs is less professional men and more good mechanics" (Sept. 6, 1900).

He was sure that any man over twenty-five who was still going to school was a troubled person, and he urged that when any kind of work shortage existed the colleges be scoured and all men over twenty-five be put to work. That might keep the loafers out of school. Perhaps the sentimentalists about education were responsible for such a state of affairs. Too many men were running our schools who were starry-eyed visionaries; it was time to return education to the men of better sense, the practical men of business.

To bring Ed Howe ranting to his feet one only need mention a school of journalism. Such institutions were unknown in his youth, but early in the twentieth century they began to appear, making college education even more scandalous than it had been.

He read of such experiments as those at Northwestern, Kansas, Columbia, and Missouri, of the founding of a "college of journalism" by editor Murat Halstead. And sour editorial observations emerged:

> It is the experience of those employed on newspapers that every man thinks he knows the newspaper business already. [June 6, 1900]
>
> As no two editors have the same ideas about how a newspaper should be run, we pity the man who is engaged to teach the business at the Kansas university. [Aug. 20, 1903]
>
> The class of journalism at the State university will result in only one thing: Making this world harder than ever for editors. When a Young Thing with long hair is graduated from this class, and returns home, he will at once begin the writing of impossible articles for his home paper. When they are refused, he will abuse the editor. He will discover that the editor, never having been a member of the class in journalism, doesn't know enough to put a barrel right side up for catching rain. [Jan. 7, 1904]
>
> There are so many editors on the average college paper that there may be some difficulty in fixing the blame, and to expel the entire staff might greatly deplete the attendance. [May 2, 1908]

When the Abilene, Kansas, editor, Charles M. Harger, was commuting weekly to teach journalism at the state university, he called upon Ed Howe (a highly unlikely choice at the time) to deliver an address on journalism before his class. Ed Howe chose to present the talk in print:

> After an editor has worked on a paper a long time, he learns to be careful, because mistakes make him trouble. But he has a great time trying to coax the younger men to be careful. Example: Lately a young man named Arthur Armstrong had smallpox. A careless young reporter printed the name "Albert" Armstrong. There is an Albert Armstrong in Atchison engaged in the grocery business. He made a roar, of course, and he had a right to. And the roar was made to the editor, not to the careless young reporter. The editor printed a correction, and again coaxed the young reporter to be careful. Yesterday Arthur Armstrong was released from quarantine. Again the careless young reporter referred to the patient as "Albert" Armstrong. This morning Albert Armstrong, the grocer, made another roar to the editor, and the editor again apologizes and explains. [Feb. 28, 1908]

If schools must teach journalism (and Ed Howe could see no good reason why they should), take an example, then, from the state agricultural college of Kansas. At the "farmers school," as he termed it, journalism was designed so that a student learned how to pull a proof, set an advertisement, feed a press, cut stock, learn mechanical processes, read proof, manage the business, learn the job department, and all in all become fitted for country newspaper work. "As we understand it," he said, "the school of journalism at the State university is trying to turn out editors and editorial writers. It isn't the editorial writers who make business for a successful newspaper" (Feb. 5, 1910).

As Howe commented with perturbation on the mistakes of college education he was looking at the same time on the foolishness of extracurricular affairs. No one ever heard anything creditable about a college student, unless one considered playing a mandolin or football creditable. Reports from colleges were as bad as reports from reform schools. The best athletes (John L. Sullivan, for example) had had no advanced education. What was a boy being fitted for in college but to come home, show off, strut about wearing "shoes a little more yellow than anyone else; ties that are gaudier, shirts of a more startling design, and their hair parted more evenly in the middle" (June 6, 1900). Was this the way to equip a young man for the harsh struggles of life?

What did Ed Howe see when he examined colleges in America (and largely, of course, colleges in his part of America)? He saw young men with banjos, singing in glee clubs, joining football clubs, yelling around the country, causing trouble in saloons and variety theaters, making wise people decide against sending their boys away to be educated. He saw youthful orators, learning elocution, causing colleges to become even more "a sort of skin game worked annually upon the parents" (Dec. 4, 1897). He saw a football team making a big eastern tour, spending good Kansas money, kicking a ball around in the mud (or "playing their fiddles and singing like calves") instead of doing their lessons (Oct. 24, 1899).

It was all a joke, and not a very good one. Those who believed John J. Ingalls to be the leading citizen of Atchison must be mistaken; it was really Hugh Todd, lately injured while playing football at a college in the East. A Missouri paper carried a headline reading: "Missouri State University Crippled!" And what had caused the injury to the great university? "The pitcher of the base ball nine has quit!" (Feb. 8, 1908). True backers of the state university would cheer the news, he said, that it had lost the football game to the University of Nebraska by a score of 12 to 0. "Now if it gets walloped again on Thanksgiving day by Missouri, there will be some hope that the students will finally come to their senses, let foot ball alone, and go to school" (Nov 19, 1900).

Where could one most easily find a troublesome young man? At a university, of course. Students of the University of Missouri had made a disturbance at a circus: "It will soon become necessary to station a regiment of soldiers permanently in every town where there is an considerable number of college students" (May 12, 1906). Students of the state agricultural college at Manhattan had been suspended for calling on Governor Hoch and demanding that the president of the college be removed. "This is carrying Liberty too far," he thundered, but "we expect that the president of the agricultural college will be removed. That's the way things are being done, lately" (Mar. 23, 1905).

So these offenses against common decency and common sense continued, and Ed Howe vowed that he would be one farmer who would not let tax money be spent to provide garages for students driving their cars to school. He would fight, too, against teachers running things, instead of parents (such as parents who needed their children at home to clean the chicken house or run an errand). He would continue to warn people that the quickest way to see a boy go bad was to send him to medical college, where he would receive experience cutting up bodies of dead women and then go out and commit outrages on the bodies of living women. He would oppose the ridiculous practice of children, not yet dry behind the ears, standing up at commencement exercises, boring their elders, and giving them advice they neither need nor want:

"Commencement exercises are foolish and unnecessary in the first place, and they become positively ridiculous when the graduates give advice in their essays to those who are older than themselves. At a recent commencement, a graduate advised editors how to conduct their newspapers, and suggested methods ministers should adopt for making their work more acceptable to the Lord. These graduates imagine, no doubt, that as soon as they have finished their orations, the people present will step forward and bid for their services. As a matter of fact people do not go to commencements to be instructed; they go to be amused" (June 9, 1899).

His concept of the mission of the press was similar to his concept of education. A man was mainly in newspaper work to make a living. And Ed Howe was making a good one. He was a newspaperman (never a journalist; he scoffed at such lofty words as "journalism"), but never in the exalted sense of a Greeley or a Bryant or a William Allen White. He did not see things the way those fellows saw them. He had the extraordinary capacity, though, to look at himself as an "opinion-maker" (even though he must have known he was an important one, especially as the years went by), and to laugh a little. He wanted to be like the Kansas City newspaperman who came to town and said nothing about "supplying a long felt want." That kind of man, in his opinion, was likely to be a good one.

Perhaps his modest protests were designed to bring praise; they often did. Yet usually he was a scoffer at the idea of "editorial influence." He was a country editor, and knew it, and liked it. Whenever he got to the big cities of the East he read the newspapers and realized immediately what marked them from little sheets like his somewhat modest *Atchison Globe*. The big boys printed as news what the country editors printed as gossip.

In 1891 he wrote about country editors for the *Century*,[17] and his ideas provide interesting revelations into his attitudes toward the life he led. First of all, there were few rich editors, he said. What editors there were had to print some rather stupid stuff: "I was once bothered a good deal by a certain man who said he could clean more chickens in an hour than any other chicken-cleaner in the world, and he wanted the fact mentioned." As country newspapers tended to be alike, so did country towns: Kansas and Nebraska towns were almost identical in their populations, banks, newspaper totals, mills and elevators, and so on. Most men seemed to think that, while they might fail as doctors or lawyers, they would succeed as editors. The reverse would be true:

"Really good newspaper men are scarce in the country, for a business man and a writer must be combined to insure success; but there is no lack of newspapers, and as half the people seem to be waiting to give the business a trial, I feel certain that the supply will always be considerably greater than the demand."

And, as some men were convinced they could be good editors, most men were not really too convinced about the shibboleth of the free press in America, there being "a strong undercurrent of opposition to [it] among our liberty-loving people."

He believed four classes of men generally owned country papers: farmers' sons who thought they were too good for farming, but not quite good enough to do nothing at all; school teachers; lawyers who had failed in the law; "professional printers" who had worked into the position. And it seemed to him that boys drifted naturally into the job of printing. "I have seen hundreds of them learning the trade, but it seems to me that in all the towns in which I have lived I never knew any boys who were learning to be tailors, or blacksmiths, or painters."

He saw a need for good local papers in his state, but not local papers run by men who spent all their time at editorial conventions or trying to dominate politics:

"The local paper, when well conducted, can become a power for good. It is always respected, when it deserves respect, but the average local paper is so poor that it is not useful, and it is not respected. The average editor of this class is hoping for political preferment, and makes his paper a disgusting party organ, to the neglect of legitimate local news and comment. He permits a boy to do work he should do himself, and the result is that the average country paper is a huge joke.

"The few good country editors are missionaries. Let them work away; in time they will reform their idle brethren" (June 20, 1902).

He had long known that he was a kind of prophet without honor, a man who would have to fight his way to achieve position in Atchison, for he had to buck strong opposition and he was too outspoken for the tastes of many. Now he was making a success, and he still knew that he lacked the leadership qualities of, say, the man he liked to call "Old Bill White" (even though White was a decade his junior). White could "utter a clarion note in the *Emporia Gazette,* and, by the time it has appeared in the *Kansas City Star,* the State is aroused, but I can't do it," he reflected.[18]

Perhaps Ed Howe simply wanted more than was being granted to most Americans of his time, and perhaps, despite his disavowals, he really would have liked to be a William Allen White and be consulted by the great of the land. He was sure that an editor could not truly have friends like other men, particularly if that editor was a successful one, and he felt that even the most respected editors would have opposition as a constant element in their lives.

Business success on a newspaper was paramount to him, but the editor must retain his integrity. He could not retain it by selling himself or letting himself be purchased. "No free lists" was his policy, and that included actresses, politicians, and notoriety-seekers in general. He clearly made a division between news and free advertising, and he was no more ready to promote the San Francisco Exposition than a dancer appearing at an Atchison hall. News and advertising might be interspersed, but all advertisers paid.

As he looked about the land the papers he admired were the prosperous ones. William Rockhill Nelson had caught his eye back in 1880, when he arrived in Kansas City and started the *Star*. He felt called upon to advise Nelson editorially about his mistake in purchasing the *Kansas City Times*—the thriving morning edition of the *Star* in later years—and changing the makeup and type style: "Go back to the old one before it is too late" (July 21, 1903). He conveyed his admiration for Nelson in a conversation with another newsman:

> I introduced a New York newspaperman to Colonel Nelson, and he said to me later:
>
> "Colonel Nelson's talk was the best lecture on the newspaper business I ever heard."
>
> Some noted general once said that the Lord is always on the side of the army that has the biggest guns—or something to that effect. That is Colonel Nelson's theory: luck is always on the side of the best newspaper. The New York newspaper man said to me, when we were riding down town:
>
> "I suppose the *Star* is in the market for the best newspaper men."
>
> "No," I replied: "it has them."[19]

And, as a man who tried to run a tight newspaper office, where there would be little nonsense going on, he admired things at the *Star* plant:

> The old fashioned idea that a newspaper office was a place where almost anyone could loaf and read the exchanges, is now out of date. When a man walks into the office of the *Kansas City Star,* a boy in uniform walks up to him, and asks whom he

> wants to see. If the visitor gives a name, the boy takes a book from his pocket, glances into it, and, in a dignified manner, tells the person at what hour the person in question can be seen. A boy ushers the visitors into the presence of the person asked for, and waits for the conversation to close, when the boy shows him directly out of the building. If the oldest subscriber should go into the *Star* office to loaf, and "josh" with the editor, he would freeze to death before he got out of the building. The *Star* office is a place to do business. The employes are paid to work, and there is no sign of idle talk. This is business as it should be. Many a business house could learn a valuable lesson from the *Star*. [Mar. 2, 1897]

The New York *Sun,* however, which bore the reputation among some newsmen as being the best paper in New York City, did not meet with Ed Howe's approval. He once visited the office, looked at the bust of Charles A. Dana, and then saw "about the dirtiest and worst arranged newspaper office I have ever seen. Some of these days there will be a fire in the *Sun* office, and fifty or sixty of the brightest newspaper men in America will do well if they get out with their lives. . . . the country printing-office towel joke would apply to the entire establishment, it is so dirty."[20] He admired the *World* much more, and believed that if the *World* was "yellow" then yellow newspapers were the best kind. He admired its honesty, its enterprise, its success, the good that it did, "more good than all the alleged reformers put together," its popularity with great masses of readers (Apr. 4, 1900). But the yellow press in general he deplored, and in referring to a certain yellow editor (William Randolph Hearst, in all likelihood) he said he "should as soon have the reputation of Captain Kidd, the pirate, as the reputation of the noted yellow editor I refer to."[21]

Yellow journalism he criticized on many occasions, but it was not the only journalistic development or tendency which he thought disgusting. Journalistic deadbeats angered him—"the drinking of free liquor, the smoking of politicians' cigars, and the doing of a hundred other things that is discreditable to any class of men" (Oct. 5, 1880). Poor writers he constantly sounded off against. Cowardly editors, who took off against John D. Rockefeller, or the Mormon senator, Reed Smoot, who was under attack because of the polygamy question—these disturbed him. Such editors were afraid to deal with critical issues of the day; their response was to go against one man and his home and family. Dull editors, filling their pages with their petty prejudices, their dry and stilted opinions—these should be eliminated from the map, but "we admit that OUR editorial page is dull" (Nov. 24, 1909).

The American press had grown too big for the provincial Edgar Watson Howe. So he was troubled by the power that was represented and the weight that was being thrown about and the dishonesty that he felt sure characterized many journals: "Probably the most insolent American is the big editor who has acquired a big circulation, a big advertising patronage, a big building, and a big fortune. Being rich himself, he advocates all sorts of public improvements, that they may become monuments to his memory; as the preacher insists on building a new and unnecessary church as evidence of his activity."[22]

Most of all he disliked what he called the "newspaper bosses," for he was never part of the Kansas club of editors, and he disliked using a newspaper to promote political fortunes, even though that had been probably the main tradition in American journalism. Editors with grievances and candidates got his dander up: "No editor has a right to abuse a candidate day after day" (Sept. 15, 1904) (as he had abused, and was still abusing, William Jennings Bryan). Kansas was in the hands of bosses, especially bosses whose newspapers had the largest circulations. This was the theme that came to characterize his observations about the press in the later years on *The Globe:*

> Kansas is being ruled by Plutocracy and Privilege.
>
> The *Topeka Capital, Emporia Gazette, Kansas City Star* and *Wichita Eagle* and *Beacon* are running Kansas as absolutely as though they owned it.
>
> And this combination of rich editors will continue to run the state so long as they avoid a quarrel.
>
> The struggling masses have no representation in the congress which meets alternately at Topeka, Wichita, Emporia and Kansas City. The people have put up Tom Wagstaff, to see what sort of an impression he can make against predatory wealth, but he isn't making much headway, owing to his poverty. [May 28, 1910]

Powerful as were the bosses, there was another class of newspapermen at whom Ed Howe looked with dislike. These were not the newspaper bosses but the "newspaper boys." Reform them—the reporters, feature writers, headline writers and the like—and you can reform journalism, he said. For these were the men who ran the world, who shaped policies on those institutions that had become the greatest power in the country—the newspapers. The newspaper boys, he said, made public opinion, colored the news, and made papers the country over look and act and read alike.

Ed Howe's attitude toward what he would have laughingly called "culture" was geared, as surely as his attitudes concerning education and the press, to the practical and the successful.

How rapidly he moved in to deride those who labeled him a critic! The word "critic" described "the meanest trait in human nature." One man's opinion is every bit as good as another man's; "you are only one of millions of critics."[23] His was consistently the mucker pose; artistic or cultural pretension was a bore. He took pride in Atchison because the town, perhaps taking its cue from him, was not a cultural town; it was "the only town in Kansas that hasn't taken a lot of flower pots containing a few, scrubby, rough head chrysanthemums, and called it a flower show" (Nov. 21, 1893). If he knew the meaning of a foreign phrase he would not admit it. "When Leavenworth puts up a few greens in a hall, gets a few fiddlers together, and the women gather in their best gowns and the men borrow dress suits, it is called a bal poudre. Now, what is a bal poudre?" (Jan. 2, 1902). Or, for that matter, what is a finger bowl?—"the most embarrassing thing in society" (Mar. 24, 1892).

Just as sure to be hooted at were the women who got together each fall to organize a Shakespeare club, which turned into a card party at the second meeting, and gave a prize at the third, and completely forgot "Old Bill Shakespeare" at the fourth. But a complete lack of local cultural enterprise also brought disapproval from *The Globe.* Howe asked in the 1880s why a city of fifteen thousand could have no musical association, no reading circles, no efforts made to enrich the mind. He was distressed that a presentation of Shakespeare did so poorly in Atchison:

> It is a fact as cold as a puppy's nose, and as undeniable as the saying that all men are sinners, that Atchison is not a literary town. Night before last the rain and the wind gave a concert that made people tremble, but there was a good crowd at the opera house to hear the minstrels. Last night the wind had a suggestion of goblins in it, and there was no rain, but the people in the opera house were as scattered and lonesome as the men will be in heaven. The occasion was the rendition of Shakespeare's "As You Like It." We suppose the people should

> blush to think that Miss Gale played to a poor house last night, but they don't seem to blush at all. They rather seem to enjoy their minstrel reputation. [Apr. 14, 1892]

He was a kind of minstrel man himself, in his tastes, the circuses of his boyhood still fondly remembered, the musical associations of his tramp printer days still present in some of his attitudes. And of the fine arts it was always music that Ed Howe enjoyed most. But it was always *enjoyment,* for he had no deep understanding of music. Music, like some other subjects, was not meant for the professorial class. It belonged to the people, and one of them, Adam Brenner of nearby Doniphan, "a plain, plug grape-grower, [was] better on the musical instrument and more competent to teach than the impressive lads at the state university" (Dec. 2, 1885).

Howe was the "brass band editor" of *The Globe,* ready to go to St. Joseph, or even as far away as St. Louis or Chicago, to hear a concert. "The brass band editor of THE GLOBE likes music as naturally as he likes milk," he wrote, "and will tell his impressions exactly as they occur to him, without reference to art or culture" (Mar. 15, 1895). His impressions, one might guess, did not always coincide with either popular or critical taste of the day; he was no admirer of that celebrated composer and leader of a big brass band, John Philip Sousa:

> Sousa . . . has one bad habit: he plays too many of his own compositions. In a recent programme of nine numbers, one-third were by Sousa, and, in addition, he played five of his own marches as encores: of the fourteen selections during the evening, therefore, eight were written by the conductor! . . . He is billed as "The March King," but he is not the march king; he is not even a fair writer of marches. Sousa's fame as a band master has made his marches popular; they are not good marches. Sousa has written a comic opera, "El Capitan," but it will not last. I have not heard it, but I am so certain that Sousa has no genius as a composer, that I know what the fate of his opera will be. [Feb. 11, 1897]

But who cared about Sousa, anyway, when there was a fine cornet player, so good that he made Howe recall his happy days at Chicago's Columbian Exposition? To make sure that he was able to hear good bands perform he brought them to Atchison, and he frequently suggested that the best kind of philanthropy would be the sponsoring of bands to play concerts all over the land. A band concert at Forest Park in Atchison drew his enthusiasm, especially its performance of "Liebestraum." "An overture was played with excellent effect, and many of the minor pieces were simply gems" (Apr. 14, 1892). In the editorial columns he promoted the concerts that his newspaper sponsored:

> THE GLOBE has long been an enthusiast on music. On the 20th, it will give two concerts at Forest park, at 3 and 7 p.m., by a band of forty-two men. These concerts will be complimentary to patrons of the paper. The people are invited to turn out, and see if THE GLOBE's theory about music is not true.
>
> THE GLOBE'S theory about music is that people are tired of amateur music, but long for good music. There will be good music at Forest park on the 20th, at 3 and 7 p.m., and it will be free.
>
> THE GLOBE is paying the expenses of these concerts with a view of interesting the people in good music. If the experiment is successful, similar concerts will be given every month. Possibly by next year, the people of Atchison will be wise enough to do what we have long contended they should do: hire a band of forty men, and give concerts three or four times a week. [June 6, 1899]

This was the true religion of *The Globe:* music, the kind of music his bands performed at Forest Park (costing him a little over three hundred dollars, he wrote, including, presumably, the fireworks at intermission). Why couldn't Atchison spend its money on such affairs, he asked, instead of on foolishness? There were six thousand people at the concert, compared with the puny sixty who patronized a preacher who was critical of *The Globe*. Which sermon was better?

This was his message. He truly believed that his greatest ambition was to organize a band that would travel about and give free concerts. His best moments, perhaps, were spent in concert halls, where he could be free from the nagging problems of home and office. In one of his long columns on music he seemed to become a different man for a while:

> A country boy saves his money for weeks, and goes to town on circus day: he likes to hear the rich rumble of the circus wagon, and he likes to look at the elephant, and the thousand dollar beauty on its back. No one finds fault with the boy for doing this: He is a better boy for his day off, and no one should find fault with me because I save my money for months, and go

> to the grand opera every year, though perhaps I have no right to write about it. I like grand opera as thoroughly as the country boy likes a circus, and I spend the money I have saved up quite recklessly so long as it lasts, and return home with my pockets full of things, as does the boy returning from the circus. [Mar. 3, 1897]

In a reminiscent mood he went back to Falls City, the town of his early printing days, and listened to the brass band, which, unfortunately, "was as bad as ever" (Nov. 24, 1901). He got to hear the great Caruso, and thought him "the new champion," even though the editor's published criticism of Caruso consisted largely of recalling how he himself had been judged the best tenor ever heard in the choir of the First Methodist Church at Falls City. He kept up his public singing, performing December 12, 1907, with Mrs. Ada Smith Fullerton, an Atchison soprano, at the Topeka auditorium, and then giving a travel lecture after the concert. And he believed that, despite such an occasion, his town was bereft of talent: ". . . for fifty years every girl in town had practiced on the piano until she had driven the neighbors crazy, but Atchison had not produced a single musician."[24]

He was a small town man, for sure, whenever he looked at a painting. He offered predictably conventional criticism, and was shocked at what he thought immodest display, always preferring the practical and the representational over the experimental. Few paintings impressed him. His taste ran to photography, to the "coldly judicial, impartial" camera. Never had he been moved in an art gallery, he wrote. Like Mark Twain he loved to poke fun at those who appeared impressed by "great art," and he quoted with approval (he probably manufactured the story) the American woman in Rome who, studying Titian's *Sacred and Profane Love,* said she could not tell which was sacred and which profane but finally decided: "I guess the naked one is sacred love; surely they ain't millinered in heaven" (Aug. 3, 1879). Realistic art (and literature) disgusted him. He could not see why the only *real* things were those which were "loathsome and unpleasant." "Because it is a fact that there are decaying corpses in existence is that any reason why these should be publicly paraded before the eyes and noses of the public?" (May 3, 1897).

Magazine illustrations were cause for hilarity, and readers of *The Globe* were treated to detailed descriptions of what Ed Howe had seen in *Century, Scribner's,* and the *Ladies' Home Journal.* Scribner's let him view "a woman as naked as the day she was born," a picture which would have caused the *Police Gazette* to be denied the mails. Such art should be termed nonsense, it being produced by young men living off their parents, calling themselves "Bohemians" when they should be called "Bums." Women should be clothed, because that is what civilization demands and that is when they look better.

Then there was a *Ladies' Home Journal* cover: "A woman is pictured with her dress cut low enough for nursing purposes, and with one foot cocked high in the air. Her lap is piled with grapes and apples, and beside her two naked children sport, also plentifully supplied with fruit. One of the children hasn't even a sash or a conveniently growing vine to cover its nakedness. We call such Art plain rot. It is probably named Harvest, Bounty, or Autumn, but we fail to see why the Lord's bounty in sending good crops should be represented by a half naked woman and two undressed children. It is the kind of a picture to adorn the saloon instead of a woman's magazine" (Aug. 23, 1897).

The good Kansas editor looked at such illustrations with eyes of wonder. And *Century* entertained him with one called "Midsummer Glow": "In the back are green trees and two women with faces redder than any powder we ever saw, and in the front a woman on her knees gazing with a rapt expression on a naked child. Is she looking him over for chiggers? The women in the back have on robes as if they had just brought him from the tub, and one has something draped over one arm that looks like a bath towel. If she is looking him over for chiggers, why make a picture of it, and why have the naked child standing out doors among the flowers where he will get more on him? Her eyes are fastened on his shoulder, and it is our experience that chiggers do not like shoulder meat as much as they like hams. Perhaps she is looking in the wrong place" (Aug. 9, 1905).

These were as bad as what he liked to label "country town art," produced by visiting ladies who put their work in store windows and got the gullible to walk by softly, speaking in muted tones, for "they are in the presence of Art." One such woman came to Atchison and painted Ed Howe's Missouri River—sand bars, atmosphere, and valley. He had lived on the Missouri for twenty-six years and felt that river and picture had nothing in common. But no one else in Atchison seemed to dare to say anything about it. He also reserved both newspaper space and humor to tell about the statue that was representing the great state of Kansas at the St. Louis Fair of 1903, "a half nude woman, with one arm thrown over the head of a bull":

> The woman has no clothes on, except a drapery across her knees, and a handkerchief wound around her forehead. The former might be a bathrobe, but the latter looks as if she had just finished dusting, and sat down to rest.
>
> But she has a sickle in her hand, and Kansas women don't use them to dust with. And there is the bull. A bull doesn't belong to a parlor scene. We never yet saw a half-naked woman sitting with one arm over a bull crouched beside her, and we have lived in the state twenty-five years. Bulls are not that tame. If it had been a cow, on her feet, with a milking bucket under her, it would have been more like. The woman's feet are bare, except for a pair of sandals. Our women don't hang around fierce bulls in such attire, but, on the contrary, run from them.
>
> If the artist insists upon a bull, then he should have a full dressed woman holding up her skirts, and running for dear life for a fence. [May 8, 1903]

Now for the literary tastes of Edgar Watson Howe, a writing man himself: they could only puzzle the critics who remain convinced that he was consciously—or even unconsciously—in the vanguard of either realism or naturalism. Start with his contemporary in the local color tradition, Bret Harte of points west. Ed Howe had no use for him. Howe would not believe that all the bad women passed through the middle states and went on to California, even though he was certain that none of them had stopped in Atchison. He was admittedly an admirer of Mark Twain, but he says little about individual works of the great man. He was more inclined to spend his time harping at a more inconsequential figure, like Bronson Alcott, of the utopian dreams and visions and impracticalities that could only make a man like Ed Howe impatient. "The man was a failure, and ridiculous: he makes this admission himself."[25] Emerson he admired, however, probably because he himself was as self-reliant a man as Emerson could wish for. Walt Whitman was a failure, a freak, who did his own cooking and housekeeping, looked funny and talked funny, "yet he is rated higher than James Oliver, who invented the modern steel plow . . . . The spirit of James Oliver is doing good to-day on almost every farm in the civilized world, yet Walt Whitman is more noted. What an outrage!"[26]

His belief was that a successful writer could not match a successful man in most other enterprises. "Did Shakespeare, or Goethe, or Whitman, or Buddha, or Tolstoy, or Confucius, or Rousseau, ever teach you as important lessons as you learned from your parents, from your worthy and intelligent neighbors, from the leading men of practical affairs in your own country and age? *They did not,* and you know it." The pen was *not* mightier than the sword, and the hoe was mightier than either. Here was a man who was at least a minor league literary lion yet he had almost nothing to say about his contemporaries, and viewed writing men as black sheep, "like the village fiddler," their work largely rubbish, none of them coming up to the wisest men in most American communities.

To him poetry was of no use. A poem by the great John Greenleaf Whittier opened the Centennial Exposition of 1876, but the real works of art—those on display at the exposition—were forgotten, with their creators. Edwin Markham's "The Man with the Hoe" made him impatient, Markham's philosophy being completely false, in that he taught that a working man is a slave. "The socialistic, sentimental, fool spirit is responsible for the popularity of the poem. It does not contain a grain of sense" (Sept. 26, 1899). James Whitcomb Riley was much more to his taste, even though Riley had too many bad imitators.

Few of his contemporaries drew real praise. Especially silly in Ed Howe's eyes was the vastly popular Rudyard Kipling, who was too much of a hero, especially when one considered how he had abused America. Kipling's "animal stories" in the *Ladies' Home Journal* drew this comment: "If they are not the rottenest stuff for which a big price was ever paid, we do not know rot when we see it" (May 1, 1900). Better in his opinion was his Kansas colleague, William Allen White, who had written *The Court of Boyville,* a book that took Ed Howe back to his boyhood, with all its trials and joys. White's *A Certain Rich Man* did not please Howe, however, though it did provide him with a satirical paragraph: "Some day we intend to write a book, entitled 'A Certain Poor Man.' The hero of it will be an Atchison man we know. He isn't worth hell room; he was born worthless, is worthless now, and will be worthless as long as he lives. The history of this man would, we believe, prove interesting. Within a month he has had five different jobs. He was able to hold one job four days, but in the others he didn't last long" (July 1, 1910).

A *Globe* plug for a book was a rare thing. The outspoken author of *The Story of a Country Town* was a literary prude. He was a realist who scorned realism in others. Zola's *Germinal,* which was receiving considerable attention, was to him a "filthy" book, Howe observing that "The American taste for filth is so pronounced that should a publisher issue a text book containing all the filthy words, and nothing else, it would have a large sale" (Mar. 16, 1885). He hated what he termed filth in literature as he hated a dirty story, and said he had never bought a book that had been advertised as being "filthy." Hardy's *Jude, the Obscure* disgusted him—too much like a doctor book, fit only for a woman contemplating marriage with a man she disliked. (And the parallels between Jude's grim existence and that of Howe's own Jo Erring are striking!)

For years he ripped away at the popular novel *Quo Vadis?,* which was full of Christian martyrdom, woodland bacchanalia, a garden party scene at Nero's villa, where torches were made of living men—all too much for him. It was the "nastiest book we have read in years," and the author, Henryk Sienkiewicz, was always "Stinkywitz" in *The Globe:*

> It is popular because it is nasty. Much as we admire men and women, we fear they like nasty things occasionally. Three or four of the chapters describe a banquet that Nero gave. He took his friends to an island, which was filled with naked women, and the drunk that followed was a corker. This incident is not historical; Stinkywitz deliberately invented it, to shock nice people, and cause them to read his book, and tell each other about it. The author weeps all through the book because of the licentiousness of Nero's age, but most of the licentiousness he speaks of, he invented. Anyway, the licentiousness of Nero's age had been almost entirely forgotten until Stinkywitz's book appeared. His occasional references to the Home and Fireside of the Christians, won't apologize for the frequent references to nastiness. Stinkywitz reminds us of the reformers who make sensational charges which are not true, in order to weep over them. [Feb. 7, 1898]

When "Stinkywitz" reported that he had been reading Zola's books, Ed Howe had *two* dirty writers to attack, and he commented that he planned to read Zola himself to see if anything could compare with the banquet scene in *Quo Vadis?*

So *The Globe's* literary critic proceeded through the years, generally flailing away at the popular—or at least widely discussed—books of the day:

Edward Bellamy's *Looking Backward*—"Books of this character do no good; on the contrary, they cause the people to become more discontented, and spend time in arguing that should be devoted to work" (July 1, 1897).

Rostand's *Cyrano de Bergerac*—"If you don't receive any copies, you may as well begin going to bed at dusk, for you are no longer in it" (Dec. 12, 1898).

Winston Churchill's *The Crisis*—"When you see a woman with 'The Crisis' under her arm, bow low: she is loaded with history, and knows more about the Civil war than Anybody. She knows how Virginia Carvel wore her hair when the first gun in the Civil war was fired; how the villain, Eliphalet Hopper, took both sides, and that Lincoln was still alive when Stephen A. Brice asked Carvel to marry him" (Aug. 7, 1901).

Alice Hegan Rice's *Mrs. Wiggs of the Cabbage Patch*—full of fine, homely philosophy, like "Looks like ever' thing in the world comes right, if we jes' wait long enough" (Aug. 21, 1902).

Edith Wharton's *The House of Mirth*—". . . imagine the reader's disgust to find that the poor miserable heroine takes poison, and the only kiss in the entire story is a very chilly one which she presses on the high forehead of the poor refined young man the night before she commits suicide" (Oct. 21, 1905).

Shaw's *Mrs. Warren's Profession*—"After 'Salome,' and the Thaw trial, 'Mrs. Warren's Profession' must seem as tame as one of the Elsie books" (Mar. 15, 1907).

Elinor Glyn's *Three Weeks*—"The nastiest book published in recent years" (Jan. 10, 1908).

Florence L. Barclay's *The Rosary*—"There is something wrong with a country where every public library buys and circulates from two to a dozen copies of [it]."[27]

Veblen's *The Theory of the Leisure Class*—no wit, no agreeable style, an obvious moral. Veblen is probably an excellent man, but he should not rule adults the way he rules children in classes.[28]

Popular literature (such as that being composed by Harold Bell Wright—"a sharp business man") generally met his disapproval. He had cynical words for the widely celebrated George Bernard Shaw, whose "jealousy of Shakespeare always reminds us of a rooster, which struts out and crows lustily after a gobbler, lord of the barnyard, has passed out of sight" (Jan. 28, 1909). An avid reader of magazines of all kinds, he provided ample reviews of their contents, and laughing criticism of their silly romantic stories and "arty" pictures. An iconoclast himself, he was disturbed at those who were taking the myths of Parson Weems, his lives of Washington and Francis Marion, for example, and saying they were untrue. He preferred to "cling to the boyish notion that Weems was quite a writer, whether he wrote romance or biography" (May 17, 1909). And when the Bacon-Shakespeare controversy began to stir up his readers he enlisted himself immediately on the side of Shakespeare. For Shakespeare was of the common people, a self-made man who had become great.

5

LAST YEARS ON *THE GLOBE*

Editor and Father

Over the years revealing little messages appeared in the columns of *The Atchison Globe,* references to family life, to the problems of being father and husband. They tell, sometimes openly, more often obliquely, what life was like for Edgar Watson Howe as he entered the late years on his newspaper. They tell more, perhaps, than the little he reveals in *Plain People* or the combination of myth and truth that characterizes what is known about the Howe family.

He wrote, for example, about the "growing science of raising children," one of the "frauds" he deplored: he thought "The ordinary catch-as-catch-can children are always the best" (July 2, 1895). (His children were scarcely catch-as-catch-can.) He wrote about the woes of being a boy, about a boy and the constant and oppressive use of the word "don't":

"He hears it from his father, his mother and his sisters from the time he comes to breakfast with an unwashed face to the moment he falls asleep at night with dirty feet. When he is grown he hears it, and when he marries he finds it is his wife's watchword. 'Nagged to death' wouldn't be a pretty phrase to put on a tombstone, but in a distressing number of cases, it would be appropriate" (Apr. 4, 1892).

As he watched his own sons grow up, and observed them and their friends, he recorded his observations on the editorial page:

"Notes about boys: A boy only washes the front of his face. . . . All boys like to see things killed. . . . No boy likes to have a man come to see his sister. . . . A boy would rather hunt than eat pie. . . . When he is telling his hunting experience, he can be heard a block away. . . . Every boy 'talks about' his school teacher. . . . There is nothing that a boy will resent quicker than the charge that he washes dishes. . . . A boy is quick to fight his sister because he knows he won't get licked. . . . When there is excitement, a boy is always in a great hurry to arrive on the scene, for fear something will happen that he won't see" (Feb. 13, 1893).

Daughters called for comment, too, and the problems of the president were like the problems of a country editor:

> President and Mrs. Roosevelt went to great pains fixing up a room for Alice Roosevelt, while she was away last summer. "It is a nightmare in yellow and blue," she says of the wall paper, refuses to sleep in the room, and Papa Roosevelt has given orders to have it repapered in red. When it comes to picking out anything for a princess, every father, whether a hod carrier or president, should remember that he hasn't any better idea of Beauty and Art than an Indian. [Dec. 15, 1902]
>
> Some time ago Daughter fixed up an Indian corner, and the Indian craze stalked through the entire house. Later it was the Dutch craze, and queer figures in wooden shoes began to appear on everything from sofa cushions to plates. Now Daughter has struck a new gait; it is the Egyptian fad. This is worst of all. The Indian and the Dutch girl were preferable to the figure built like a triangle. [Nov. 19, 1904]

And popular sentiment of the day reminded Ed Howe of what life was like for the husbands of the world: "Some one once wrote a sentimental song about the 'light in the window for me,' and ever since that time the 'light in the window' has figured in poetry and song to a great extent, and in a more sentimental manner, than it is entitled to. The cold truth is that when there is a light in the window, it means some one is sitting up to give the last one to come home a scolding, or advice about the good sense of going to bed earlier. A light in the window is something that a nagged person never fails to see, and when his eyes first see it in turning a corner he gets a cold chill and longs for a home in a boarding house" (Dec. 24, 1898).

Ed Howe thought he could escape the problems of being father and husband. He apparently believed, one of his good friends thought, that an author should be on the eccentric side, or at least that an author should escape the pressures of home life. Beside his big red brick home he had built a tiny house, consisting of one room, that contained a couch, chair, table, and stove.

"Here he thought genius would adopt him for its own and that all his future efforts would be crowned with popularity," a friend wrote. "It is generally believed that his recent literary failures were written there." But soon he returned to his library to do his work.[1]

His wife comes through in his writings and family reminiscences as a shadowy figure only, the reader treated mainly to impressions of bitterness and tears and quarrels, though never described specifically. Of his sons the favorite was Gene. Jim tried for his father's favor but couldn't get it; he once told a friend that he would work at *The Globe* day after day without his father saying even hello.[2] Though Gene was favored, his own testimony was that life with father could be pretty grim, that Mrs. Howe was a woman who "never spoke a harsh or unkind word to anyone." The children saw Ed Howe in terrific rages, and all of them grew to be frightened of him. Gene's recollections, colored though they are, provide perhaps the best insights into the home life of the Howes in the 1890s:

> I can remember approaching him in the evenings or mornings timidly, furtively, as a rabbit ventures from the weeds into the open road in the evening, to find out whether he was in one of his black moods or was in good humor.
>
> Father was upbraiding mother most of the time. She was often crying openly or trying to hide tears from the children, and he was spending more and more of his time away from home. When she was not outright displeasing him or arousing his wrath, she was "getting on his nerves." No spirited woman could have lived with him as his wife; his demands were so exacting, his whims so impossible to anticipate.[3]

The editor carried his ideas about religion into the home. He opposed his children's attending church services, and this led to a clash between husband and wife, for Mrs. Howe was a Methodist who wanted her children to be brought up in a church. In late life, Gene wrote that he *thought* he had been baptized, but that he was not sure. Jim also offers a memory of family life from the vantage point of many years:

> Well along in the twilight zone and as the shadows deepen, I have but one recollection of anything I ever did having father's approval.
>
> This concerned my Sunday school record. And it was a

> record. In Atchison, though long forgotten, the record probably still stands.
>
> Mother used to escort me to the front door of the church Sunday school class and, I suppose, probably with pride, watch me enter. But what she did not see was my exit a few minutes later through the back door.
>
> Of course the neighborhood talked of this. And eventually my hookey playing from Sunday school came up at home.
>
> Father uttered not a word of approval or disapproval. But from his facial expression (probably with atheistic satisfaction) I took it for granted that he was pleased.[4]

Jim, the oldest of the children, had ambitions and ideas of his own; he wanted to be a doctor but his father refused to send him to college: "Jim was to be a newspaperman and any suggestion otherwise was an insult." Gene learned never to ask his father for things; that attitude helped make him the favorite. When the boy was ten or twelve (Gene's vagueness in his recollections resembled that of his father) he and his father moved into a cottage in the yard, a six-room building, the rest of the family staying in the big house, for Ed Howe was not talking to his wife.

"This was a town sensation, naturally, and my life for a few years was bewildering. Neighbor women, some of them, accused me of abandoning the others by living with father. Mother herself was hurt and tearful. The big house, where I visited every day, of course, was a place of sorrow and despair. Father was having his terrific black moods. Other children were repeating terrible tales to me on my father which weren't true, and the newspaper was being boycotted, and father was being threatened."

The black moods must have been frequent, and they always brought on Ed Howe's most violent attacks on religion and women. Howe would "begin to react to the favorite attention he was attracting because of the excellence of his newspaper, and he would enter a period of exhilaration," Gene recalled. Up and down, then, would go his moods. His son calculated that his father was depressed eighty per cent of the time, and that when he was home his downtown politeness disappeared.

"And then would come one of his periods of exaltation. I do not know what else to call it. His joy of living would embrace everyone close to him. Happy days were back, life was grand and wonderful. He would come into my bedroom in the morning and awaken me by jumping into bed with me. He'd take me swimming out at Deer Creek. The two of us would drive out there together and we'd swim in a swimming hole. He'd take me down to the office evenings and teach me how to set type; he wanted me to be a 'swift,' as he was rated when he worked on Brigham Young's newspapers. He was lavish, rather than generous with me, at these times."

But the respites were brief, and soon he would be back tossing in his bed at night, and the boy would tiptoe around for fear of angering his temperamental father. Another of Gene's recollections was even more revealing of the moods and attitudes of Ed Howe:

> I remember a high spot of my youth when I was about twelve years of age. He said I was engaged in too much duck hunting; he said he realized how much I enjoyed it, but he believed it was having a bad influence on me. So he offered me $500 cash to stop. And I took it. That was a fortune to me in those days.
>
> It wasn't two weeks later until he saw me standing on a corner overlooking the Missouri River. A norther was blowing and ducks in great droves were streaming down the river. I was standing there big-eyed, looking at them and bleeding inside.
>
> Father slipped up on me before I knew it.
>
> "How are you feeling?" he asked.
>
> I gulped out that I was feeling all right.
>
> "No, you're not," he said, as he laughed out loud. "You want to go hunting, don't you?"
>
> "Yes," I replied.
>
> "Well," he said, "go on up home and get your dog and gun and drive down to Sugar Lake, and don't be in a hurry coming home."
>
> I got to keep the $500, and I kept on with my hunting.[5]

One of Gene Howe's boyhood friends was Ray Holland, who became editor of *Field and Stream* magazine, and he too remembered what Howe was like. He knew the entire family, and he regarded the father with awe. He was a carrier for *The Globe,* one of the few that the great man recognized. "All the carriers would be grouped inside *The Globe* office waiting for our papers and Mr. Howe would walk past. He'd look at me and nod slightly and grunt. I rated that distinction because I was one of Gene's friends." Ed Howe apparently believed that Ray was a bad influence on Gene, because he, like Gene, liked to hunt too much. Gene would tell his father about Ray's hunting success and a story about it would appear in the newspaper, and that didn't seem to the boy to be very good publicity.

> An item saying Ray Holland killed 19 quail northwest of town would be read by farmers on whose land I had hunted and that was bad. If my farmer friends thought I killed too many quail I might find myself unwelcome on certain farms.
>
> One day I met Mr. Howe on the street and asked him not to print such items, explaining the possible reactions. "Most people like to see their names in the paper," he growled. "If you don't want your name in *The Globe,* you won't have to worry about it from now on." For a while after that it would have been necessary for me to shoot somebody on Commercial street if I wanted my name in the paper. I have always thought that had something to do with his feeling that I was leading Gene astray when we went duck shooting together. [Oct. 19, 1952]

Jim Howe's life was that of a boy who worked, with little parental encouragement or friendship, in the printing office. As a man he too looked back to boyhood days in Atchison, of roaming with his friends, stealing grapes and watermelons (as a grown man, living in California with a vineyard of his own, he had to contend with boys raiding *his* plants, and Ed Howe told him: "Serves you right. It's retribution for all those raids you made at St. Benedict's college!"). Jim would watch until the grapes were ripe at the college, which was not far from the family home, and then make his move, or he would go into the Missouri Valley countryside to find the patches of ripe watermelons. His special friends were the nearby Negro boys of Atchison. When he grew older he would hop the Missouri Pacific and take a ride to Omaha, twelve hours away. Or he would think about joining "Harry Ward's Magnificent Minstrels," a plan that did not meet with his father's approval, especially when Jim and a friend, a brother of Harry Ward, went as far as Henderson, Kentucky, and had to be brought home on railroad transportation money provided by Ed Howe.

Anecdotes, for the most part, provide details of the last years of Ed Howe's marriage and the break-up of the family. Gene Howe accounted for the divorce in his descriptions of his father's mysterious and volatile temperament. Others suggest that it was Ed Howe's talent, if not his genius, that made him a difficult man to live with. The marriage seemed doomed, and divorce finally came in 1901, probably as a relief for all parties, especially the children. *The Globe* itself reported that the divorce petition had been filed, by B. P. Waggener, attorney. The date was June 1; the hearing was the following day. Witnesses were listed as James P. Howe and Miss Anna Nicklaus.

"The petition alleged abandonment, charging that the defendant had not lived with the plaintiff for over two years. It recites that they were married in Falls City in 1874; that the plaintiff has always conducted herself as a dutiful and affectionate wife, and that the defendant abandoned her without cause. It was estimated in the petition that the defendant was worth in excess of $25,000. By the terms of the decree, Mrs. Howe is to receive $15,000 alimony, to be paid in monthly instalments of not less than $100 until the obligation is charged."[6]

The editor made little reference to either marriage or divorce in the next several years, but when *Plain People* appeared in the 1920s he finally wrote in some detail about his marriage and its aftermath:

> The world has decided a gentleman may not tell his side of a controversy with a lady, and as my former wife was that, I shall observe the conventions. Perhaps I will be excused for saying our friends generally agree that our divorce was a success, if such a thing is possible. There was no scandal, and separation resulted in no disturbance in the life of either party, except to improve it. Divorce was granted on the application of my wife, abandonment being charged, which was true to the extent that I lived in the house in the yard now occupied by my brother Bruce.
>
> We mutually agreed on an amount I should pay, and this contract was performed punctually. When these payments were met, and there was no longer legal obligation, without suggestion from anyone I continued the payments, and do to this day. My relations with my father-in-law continued so cordial after the divorce that it was publicly remarked by Kansas newspapers.
>
> I have always been able to get along with women rather well, except as a husband; I do not believe I have much genius in that direction. No one has heard me say I would have been an ideal husband differently situated, and I have never had a desire to try the experiment a second time. I enjoy home and children as much as anyone, but unless wife and husband are well suited to each other, there are difficulties in marriage I have found greater than in any other phase of life. Possible

> divorce causes me my greatest regret, but I have no doubt it was best for both of us. Being married, in many of its phases, is almost as mean and necessary an experience as being born, dying, correcting children, eating food and getting rid of it. I have been husband, son and father, and sometimes think I have had most reason to blush as a husband.
>
> I have been accused of being "a woman hater"; of making too light of women, sentiment, spirituality. The truth is, I think too much of all these. I am actually the most sentimental of men; the grand gallantry which has distinguished the world has impressed me: I believe a lot of the compliments, in spite of my knowledge that the world does not mean half of them. I have assisted in building a false story, and almost believed it.
>
> If the world would pardon complete candor, I might write a book of some benefit to it: not because I am wise, but because I have made so many mistakes I am willing to acknowledge. In writing these memoirs I am frequently confronted with the necessity of cutting out what should go in, if an old man's book is to be of any real value. . . .
>
> I have a tremendous awe of a marriage ceremony. Now that I am not a married man, I find myself trying to be a good husband. Nothing would induce me to distress my former wife. Although we have not seen each other, or had any communication whatever in more than a quarter of a century, our relations have been genteel. If I should learn that she wished a certain thing done, I should do it, if within my power; and am certain she would do as much for me. We are actually two fairly worthy old people who should not have married each other, but who have a good deal of respect for an old union now that it has been dissolved. If there was bitterness on both sides when we were man and wife, it has entirely disappeared: in its place has appeared a kindness more like ourselves before we knew each other.[7]

After the divorce, Clara Howe went to Emmett, Idaho, with Jim and Mateel, where Jim had gone shortly before to buy a newspaper. Howe and Gene moved back into the big house, and Gene worked for his father on *The Globe,* setting type and selling advertisements and paid locals. One week he went with friends on a steamer excursion down the river to Leavenworth. Gene got drunk, passed out, and was left behind. And there followed a characteristic action from Ed Howe, consisting of a short story he wrote and published in *The Globe:* "Three Atchison young men disgraced themselves in Leavenworth Saturday. The publisher's son was the drunkest of the bunch."[8]

After a short time Gene, too, was off to Idaho, where he worked for Jim for a short time, and then on newspapers in Oregon, including Harvey Scott's celebrated *Oregonian.* At twenty-one he returned to Atchison to work again for his father.

The picture of Ed Howe that emerges is largely that of a cruel and unreasoning father. Yet he had many moments of understanding, and he was especially proud of what his boy Jim—the usually misunderstood Jim—was doing in the West:

"If you move to another town, don't talk about the town you came from. The people in your new home will not like it. They are apt to think, 'If you like that town so well, why don't you go back there?'

"There is a remarkable paper printed at Emmett, Idaho. Its editors and publishers are three mighty fine young people from Atchison, Kansas. But the word 'Atchison' has never appeared in their columns, and we think it's a smart trick, even if we did advise that course" (May 6, 1904).

Teacher and Leader in Atchison

An editor, unfortunately for him, must be a bit saner than most of his readers. When he defaults in leadership his community suffers. When he expresses foolish or dangerous sentiments, especially if he is a man of known influence, his opinion-making can be harmful, and even criminal.

Edgar Watson Howe, unhappily, was too erratic to be depended upon for sound editorial guidance at all times. Yet frequently he gave good instruction to his little city. In his late years with *The Globe* he seemed to spend much time scanning other newspapers, reading dispatches from the telegraph, and voicing his opinions on what was happening in the world. His views represent almost a cataloguing of the American experience early in the twentieth century.

He and his newspaper had emerged victorious from the election campaign of 1896; Atchison had been kept safe from free silver and Bryan. But soon there was wild talk about war, and Ed Howe was realizing as early as 1896 that the manifest destiny gang and the disciples of Admiral Mahan's seapower theories were a force to be dealt with. A carefully detailed editorial expressed his feelings about the imperialist impetus:

> Americans have an exaggerated idea of their own importance: they do not realize that their country is not the world. Suppose war should be declared between America and Spain, and suppose that all the powerful monarchies should be drawn into it, on the side of Spain. The war-ships of the allied powers would sweep our great coast cities off the face of the earth, and absolutely destroy our commerce, for compared with the navies of the great powers, our navy is about as effective as would be a pop-gun compared to a Winchester repeating rifle. Our preparations for war would saddle billions of additional debt upon the country, to say nothing of the murder of the flower of our young men, and the sorrow, and commercial disaster. And what would be the cause of all the trouble? Falsehoods, manufactured by irresponsible adventurers: Jingoism indulged in by a lot of men who have more respect for wrong than right. Uncle Sam has been swaggering a good deal of late, and foreigners are in bad humor. Uncle Sam has been daring England to fight, over the Venezuelan question; he has been brow-beating Turkey, and just now his friends are holding him to keep him off of Spain. Germany is not in very good humor on the Uncle Sam question, either, and some of these days, if we are not more careful, we will be compelled to carry our distinguished relative home on a stretcher. [Dec. 21, 1896]

To Ed Howe's credit he was never stampeded into an enthusiasm for doing battle with Spain. The extravagant newspaper accounts of the supposed mistreatment of Evangelina Cisneros, which were ballooned into prominence in Hearst's *New York Journal,* were, as far as Howe was concerned, merely a sharp publicity stunt, and he anticipated that Miss Cisneros could go on the road and pick up as many followers as Mary Elizabeth Lease. Long before the episode of the battleship *Maine* he had guessed the role that was being played by Hearst, who was rumored in late 1897 to be planning an expedition to Cuba. Howe would have had Hearst arrested, that editor who was "willing to do anything to become notorious" (Dec. 6, 1897). War talk was dominating some of the nation's biggest newspapers; Howe's *Globe* carried a cautious overline: "Americans Believe That All They Have to Do Is to Declare War, and the Other Fellow is Licked" (Feb. 15, 1898). On the day of the explosion of the *Maine* an overline read: "A Fierce American Battleship Which Went to Cuba to Terrify the Spaniards, Blew Up and Killed 270 Yankees" (Feb. 16, 1898). In accompanying editorial comment Howe strove to keep himself and his readers from shouting at the tops of their voices:

> Accidents happen to warships regularly. They are so intricate and expensive as to be dangerous. They are not seaworthy. The modern battleship is a terrible fighting machine, but it is not safe at sea, or anywhere else, judging from the explosion on the *Maine* in Havana harbor.
>
> ———
>
> This morning, when it was thought that the *Maine* had been blown up by the Spanish, there was a strong war feeling on the streets. But there is no doubt that the accident was due to American carelessness. It is a pity that the warship was not blown up by a Spaniard, since it was blown up: war would be more comfortable than the thought of the terrible loss of life as a result of carelessness. [Feb. 16, 1898]

Thus the mood of *The Globe* in early '98. "The Destruction of the 'Maine' at Havana, Was Due to American Carelessness, Not to Spanish Treachery," the paper declared. Howe had never fallen into the Cuban propaganda trap; he never believed the Spanish blew up the *Maine;* he was fully aware of what Hearst and Joseph Pulitzer were doing.

Perhaps it would be best, he thought, to laugh at the whole unfortunate mess: "The very latest war rumor is that a huge Spanish battleship, believed to be the *Carmelita,* arrived at a point three miles below town at four o'clock this afternoon, and that it will shell the city at daylight from a point near the brick yards. The member of the local militia company who is devil at this office, informed a reporter that so far as he knows, he has not been called out. How does it come that the lives of Atchison people are thus menaced by the Spanish, and no American battleship in sight to protect us? Is this the best old McKinley can do?" (Feb. 21, 1898).

There must be no war with Spain: that was his platform. The jingo crowd had not reflected on the seriousness of war, the need to send an army to Cuba, to feed the starving, nurse the sick, furnish seed and implements. To stress his opinion Howe even did what the modern press would consider reprehensible: he injected editorial observations into news copy, inserting his opinion, in a telegraph story on the matter, that the *New York Journal,* "the most unreliable paper in New York," quite likely had faked the letter purportedly written by Spanish General Weyler to a friend in Havana (Mar. 17, 1898). Howe scolded the American people for their ridiculous behavior, their apparent unwillingness to learn the truth about Cuba, their acting like town gossips who insist on believing a choice item about a man and woman in trouble. He believed that the American people had been defrauded, that few newspapers had printed the truth about Cuba, that the Spanish side had not been heard at all, that a great majority of those stories printed about Cubans had been designed to push this country into a war with Spain, a war to help free Cuba.

Editorials and page one overlines continued to spell out *The Globe*'s opposition to war. When *The Globe* finally presented its headline that read "WAR DECLARED," Howe was mild in his accompanying editorial statement: "Something is wrong with either the gun boats or the artists. All the gun boats in the papers have their guns pointing toward heaven. Do they expect to find the Spanish there?" (Apr. 25, 1898).

It is also to Howe's credit that when war was declared he accepted the decision and put his newspaper behind the President and the nation: "And Quit Talking, and Enlist: A Recruiting Office Will Be Opened in Atchison Next Saturday, April 30." "Now that war cannot be avoided, the people generally are in favor of a vigorous campaign. The sooner Spain is humbled, the more respect other nations will have for us" (Apr. 26, 1898). Thus he changed the Cuba policies of *The Globe*.

In the summer of 1898 most of the attention of *The Globe* was focused on Cuba and the Far East. Admiral Dewey's naval victory at Manila made a new war hero for the nation, and Howe offered early speculations on the likely politics of the gentleman. He commented on the high enthusiasm in Atchison when the story arrived from Manila, and in most respects he proved that *The Globe* had become an all-round newspaper—maps and diagrams, sketches of the Philippines, pages of stories about Cuba, descriptions of relations that had existed between Spain and the United States, even a page of war songs, with words and music. The paper was light on comment for a few months, and heavy on news, with some shifting to exposure type stories about the Spanish (a predictable, though not commendable, action for a newspaper to take in time of war). For Spain was becoming now somewhat of a villain in the eyes of Ed Howe, who temporarily had shifted his attention away from William Randolph Hearst.

During the war the suddenly chauvinistic newspaper had carried a drawing of an American flag on the editorial page; the flag disappeared with victory late in the summer. And Ed Howe was free to get back to the theme of anti-war and anti-imperialism that so characterized his paper's policies in late century.

In opposing the Spanish-American War and the decade of expansion that followed, Ed Howe was out of step with the leadership of the Republican party, which he normally preferred. Expansion was our duty, even our Christian duty, said party chieftains. It was a notion that some intellectuals were drawing from the theories of Darwin, and business prosperity, national prestige and enlightenment for the downtrodden became part of the imperialistic mood. The Atchison editor, for a change, was more in tune with the Democrats, who remained anti-expansionist through much of the period of expansion. He saw as little sense in our impending actions in the Philippines as he had seen in fighting over Cuba, though he was able to see some humor in the situation:

"The only redeeming feature in assuming the responsibility of providing for the Filipinos is that they don't wear much, and their dry goods bill would not be considerable" (Dec. 14, 1898).

"We wonder that some babies are not named Aguinaldo. They are yelling kickers like him, rebel against every order, and though they are very young, try to run things. Aguinaldo would be a very appropriate name for a boy baby" (Sept. 16, 1898).

He could not believe that America's true leaders—in business or politics—could favor expansion. He foresaw that the Republicans would have to relinquish the issue, as it had been relinquished by labor. Howe was becoming troubled that William Jennings Bryan was on his side, but he was forced to accept this as one of the unfortunate circumstances of life.

His interest in, and enthusiasm for, Admiral Dewey weakened as the postwar years proceeded. Please refrain from opening your mouth, he suggested to the great hero. We know you are an expansionist man; after all, you are navy. But there are many who cannot agree with you. And even though Howe opposed imperialism he thought his country should crush that despicable fellow Aguinaldo, drive "his ragged vagrants" into the sea, and settle the Philippine question. He was sure that no one really wanted to stay in the Philippines any longer than necessary: the whole venture was consuming taxpayers' money and taking American lives. He also was having editorial fun with a Kansan, Brigadier General Frederick Funston, who had become a celebrity through his capture of Aguinaldo. Some papers were booming Funston for high office (all eighty-five pounds of him, as Howe would put it); he was surprised that Funston would consider being a mere congressman when he might have a future in the White House.

He continued sounding off on American interference in faraway lands. War hero Dewey had become—of all things—a ridiculous Democrat, with a busybody wife in the background. Fred Funston, unlikely hero as he might be, was giving Kansans a relief from the antics of Carry Nation. The war in the Philippines continued to be the silliest war in history, one caused by politicians and yellow newspapers. Cuba was turning out to be just as expensive as he had predicted, and Howe was suggesting that America adopt the platform of *The Globe* with reference to Cuba and the Philippines: "Let go and run." He would be glad to sell the Philippines, and throw in Cuba, the Hawaiian islands and Puerto Rico.

Here, then, was that almost stereotyped Midwestern isolationism in the columns of *The Atchison Globe.* For coupled with the sanity Ed Howe expressed over the Spanish-American War and American involvement in the Far East and the Caribbean was an attitude that some regard as being typically Kansan, an insularity born in part out of the decided inferiority complex that many residents of the centrally located state of Kansas still demonstrate on occasion. Howe preferred to see Kansans—and all Americans—stay home. "We Don't Care Anything About Alaska: The Sight of a Kansas Wheat Field Is Enough Gold for Us" (July 20, 1897).

Foreign affairs interested him because they were news, but for that reason only. As *The Globe* carried stories about Cuba it also offered opinions about the controversial Dreyfus case in France, with the editor at first anti-Dreyfus and then wholeheartedly on the side of the wronged captain. "Other people's wars" drew as little sympathy from the editor of *The Globe* as wars fought by Americans. World developments, however, could alter his view somewhat. Though he admired the bravery of the Boers of South Africa he could not comprehend their ignorance in believing they could whip the mighty British. As for the British, they had suffered indignities from the Boers, so they had a case in making war. There was no real reason for any war, for the world had progressed past the time "when men did not know any better than to hack each other with battle axes" (June 3, 1902). Ed Howe also anticipated much bloodshed when war threatened in China, a war being fought over a missionary, of all people. He was perplexed about the Boxer rebellion: the Boxers had attacked both a Catholic mission and a Methodist Bible house. What did the Boxers want? What was this "yellow peril" newspapers were talking about? Could it be "the stuff called salad dressing, which the women insist upon smearing upon every thing on the table"?

The home scene remained dearer to *The Globe* than those exotic foreign places where outsiders were causing trouble with the rightful possessors of a piece of land. From his newspaper office the aging (in his opinion) editor could watch what was developing in the election campaign of 1900. He had forecast in 1898 that Bryan would never again be the Democratic candidate (perhaps the candidate of the Populists or Greenbackers, as another John St. John, but never of a respectable party—even the Democrats). And as the Democratic national convention at Kansas City drew nearer he issued warnings against attending such things; he would send a man who would "enjoy the hurrah, and the crowd, and the robbery" (Mar. 3, 1900). He was cheered when Bryan, the Democratic nominee despite everything, dropped the old song of sixteen-to-one, and he tended to favor the criticisms Bryan made in his acceptance speech as he denounced Republican imperialism. But Bryan's subsequent campaign, in which he called for arbitration for labor, shorter hours, and breaking up of the Republicans' "industrial despotism," angered him.

He would comment on how Bryan had come to dominate the Democratic party, and how statesmen were going to Bryan to give obeisance, all this for a man who was as statesmanlike as John P. Altgeld or General Jake Coxey. And as the election approached he would issue another dogma from *The Globe* office: Bryan may be a candidate four years from now, but not for the Democrats; surely the Democrats would not nominate this "disturbing element in politics" again.

William McKinley was another matter. From the day McKinley had entered the White House (except for the President's unfortunate yielding on the Cuban question) Ed Howe had admired him, and had praised "Mother McKinley," too, a fine woman who knew her place. McKinley was of course a sure thing for the 1900 nomination; it seemed a pity, in a way, that the Republicans could not nominate the brash young Theodore Roosevelt for President, because he was so much like Bryan that he might cancel out some of the appeal of the Boy Orator. It was Roosevelt who was attracting attention as the Republicans met at Philadelphia, but this man was too much of a fuzzy liberal for the conservative Howe. Yet Roosevelt was nominated for Vice President.

Many things troubled Howe about the Rough Rider. Roosevelt was a "fighter for the Lord" who had stopped in Chicago on his western swing to go to the Dutch Reformed Church. (Howe disliked all politicians who worked the church, as he phrased it, in trying to obtain office.) Roosevelt talked too much; he bragged about the Battle of San Juan Hill, where he had become a national hero, where he had "turned the retreating negro soldiers back with his revolver." Roosevelt actually had very little to do with the battle, said Howe, but Republicans should take heart: "Teddy is not the whole cheese; . . . he is more or less of an accident" (Aug. 31, 1900). The Republican campaigners were leaning heavily upon the recent war, Howe thought, and he was disgusted on hearing that the Republican National Committee had been behind a story that Spaniards and Cubans in New York had tried to assassinate McKinley. "It is as weak an invention as the story of an actress losing her diamonds. . . . What colossal asses the politicians seem to think the people are!" (July 11, 1900). The election results were a foregone conclusion; America was riding too high to turn out the successful McKinley.

It was slow between elections on *The Globe*'s editorial page, despite the constant protestations of the editor that he and his newspaper were non-political. But Ed Howe could always beat the dead horse of Populism: "A Populist is a man who declares that industry is discreditable; that thrift is a crime, and respectability suspicious" (Nov. 8, 1900). He could hit at Bryan, a perennial target: ". . . he will never again be taken seriously by the Democrats, or by any respectable proportion of the people." He could laugh at the receipt of photographs from Washington showing the McKinley inauguration: "Nothing makes our heart so swell with patriotic pride as a dim looking picture of a lot of umbrellas in the rain" (Mar. 13, 1901). He had much more to write about in 1901, for the President went to the great Pan-American Exposition at Buffalo and was shot down by Leon Czolgosz. Editorial comment in *The Globe* consisted first of words from the *Kansas City Times* and praise from Howe for the President's behaving like a true soldier after he had been wounded, and then came dozens of short, crisp editorials in the by then familiar style of Ed Howe:

> History Grows More Difficult to Learn: Booth Was Easy; Guiteau Harder, But Who Can Remember Czolgosz? [Sept. 9, 1901]
>
> Shollgosh, the man who attempted to assassinate the President, occupies comfortable quarters, gets three meals a day, and will be allowed a lawyer to defend him. Aren't the Americans too good to criminals? [Sept. 10, 1901]
>
> The Rough Riders will now make the sudden discovery that their place is in office instead of in the saddle. [Sept. 14, 1901]
>
> Emma Goldman Isn't as Guilty in Inspiring the Assassin of McKinley as W. R. Hearst, of the N. Y. Journal.
>
> Didn't Tom Platt play a rather severe practical joke on himself when he "shelved Roosevelt" last summer at Philadelphia? Roosevelt is now president.
>
> The people will learn to like President Roosevelt, but they loved President McKinley. There will always be this difference, no matter how long Roosevelt is in office. No man since Lincoln has been loved like McKinley. [Sept. 17, 1901]

This was American social history, written in editorial paragraphs, with both the sense and the sentiment of the times. Ed Howe was convinced that William Randolph Hearst's newspaper utterances had played a part in the assassination; he was just as sure that Carry Nation of Kansas was at her most shameful when, during the period between the shooting and the death of the President, she had said: "Bill McKinley deserves to die. He is the friend of the brewer and the drinking man" (Sept. 18, 1901). He was disgusted at delays in the Czolgosz trial, but he predicted that Czolgosz would be "electrocuted some time before November 30, and in hell one minute later" (Sept. 20, 1901).

Came then a new age in American politics, and Ed Howe was

unready for it, even though Theodore Roosevelt provided him amusement and inspired occasional admiration. He laughed at the Roosevelts' going to two churches on Sunday, T. R. to the Grace Reformed Church and his wife to the Episcopal, and recommended that the patronage of the six children should be divided, to "make the church vote more solid" (Oct. 4, 1901). He did not like the way William Allen White, his fellow Kansan, was becoming a Washington politician, "the solid Kansas man with the Roosevelt administration" (Oct. 11, 1901).

The first Roosevelt message was a shock to Howe, even though he had not expected too much from the new man in the White House. It seemed a call for everything the *New York Journal* wanted—a larger navy, a Nicaraguan canal, no changes in the pension department, visionary irrigation schemes in the West, no changes in the tariff laws. Roosevelt sounded like a wastrel, a spendthrift. Ed Howe was sure that Roosevelt was unpopular—with the people, the politicians, everybody but the Rough Riders.

In the fall of 1902 there was much talk about the pending visit of Roosevelt to Kansas, but Howe was relieved—he wrote—to hear that the President had bruised his left leg, that an abscess had developed, and that the trip would have to be canceled. This brought Roosevelt a scolding from Atchison, because if Roosevelt had not been "gadding" about he would not have been injured. McKinley had been assassinated while "gadding"; before that he had been wandering around in California while his wife was dangerously ill. Hayes had been a "gadder," and so had Cleveland, and Presidents should stay home and keep their health. Recovery soon came for Roosevelt, and Ed Howe had something new to write about:

> The president put his leg on a pillow, and rode forth this morning to see several thousand old, and bent, and diseased, and worn out old soldiers march by. When they remembered what they had endured during the Civil war, how that leg must have appealed to them! Wrapped in its pathetic folds of white linen, lying gracefully upon a downy pillow, and with a half dozen anxious surgeons near by, how touchingly it must have reminded them of the legs and arms they lost on the battle field, with no one to help, or care if they lived or died.
>
> Three cheers for the president's leg! Long may it wave when it brings hearts to hearts in such tender communion as

upon the occasion of the G.A.R. review in Washington this morning. [Oct. 8, 1902]

In 1903 the President was able to make a tour after all. Topeka, that trouble-making town, was listed as one of his stopping places, and the capital city of Kansas was rocked by a controversy over whether the governor or the YMCA would entertain the President, a row "worse than [that] between Mrs. Nation and the Rum Fiends" (Mar. 27, 1903). All the more reason, then, for this busybody President to stay home. In the little Kansas town of Sharon Springs the President was to be the subject of another dispute, for there were three churches in the town and there was competition among them to see which Roosevelt would attend. There was also word that the President would attend about a dozen commencement exercises while on tour: Ed Howe was sure that "the people are omitting nothing that will make the trip a delightful one" (May 14, 1903). And the editor offered a typically small-town touch in commenting on a special family problem facing the President: "Some one who has kept a diary finds that Alice Roosevelt has had some social engagement every day and evening since they moved into the White House, and that her collapse is a result. The president may know how to run the country, but his daughter goes at a pace that would startle even Emporia" (May 25, 1903).

Like other Kansas editors since his time Ed Howe could always be counted upon to return to the Republican fold every fourth year, no matter where he had been in the preceding three (he had usually been with the Republicans, sniping away at them, of course). To Howe, Roosevelt was no McKinley, but he was much better than a Bryan—or a Hearst. Hearst was the No. 1 villain, as he had been for *The Globe* since the days of the Spanish-American War, and Howe feared—or appeared to fear—that the Democrats might take the Hearst candidacy seriously in the election of 1904.

"It is not at all improbable that he will be the next president of the United States, and that we will be punished by seeing pictures of Mrs. Hearst, and pictures of her children: Algie, Waldace, Henrietta, Mayme, and Lorna. We will hear what a great statesman William Randolph Hearst is, and read stories of how he longed for learning in his youth, and studied good books until late at night, in the attic, although the facts are he was the son of a nabob, and wouldn't accept the education that was offered him.

"Hurrah for Hearst!" (Nov. 13, 1902).

For a change William Jennings Bryan was out of the calculations of either the Democrats or Ed Howe. But Howe was still disgusted that Bryan's voice had been so loud at the St. Louis convention and that the Democrats had spent so much time vilifying their own nation ("In 1896 it was about to be crucified on a cross of gold to gratify the malevolent aspirations of England. . . . This year it contents itself with denouncing the president as a usurper"). But their candidate was such a nobody that the Republicans could not help winning (July 11, 1904). Overnight Roosevelt had become, to Howe, a more admirable man ("vigorous, pushing, creditable . . . with ideas, and courage to enforce them"), running against poor old Alton Parker, a man nominated only for the reasons that he was from New York and had no notions that would offend anyone (July 13, 1904). It was a campaign of incredible dullness, and Ed Howe announced in November, "We are to have four years more of Kermit, Quentin, Theodore and Archibald" (Nov. 9, 1904).

The Roosevelt years were relatively placid ones, and perhaps they needed such a flamboyant President. Those were the years in which Roosevelt distinguished himself for his part in one of those foreign wars that the anti-imperialistic Ed Howe so disliked, for war had broken out between the mighty Russians and the insignificant Japanese, and Howe wanted to know what the war was all about. It was another silly war, and on top of that it was being ridiculously reported. Howe refused to treat the story of the capture of the Russian cruiser *Variag* by the Japanese as other editors were doing; he kept seeing pictures of the cruiser and realized that some of the pictures showed a vessel with two smoke stacks and some with four. The New York papers, brighter than most, were carrying front end views, with no way of counting the stacks. There also were all kinds of "official" accounts of the Japanese blockade of the entrance to the harbor at Port Arthur, accounts from Berlin, Paris, London, Port Arthur, Vladivostok, Chemulpo, and Kalamazoo. Only one "official" report to a story, *The Globe* ruled. Nor could *The Globe* offer interpretative enlightenment about the war, for the town of Atchison had no Chinese laundrymen to be interviewed. Howe blamed the Associated Press, in part, for "The most worthless rot ever printed in American newspapers," and he said he was losing hair, pulling it out in his rage over the war news his poor newspaper had to print (May 25, 1904). His forecast of the Japanese future, after the Russians had been defeated, must have seemed pretty silly to some readers, but to others it was probably both prescient and frightening. It pointed to comments he would make on his trip to the Orient a few months later:

> There is something in the Yellow Peril. The Japanese, flushed with their success in whipping Russia, will become impudent, and we will have trouble with them in the Philippines, where we have no business.
>
> The Japs are powerful because they have plain common sense. The Japs pull together. However much they may wrangle among themselves, they are united when in public. They live simple lives, and are industrious. When they agree upon a policy, they accept it. When they elect a leader, they obey him.
>
> But in Yankeeland, as soon as a leader demonstrates unusual ability, a lot of crazy fools jump him, and invent stories about him. In Yankeeland, there is always a crowd to tear down. In Japan, men of unusual ability are honored, whereas in Yankeeland, they are maligned, and discouraged, and accused of crimes they did not commit. . . .
>
> If the Japanese keep their heads, and practice the principles they have practiced in the last half century, they will become the greatest nation on earth, for the reason that the people of other nations have gone crazy. . . .
>
> Have you not lately remarked the tendency toward simplicity? Japan is a wonderful nation because its entire people live the simple, temperate, useful, industrious life. [Apr. 29, 1905]

In early August of 1905 the peace conference to establish terms between the former enemies opened at Portsmouth, New Hampshire. Howe was cynical about prospects for success there, the town of Portsmouth being too cool, the hotel view too attractive, the delegates too well paid and well fed. He was dubious about Roosevelt's being able to make terms between Russia and Japan, but he felt the President stood a chance of becoming one of the great men of the world. Roosevelt was probably better at making such deals than at controlling his own household, Howe suggested; "Sakhalin is a trifle compared with the points of dispute between a woman and her step-daughter" (Sept. 2, 1905).

Peace was achieved, then, in this ridiculous war, but Howe could not trust the idealistic notions that true peace could be achieved in the world; look at all the minor wars of recent years. Efforts at The Hague to establish world peace amused him, such conferences being "as big a joke as the bloodhound: Turn a bloodhound loose and he will sniff around and then make a bee line for some innocent man's front door, and squat there in triumph" (June 17, 1907).

Reformers continued to annoy him, and his real battle with reformers was with the group that came to be called the Muckrakers. But not *all* the Muckrakers. There were good ones and there were bad ones. The worst was a woman named Ida M. Tarbell. His grievances against Miss Tarbell were several. She was attacking a man Ed Howe greatly admired, John D. Rockefeller. She was the daughter of an oil operator who had failed and she therefore hated Rockefeller, the very symbol of success in his time. She was writing the articles because Rockefeller had been able to obtain rebates from the railroads. She was writing because other "reformers" in the oil fields had failed. On and on the editor raved. And how viciously this woman wrote (just being a woman was bad enough): calling Rockefeller an "associate of horse thieves, and a disreputable character, generally. . . . In the interest of Reform, is it possible that a gentle, refined woman has been lying about an inoffensive, worthy old man?" (July 13, 1905).

Ida Tarbell was the worst; she was making her attacks upon reputable and successful businessmen. Thomas W. Lawson was almost as bad, a "rank humbug," writing his articles about high finances in a cheap fifteen-cent magazine. Such writers were exploiting the people and the institutions that had made America great. There was absolutely no reason to become panic-sticken about life insurance, despite what the magazine writers were saying. What was this crazy new passion for "Reform"?

So the reformers, Miss Tarbell and Lawson, were scoundrels. Lincoln Steffens was another matter; he was a *good* muckraker. And why? Because he was pointing to the evils of *government,* and he was placing the responsibility where it belonged, upon the *people.* Tom Lawson blamed the trusts; Steffens blamed the people. Steffens was right. Ed Howe greatly admired *The Shame of the Cities,* which ran concurrently with Miss Tarbell's series on the Standard Oil Company. Howe believed that the people could have honesty and economy in government if they demanded them of the politicians (and in this Howe's optimism surpassed—temporarily—that of Lincoln Steffens himself). When Theodore Roosevelt began to make war upon the Muckrakers he might have expected the old editor in Kansas to be an ally, but Howe, in his ambivalent attitude, continued to praise some reformers and revile others, including the President. He must have had some confused readers about that time.

What was wrong in muckraking, to Ed Howe, was the disposition to believe every man a thief, especially if that man were a business or industrial leader. This was socialism, a vile doctrine spreading far too rapidly throughout the country, one that said that when a man was not doing well that it was due not to his idleness or dissipation or lack of success but to the existence of industrious and temperate men. As the fame and popularity of Ida Tarbell began to wane, Ed Howe had another reformer to knock, a socialist named Upton Sinclair.

First Howe observed editorially that Sinclair had written a book about the packing industries in Chicago called *The Jungle*. Then he said Sinclair was "so prejudiced, and unfair, and untruthful, in the interest of Socialism that his book will not attract much attention." No one could believe the details Sinclair included; this kind of thing could only be false. "The packing houses are conducted with as much cleanliness as possible, and their food products are put up under the most perfect sanitary conditions. The statement that an occasional workman falls into the vats, and that his body is used in the manufacture of Pure Leaf Lard, is as revolting as it is silly and untruthful" (Apr. 26, 1906).

Sinclair was a handy new target, a wrong-headed man and a socialistic agitator on top of that, the son of a whiskey salesman and the grandson of a rebel soldier, a disturbing force trying to injure the livestock business of Ed Howe's part of America. But in making Sinclair an editorial page target Howe did not suppress the contrary evidence that began to pile up as investigations were made of the Sinclair charges, even though such evidence still did not convince Ed Howe. This "eastern Reformer" was weeping because no good, clean meat could be bought anywhere. Rubbish! "Every sane man knows that good meat may be had in every town in the United States. . . . How unfair to unnecessarily and unjustly abuse the great live stock interests of the country!" (July 14,

1906). Sinclair had no sincerity; he was out to make a record and he was out to make money. He had never been a worker, a productive man, one who gave jobs to others, and now he, an "adventurer and destroyer," was even receiving good notices from the President himself.

"Why don't one of the Reform magazines attack some of the follies of the Pee-pul?" Ed Howe asked. "The Pee-pul do many silly things, and a good jacking up would do them good" (Oct. 11, 1906). What could be in the mind of a fellow like Jack London, writing about his days as a tramp, complaining about a jail where he once spent time—the food, the work, the treatment of prisoners. London went "on the road" from choice, and why should he expect city prisons to be "modeled after Buckingham Palace, Delmonico's, or the Waldorf-Astoria" (July 29, 1907)? Here was another reformer, and this one made money at reform, through the literary route, and was able to cruise through the South Seas in a thirty-thousand-dollar yacht. "Human nature is a good deal the same, whether it claims to be a Socialist or an autocrat" (Aug. 26, 1908).

It was a time in which the kind of people Edgar Watson Howe had always disliked were living well and gaining the applause of the crowd: people who wanted to reform interstate commerce, and already had harmed businesses of respected men. Socialist bums like Sinclair and London. Prohibitionists, Carry Nation and worse, old harridans like the ladies of the WCTU who heard that President Roosevelt had been given sixty bottles of beer, and wanted to know whether this was so. "President Roosevelt has informed the W.C.T.U. that he sent back those sixty bottles of beer, and the W.C.T.U. declares he is a 'dear' " (Sept. 18, 1905). People like Judge Ben Lindsey, a starry-eyed idealist whose views were appearing in one of the muckraking magazines. Pure food and drug nuts like Dr. Harvey W. Wiley, who were giving trouble to health boards and business men and prowling through soda fountains and restaurants. "Everything is impure, here lately, according to the experts and cranks. Meanwhile, people are living longer than ever before" (Mar. 16, 1909). Or the ladies, sitting in their parlors in their study sessions, looking for new hell they could raise for decent citizens:

"The desire to Uplift the Sisterhood has many drawbacks and discouragements. Mrs. Lysander John Appleton recently conducted such a meeting. She spoke of the blind groping of her sisters for Higher Ideals, and the troubled questions that obtruded themselves upon their subconsciousness all through the day and night. 'I would like to hear from you,' she said; 'Perhaps in your yearning for a solution of the problems that confront you, I may be able to help you. Mrs. Boogs, tell us what is the Great Question of your life.' Mrs. Boogs rose pale and trembling: 'It is this,' she said; 'What shall I get for the next meal?' " (Jan. 1, 1910).

And though he could still have fun with reform, these were not good times for Howe and others like him throughout the country, and perhaps much of the trouble could be laid at the door of Teddy Roosevelt himself, a man whose reforming tendencies were coming to rival those of the Populists (though he was stopping short of the tariff, the one thing Ed Howe dearly wanted to reform). Or perhaps at the door of that forgotten man, Bryan. Howe was inconsistent in his views about Theodore Roosevelt (as he was about many people), one day commenting that the President's popularity was due to his honesty and understanding of the problems of the people, another day (in the same year) criticizing the President for making a demagogic appeal, for catering to popular opinions, for telling the masses that "when an employe is injured, through his own carelessness, the employer should pay him damages" (Dec. 4, 1907). More socialistic nonsense, thought Ed Howe.

There was another concern for Howe in those last years on *The Atchison Globe:* Roosevelt was continuing the imperialistic tendencies that had marked him back in the 1890s. This business of sending the Great White Fleet into the Pacific, for example. Let the Japanese take warning, Howe said, that our Navy is not preoccupied with vodka and whiskers, and sending torpedo boats and destroyers after our ships might not be wise. The chief danger Howe saw in the voyage was in an accidental explosion like that which sank the *Maine* in 1898. No explosion, no war, he believed. He saw no reason for the officers of the vessels to take ten days at Rio de Janeiro, spending taxpayers' money, and he resented the way the Navy-minded Roosevelt was apparently using the White Fleet's travels as a way to impress an economical Congress with the need for a bigger navy.

The days of Teddy and the Muckrakers were coming to an end; so were the exciting issues. For Ed Howe the coming into popularity of William Howard Taft was a kind of relief. There were objections, of course (there were objections to every President), but Taft proved to be more Howe's kind of man. He liked him even more after he shook loose from the influence of Theodore Roosevelt and stopped his personal boom for higher office and his trips and receptions. As *The Globe* entered 1908 the name of Taft appeared on the editorial page as frequently as had other great names in the past, even (or perhaps especially) in the one-sentence paragraph that was Howe's trademark: "The only objection we have to Taft is that he looks like a grown up advertisement of Mellin's baby food" (Feb. 14, 1908). There was another objection: he would have to hear about the little Tafts as he had heard about Quentin, Kermit, and company; he was sure that little Charlie Taft was a nice little chap but he hoped that little Charlie would not keep advertising himself and the family in the nation's press.

The Republican convention at Chicago was one more nauseating political affair to have to publish news about; it was on a level of dignity with the eighth grade commencement in the Atchison theater—yelling, hissing, cat calls, groans, outbursts. The Ed Howe who hated politics was again in good form. Newspaper pictures of Taft at the age of three failed to impress Howe much, except for the child's panties, which came to his ankles and were trimmed with embroidery and quite unlike those worn by other babies fifty years before. ". . . the picture of William Taft at 3 is interesting only because of his panties" (June 20, 1908). He foresaw antagonism (justified) to Taft because of his Unitarianism (the old refrain: "A Unitarian is a first cousin to an infidel") and because of popular support for Bryan, a man who believed "that the whale swallowed Jonah, and has long been more of a preacher than statesman" (June 22, 1908).

Little impressed Ed Howe in the campaign of 1908. The supposed conspiracy to assassinate Taft from a Chicago skyscraper was a bore. The parties were almost alike. Atchison, poor town, would get to see Taft—fat, almost bald, hair parted in the middle, a man who talked with his hands and his smile. And Democratic efforts to stir up trouble and make the voters think they were in disastrous times brought editorial denunciations.

November of 1908 brought the third repudiation of William Jennings Bryan and the endorsement of Taft by the safe business men of America, those "men who do things, and provide employment for other men: men who are reliable, conservative, industrious: the best men in the country" (Nov. 4, 1908). Faith had been demonstrated once again in the capacity of the Republicans to bring confidence and prosperity, in the fact that Republicans over the long haul had provided the best of times for the American people, in the successful candidate himself—his work in the Philippines, his serving as Secretary of War. Now Theodore Roosevelt could go to Africa, and fight lions, insects, and diseases. Now the American people could deal with a new insanity: Would "Billy Possums" take the place of "Teddy Bears," because Taft had attended a 'possum dinner in the South?

Mostly, for Ed Howe, the Taft years were years of controversy about the tariff, the continued rise of the industrial barons, and the development of progressivism. Generally speaking Howe remained one of the stronger newspaper proponents of the men of wealth, but he separated radically from his conservative colleagues on the question of the tariff, and he was depressed that William Howard Taft would permit a contrast with his predecessor so radical as to serve as a defender of Senator Nelson Aldrich of Rhode Island and the man's high protective tariff. *The Globe* had opposed the tariff from the beginning, feeling that it was injurious to the interests of northeast Kansas and the farmers throughout the country. In 1902 Ed Howe had written that he had never been able to understand the Republicans on the tariff, which was simply to him a tax on consumers in the interest of manufacturers. He conceded that had he lived in Pennsylvania, say, he might have been able to see the point of high protection, but being a Westerner he could not. He was sure that a vast majority of the American people wanted a reduction in the tariff, that both parties had pledged reduction, that Congress was simply ignoring the wishes of the people on this critical point. As discussions continued he made Aldrich more and more the butt of his attacks, and he even came to deny that the tariff was a political question, contending that it was a question of graft, graft belonging to men of both parties.

From Atchison he looked to the nation's capital where the oversized President (automatically an offense in the eyes of the slim Ed Howe) was spending his time on the golf links when he should be trying to bring about a lower tariff. And he was angered. Where was the old fighting streak? Where, for that matter, was the streak that one might have expected in the hand-picked successor of the blunt Teddy? Taft had said the Payne-Aldrich bill was the best tariff bill the country had ever had, and that one statement, said Howe, led the American people to look toward Africa, where Roosevelt was hunting lions. Howe began to speculate on whether Roosevelt was going to be interested in running again for the presidency; after all, his man had not worked out. The one place where Howe saw good sense emanating from the White House was in the area of trust reform; reasonable regulation of corporations, not persecution, was all the country was entitled to have.

Those were times of insurgency, when both parties were viewing with interest certain matters the Populists—and now the Progressives—had been talking about for years. William Rockhill Nelson of the *Kansas City Star* had suggested that a new party be formed from progressive Republicans and Democrats, and Ed Howe offered his own ticket, with a number of Kansas names to lend familiarity to the proceedings:

> There may be more to the new party which the *Kansas City Star* proposes to organize than has occurred to you. Here is a ticket we propose for the Kansas City Star Party:
>
> For President–W. R. Nelson.
> For Vice-President–Arthur Capper.
> Secretary of War–Senator LaFollette.
> Secretary of Navy–Senator Cummins.
> Postmaster-General–Vic Murdock.
>
> We had old Bill White picked out for secretary of war, but decided the president would need him as his right hand man, to issue Clarion Notes, so we will make him secretary of state.
>
> Governor Stubbs has been fighting the railroads so much we will make him the interstate commerce commission.
>
> The noble little man from Denver, Judge Ben Lindsey, can be the supreme court. . . .
>
> Gifford Pinchot will have to be secretary of the interior, so he can put Ballinger in jail.
>
> Henry Allen is really too decent a man to be caught in the company he is now in, so we will give him something nice and easy: make him minister to England or Germany. We are just a little afraid to trust him in Paris.
>
> Fortunately, there are enough good positions left to accommodate all the present members of the new party, so no trouble

will arise from having more Good, Noble Men than offices. [June 16, 1910]

These were in part the newspaper bosses about whom he was then complaining in *The Globe.* Insurgency was a bore to him, but he wrote about it frequently. The year of the Bull Moose still had not arrived, so he was still interested in the prospects of Theodore Roosevelt, even though Roosevelt had enough potential insurgency to make a standpatter like Ed Howe quite shaky. On one point (other than the tariff) Howe joined forces with the men calling for reform in government: he did not care much for "Old Joe Cannon, who runs the House of Representatives" (Mar. 27, 1908). It was old Joe who was controlling Congress and making things like the Payne-Aldrich tariff possible. And if Cannon was as bad as his opponents were saying then he should be removed not only from the House Rules Committee but from his post as speaker.

In their zeal to curb the power of Cannon the reformers were laying off the men of business and industry for a change and that, for Howe, was just fine. How he admired Carnegie and Rockefeller, and he had years ahead of him in which he would admire them even more. His admiration for them, especially for Carnegie, was lessened a bit in his puzzlement over the idea of spending money for public libraries when children were dying in large cities because of the heat, because their parents were unable to afford ice. Rockefeller was generally a more sensible custodian of his money, thought Howe, for he was meeting the endless abuse directed at him by authorizing a great foundation to give away his fortune to help the public. Ed Howe thought this a good idea, though he did not believe the public would be grateful. It seemed more likely that people would take a cue from the *Kansas City Star,* which was attacking Rockefeller and Standard Oil and forgetting that the *Star* was as big a monopolist in the newspaper field as Standard Oil in the oil field. Why this constant moaning about the great men who had enriched America? What was wrong with Jim Hill and E. H. Harriman? They were merely men who knew and understood how hard it was to make a dollar, and had gone out and met the competition and won. The world was a dog-eat-dog place, and the fittest survived; this was the gospel being preached in America, and Ed Howe, who had survived against the competition in Atchison, Kansas, believed that gospel.

Our admiration should go out to the men who rise above the crowd; there's always someone fighting for your job, even if you are only a simple mechanic. "It is a fight from the cradle to the grave, and the man who makes a great success, is a genius, and entitled to admiration" (Jan. 29, 1907). Carnegie had made the fight, and so had Rockefeller, and so had James J. Hill, of the Great Northern, one of the most useful men alive, in the opinion of Howe, even though Hill was "abused like a thief."

Reformers—they were the "Good Boys" to the American people. The industrialists—they were the "Bad Boys." But which of these were really trying to help the American people out of their problems? Which, in the Panic of 1907, had loaned millions at six per cent? Which were trying to institute a temperate and less revolutionary approach in American life?

And if one wanted to find an American trust that really needed to be busted, here was one to consider:

> You who have tipped the waiter, the barber, the porter, the steward, bellboy, and numerous others who receive that form of public patronage, have doubtless imagined you were helping swell a small wage, and feeding hungry children. It is an established fact that the Pullman porter depends upon the traveling public for most of his pay. But a recent strike of hotel porters has developed the fact that they were required to turn in their tips. It is also alleged that many of the cloak and hat stands in theatres, etc., are operated by one thrifty individual who employs young men and requires them to turn in their tips, which usually amount to more than their wages. This knowledge may curb American generosity, for Americans hate to fatten a trust, and tips seem to be following oil, steel, sugar and electrical appliances in that direction. [June 19, 1909]

Thus a cause for a crusade, as revealed by the editor of *The Globe!*

Country Editor in a Changing World

In 1876 Ed Howe could go to the Centennial Exposition and, country boy that he was, gape open-mouthed. In his other travels he would see things that would capture his admiration. But a streak of skepticism was always there in Ed Howe, too, combined with a strange kind of anti-intellectualism from a man who showed considerable intellectual ability, despite his almost nonexistent formal training in schools.

Ed Howe just couldn't believe that certain things were possible. If he saw it work, well, it might be understood. He believed in progress, of course, but doubt was always in him, too, like his doubt about the perfectibility of man or the infallibility of the Bible.

One can almost predict the way Ed Howe would respond to developments of his time. For example: he heard about a Professor Roentgen who said he had discovered a process whereby the bones of a living man might be photographed, and that he had a powerful new light that could see inside a locked trunk. "Prof. Roentgen is not a great scientist: he is simply a great liar" (Feb. 3, 1896). Don't be credulous about such things, he warned the public; colleges and college professors believed in advertising as much as did the next man. "Nine tenths of the X ray business is foolish, and the other tenth experiment" (Apr. 29, 1896).

He was similarly skeptical about the value of discovering the North Pole, which a fellow named Peary kept talking about. Wireless telegraphy was a fraud, and Ed Howe knew that he was in trouble with some people because he thought it no more than an interesting experiment. Too much big "talk" in the business of electricity; "There is a little something in the wireless telegraphy talk, but not much. It will never be of practical use. . . . Marconi is a joke. Mark the prediction from a little old country newspaper" (May 12, 1902). The only people Marconi really impressed, he thought, were the newspaper reporters; why doesn't this "man of colossal brain, really do something?" (Feb. 17, 1903). Four years later there appeared the same chant in *The Globe:* the wireless telegraph had swindled people of millions of dollars, because it just wouldn't work. If it was such a good thing, why were the telegraph companies using wire ten or twelve years after the wireless was discovered?

Another touch of American stupidity was in this wild talk of the Panama Canal, and, sure enough, a scandal and an investigation had resulted. The government would find itself unable to build such a canal, and after twenty or thirty years it finally would be admitted (by whom he doesn't say) that construction would never take place.

One invention that Ed Howe *did* admire was the telephone; he marveled on hearing an Atchison man talk with a friend in St. Louis by telephone. "Thousands of other things new and strange have been invented in this wonderful age, and are being invented all the time" (June 12, 1907). Why couldn't this Kansas editor, a man of undoubted intelligence, extend his optimism and interest to the wireless, or to the "flying machine"? The Wright brothers had tested their first plane; now they were trying one in South Carolina and barring the press from exhibitions, "another effective way to secure free advertising" (May 14, 1908). Flying machines would not work. Quit worrying about them and make a bet that airships will stop before the end of their journeys. Flying machines able to carry many passengers were impracticable. Whatever you do, don't sink your life savings in flying machines; pay to see one of them at a county fair but go no further than that. As for the Wright boys, they were a nuisance that would go away in time:

"On a farm near Tonganoxie, Leavenworth county, lives a brother of the Wright brothers, who are trying to fly. The Kansas member of the Wright family is a farmer, and wiser than his noted brothers. Some day the Wright brothers who are trying to fly will have a tumble, and will be mashed to a pulp. Then the Kansas member of the family will realize that he is the real genius of the family" (June 8, 1909).

So the doubting words continued. "It is occasionally said of *The Globe* that it is not Progressive, because it doesn't believe that in a few months people will sail everywhere in airships" (Oct. 20, 1910). Balloons? Men would never be able to fly them.

And the automobile? A new specialty in which to get yourself killed (one of the editor's sounder prophecies). "There is really less pleasure in riding sixty miles an hour than in riding six, unless the exciting sensation of being jolted, and having your breath taken away, be called pleasure" (Aug. 13, 1908).

The North Pole again, and the controversy over whether Peary or Cook discovered it: "We are willing to give up our interest in it without a controversy" (Sept. 14, 1909).

Radium: "If we had our way—incidentally, we may remark that we never have it—there would be less in the newspapers about Radium" (Jan. 20, 1904). Worry instead about a better way to can tomatoes, a more important matter by far than radium.

And yet, in less exercised moments the grumbling editor could come forth with opinions as optimistic as those of any reformer. In rare moments he could sound like a Condorcet of the Kansas plains:

> We are not one of those who believe the world is in danger. The people are becoming wiser and better every day, as a result of experience. The people, now in control everywhere, were formerly slaves. The progress made within the past century has been marvelous. The man who said, "There is nothing new under the sun," didn't know what he was talking about. Sometime soon, men will begin studying the science of Comfort. They will quit worry, and lying, and drunkenness, and other sins that make men miserable. They will practice the common sense doctrine that for his own sake, man should behave himself; that the best way is the easiest way: that it is as foolish for a man to be a drunkard, loafer, liar or thief as it is to cut off a finger. In the immediate future men will study the science of government, and rid the world of unnecessary taxes, official thievery and public waste. [Dec. 9, 1907]

In those years, too, Howe was pontificating on matters of less significance than science or government. His newspaper took special interest in the great San Francisco earthquake of 1906, devoting a rather overpowering headline in seventy-two point type to the story and allowing the story itself to use up most of the news space. The activity of Congress in investigating plural marriage in Utah brought denunciations of both investigators and practitioners of polygamy (*one* wife was too much for Ed Howe). He loved to write about the Boy Scout movement, which he believed could promote militarism in good clean American youth, a movement that took boys out with their rifles so they could shoot each other when they should be at home helping their mothers weed the garden. And he devoted considerable attention to the sordid story of Evelyn Nesbit, the wronged woman; Harry Thaw, the wealthy playboy; and Stanford White, the murdered architect. He hoped that Thaw, the murderer, placed in an insane asylum, was where he belonged, and that punishment there might be worse than the death penalty.

Paris and Atchison

As Edgar Watson Howe entered the first decade of the century and the last decade as editor of his newspaper he was the undisputed leader of journalism in Atchison. The *Champion* had had several owners after the passing of Governor Martin in 1889, including Ewing Herbert, a Hiawatha, Kansas, newspaperman, J. E. House, later of the *Philadelphia Public Ledger,* and Walt Mason. The *Patriot* had collapsed and was renamed the *Atchison Morning Star and Daily Patriot,* lasting under that name from late 1895 to February 1896.

Both Howe and the House-Herbert combination learned much from the unsuccessful effort to beat *The Globe.* House and Herbert apparently had decided that vilification of Howe would be profitable; the local Catholic Church had been induced to boycott *The Globe,* and other efforts were made to hurt the reputation of both editor and newspaper. But eventually an editorial calling it quits appeared in the *Champion:* "The people of Atchison have been given a fair opportunity to decide between *The Atchison Globe* and *Atchison Champion.* They have decided in favor of *The Globe,* and with this issue we quit. And the decision is just, as *The Globe* is an honest, capable newspaper, owned by an honest man."[9]

At the same time Ed Howe was becoming even more of a figure in his part of the state, and was making observations about editors in other communities. He admired Dan Anthony of the *Leavenworth Times* and promoted Anthony for Congress: "Leavenworth people like him, and once elected him mayor, which is the supreme test of a man's popularity in a small city. . . . He is backed by good neighbors, good kin, and a good town" (Jan. 15, 1907). He liked William Allen White, of course, though he frequently disagreed with White's publicly stated positions, and he admired Victor Murdock of the *Wichita Eagle.* But the "Mutual Admiration Society" of Kansas editors continued to annoy him, and he reserved special scorn for newspaper enterprises in the capital city:

"Isn't this Topeka way of writing up a wedding Just Too Sweet? 'This match is thought to be a Simon pure love affair, and as their boat slips gently down the ways at its launching on life's eventful sea, with Cupid at the wheel, they will bear away our hearty congratulations and all our good wishes for a long, happy and successful voyage' " (Oct. 20, 1904).

Mainly Ed Howe was losing touch with the Kansas scene, and his observations about the state were becoming almost perfunctory. Not since the 1880s, when he was still a youthful editor on *The Globe,* had Howe been abroad. And in the spring of 1900 he left on the first of four extensive trips he would take in the next several years; on each occasion he sent back dispatches, as he had done on the trip to Europe. On each occasion, too, the accounts appeared later in book form.

The first of these trips was the one that became a book called *Paris and the Exposition.* On May 8, 1900, he and his son Gene sailed for Paris on the North German Lloyd steamship the *Kaiser Wilhelm der Grosse.* He took a cab to the docks in Hoboken, and observed the sentimental scene at the ship: "There is something about going to sea that moves people deeply." Something else about going to sea moved Ed Howe: the sea. Soon after sailing he became seasick, and he gave his readers a vivid picture of the rolling of the ship:

"A ship rises and falls about as regularly as you breathe when in repose: when you inhale a breath, the prow rises; as you exhale, the prow goes down, and the stern up, and this goes on throughout the voyage. When the weather is bad, the motion is quicker: the ship seems to fall at times, as if to catch up with your breathing."

He was always seasick when he embarked upon a voyage, and he always threatened never to step on a ship again. But this did not stop him from eating heartily at sea, and in good reportorial fashion he described the bill of fare, which was too fancy for such a simple man. He took a good Atchison breakfast of orange, oatmeal, bacon and eggs.

The ship had several notables aboard—Maude Adams, Anna Held, Colonel Astor, one of the Vanderbilts. Howe made a tour of the liner on invitation of the captain, and he observed life at sea: always a lot of gossip, a lot of flirting, a lot of talk about the gambling in the smoking room. Six days after sailing the vessel reached Cherbourg, entering the harbor at eight at night, delayed five hours because of head winds. The next morning he arrived in Paris, where he met Frank Fava, who had lived two years in Atchison and worked at a restaurant there. He was to be Howe's guide, and within two hours Howe had gotten back his health and was riding in the streets of the city looking for amusement.

The Paris Exposition, in his American eyes, was inferior in some ways, superior in others, to the Chicago fair, which would always be the standard for Ed Howe. The grounds at the 1900 exposition were too small, only half as large as Jackson Park in Chicago. The Trocadero was ugly, not light and attractive like the white buildings of 1893. The Eiffel Tower was a worthy relic from previous days, and the Assembly Hall was worth looking at. He wrote about how the Seine cut the exposition into two parts, with each bank lined by beautiful buildings. He missed a midway, but thought the foreign exhibits were very good. And he learned to save money by standing outside shows and then, when a Frenchman came out, asking him, "Well, how was it?" He could tell from the shrug whether the show was worth seeing. In the city his quarters were the Hotel St. Georges, where he was surprised because he found that, contrary to his expectations, he was not being cheated. Generally speaking his visit to Paris was thoroughly enjoyable: he ate in several quarters of the city, had praise for the police department, and always found a need for an interpreter. America's role at the fair seemed shameful—there was no beautiful building to be seen. But there was a place on the exposition grounds where American food, such as corn bread, was prepared by colored women. That he liked.

He and Gene spent fifteen days in Paris, looking over the city itself as much as the exposition. Wandering about the streets always entertained him, and he liked his hotel. Every other day he received copies of *The Globe,* and he recorded that his happiest hours in Paris were spent checking on happenings at home. He went to the Hippodrome—a circus in a modern building, with seven thousand persons in the audience, one thousand performing, and seventy-eight in the orchestra. On returning to the exposition he was impressed by the illumination of the Electricity Building, a wonderful sight in his opinion.

There were plenty of things to do in Paris other than go to the exposition, even though that was the main attraction. He was interested in the French system of money, learned how to get around in Paris, compared prices (flour cost most in Paris but bread was cheaper, "And all French bread is excellent, which may be said, also, of all French cooking"). And there were the women of France:

"The French believe that women should be useful as well as ornamental. That they are ornamental, admits of no question, for there are more good looking women in Paris than in any other city in the world. They are also useful. Nearly all the shops are operated by women. . . . Women sell the tickets at the theatres, and women sell the tickets in the exposition offices. They are the ushers at the theatres. They sell flowers and vegetables on the streets."

But this raised a question in his mind: "Since the women of France work so much, what do the men do? I don't know; possibly they are in politics. The men seem to be busy. I suppose that at the bread shops, the men are the bakers, and that there are other places out of sight where men may be useful" (June 15, 1900).

French streets interested him; there was no squared-off regularity like back home, but instead wild and wandering thoroughfares, some wide, some narrow. As a city Paris did not seem the equal of New York or Chicago, its buildings being less imposing, but it tended to grow on the visitor. The Louvre looked old and wrinkled at first, as did Versailles, but both improved on later visits. What Howe saw inside the Louvre was another matter; his artistic prejudices were revealed to the folks in Atchison (as if they hadn't known already): "I saw paintings—examples of early Italian art—that I would not take as a gift, except that they came from the Louvre: if a second-hand dealer should offer me one of these paintings, I would not accept it as a gift. Yet they are valuable. We must not measure other people's goods in our half bushels."

There were playhouses to visit, and of course the Moulin Rouge, which, with its notorious can-can, did not seem nearly as wicked as he had been led to believe (or maybe hoped) it would be. The wine market impressed him, and he was coming to feel that taking such a trip tends to universalize a man: "In all countries, you will find flour, fish, wheat, corn, potatoes, oats, boats, railroads, oil, wine, and so on. A trip abroad takes the conceit out of a man" (June 16, 1900).

So went the trip, a fine experience for a provincial man. He loved the Swiss village, with "a real cascade pouring down the mountains, and an artificial brook flows through the grounds," and the Swiss milkmaids serving milk and cheese, and the Swiss stables. He witnessed a moving sidewalk, which carried visitors at six miles an hour for a fare of ten cents. There were few nights out for the old man: he advised the younger fellows that the sights of Paris were not worth seeing. As he toured the city he recalled what he knew of history and literature: Sydney Carton, for example, of *A Tale of Two Cities;* the Place de la Concorde, which conjured up Carton for Howe more than it did Louis and Marie Antoinette; the site of the Bastille, where Dr. Manette was imprisoned; a wineshop like that of Madame DeFarge; Tellson's Bank, in the old section of Paris, where Jarvis Lorry worked.

"As I stood by the site of the guillotine, I did not think of Louis XVI and Marie Antoinette, famous in history, prominent in every art gallery, and in every museum, but of Sidney Carton and the poor little seamstress who held his hand; these children of misery, of fiction; these types of the people who went mad from oppression, and the fruits of whose victory may be seen in Paris to-day" (June 18, 1900).

After he and his son left Paris, they had a chance to admire the countryside between Paris and Cherbourg. They sailed home on the *Lahn,* and the weather, except for fog, seemed almost perfect. Then back to New York, and a trip to Niagara Falls, and, "At 11 o'clock one Saturday night, a grateful man carrying three grips, and leading a sleepy, stumbling boy, got off a train at Atchison, and greatly admired the town" (June 19, 1900).

Ed Howe was still just a simple country editor, in his opinion. As the new century came in he was still setting some type with his staff, always making the two-column head on page one his specialty, always checking the overline. *The Globe* was usually a four-page paper, though on Fridays, in readiness for the Saturday specials at the local stores, it had eight pages, and sometimes on other days of the week as well. There were many feature articles, and many halftone illustrations, as well as drawings. Advertising was extensive—patent medicines, Henry George cigars, Dr. Lyon's tooth powder, railroads, local stores. Ads continued to occupy part of the front page—an endorsement of Paine's Celery Compound, a boost for the Burlington Railroad. The reader generally would find the lead columns carrying Associated Press news, nothing of a detailed nature, but a series of rather brief stories; market information from Kansas City; news from Washington; "news and comment," largely national news, written in an informal, chatty style. "Globe Sights" remained a standard, but Howe's paragraphs could be found throughout the paper. Makeup was unimportant on *The Globe,* as it was on most country papers (and on a good many in the big cities).

The affairs of Kansas and of Atchison were being subordinated, perhaps out of mere tiredness, to developments in places removed from Ed Howe's immediate sight. What happened in Kansas continued to attract some interest, of course. The summer of 1901 brought a drought, and Howe wrote that neither corn nor hell would be raised that year, that both Iowa and Nebraska were praying for rain.

The elements in Kansas are freakish; by fall Howe was back in an ecstatic mood, recommending that people stay at home, for Indian summer, "the poetry season of the year," was about at hand, and the drought and heat of July, the canned goods Kansans had had to eat in midsummer, and the discomforts and miseries would be forgotten "in the glorious days of Indian summer" (Aug. 28, 1901). "What's the matter with Kansas?" he asked in 1902, and replied: "Watch the Washington list of patents granted, and you will see that Kansans are always granted patents for inventing trusses" (June 11, 1902). So in the midst of his joyous editorial utterances a dig for the state.

In 1903 drought had yielded to flood, one of the worst floods in the history of Kansas and Missouri, and *The Globe* editor printed a colorful and factual description of the destruction:

> If you cannot see the flood at Kansas City, imagine it. Imagine six feet and a half of water on the floor of the union depot. Imagine water over that populous valley ranging from a depth of six feet and a half to fifteen; imagine strong currents of water through streets lined with great wholesale houses and manufacturing institutions; imagine entire suburbs, containing twelve to fifteen thousand people, submerged and houses and box cars floating about; imagine sixteen bridges washed out across the Kaw; imagine homeless and hysterical people; imagine people in great danger, and efforts being made to rescue them; imagine twenty to thirty thousand people being cared for by relief committees; imagine business paralyzed, and the greatest flood in the history of this section, for there is good reason to believe that the water was higher in Kansas City on Sunday and Monday last than it was during the flood of 1844,

> when there were few people in the country. If you have an active imagination, you needn't go to Kansas City or North Topeka. [June 5, 1903]

In the summer of 1903 President Roosevelt made the trip to Kansas that Ed Howe had written about as being so unnecessary, and the editor attended the dinner given by Governor Bailey in Roosevelt's honor. He wrote a detailed description of the Governor's mansion, then described the gentlemen attired in tuxedos (three men) and the rest in swallow-tailed coats. He reported five black ties and twelve white ones, three of the ties "tied," the others apparently "dickies." (Details, he said, came from Old Bill White.) There was a fruit salad to start off the dinner, and fixings a bit fancy for a boy from a country town. There was a shrimp salad, and a sally from Roosevelt: "The President inquired here, 'Governor Bailey, did these shrimps come from Kansas?' the governor having said that the bill of fare was made up largely of Kansas products. You know how a preacher's joke goes; well, it's nothing to a President's joke; we all roared." He heard a lot of good stories (and some apparently not so good, but he laughed politely). He promised to save them for private use so that he could say, "The President told me an interesting anecdote at Topeka."[10]

There was another party that summer, one that *The Globe* held for the press on August 2 at Forest Park. The guest was Governor Bailey, and he talked about good citizenship, which must have excited editor Howe. *The Globe* reported: "At the conclusion of the governor's address, there were calls for 'Howe, Howe, Howe.' Governor Bailey introduced Mr. Howe to the audience, and he said: 'Ladies and gentlemen: I am very fond of the people of Atchison, of Ellery's band, and of Governor Bailey, and they are all present' " (Aug. 3, 1903).

"Vacation Notes," an annual feature for *Globe* readers, were published in September, as Ed Howe left September 24 for the Pacific Northwest. He sent back articles about railroads, about traveling on trains, about crops and irrigation projects in Idaho, about the need for dams in the Snake River country, about the towns (Emmett, Idaho, where "an Atchison young man lately bought a weekly newspaper"), about the mountains and the mines. He traveled along the Columbia River, visited the newspaper plant of the *Oregonian,* and was generally of the opinion that Westerners—ticket agents, hotel clerks, waiters, and porters—were pretty rude people. Local notes always got attention: there were Atchison people in the West who subscribed to *The Globe,* and he concluded that "You will find formerly of Atchison people everywhere except in hell" (Sept. 26, 1903). Howe could be a great talker, contrary to the general impression that persists of a grumpy, taciturn man, and he loved to converse with men in smoking cars on the trains. He complained a bit about expenses: ". . . if the passenger does not look out, his bill for one meal will be from a dollar and a half to two dollars" (Sept. 28, 1903).

Ed Howe wrote most interestingly when he described his journeys beyond the confines of Atchison. In May of 1904 he was preparing to go to the St. Louis fair, and he provided a disputatious little note concerning the annoyance felt by many because the state flower was not in the Kansas decorations at St. Louis:

". . . the sunflower at Chicago was obtrusive and ugly, and made the building look like a nine spot. The sunflower is not pretty; all that can be said of it is that it is cheerful, and refuses to be downed, and shows a perseverance worthy of a prettier flower. Besides, it is not a Kansas flower. It may be treason to say so, but more sunflowers grow in Missouri than Kansas ever saw.

"It is possible to love Kansas without waving a sunflower at the world" (May 12, 1904).

On that heretical note he went to St. Louis, and spent two days there, in almost continuous rain. But he was much impressed. He thought the fair might be regarded in time as one of the greatest, and he liked St. Louis people and the St. Louis spirit. He was taken with the "Inside Inn," a structure that could accommodate four thousand guests, and he was interested in learning that what was known as the "midway" at Chicago was called the "pike" at the new fair. The disputed Kansas building seemed creditable enough, and well located, with attractive work by Kansas artists, but it was little more than a meeting house for Kansans. Atchison had a display in the Agricultural Hall, built around the corn Indian of the last Corn Carnival, a display provided by the Santa Fe Railroad at a cost of six hundred dollars. A good fair, all told, he thought.

He wrote from the north woods in late August, the closest thing to nature notes ever achieved by this practical editor, who preferred to write about what he was eating, how much things cost, what the grocery stores were like.

On December 8 *The Globe* published a twenty-eighth anniversary edition of eight pages, signaling a move of the paper into a new building. There was a dedication ceremony, with potted palms, roses, ornamental plants, and chrysanthemums, and a string orchestra played. An overline on page one read: "The Globe Begins Its 28th Year To-Day, With Some Prosperity, but With More Humility and Thankfulness." And Atchison of 1904 was the center of interest.

It was a time for sentimental reflection by the old editor: "With this issue, I begin my twenty-eighth year as editor of *The Atchison Globe*. I began at twenty-three: I passed my fiftieth birthday last May. I fear that during these twenty-seven years I have offended a good many people. . . . I am not afraid to denounce that which is palpably wrong, but I am sensitive about wounding the feelings of worthy people. . . . I suppose that twenty years ago, like most men of thirty, I thought I knew it all, but I do not think so now. I fear that years ago, I cut and slashed a good deal, but it was due to a lack of judgment, and not to viciousness."

He talked about what it was like to publish a newspaper, of how most people in town always think they know how to run a paper, but that they don't. He made no pretensions, he said, about knowing how to run a department store, or a law office, or a doctor's office. He modestly disclaimed knowing much, but reminded his readers that he had survived a good deal of competition. He wrote again of his lack of religion, and said that he could not help it, that "if I should pretend to believe that which I do not believe I would be open to the charge of dishonesty and hypocrisy." He did not intend to change his habits of work, and would continue to "haunt Commercial street."

He had arranged, in planning the new building, that his room should adjoin that of the cashier, because he never came in from the street without money for subscriptions. And he speculated a bit about his future, with some uncertainty:

> Years ago, I used to say I would retire at fifty. Yet on my fiftieth birthday I was busily engaged in building a new office, and getting in deeper. My hope is that within a few years, I will be able to surrender *The Globe* to my three principal asso-

> ciates, who have worked with me so long, so faithfully and so acceptably.
>
> I have often referred to my ambition for old age: to retire to a small farm near Atchison, and print "Smith's Quarterly," a publication appearing four times a year. In "Smith's Quarterly," I will be free to say what I really think, which no editor of a daily newspaper is ever able to do.

There was a page of letters (Dec. 8, 1904) from readers of *The Globe,* letters attesting to the national recognition Edgar Watson Howe was achieving: Edward Bok, whose *Ladies' Home Journal* had been lampooned by Howe; Lincoln Steffens, then editing *McClure's;* Henry King, Kansan and editor of the *St. Louis Globe-Democrat;* Eugene "Ironquill" Ware, poet, old Indian fighter, and commissioner of pensions; William Rockhill Nelson, editor of the *Kansas City Star;* William Allen White of Emporia; Paul Morton, Secretary of the Navy; Governor-elect B. B. Brooks of Wyoming, a north woods tramping friend of Ed Howe; editors of newspapers all over the land; and the common folk who had come to know *The Globe,* like a woman in Cordelia, Pennsylvania: "Of all the papers I see, *The Globe* is ahead of all of them in wit and sound sense. Even if the editor sometimes unmercifully soaks we women, I will stand up for him."

Howe had left his family but his children had not left the newspaper. His daughter Mateel wrote dispatches about the Portland exposition of 1905 for Atchison readers. Jim was sending stories bearing New Orleans datelines, and his father was following the career that would take Jim to Honolulu, Washington, San Francisco, Philadelphia, Portland, and New York; to the foreign service of the Associated Press and war correspondence in World War I. A few years later Jim sent a dispatch describing his work on the *New York Journal:* that must have been something of a shock—the son of Ed Howe working on a newspaper owned by William Randolph Hearst!

A Trip Around the World

Howe took five hunting trips to the north woods. He attended most of the expositions in exposition-minded America. He traveled abroad, and he believed all this traveling had done more to round out his education than anything else in his experience. But the most extensive of his journeys was that which started October 26, 1905, and ended March 10, 1906, all reported in detail in *The Globe.* It was a round-the-world trip that covered thirty-one thousand miles and employed twelve different steamships and trains in eleven different countries.[11] He took Mateel with him, and he calculated that the whole thing cost him thirty-five hundred dollars.

His trip took him through the American Southwest—the Arkansas Valley, Colorado, the land of the Pueblo Indians and the Navajos and the Japanese settlers, and the Grand Canyon. At the canyon the conductor of the train told him that a hundred excursionists representing the WCTU had visited there, stopping at the Bright Angel, and the editor was amused to hear that the total receipts of the party were twenty-two dollars; knowing that the women did not drink he concluded that they also did not eat. He gave his readers back home a description of the canyon—the fantastically shaped mountains, the winding river, the rapids. Impressing him almost as much as the natural wonders was the new hotel at the canyon, the El Tovar. He also was amused by the propensity of Westerners (all busy looking for water) to shorten the names of their cities: "Flag" for "Flagstaff," "Albuqu" for "Albuquerque," "San Bedo" for "San Bernardino," "Los" for "Los Angeles," "Frisco" for "San Francisco" (I, 26).

The ship was to sail from San Francisco, where he was to meet Mateel and Gene; meanwhile he was being harassed by a missionary, his wife, and their five noisy children. He looked around California and saw what seemed a new world, "as well known as Uneeda biscuit," one dominated by advertising, full of stranded tourists who had decided to stay and hustle for a living. Readers in Atchison were spared none of the needling little touches of the editor, and his daughter apparently would have to suffer the bite of his comments. He took Mateel and Gene to hear *La Traviata,* and his attire, notably a colored tie, shocked the "young lady," as he called her, who asked: "Haven't you a black tie?"

"As soon as the young man caught me alone, he said, referring to the incident: 'She is beginning on you, too.' At the theater, when the young lady took her hat off, I noticed that she had her hair 'done up' in the fluffy way young girls are just now affecting.

I really admired it; it looked well, but I said to her: 'Haven't you a comb?' The young man was amused, and said: 'You got back at her all right. You will have to assert yourself on your trip, or you will come back as meek as I am. I shouldn't dare act as I do here, if you were not around' " (I, 44).

The *Siberia* was the ship on which the Howes would travel first. It left San Francisco November 4, and the editor was seasick, of course. Then the short, informal dispatches commenced for *Globe* readers. Howe was beginning to wish he was home, and he was tiring of the other passengers, the fire drills, the meals, the rough sea.

On November 10 the *Siberia* reached Hawaii, where Ed Howe was impressed by the tropics, the trees, the flowers, and the vines. He gave factual descriptions of the taro crop, and how it failed, and of how the natives were forced to make poi from American flour. And he made an apology quite in keeping with his constant refusal to be known as the least bit intellectual: "I hate a man who, in writing travel notes, frequently uses queer words taken out of the guide-books. I apologize for 'taro,' and 'poi,' and shall not offend again" (I, 72).

Aboard ship the misery of his life was a little boy, the son of the missionary couple he had seen on the train, whose name was, happily for Ed Howe's purposes, "Henry George." Henry George was a terrible pest. He bothered the Japanese, who liked to play a kind of checkers game in the smoking room, and he was told to get out. This increased Howe's admiration for the Japanese nation. Henry George next appeared in the smoking room and "attempted the Carrie Nation act: that is, he upbraided the men for smoking, saying it was a shame to waste money in that way when money was so badly needed in missionary work" (I, 114).

Except for the missionary family Howe liked the Americans aboard the ship, and he was coming to believe that stories of "loud" Americans abroad were myths. He thought it likely that Americans invented and circulated stories about each other. The ship reached Yokohama November 21, after a delay caused by a heavy headwind. Soon Ed Howe developed a deep admiration for the people of Japan and their country as well. But there seemed to be a sameness to things; he did not need to see every city in Japan to know what the country was like. After all, "if you have seen Kansas City, you can imagine Topeka; and after you have seen Topeka, you can imagine Atchison" (I, 147). He went for a rickshaw ride, and he received constant descriptions and commentaries from the "Educational Bureau"—Mateel. It was a crowded, cosmopolitan land, and Tokyo itself had thirty daily papers, with a newsboy who excited attention to his "extras" by tying a bell to his feet. The newspaper offices and facilities were not impressive: *The Globe* could print more copies in an hour than these presses could print all day. The mailing room of one newspaper had a dirt floor; the press room was heated with a coal stove; the Japanese did not know what the word "Linotype" meant.

Tokyo fascinated him, and an incident occurred there that gave him cause to laugh at himself and at the rest of the world too:

"And when it is recorded in the archives of the State Historical Society at Topeka that the two young daughters of His Majesty, the Emperor of Japan, bowed to the Atchison party in a public park in Tokio, let it be specifically mentioned that the bows were directed at me: my daughter admits it, and is vexed about it. The Federation of Women's Clubs at the next meeting at Hutchinson will probably pass resolutions condemning the bad taste of the princesses, but the fact remains that the princesses bowed to me" (I, 163).

Buddhist lore impressed the editor, and Tokyo with its bustle reminded him of American cities: its rail station was like St. Louis at rush hour. From Tokyo the Howes traveled to Kyoto, a city then caught up in festival time, for Admiral Togo was in town. Ed Howe wondered how two Japanese might be treated on the streets of Atchison, visiting the site of Ben Holladay's stage office, the office of the wharf-master, and the like. "We were treated better, I imagine, than two Japanese would have been treated in Atchison on Corn Carnival day, for we saw only one or two intoxicated men, and only one fight" (I, 177).

The potential of the Japanese nation both impressed and worried him; war against Russia had made Japan a world power, and he frequently reflected on this in his conjectures about Japan. He investigated the rumors of Japanese immorality—girls undressing male travelers in their rooms and giving them baths, things like that—but he found no evidence of the Japanese being any more immoral than anyone else. He obtained insights, too, into the contrasts between the thriving commercial cities and the poverty-stricken towns of the countryside: "We arranged for lunch at a Japanese hotel, and visited a fishing village; the poorest lot of people I have ever seen anywhere. The place was so frightfully dirty that we did not remain long. The poorer the town, the narrower the streets: in the streets of this town there was barely room for two people to walk abreast. We saw here also a native school. All of the children were foul, and many of them had great scabs covering their heads. . . . Nearly all the children I saw had bad colds, and showed it in a disgusting way. Most of the people are barefooted, except that they wear sandals" (I, 202).

From the port of Kobe the Howes returned to a ship, where Howe had quite a shock, one of many that occurred on his world travels—he saw a half-naked woman and was forced to turn his head from the revolting sight. Next the ship sailed to Shanghai, where Ed Howe formed impressions not very favorable to China. Thanksgiving Day was spent at the Astor House in Shanghai, and he then went out on the streets of the city, noting the behavior of Chinese, hearing about the treatment of the Chinese by both English and Americans. His contempt for this alien people became considerable; he observed their size and wanted to ask them: "You miserable devils, why didn't you whip the Japs? Why don't you try it again?" He concluded that the Chinese lacked "spunk" (I, 211-12).

On December 3 he left the ship at Hong Kong, where he reflected that the Chinese were coming to look alike to him and that he was getting tired of the whole trip. He stayed at a hotel recommended by a friend, and wondered at the straw pillows and another furnishing: "In the room hangs a blackboard, although no chalk is supplied with which to do problems. Now in the name of all that's curious, what is that blackboard for?" (I, 241).

From Hong Kong he left for Manila aboard the *Tean,* which was little more, in his opinion, than a cattle boat. He found Manila a little like Tokyo and the Filipinos like the Japanese, though less industrious. In Manila he was entertained by Major W. H. Bishop of Salina, a lawyer from Kansas. And he was generally impressed by the modern city, by luncheon aboard the battleship *Oregon,* by a cockfight, by the prevalence of Catholics in what looked like a heathen land, by the ignorance, the heat, and the mosquitoes. He had delivered himself of many opinions about expansionism in the Far East, but was not prepared to say any more at the moment.

Life in general in the Philippines did not impress him. He was afraid that just being there would make one lazy—no winter, thatched roofs, bananas growing wild, a man able to live on two cents a day. This kind of life was not for the enterprising editor from the Midwest. He also was amused by the impact that the recent war and occupation apparently had had on the culture of the Filipinos:

"When the American soldiers came over here, their bands brought many tunes with them that struck the Filipino fancy. One of these was 'A Hot Time in the Old Town,' which is frequently played by Filipino bands at funerals, as the Filipinos do not know the character of the song. The Filipinos are very fond of moving-picture shows. Recently the Passion Play was being given before a Filipino audience, by means of moving pictures, and the band played 'A Hot Time in the Old Town' during the crucifixion" (I, 295).

The trip to Manila had been only a side excursion; he returned to Hong Kong on the cattle boat, going through a monsoon and coming to hate the ship—and ships—even more. In Hong Kong he stayed in a different hotel, the King Edward, then on December 16 boarded the *Simla,* an English ship, for Singapore. Sea travel was becoming a bore—little to see or do, and nothing like being in Atchison and hearing the big news that Big Creek was out and a friend had to go around six miles in order to get to town. The *Simla* landed at Singapore on December 21, and Howe found the city a pretty one, and the Raffles a fine hotel. He was becoming afraid that his days in the Far East would turn him into an Englishman, a man who wore pajamas and kimonos, and drank whiskey and soda and used the broad "a" when he said "pass." He also was worrying a little that he had criticized the missionaries too much, but he did believe that no one in the Orient had a good word to say for them, that even the good Methodists and Baptists and Presbyterians would not support missionaries in the future.

From Singapore the party sailed for Ceylon, spending Christmas day on the ship, and going through an Indian Ocean storm (he was coming to think that ocean storms were a part of his way of life). The vessel reached Colombo December 27, and the Howes stayed at the Galle Face hotel, where crows flew in and out the window and oxen drew carts through the streets. He found the coffee in Ceylon terrible, even though coffee was grown there—and he reflected that back home all the good Kansas beef was shipped to other parts of the country. Perhaps all the good Ceylonese coffee was shipped to America. His attention also was drawn to a local beauty:

> From the windows of my room, this morning, I had a good view of a native hired girl. Below my windows is a pretty fair native residence, and the hired girl was seated in the passageway between the main building and kitchen; evidently breakfast was in progress, and there being a dull moment, the girl was resting. She was rather good-looking, barring her bare feet, and, as she rested, she chewed the betel-nut, and spat a red juice around as a railroad brakeman off duty squirts tobacco-juice. As the girl chewed and spat the red juice about her, she lazily scratched her feet. And the girl was rather young and good-looking: she would attract attention at a native Grand Ball. [I, 364-65]

Ed Howe spent New Year's day in Ceylon. He was getting tired of his pineapple-a-day diet, and he decided that he preferred Atchison people and the town of Atchison itself to anything he had seen elsewhere. He thought that when he finally got home he would not talk too much about the trip but would hire a hall and tell all about his journeys in two hours. "At this 'talk' I will wear the different suits I have purchased," he said. " 'This suit,' I will say, for example, 'is the one I wore down in Ceylon. It was made in two hours.' (This will give those present a chance to say, 'It looks it.') Then I will make a quick change, and put on the suit I wore in India; price Rs. 10; etc., etc." (II, 8). In Ceylon another half-naked woman gave him a shock, and he spoke with distaste of the native practice of allowing children to run around with their clothes off. Men seemed to go naked more than women, he reflected, and he wondered if the female form might not be as symmetrical as that of the male. "The female form needs the addition of dry goods to make it effective," he concluded (II, 9).

On January 3 he sailed for Calcutta on the *Somali,* reaching India January 8. His travel writings were revealing to the people back home how mysterious lands looked to a man of simple background. India proved to him the superiority of the white race over the black—a land where 150,000 whites ruled 400 million blacks. Tipping bothered him; why should he have to pay four coolies who took his baggage into town, four who took it to a room, then a table waiter, a room man, a scavenger, a man who brought hot water and so on. "I have said nothing of the men who are constantly in front of your room offering to sell you a snake, tell your fortune, make a tree grow out of the ground, make music, or perform athletic feats" (II, 60-1). He took a train to Benares on January 10 and noted the resemblance of the countryside to the short-grass country of Kansas. He thought about how several of the rivers might have been the Solomon or the Republican, how a lack of water was like the problems of western Kansas, how the soil and the clouds of dust made him think of parts of his home state. If you put Colorado, Wyoming, Idaho, Montana, New Mexico, Arizona, and Utah together, and gave them a climate like that of Southern California, you would have India, he thought. There was nothing naturally fruitful like the Midwest that he knew so well. The Indian culture astonished and annoyed him, especially the "fool notion" of the Hindus that monkeys are sacred.

In his travel letters he always demonstrated a capacity to universalize a situation, to make his readers understand something by relating it to their own lives. For example, he compared the life of an Englishman in India with the life of a Kansan, and he suggested what the life of Ed Howe would be like at home—on the Indian model:

> Early breakfast at 7; then Eugene Lett would arrive, and shave me. At 8 or 9 o'clock I should take a bath, the water being brought to my room in tin cans used originally for the shipment of coal oil. At 9:30, regular breakfast, after which I should call my gun-bearer, and go out and shoot a tiger. . . . I should have a head man; that is, a man to act as butler, and overseer of the other servants. This head man would be either Joe Henderson or Goat Edwards, colored neighbors of mine, and I am inclined to think it would be Goat Edwards, as I have a suspicion that Joe Henderson tramped up my cucumber vines when we were gardening together last summer. It would be the business of Goat Edwards, my head man, to hire coolies to do my work, at two cents a day, out of which he would exact a small commission, without letting me know anything about it. . . . At two o'clock, tiffin; at 5 o'clock, tea; at 8:30 dinner. After dinner, I should sit out on the porch and smoke excellent cigars costing two cents each. [II, 73-4]

The palace of the Rajah interested him; so did the Ganges. He visited Lucknow, the site of the 1857 mutiny, was impressed by the Taj Mahal, went to Delhi and took a train to Bombay, which he reached January 18. He found Bombay a beautiful city, but the customs of the place irritated him, particularly ideas about marriage and religion.

Nor was he taken with the Muslim faith, a belief that bothered him and that he discussed in many future paragraphs: "Some day it will become necessary for the white races to suppress the Mohammedan religion; it is so intolerant, brutal, and so mixed up with filth, inhumanity, murder and disorder. . . . The religion which teaches that American bacon is unclean food, and all white men are worse than dogs, is becoming entirely too gay of late" (II, 137).

Sounding angrier and angrier, the Atchison man left India January 20 on the *Persia,* whose passengers were all agreeable, even though they were almost all British. The travel letters became shorter, to fit, probably, the editor's temper. The ship stopped January 24 at Aden, and it reached the Suez Canal January 28. In Cairo he stayed at Shepheard's Hotel. He looked at the Nile Valley, which resembled the valley of the Missouri at Atchison when growing wheat covered the countryside in the spring, but there were neither trees nor vegetation on the bluffs of the Nile. He thought that Saturday in Cairo was a lot like Saturday in Atchison. Too many hours in the Cairo museums tired him; antiquities were as big a bore as paintings. The Pyramids also were a disappointment. The Sphinx startled him: it was not only much smaller than he had expected but it was in a gully. And like Mark Twain back in the sixties he was revolted by the "pilgrims" who had to leave their mark everywhere they traveled.

On February 4 the ship left for Palestine and arrived the next day at Jaffa, where a train took the Howes through the mountains to Jerusalem. Howe was attracted by the arched streets, the flagstone footways, the shops and markets and beggars. The Church of the Holy Sepulchre was probably a noble structure, he thought, but it was also like temples in pagan lands. And the pilgrims were like Christmas shoppers in Atchison, "women with the Christmas trot." He visited Bethlehem, Jericho, the Jordan countryside (where the rainfall totals were similar to those at Hays, Kansas), the Wailing Wall (where the Russian peasants reminded him of people at a Methodist camp meeting). He reported that at Bethany he asked for forgiveness for the sins of the people of Atchison:

"If the people of a Russian town can send a representative here, and he can cause the sins of his fellow-citizens to be wiped out, I don't see why I can't do the same thing for my fellow-citizens. True, they didn't appoint me as their ambassador, but that, no doubt, can be easily arranged after my return" (II, 203).

Noise and filth and wretchedness—these were his impressions. Though he wasn't sure he should be doing it, he smoked while passing through the Jewish quarter of Jerusalem, as he had done in old Shanghai. He was appalled by "how the people breed here, Arabs as well as Jews!" (II, 206). The walled cities intrigued him; he said the people of Atchison, to comprehend the walls, should imagine a wall thirty to fifty feet high around their city, with towers and gates: the south gate would be the Leavenworth gate, the west gate the Topeka gate, the north gate the Doniphan gate. On the outside would be a deep ditch or moat, with access to the city only by drawbridges. And the wall would be designed for fighting invaders from Missouri, Iowa, or Nebraska.

From Palestine the party went on the *Republic* to Alexandria, and sailed from there February 15. Ed Howe saw Stromboli in eruption, but the greatest delight yet was in seeing the American flag in Naples, which the ship reached February 17. Vesuvius, hot and smoking, and Pompeii—these were reported in conventional travel folder fashion, and then the travelers went to Rome by rail, passing Monte Cassino, which impressed Howe, as did the well-cultivated fields. Rome he liked, with its churches, its hotels and electric rail system and cleanliness. But the Coliseum "was too big and became a ruin, and that will be the fate of Convention Hall" (II, 274). He reached Paris February 23 and visited the Luxembourg galleries and stayed at the Hotel de l'Athenée, where he had had lodgings twenty-two years before. And he was disgusted by the indecent sculptures and paintings in the Louvre:

> In the Louvre, I can point out an "art gem" by Rubens that is as unnecessarily indecent as is a filthy word written with a stick in the snow. . . . I can point out hundreds of religious pictures in the Louvre that are ludicrous: people laugh at them in spite of the sacredness of the subjects treated. In one picture is shown a cherub sliding down the sky on a sled, belly-

> buster fashion .... The bosom of a woman should be sacred to her infant children, but it is exploited in art. Rubens, the nastiest of painters, transcends the limit by painting an angel with three sets of bosoms. This may not be a nice thing to print, but there is such a picture in the Louvre, in Paris, the finest art gallery in the world. Where could such a woman find a corset? [II, 282-83]

The "Impressionists," whose work was in the Luxembourg, were even worse, for they were crazy. He would not accept an impressionist painting as a gift, and their work should be displayed as curiosities, not as art.

He was off to London on February 25, getting his mail from home (a great joy), and leaving February 28 on the *Baltic.* The ship anchored off Sandy Hook March 9, and he reached Atchison March 11.

A mild kind of fame came to Ed Howe when the travel letters were published in 1907 as *Daily Notes of a Trip Around the World,* in two illustrated volumes. The notes received considerable praise, and they still have some of the charm and humor of Mark Twain's *Innocents Abroad.* Henry King of the *Globe-Democrat* commented on their "unconventionality," on how Howe "can not get away from the habit of expressing complete, detached observations by means of short paragraphs, and the 'pertness' and shrewdness of these observations are among the distinguishing qualities of the work."[12] The *New York Times* gave the notes another boost:

> Possessing the agreeable qualities of freshness, spontaneity, and unself-consciousness in a degree rarely to be found in travel books, ... The subject matter ... is, not Hawaii, Japan, China, the Philippines, India, etc., but the unspoiled citizen of Kansas as he is revealed by contact with outlandish places, and manners. Naturally, but not without humor, Mr. Howe assumes that these outlanders are all somehow (though the fault is not theirs) wrong, freakish—as deviating from the Kansas model, but he reveals himself as a very likable provincial, and he records incidents which, though they may not strike you quite as they strike him, will strike you entertainingly, nevertheless. [May 6, 1908]

The *Independent* called the notes the most entertaining in many a year. Other praise came from S. S. McClure, William Dean Howells ("The Howe travel letters are delightful"), Edward Bok, and Elbert Hubbard. The New York *Sun* compared the notes with *Innocents Abroad.* And Ed Howe, for years, carried advertising for the *Daily Notes* in both *Globe* and *Monthly.*

The Road to Retirement

They were the years of success, those *Globe* years when the pattern of the paper was established and Ed Howe could go off "gadding" around the world and achieve status that he often felt his town had denied him. He was becoming prosperous; he was making, in his best years, $24,000 to $25,000. Periodically he published boastful claims about the paper, and its advertising and circulation.

His pride remained Atchison and Kansas; at least it must have seemed so to his readers. The New York magazines that printed photographs of beautiful actresses could find better examples of beauty in the vicinity of Atchison, Kansas, he thought; he knew a dozen girls whom "the actresses can't touch." His town was the best town morally in the state—fighting, drunken rows, scandals, shootings, and public dishonesty were seldom in the news. The people were hard-working and known for their charity and friendliness; parents could look forward to their children spending good clean lives: "The evils that stalk around in other towns seldom show their influence here" (Aug. 29, 1908). About this time a Philadelphian wrote that Atchison was the best-governed city of its size in America, and that it was governed by a newspaper, *The Globe:*

"In Atchison a man is mighty careful about cutting up the daddles or getting drunk for fear his misdoing may be noted in *The Globe* that afternoon or the next. Yet, such reference is always made in the spirit of kindly warning. In Atchison there is no such thing as graft. *The Globe* won't stand for graft. Its city editor has been a member of the City Council for many years, and its editor is in reality the Mayor, chief of police and moral guide of the place."[13]

Ed Howe remained an editor who could not, except for a few minor things that became subjects of his barbs, see much that was the matter with Kansas:

> Kansas is the only place worth while to those who have dwelt long within her borders. But no one, however prejudiced, doubts that some of the abundant advertising this state has received from the time of its territorial infancy up to date, has been of a kind that brings no valuable results. There were the Border Ruffians, Indians, grasshoppers, hot winds and Populists, all bad enough in their way, and not intended to boost the price of real estate, or the figures of the census report. Each of these, however, has had its little day, and has journeyed backward into history; forgiven, if not forgotten. The one source of ridicule abroad and trouble at home, which, like the poor, is always with us, is our prohibitory law, beautiful enough in theory, perhaps, but disgusting, ludicrous, assinine [sic] in the efforts to put it into practical use. [Aug. 12, 1907]

The way to keep the state a good state was to be a booster, a boomer, like those boomers he had laughed at in his newspaper and novels. He published what he called the "GLOBE'S GREATER ATCHISON HOME PATRONAGE SECTION." "CRUSH THE EVIL," cried *The Globe*. "Stop Patronizing Mail Order Houses and Trade With the Legitimate Merchants." On the front page of the paper appeared a four-column cartoon of a huge pig, labeled "Mail Order House," eating in a trough labeled "Trade." A skinny little pig labeled "Country Merchants" was trying to get to the trough, and having little luck; the caption: "ROOT, 'LITTLE HOG,' OR DIE" (Oct. 6, 1908). Ed Howe opposed the mail order houses and also fought the parcel post bill being advocated in Congress. The greatest opposition to the bill came not from express companies, he wrote, but from country merchants who already had been crippled by the big mail order firms: "With a parcels post, they wouldn't have any more customers than the keeper of a bird store" (Aug. 14, 1907). He had changed his tune by November 23, 1910, when he once again was writing about parcel post but this time was contending that the express companies were flouting the will of the people.

Several special editions appeared over the years. One of them was published February 16, 1909, a giant for its time, with forty-four pages; its overline: "The 'Little Globe' First Appeared in 1878, With Two Pages. You Are Entitled to Forty-Four Pages To-Day." Lincoln Steffens and Arthur Brisbane sent him letters of congratulations. Advertising and feature articles were extensive —the Indians of Kansas; old John Brown; the big new high school building, Mt. St. Scholastica Academy, and St. Benedict's, all in Atchison. Howe himself wrote a primitive western tale called "Hat-Six Ranch." There was a gallery of photographs of Atchison homes, local industries, and community leaders.

The editor went traveling again in early 1910, leaving for the West Indies January 18 with his daughter, Mateel, Miss Eleanor Havens of Leavenworth, and C. D. Walker and his daughter, Isabel. He was going for his stomach's sake, he wrote, for "Nothing does me so much good as a sea voyage" (he knew he would be seasick, and therefore unable to eat, and therefore forced to sleep a lot).[14] He traveled through Indiana and recalled his boyhood days there. And once again he sent back travel letters to *The Globe.* In New York City he went to the office of the *World,* where he stared with wonder at the sixty-eight Linotypes in the composing room. He looked through the Italian, Jewish, and Chinese quarters; and in stereotyped outlander fashion commented that he could visit New York, but would rather not live there. On January 22 he boarded the vessel *Moltke,* which sailed the next day. It stopped January 26 at Charlotte Amalie on St. Thomas in the Virgin Islands, and at San Juan, Puerto Rico, where he was impressed by the natives and talked with a Wisconsin man engaged in pineapple growing. Always the reporter, Howe noted that the man was making a hundred dollars an acre, that net profit on sugar cane was sixty dollars an acre, that grapefruit and oranges also were profitable but that bananas were for home consumption only. Such information led the Kansan to reflect on the benefits of American business abroad, especially the United Fruit Company, which had made fruit both cheap and abundant.

The *Moltke* arrived at the Panama Canal February 1, and there Ed Howe met Colonel Goethals, the chairman of the Canal Commission, who described what Howe (who had scoffed years before at the very idea of such a canal) was now seeing as the biggest undertaking in history—with the possible exception of the Great Wall of China. Once again reportorial details engrossed him more than anything else, and helped to make his comments on the West Indies easily his dullest travel writings. Aboard ship he watched the behavior of other people, especially those young women who were smoking cigarettes. "One of the more modest women on board shocked me by saying: 'If I were as good-looking as she is, I believe I would dare call attention to myself in that way.' "[21] The *Moltke* had not stopped at Haiti, and Ed Howe had learned why—many grown men went naked there:

> In order to see that country, I shall be compelled to accompany an excursion for Men Only. . . . But I do not understand why the women on the "Moltke" are suddenly so squeamish: at Fort de France, on the Island of Martinique, some of the men divers who surrounded the ship were entirely naked. The women stood about the decks, as usual, and watched the divers, but I did not see any of the women passengers faint. Indeed, some of them threw coins into the water, to see the naked men dive; and, perhaps, I need not add that to see a naked man go over the side of a boat, wrong end up, is not an inspiring sight for ladies. It shocked me, careless as I am about some things.[22]

The *Moltke* went from the canal to Caracas, Venezuela, where Howe took a train to Porto Cabello. Always he was reporting on the crops he saw (a good Kansan on tour), and the local habits, the seclusion of women, the art, carnivals, markets, how much things cost, and the endless statues of Columbus. At Port of Spain, Trinidad, he commented on the prevalence of Hindu laborers, and from the ship he complained about having to hear music by John Philip Sousa, still one of Ed Howe's more forgettable composers. At Fort-de-France, Martinique, he saw the prettiest girl yet on the voyage, and at St. Pierre he saw a city still in ruins after the eruption of Mt. Pelee and the terrible earthquake that followed. At Havana, where the wreck of the *Maine* was still in the harbor, the *Moltke* was unable to dock, and Ed Howe told why: the people aboard were Americans, and Cubans hated Americans. On February 15 the ship stopped at Nassau, but there was too much high life there for him, and he was glad to go home, as usual. He returned to Atchison February 21.

The letters from the Indies were in general weak—too much travel reporting, too little commentary—but they appeared in book form, as *The Trip to the West Indies*. One gathers that Ed Howe was getting tired about that time. He had success, financial and journalistic, though his personal life had been more or less a failure. As early as 1902 he had written a reflective editorial on the problems of becoming old:

> We wish we could spend the Fourth of July in one of the Philippine islands, where there will be no celebrating.
>
> We do not object to the enthusiasm of boys on the Fourth,

> but we are getting along in years, and no longer enjoy noise. Our nerves are somewhat unsteady, and we require rest. The same is true in every day life: old people and young people do not enjoy the same things, but an old man is abused unless he has the "enthusiasm of youth." A perfectly ridiculous proposition, but it is a universal custom in this country to abuse an old man who does not enjoy the noise of his "young folks."
>
> Some of these days we intend to establish an Old Man's Place. It will be conducted on a plan calculated to satisfy an old man. Young people will be permitted to be as noisy as they please, off the Old Man's Place, and we will grant the necessity and right of the young to be youthful, but we will be in position to live as an old man should. The Old Man's Place will close promptly every evening at 8 o'clock, and the nights will be quiet. No courting; no babies, and breakfast at 6 a.m. In short, the Old Man's Place will suit our age and our prejudices, and those who do not like it can move out. [July 3, 1902]

He still had thoughts about the hypothetical publication he planned to call *Smith's Quarterly*. The job of an editor was frequently frustrating—the work itself, the public and personal protests, the occasional need, much as he disliked it, to suppress, even though he knew that suppression ultimately would come back to haunt the suppressor. The small town suited him, of course; he and William Allen White had learned, or had assumed, that their niche was the Kansas town, that the big city was not for them. He had tramped the streets of Atchison for thirty-two years, notebook and pencil in hand, finding stories and writing about things that less perceptive writers would have ignored, as Walt Mason would say about Howe in *The American* even after the editor had retired from *The Globe:*

"If you journey the length of the main street of Atchison, Kansas, any fine morning, it is more than probable that you will be accosted by a middle-aged man of a serious cast of countenance and polite bearing, and if you have anything in the way of news to impart, it will be received with gratitude and jotted down upon the back of an envelope or any fragment of paper that the serious-faced man can dig from his pockets."[23]

Mason said Howe worked as hard as his staff at gathering news, that his life was a routine one—at work at eight, the forenoon on the streets, gathering stories:

"His hand-writing is the worst in the United States. He starts a line at the upper left-hand corner of a sheet of paper and when it is ended it has reached the lower right-hand corner. His typewritten copy is a trifle more illegible than the product of his pen. . . . He is quiet, courteous and amiable, and when he is tired of hard work he starts to work a little harder as a relaxation."

He had always had a good staff, and he was close to his associates—Miss Frances L. Garside, Ralph "Doc" Tennal, Miss Nellie Webb, J. E. Rank. Tennal was the first of these to leave, "a remarkable reporter of local news, but being ambitious and realizing the limitations by which he was surrounded, he concluded to acquire a newspaper property of his own" (that being the *Sabetha Herald,* to which he went in 1905, then becoming editor of the *Kansas City Star's* weekly edition, and returning to Sabetha to become editor again of the *Herald*). Rank left a few years later for Bartlesville, Oklahoma, then returned to Atchison. Frances Garside went to the *New York Journal;* Nellie Webb remained on *The Globe* and became a mainstay under Gene Howe's editorship.[24] She already had been a key member of the staff for many years. The story was that she had applied for a job in October, 1898, at $2.50 a week, even though, according to one report, Howe had said: "Nellie, I like you, but you're worthless. You are too fond of card-playing and having fun." She became known for her column, "Wreaths and Wallops for Women," which was quoted all over the country.

Ed Howe had acquired a home in the countryside near Atchison, and the *Topeka State Journal* reported on August 16, 1908, that its Atchison competitor was now living there. Howe called the place "Potato Hill"; when he was in Colombo, Ceylon, he had sent an article home saying he would call his home that, giving it such a name to make fun of the ostentatious titles many people were giving to their homes—Oakhurst, Pinecrest, Chestnut Hill, and the like. Howe built it as a place to retire when he became old, because he believed that old people tend to stand around and get in the way of others. So, the "Old Man's Place" was a house with two bathrooms, an important thing to Ed Howe; one of his early paragraphs had read, "A man rarely wants to go to the bathroom that he does not find a woman in it, or waiting to get in." At Potato Hill he also had what he thought was the best bedroom in the state, with a private bath. The house was high on a hill, surrounded by hard maples, which he himself had planted, and it became the delight of his retirement:

"A windstorm does not worry me at Potato Hill, although the bungalow is built on a high point, overlooking a wide sweep of the Missouri valley; from the east veranda, there is a view probably unsurpassed in the West. The house has modern improvements, and I shall be as comfortable there as a town man. The room where I shall work in future is 24x19 feet, with two closets, fireplace, private bath, and light and air on three sides. Think of a man having two closets of his own; one supplied with hooks, and the other with drawers!"[25]

A few years later he wrote about how he had acquired the farm, which had belonged to a business woman who had heard that he wanted it. One day she had invited him to visit the farm, and she and her pretty niece provided lunch, which they ate at a spring. "The two women had taken me out to rob me; no doubt about it. The bait was the picnic lunch; in addition to that, they let me do the talking, and gave me the impression that I was interesting. My wit was so promptly and keenly appreciated that afternoon that I realized that I wasn't as smart as the two women robbers pretended, although I suppose I am as conceited as anyone."

"The robbers closed in" on him, talked about his desire to own the farm, and the woman told him she did not like haggling and that she would sell the farm for ten thousand dollars. Howe replied: "It is a pleasure to deal with one who dislikes haggling. I, too, like to deal with a business person; one who is fair, and who doesn't ask more than a thing is worth. So I'll meet you in the same spirit of fairness. I'm a fool to do it, but I'll give you four thousand dollars." And, said the hard-headed business woman: "I'll take it." So they gathered up the picnic dishes "and drove home in the gloaming" (January, 1912).

He had thought of retirement for years, discussing it in numerous editorials, commenting in 1909 on the good life being lived by James Gordon Bennett, Jr., of the *New York Herald:* "Mr. Bennett does not visit his newspaper office more than once in two years, yet the *Herald* is one of the great papers of the country." A few weeks later he was writing that there should be no limitations on a man, that he should keep working, or be permitted to keep working, as long as he is doing the work well. So he mulled the matter over. By late 1910 *The Globe* was an eight-page paper almost every day of the week, with still no Sunday edition. It still carried advertising on the front page, still put "telegraph news" in the central position, once in a while placed a display head over a big story. "Globe Sights," longer editorials, many reprints, much advertising, "label" heads, such as "City News"—these identified the paper. There had been no radical changes in recent years, although Ed Howe was writing less and less.

On December 31, 1910, Ed Howe published his last issue of *The Atchison Globe.* On that day "Globe Sights" read about the same as usual. There was no comment on his departure; there was nothing in the editorials to reveal that a change was about to take place. He turned the newspaper over to his sons, Gene to serve as the editor, giving them majority control if they would induce old employees and friends to raise funds for the minority stock. He then took his old typewriter "and went home to sulk." Things had been going badly, he thought. He had been getting nervous, was having difficulty sleeping, was tired of callers and petty details and other editors trying to get his specially trained men to quit. He also was tired of others trying to get credit for what he had done.

A few months later, in an article for the *Independent,* he wrote that he was tired and preferred to "rust out rather than wear out." And he recalled a conversation he had had with a farmer acquaintance:

" 'I am fifty-seven years old, but still able to do a good day's work,' the farmer had said.

"Is there nothing in this world beyond a good day's work? I didn't applaud the statement as much as the farmer evidently thought I should. Think of the millions of elderly men wearily earning money they can never use! They continue in the harness because they fear idleness will kill them."[26]

He also wrote about an old dog and a young dog on the farm. The young one was always looking for excitement: many fights, many scars, many dashes for rabbits, and much time spent digging for foxes. "But the old dog, having been a long time out in the world, knows that little of interest is going on, and spends much of his time sleeping in the sun. The old dog has accepted a hint from Nature; it is a pity men are not equally wise."

The old dog of *The Globe* thought he had been wise. The January 4, 1911, *Globe,* now being edited by Gene Howe, carried

"A STATEMENT FROM E. W. HOWE." First it reported that he had retired permanently from *The Globe,* that his successors thought public curiosity called for a statement, and that he was carrying out an intention he had had for several years. *The Globe* was never more prosperous, but he believed his retirement would be a good idea. He planned to publish within three months two books—*Country Town Sayings,* which would be a collection of his best paragraphs (the book became a standard volume), and *Country Town Sketches,* a collection of longer pieces. He planned to write a play based on *The Story of a Country Town:* "If I cannot make a play out of it, I shall at least enjoy trying it, and failure will not greatly disappoint me." *Country Town* had been a successful book, and he hoped other books might appear, books better than the failures of the later 1880s.

All his friends knew he had long contemplated retirement. Five years earlier he had tried to make arrangements with his staff, but nothing had come of the attempt. Six months before retirement he had offered the paper to his principal associates; again the plan had not succeeded. Now he was retiring—"It is the rule of the world: old men retire, and young men take their places." He had no bitterness; Atchison was his town and he hated no one there. No resentments, no enmities, but many good friends.

"I know that so long as I remain in active business, I should do my work with good nature and patience. This was becoming more difficult every year, because the annoyances around a newspaper office, I have always believed, are particularly burdensome. I was the 'old man,' and most of the annoyances came to me, and they wore me out."

For thirty-three years he had "pottered up and down Commercial street," and those years were at an end. Late the preceding Saturday afternoon he had realized he was making the last trip, and it had been a shock to him.

At Potato Hill he planned to publish a magazine: *A Farmer's Magazine for Town People*—the *Smith's Quarterly* he had long talked about. Perhaps it would resemble Elbert Hubbard's *The Philistine,* but he would do more writing than Hubbard normally did. He would be happy at Potato Hill. He had his brother Bruce; his niece, Adelaide, Bruce's daughter, as his housekeeper; and the family to assist in publishing the magazine. "If at any time *Smith's Quarterly* does not suit me, I shall suspend it and return the money to my handful of subscribers. I intend to do, so far as possible, what I please, so long as I do not interfere with the rights of others."

Would he attempt to come back, as Jim Jeffries had done? "Probably not, knowing what happened to Jeffries." He might send contributions to *The Globe,* but the editor could accept or reject them as he saw fit. But there would be no attempts to fight Jack Johnson:

"I have no championship belts, but I have a gold watch given me by citizens of Atchison; also a silver water service, and a loving cup, attentions I believe no other Atchison editor has ever received from the people. These I will cherish, and try not to disgrace, but I will not fight Jack Johnson, and have my friends bet on me, and lose."

He was unnecessarily (and unconvincingly) modest in disclaiming success or fame or ability: "I have written some terrible stuff, from being hurried, and lacking judgment and sense. Within the last few days I have gone over six and eight copies of *The Globe* without finding a paragraph worth preserving; but I found much that humiliated me [this was his gleaning for *Country Town Sayings*]. After an experience of that kind, a man feels modest, and I feel modest as I write this."

He would not leave Atchison; he would rather live there above all places. But newspaper work had become too wearing. Farming would be easier. His conclusion:

"There are two schools of philosophy. One declares that when a busy man retires from business, he mourns, and shrivels up, and dies in a few months, he is so sorry he has nothing to do. The other school of philosophy declares with equal positiveness that after reaching the prime of life, or as soon as possible thereafter, a man should retire, and refuse to become money mad. I have forgotten the exact language of this school of philosophers, but the idea they express is that a man should give his soul a chance, and not worship the dollar. I don't know which school of philosophy is right, and not knowing which good advice to take, I have acted on my own judgment.—E. W. HOWE."[27]

The retirement brought dozens of statements of praise to *The Globe.* All were duly carried on the editorial pages of two issues. They ranged from praise from Charles Finch, editor of the *Lawrence Gazette,* to that from Frank Cobb, editor of the New York

World, who said Howe had "put Atchison on the map and has kept it there year in and year out."

And there was doggerel, from "Doc" Bixby, in the *Nebraska State Journal:*

Some day, when he is at the plow,
I'm going down to see Ed. Howe;
And, not to count among the bores,
I'll peel my coat and help do chores.
For style I do not give a darn;
I'll feed the pigs and clean the barn,
Out to the pasture gaily treck [sic],
And milk the spotted cow called Speck,
Hike back, and, when I've cleaned my feet,
Show how a working man can eat.
If he says "Come," then I shall fix
To see him when the grass grows.—BIX

And from Franklin P. Adams, in the *New York Evening Mail:*

Ed. Howe has quit, that good old scout,
His stuff we'll ne'er see more;
He used to write about the things
That made him very sore.

His stuff was honest as the day;
He hated bluff and sham;
For phony hair he did not care
A whoop in Hepsidam.

He always had a word to say
On every sort of question;
He let the chips fall where they may,
He had a bum digestion.

He did not have the patience of
The wise and well-known Job;
If there was that he did not love
He'd say so in "The Globe."

And so Ed. Howe has quit the game;
He quit the first of Jan.—
And everybody said he was
Considerable Man. [Jan. 11, 1911]

And, in the unsophisticated fashion of a less sophisticated age in American life, the *Independent,* like "Bix," the Nebraska poet, and the popular Franklin P. Adams, also turned to verse:

> Ed. Howe has quit, quit ere his prime
> Old Edgar Howe, and hath not left his peer.[28]

So to Potato Hill he went. He had quit voicing his opinions, on any and all subjects. Or so people thought. He had taken a few months off, and he would become a still better-known national figure in the more than thirty years in which he would be publishing what, in the late days of 1910, he envisioned as *Smith's Quarterly.*

6

E. W. HOWE'S MONTHLY

A Magazine Is Launched

Behind him lay a career that already had made him well known in American letters and journalism. He had had a national audience, but with the new publication a national circulation would be his aim.

The new editor of *The Globe* gave his father three full columns in which to make his announcement of the new magazine. Ed Howe wrote the announcement himself, he said, because one of *The Globe* men had had to go to a funeral and asked him to write the story.

He had planned to call the magazine *Smith's Quarterly,* but when he decided to issue it once a month, the name did not seem suitable. He thought about calling it *The Rebel,* but finally he decided to call it simply *E. W. Howe's Monthly.* It was to appear about February 10, 1911, "maybe a week earlier and maybe a week later. That's the joy of a magazine; its publisher is not compelled to go to press every day at exactly 3:45 p.m., a problem which has been hounding me for thirty-three years." Whether people subscribed to the magazine was not his worry. No one would be asked to advertise in it. It would not be stereotyped; when copies were exhausted none would be made available.

He had been in retirement for little more than a week, but already he had a comment to make: "I am having (as the ribald young men say) the time of my life. I do what I please when I please, and no one to suggest or hinder. I have not been out of the house for eleven days, except that I went to Topeka last Saturday, and returned by way of Kansas City. . . ."

He was on his own, too, bossed by no one, except the "young

woman," his niece Adelaide, who was living with him, "one of those benighted but agreeable women who believe that their 'men folks' amount to something." Another niece, Adelaide's sister, Edna, also was living with him, and he was sure that he was in control of the household.

Soon there would be a play from the Ed Howe typewriter; he had been thinking for twenty-seven years about making a play out of *The Story of a Country Town,* and he had written one—in three days. But it needed polishing. He was confident the play would be a success; the country town had a story to tell that would be understood by anyone in the audience.

The new routine was enjoyable, this being out of the office and on the farm. He had been sawing wood with Nick Preston, whose wife worked around the Howe house. He had been talking a lot with his brother Bruce, who was becoming a good friend. Bruce had come in to talk with him about the family cow he had killed, and about the garden, and was especially enthusiastic when the subject of radishes was mentioned.

"I agreed to write two columns, to help out; I think this will fill it. I will only add this: In the old, old days, when I rushed around after news like a chicken with its head cut off—before I retired, in short—a restless night always resulted in a bad day. If I fail to sleep well now, I do not mind it the following day. My retirement has accomplished that much, anyway.—E. W. HOWE (retired)."[1]

Retirement was far from complete. He dropped in at *The Globe* office from time to time, and Gene once testified that he hated to hear the telephone ring because it might be the old man calling to offer criticism. The son, who had been treated well by his father, tried to oblige by accepting the criticism, and the two succeeded in maintaining a close association through the years.

E. W. Howe's Monthly, Volume I, Number 1, appeared in March, 1911, about a month after its editor had announced it would be launched. It was a little magazine, pocketbook size, at first consisting of sixty-four pages, costing a dollar a year or ten cents a copy. Howe wrote everything in it, and it was mainly a collection of his views and prejudices. The subtitle was "A Farmer's Magazine for Town People." Anyone who did not want to know about all the affairs of Ed Howe would not want the *Monthly,* for it was a highly personalized publication.

In that first issue he told why he had quit *The Globe,* promised that the *Monthly* would be one magazine that could not be killed off (except by success), stressed the fact that his dream was not to become rich, recalled his boyhood and newspaper experiences—stories already told over and over again—and discussed anew the reasons for his retirement: tiredness, pressures, nagging people.

His income, he wrote, was sixty dollars a day, not much to a New York man, but to the average editor proof that a man has to work hard. He would continue to work because he preferred work to idleness.

One theme ran constantly through the early years of *E. W. Howe's Monthly,* a theme that provides a picture of gruff old Ed Howe quite different from the grim portraits provided by Gene Howe and others. It was the theme of his devotion to his niece, Adelaide. For nine years prior to the arrival of Adelaide his housekeeper had been Katie Jurgensen, who had spoiled him and waited on him like a child. Women who came to the house to look for dirt were never able to find it. Now it was Adelaide, and she continued to give him good care. His affection for her was truly remarkable. She was only twenty when she started to work for him, "a farmer's daughter, and the largest town she had seen was Omaha, across the river from Council Bluffs, Iowa, where she was born."[2]

His deep love and admiration for her were obvious in all he wrote. He watched her as she worked quietly about the house, and thought about the contrast with his more miserable early years. Her parents said she had never given them a moment's trouble, and he said he always praised her to his friends. Playfully he policed her reading, writing in *The Monthly* that he had ordered the *Ladies' Home Journal,* which she had been reading, kept out of the house. "I shall not be placed in competition with a Scotch hero who owns a farm of twenty thousand acres, covered with lakes, fens, and game preserves. There are only a hundred and nine acres in Potato Hill farm, and I cannot stand the competition of the Scotch hero" (October, 1911).

He liked Adelaide because she never complained about housework, because she baked the best bread he had ever eaten and made fine butter, and because she provided good things to eat from New Year's to Christmas. And she was neat, and quiet, and told people she was happy. ". . . when I buy her a tailor made suit, she has a figure fit for it; she is healthy; she isn't expensive to keep, since she doesn't eat much; I never saw her in tears; she does not engage in Tag Days." And her parents did not bother him. Her pastor did not call on her. She laughed at his jokes, and she did not express contrary opinions. In short, she was not a useless actress, literary woman, suffragette, a woman with headaches, churchwoman or lodge woman.

"I love Adelaide, my niece, for many reasons, but probably most of all for this:

"During these hot days, I find my 'den' rather stuffy, so I take my writing and reading to a cooler room up stairs, where I loiter my time away. Every morning, after Adelaide has completed her duties down stairs, she comes up quietly, and sits down near me, with her sewing. Very soon the cat appears (for everything around this house loves Adelaide), and goes to sleep at her feet. If I choose to remain quiet an hour, or two hours, not a word is spoken. What pleases me is, that Adelaide follows me" (August, 1912).

To her he was "Uncle Ed," and he was greatly entertained because one of his correspondents had found fault with Adelaide's name, saying he would as soon have a girl named "Lemonade" or "Orangeade" as "Adelaide."

"Adelaide is so generally admired that this letter amuses me. To my knowledge, she was never found fault with before. If you desire to live to be twenty-two and be found fault with but once, here is the way to do it: Be quiet. Adelaide is the quietest person I ever knew. I am found fault with so much that I do not mind it. When people cannot find anything in my own conduct to pick at, they make up something: here is a person who growls because I am harboring in my home a young person named Adelaide" (January, 1912).

He was surprised and impressed by the attention his niece attracted, and all, he thought, because she was "quiet, capable, modest, useful and womanly, since she can neither sing, play, nor speak pieces. . . . The woman who is an asset and not a liability is the woman men always admire" (April, 1912).

He also drew enjoyment from his relationship with his brother Bruce and Bruce's wife, Aunt Fanny. Bruce Howe was entirely different from his brother—calm, easygoing, quiet, never known to flare up or become angry. But the two got along well as they lived together at Potato Hill. Ed Howe worked with Bruce in the fields, and he talked with him about farm matters, such as the habits of setting hens, or of bees; he duly reported all this for his readers in *The Monthly*. He also discussed in intimate details the religion of his relatives, a *Monthly* article that may have created a bit of consternation in the family:

> Not having much to do, I have lately been investigating the religion of Uncle Bruce and Aunt Fanny. As near as I can make out, Aunt Fanny joined the church because it had an organ to play, with a salary of five dollars a Sunday to the organist, although she has always been compelled to fight a movement to reduce the price to $3; while Uncle Bruce joined because he fell in love with the organist. They have belonged to, or, at least, attended a good many churches: I have heard them talk about attending the Congregational, the Catholic, the Presbyterian, and the Baptist, and for a few months Aunt Fanny played the organ in a Jewish synagogue. Uncle Bruce took her to and from choir practice and services, but I believe he never actually joined the Jewish congregation. He seems to leave a church on slight provocation: I have heard his children say he was once beaten for superintendent of a Baptist Sunday school, which caused him to find fault with that denomination, and he soon after began attending a Congregational church where his wife was organist. But they finally landed in the Presbyterian church. Since I have known them, they have never attended church, to my knowledge, but they have a "letter" which will admit them to the Presbyterian fold whenever they find time to attend. Adelaide is included in the "letter"; it seems she joined when she was twelve or fourteen years old, but she never knew it, until her mother recalled the incident. Adelaide says she didn't know she was joining; she says she stood up with some other children, and thought they were agreeing to take part in a Sunday school entertainment. . . .
>
> But, in spite of their rather checkered church record, Uncle Bruce and Aunt Fanny belong to the great army of Christians who are Fighting Sin. They look at me with a good deal of pity because I have no "letter." They do not have family prayers; they do not ask a blessing at the table; they do not read the Bible; they do not say their prayers at night. Uncle Bruce's father did all these things, and I have heard Aunt Fanny speak of her father as a very religious man. Still, Uncle Bruce and Aunt Fanny are on the rolls as church members; they are among the sheep. If they could attend a revival, and the revivalist should ask believers to stand up, they would promptly and proudly arise. No wonder preachers are not getting results;

so many church members are like Uncle Bruce and Aunt Fanny. If I believe in a thing, I put in my "letter." [October, 1911]

The dramatic version of *The Story of a Country Town* on which Howe had been working had a brief career only, with its opening at the Majestic Theater in Topeka in late January, 1911. Several persons, he recalled, had wanted to make a play from the book, but he decided to do it himself, and sent a copy of the play to William Dean Howells (whose response was unrecorded). The play, in contrast to the book, had a happy ending, and perhaps Howells was not pleased enough to provide the help he had given the novel. *The Story of a Country Town* was staged by the North Brothers Company, and the leading roles were played by Sport North and his wife, known as Genevieve Russell. Topeka had the play for a week; then it was moved to Atchison. And even though Kansas was a bone-dry state, for one of the scenes champagne was opened on the stage every night.

In those unsophisticated days of the theater the play perhaps could have gone to Broadway. But Howe did not like the idea of a Broadway star playing one of the central roles. (It is more likely that the play was not good enough. Its place in theatrical history is virtually non-existent.) The *Topeka State Journal,* in friendly home-state fashion, wrote that it liked the play, praising the production, the "brilliant audience," the interest in the story, the entertaining comedy, especially the built-up characterization of Big Adam (who had been liked so much in the novel by at least one person, Mark Twain, that the great man had told Howe he should build a play around him). "His quaint sayings, his country boy actions, his imitation of the cork pulling and the gurgle of the liquor from the bottle brought forth repeated laughter and applause."[3] Ed Howe was at the opening, and he was given an ovation and came before the curtain to give a brief talk. The *Topeka Daily Capital* wrote a more probing review, noting strengths and weaknesses, saying, ". . . with all its faults, the piece is a mine of tense and striking situations and its comedy vein is both rich and unusual in its formation."[4] There was a friendly audience; people apparently *wanted* to like the play by the Kansan. The *Capital's* reviewer thought Howe had overwritten scenes; that speeches needed cutting, that the atmosphere of the book had been lost. Such a play could take place "Anywhere." But, worked on and pared down, it conceivably could become a good thing.

The Story of a Country Town disappeared into the realm of forgotten plays, and Ed Howe scarcely mentioned it again. It is not likely that he cared much about its disappearance. For he was learning to relax. He didn't even care what people thought about the magazine, he wrote, and if they didn't like the magazine they should just quit taking it (there was some edginess about the matter: he preferred not to get the abusive letters). No time to quarrel; a man cannot be argued out of his way of thinking. To one man he had returned the dollar subscription after the subscriber had said he expected to quarrel with Howe and would write and say so.

Humor and observations in *The Monthly* (June, 1911) were in the familiar vein of the past:

"In last month's issue of this magazine, I made the statement that a successful man, providing he is honest, is as good as a poor man. You may imagine that this unusual statement brought a flood of letters from the rich, ordering the magazine. But it didn't; indeed, the only rich man who wrote me said:

" 'For heaven's sake, quit saying successful men are as good as the poor; you only make the people more cruel in punishing us.' "

On women: "A certain woman who is scrawny, is always wearing lowneck dresses, whereas her sister, who is plump, never wears them. 'You have talent,' the scrawny sister often says to the fat one, 'but make no use of it.' "

On marriage: "A man came home who hadn't seen his wife in four months, and, as he opened the door, his heart beating high, his wife greeted him with: 'Don't hold the screen door open so long! You're letting in the flies!' "

He was insistent about enforcing the policy of not arguing with subscribers. He gave his "country-girl secretaries" instructions to burn all letters that were disagreeable, but dissatisfied subscribers were to get their money back. He told about a man who had written him: "I wish you would send my sister your magazine. She is losing her mind." Howe's comment: "I don't know that he intended it that way, but that's the way his letter read."

He carried advertising for his books, and as the years progressed he put in other small ads on occasion. Generally *The Monthly* had a no-advertising policy:

> Since I do not solicit advertisements for this magazine, you may think I will not get many. You are right about it. But if you will look on the outside cover page of this issue you will see that I have received at least one. In writing to this advertiser, you need not mention this magazine. But I express the hope that you will ask for Bulletin 40A; that is evidently my key number. This advertiser sent me a booklet with his copy, and I read it with interest. The name, "The Holt Caterpillar Gasoline Traction Engine," attracted my attention, for one thing, and, for another, I was interested in the fact that thirty of these engines are in use in constructing the great dam to supply Los Angeles with water. The "Holt Caterpillar Gasoline Traction Engine" lays its own track, and is something new; probably the booklet describing it will interest you, as it did me. But if you send for it, PLEASE ask for Bulletin 40A. [June, 1911]

Ed Howe was not a sentimental man about most things. What kept both *Globe* and *Monthly* going was the astonishing quantity of his prejudices. And the humor. His words about nature were few; and even when he did choose the subject he had the knack of making it an attack on the people he disliked in public life, as in a delightful editorial like this one in the first year of *The Monthly:*

> I am inspired by nature; by birds and flowers, and children, and landscapes, but in admiring nature, I do not see a thousand things that are not there. How some people rave about birds! I love them, when they deserve to be loved, but some varieties of birds I find a nuisance. There is the impudent pest known as the English sparrow, introduced into this country by a Good Gentleman to rid our fields of insects, and which has become a menace to the country. There are the swallows, which flutter in my chimneys when I am anxious to sleep. There are the whippoorwills, and the nighthawks, which go to work at night, like the girl piano players in your neighborhood, who sleep all day, and become a nuisance about the time industrious people are thinking of bed. Then there is the phoebe, which nests around my porches, and makes a mess, to say nothing of the pigeons which light on the roof, and befoul the cistern. True, I catch an occasional sight of a scarlet tanager, or a cardinal, or an oriole; I follow these with a glass, and admire them. But these modest birds are no apology for the impudent jays, who, when I enter my own cherry orchard, scream a protest as though I were an interloper. The best birds, like the best men, are modest. Among men, those most like English sparrows, swallows, nighthawks, whippoorwills, crows and blue jays attract most of the attention. Bob LaFollette, to me, is wonder-

> fully like a blue jay, with his tremendous activity and shrill screaming. The nighthawk is forever complaining about something, like Bryan. And the whippoorwills: how insistently they demand that poor Will be whipped! Their cry is not a protest because poor Will *has* been whipped, but because he is not whipped when he does not deserve it. How like the whippoorwills are Hearst, and Champ Clark, and the Insurgents generally, with their tiresome and never changing cry! The English sparrows, originally thought to be Reformers, are greatly annoying the really useful birds. Better get your gun. A pot shot at English sparrows is no sin. [September, 1911]

He had rivals in those still pleasant teen years, when World War I still had not broken out, when life seemed relatively quiet and pleasant and casual. The best of these was Elbert Hubbard, who was publishing *The Philistine* and *The Fra;* he praised *The Monthly* frequently and helped Howe get more than a thousand subscribers. Another was the *Haldeman-Julius Weekly,* which also boosted the little magazine and helped gain eight hundred subscribers for Ed Howe. There was sniping back and forth between Howe and Hubbard, always in a friendly way, two arch-conservatives who had much in common, despite the fact that one was so much the sophisticate and the other so much the country bumpkin (or so he viewed himself). Howe regarded Hubbard as one of the great men of the country, though he often said Hubbard used too many big words and charged too much for his publication. A dozen or so issues of *The Fra,* from 1911 to 1916, carried several comments picked up from Howe's *Monthly.*

Ed Howe continued to say that writing was no easy task. On one occasion he wrote that his paragraphs seemed pretty bad after he had read them over two or three times, and after reading the proof twice he was ready to throw them out altogether.

He did most of his writing at Potato Hill. Once in a while he would go into town, where he was still well known, but when he walked on the street "all the bores in town would turn up."[5] He was generally content, for a few years at least, to remain at the farm and write and reflect. He had the answer to the endless demand for an "Endowed Magazine," he thought; it was *E. W. Howe's Monthly.* And he had no worries about advertising or subscriptions. No Uneeda biscuit man, or Gold Medal flour man, or American Radiator Company man; they had all cut him cold. No one representing Little Pig Sausages or Post's or Duffey's malt whiskey or Castoria, Lydia Pinkham, Dr. Pierce, and Doc Munyon. Only the automobile supply man in Kansas City, his sole advertiser.

In February of 1912 he wrote that he was having a good time on the first anniversary of his emancipation. Like Eliza crossing the Ohio he had broken out of slavery and evaded the bloodhounds. Running a house he found an easy job; why should women complain about it?

Kansas politics and Atchison affairs no longer interested him much. There were so many people on the national scene and throughout history for him to complain about:

"Readers of this magazine may have observed that I find a good deal of fault with Emmeline Pankhurst, T. R., W. J. B., LaFollette, Ferdinand and Isabella, Jane Addams, Ben Lindsay, King Richard, Mahomet, Colonel Buddha, Columbus, Maud Muller, and other popular heroes and heroines. I do find fault with them, and justly. My contention is that some of the compliments that flow in such a generous stream to these people, should go to YOU, providing you are as modest and worthy as you should be" (February, 1912).

There was always Gifford Pinchot, a trouble-maker from 'way back. And of those on his list the most cutting comments were reserved for that woman who should be at home, washing the dishes:

"By-the-way, I do not admire Jane Addams; let me confess my shame, and run away and hide. Why do I not admire this worthy woman who is the idol of Chicago, Evanston, Aurora, and other towns in the vicinity? Because of that extra d in her name. "Addams" is not the proper way to spell Adams, any more than "Billy Burke" is the proper way to spell a woman's name. Doing good is as much Jane Adams' work as robbery is the life work of Andrew Carnegie. Had she displayed as much genius in her life work as Carnegie, there would be almost no distress in the world" (December, 1911).

His candidate for President in 1912, offered perhaps facetiously but still out of heartfelt admiration, was the man he had memorialized for twenty years:

> John D. Rockefeller would make a better president than Bob LaFollette, and is more entitled to the honor. You may decide promptly that the above is a foolish statement. But is it?

> Is it your fault, and not mine, that it seems foolish? Rockefeller is one of the greatest executives the world has ever known; you will at least admit that. Do we not need such a man at the head of this nation, instead of a politician? Make Rockefeller president, with freedom to give the people better service for less money, and he would do it. There are thousands of government employees who do not earn half their pay; one-half of one-half of the government appropriations, is wasted. If Rockefeller should be elected president, and say: "You people have been demanding reform a great many years without getting it; I intend to actually give it to you," it would be an accomplishment worth while. [December, 1911]

There were no limitations on subject matter in *The Monthly*, except personal ones. He could write what he wanted and take as much space as he thought necessary. There was no curb on his prejudices; no fear of advertisers, not even a fear of subscribers. Nonsense could take up space; nonsense it was that marked some of the early issues of *The Monthly*. There was "The 11 to 3 issue," for example, an issue based on his observation that Mexico had fourteen million persons, eleven million of them ready to listen to unreason, the other three million reasoning people. From that he drew the conclusion that 11 to 3 is the proportion one finds everywhere:

"The newspapers appealing to the ELEVEN have the large circulations; the THREE have almost no representation in the public prints. In political platforms, the THREE are denounced, and the ELEVEN praised. In plays, maudlin sentimentality is exploited, because the ELEVEN like it. . . . The proportion is not only ELEVEN TO THREE in fairness, but in taste" (September, 1912).

Some readers probably thought all this silly; he wondered what his beloved Adelaide was saying to herself when the mail was light and the magazine slumping. Because Adelaide believed the magazine to be important, and she thought everyone should subscribe to it. What, then, was wrong with those who did not subscribe to it? "My opinion is that she knows the truth about her uncle Ed., to-wit: that he doesn't amount to much" (October, 1912).

There were issues of *The Monthly* that he labeled "The Illustrated Number" (carrying a rare thing in the magazine—pictures), the "Fat Woman Number," the "Stand Pat Number," and the "Riddle of the Sphinx Number." These may have bored some readers; more likely he was appealing to the literate reader because of his clear and entertaining style, and even more for the iconoclastic comments he put forth. The special numbers were not representative of *The Monthly,* and do not hold up well. But they—and the magazine as a whole—were an outlet for his views, his beliefs, his trivial pursuits. Life at the farm, the foods he liked, his attempts to quit smoking—all found their way into *The Monthly.* He said that he saw no great importance in the publication. A. B. Macdonald, a *Kansas City Star* newsman who checked at *The Globe* office in 1933, found that only scattered copies of it had been kept.

Another Trip to Exotic Lands

In the December, 1912, *Monthly* came news that he was off to Australia for a six-month trip. It would include much more than just Australia, however: New Zealand, Africa, Arabia, and even part of Europe were encompassed in the journey. This time Adelaide went with him, "the only youngster on the ship," the *Sonoma,* on which they sailed for Sydney. As usual he sent home letters, all of them carried in subsequent issues of *E. W. Howe's Monthly.* Many of them were prosaic, describing things that had been part of the travel experiences of many persons—the ceremony of crossing the equator, for example, a visit to romantic Pago Pago and American Samoa. And a homesick note: the wireless buzz sounded like the locusts in the trees at Potato Hill.

On January 5 the *Sonoma* went through a storm, the worst Ed Howe had ever seen at sea, and the next morning Adelaide was the only woman at the breakfast table. The ship reached Sydney on January 6, and it was a land of people resembling Americans, but quite unlike Americans; Adelaide was particularly amused by these strange souls. The pronunciations of the "Austrylians" intrigued the Kansans, and Ed Howe reflected on how one of his favorite characters in literature, Magwitch in *Great Expectations,* had made his fortune in sheep while down under. Labor conditions were of special interest, and he commented on how economic issues were treated in the Australian press as compared with papers in the United States:

"At least one of the leading newspapers here, *The Morning Telegraph,* denounces unionism, saying it was originally in the interest of workingmen, but lately it has become political despotism, and union labor leaders political adventurers. 'Capital,' said *The Telegraph,* in an editorial this morning, 'will leave Australia, and go where labor is not a political despot.' I do not know of a leading paper in the United States that would care to print a similar editorial. Plenty of such editorials are printed in the United States, but in trade papers, and not in leading daily newspapers."[6]

On January 12 Howe went to Auckland, New Zealand, and two days later made a rail journey to Rotorua, land of the geysers. For Ed Howe these phenomena could not equal the geysers of Yellowstone Park, especially when he heard that soap was put into some of them so that they would show off more for the tourists. The Maoris interested him; they seemed to be much like Indians in the United States: lazy, shiftless and good fighters. Always the homey reporter, he commented that potatoes in New Zealand sold for three cents a pound, cabbage eight cents a head, green peas thirty-two cents a peck, sugar six cents a pound, flour three dollars a hundred pounds, and that the movie palaces were like those at home. The popularity of horse-racing, the prevalence of tea-drinking, the politeness of the people—all drew favorable comment. Americans would feel at home there; the Maori wars resembled our Indian wars, and the bush-rangers were like the cattle thieves, gamblers and gun-slingers of the old West. He went to Wellington on January 25, where he was especially drawn to the lady bartenders, and where he observed that the English do not speak English properly. Wellington was as fine a town as St. Joe back in Missouri, he thought.

He was back in Australia January 31, and he looked some more at Sydney—a handsome city, its people unashamed to use the word "trust," which Americans were being taught by the politicians and newspapers to despise. As an example, the street railway company, with no apology, called itself the "Tramway Trust." He sensed that there was much interest in the United States, in Teddy Roosevelt and in the Panama Canal, but he could find few American publications, except for the *Ladies' Home Journal,* and occasionally the *Saturday Evening Post,*

American, and *Cosmopolitan,* popular magazines that Ed Howe liked to read. The many rabbits, the parks, gardens, and hospitals were other attractions.

On a different vessel, the *Anchises,* the Howes were off to Africa on February 12, the editor engrossed in a book about oceans and dwelling on the technical data therein for some time in his letters. Life aboard ship irritated him; he preferred to go his own way but there was always a group of busybodies to make life miserable:

"It has probably never occurred to the members of the Sports Committee that they are a nuisance rather than a blessing. It would be very much pleasanter on board if a Gay Time had never been thought of. I do not care to dance; nor do I care to have members of the Sports Committee urge me to dance. If I care to play quoits, or any other of the deck games, I do not need a Sports Committee to urge me. The members of the Sports Committee think it an outrage that Adelaide does not dance, and look at me reproachfully. I tell them I had nothing to do with it; that her parents are church members, and do not believe in dancing. This also greatly astonishes them."[7]

He got a glimpse of South Africa on March 2, and the vessel landed at Durban, which he found an admirable city. Despite the steady rainfall he took a rickshaw to the beach and visited the Hindu market, where he was intrigued by the sale of sheep's heads and feet. Negroes seemed omnipresent to him, of course, and the racial problem of South Africa seemed to him much like that of the United States. He and Adelaide stayed at the Marine Hotel, where he attracted attention by eating roasting ears of corn American-style. The Hindu waiters stood around and watched him, he said, as did some of the other guests, and when he saw a man standing at the entrance, viewing the lighting as though he contemplated making a moving picture of the curious American visitor, he elected to have his corn cut off the cob, as other people did in Durban.

From Durban he left March 8 for a 483-mile trip to Johannesburg, and he had a chance to look over the farm country, always an obsession with Ed Howe. He concluded that he would be quite content to live in South Africa:

"I have never enjoyed a railroad ride more than I enjoyed the ride from Durban to Johannesburg. The weather was cool, and there was no dust. We left Durban in a pouring rain, but this morning the rain ceased, and by noon the sun was shining. For hours we passed through a prairie country which greatly resembled eastern Kansas as it was forty or fifty years ago."[8]

Johannesburg provided a different view of life. It was a new, clean place, a boom town in the American sense, where gold was the magic word. Boers, English, and Hindus—these were the main groups; but the color problem was even greater than in Durban. He was sure that "an American Negro would scream his head off in Johannesburg"—no rides on the street railways, no walking on sidewalks, a system of separation very much in effect. In Johannesburg he met and talked with business leaders, always to him the most respectable segment of society. He visited Pretoria, and recalled the career of Oom Paul Kruger and the Boer War and saw what seemed to him to be the best zoological garden in South Africa, with a rhinoceros so tame that children were allowed to feed it. "But how viciously these animals charged Colonel Roosevelt in his articles in *Scribner's Magazine!*" he hooted.[9]

Then to Kimberley by train, Africa continuing to appeal to the Kansan as he thought frontier America might have appealed to the pioneers going west. There was a "spirit of the Veldt," where Africans were working out problems of dry farming and irrigation and fighting with a soil not nearly as rich as that of eastern Kansas. In Kimberley he stayed in a rough hotel, which had tallow candlelight in the rooms, and he amassed all kinds of technical data about diamond mining operations.

In Africa there were many kinds of American products—Eastman Kodaks, National cash registers, Selig's moving pictures, Colgate perfumes and soap, Chamberlain's cough syrup, the ubiquitous *Ladies' Home Journal,* the novels of Robert W. Chambers (which he thought trashy), and Mr. Rockefeller's gasoline. Another export of so-called civilized lands was entirely dispensable to him—the missionary:

"One man said the superintendent of a penitentiary told him recently that ninety per cent of the convicts had been 'converted' by missionaries. A mining man testified that Negroes who had been under the influence of missionaries were nearly always less honest and less useful than natives who had had no such experience. . . . Wherever I have gone, I have heard the missionary experiment denounced by white residents. I am taking no part in the controversy, but record as a remarkable fact that in Africa, China, Japan, India, etc., the testimony of white residents is nearly always against the missionary experiment."[10]

Victoria Falls was a thing to be admired, and he made the inevitable comparison with Niagara. There was a boat trip on the Zambesi River above the falls, and more time on a train, dusty and dirty. On April 2 the party left Victoria Falls for the east coast, and Ed Howe saw the prettiest country yet, as Illinois must have looked one hundred years ago. He went from Rhodesia into Portuguese East Africa and then to Beira aboard the *Burgermeister,* going ashore at the town of Mozambique. There he visited the public market, where the Kansans were curious about the Negro women, many of whom had their faces whitened like circus clowns in order to look like white people.

"Adelaide weighs only a hundred pounds, and has rather a small waist, and all the negro women thought her waist was disgracefully small. One of them asked if she might measure it with a string. Permission being granted, and the measurement made, the string was passed around, and attracted a babble of disgusted comment from black ladies with the middle-age spread."[11]

This latest set of travel letters began to turn into conventional reports—Zanzibar, German East Africa, Mombasa; lions and big game; skepticism about the practice of shooting lions, which seemed pretty cowardly animals to Ed Howe; comments on the lower-class Hindus, the "world's dirtiest people"; a trip across the equator; a surprisingly cool evening at Aden, Arabia; a pleasant trip through the Red Sea; the Suez Canal; a private poll he took which revealed that few of the passengers knew the importance of Mount Sinai. The vessel reached Naples May 1, and he stayed at the Hotel Vesuvius, and then left for home on the *Canada,* a French ship, reaching Atchison May 18. His journey became the book called *Travel Letters from New Zealand, Australia and Africa.* Of the volume his old Kansas associate J. E. House said in *The Forum:* "No other American, living or dead, has written more interesting books of travel." Similar praise appeared in the *Literary Digest* and *Los Angeles Times,* and the comments in these publications became part of an advertisement that became a staple in *E. W. Howe's Monthly.*

In February, 1914, *The Monthly* took on a newspaper format, which must have been a more comfortable arrangement for the Atchison editor, and it maintained that format from then on. He wrote later in the year that the change had disturbed some subscribers, but that he had learned *The Monthly,* at a dollar a year, had not attained a large circulation, and at the extravagantly low new price of ten cents a year it had great circulation. "I never knew how much people thought of ninety cents until I reduced the price," he said (October, 1914). Not only could it be purchased for ten cents a year, but it cost only twenty-five cents for three years, or a dollar for a lifetime subscription.

He was writing constantly and indiscriminately. Advertising in *The Monthly* listed his works, the familiar titles and also booklets bearing such titles as "A New Bishop in the Old Church," "The Sob Squad," "The Confessions of Ananias," "The Newspaper Boys," "The Irish," "The Hook Worm People," "Colonel Buddha, Reformer and Fraud," "About a Fat Woman," "The Baby Blue," "The Suicide of Mexico," "The Brass Band Evangelist," "The Crime Against Richard A. Ballinger," "In Declining a Nomination for Vice President." These were writings taken from both *Globe* and *Monthly;* all were examples of his views and prejudices. But in the ads he boosted, mainly, *The Story of a Country Town,* with the famous quotes from Mark Twain, Howells, Charles Dudley Warner, and William Allen White.

He was writing frequently about the things he admired—the ten-cent store, Sears, and Ward's. He commented frequently on his retirement, the event which had caused him to reduce the total of his annoyances, for at the farm there was little to bother him. In April, 1915, he described an operation which he had undergone the month before, and the sometimes prudish editor gave an almost anatomical description: a V-shaped piece had been taken from his lower lip on the left side, leaving only a slight scar but fortunately proving to be benign. The operation had been performed by Dr. Sam Murdock ("a great doctor") at the hospital in Sabetha.

He wrote about visiting friends, such as B. B. Brooks of Casper, Wyoming, whom he had met twenty-eight years before on a hunting party that had included General George Crook, the famous old Indian fighter. There was a visit by Alice Hubbard at Potato Hill the summer of 1914, a visit that Ed Howe would recall in print after both Elbert and Alice Hubbard went down with the *Lusitania*. He liked the way Mrs. Hubbard showed such regard for her husband, and he liked her for not actively propagandizing for woman suffrage, even though she advocated it.

The old iconoclast was mellowing somewhat about higher education. Merle Thorpe was running a department of journalism at the University of Kansas, and Ed Howe—who once had leveled his sights at education in journalism—was visiting the university, talking to students, and making his *Monthly* available, at no charge, to students and to teachers of journalism. He also went to the University of Missouri to give a talk after appearing earlier at Lawrence, and described the visit in a letter to Thorpe:

May 10, 1916.

Dear Mr. Thorpe:

I had a fine time in Columbia. Dean [Walter] Williams gave a dinner for some of the visitors, and a rich old Southerner living near town gave a breakfast the following morning. One of the guests at the breakfast was W. J. Bryan. About eighteen were present, and the affair was one of the most agreeable I have ever attended.

We were delighted with Columbia. I have always had an idea that I would like the South, and Columbia seems Southern.

I made a talk forty minutes long and was fairly well satisfied with it. Harvey Ingham, whom I greatly admire, preceded me, and talked about thirty-five minutes. That constituted the program for the evening, except that an orchestra played before we began.

I have turned your letter over to Eugene.

Sincerely,
E. W. Howe[12]

Later in the year he spoke again at Lawrence, writing to Leon N. Flint, then of the journalism faculty and for many years the departmental chairman:

October 26, 1916.

Dear Mr. Flint:

I shall be very glad to come to Lawrence on Monday, November 6, and deliver an address at 4:30 in the afternoon. My subject will be, "Why It Is Difficult to Entertain a College Audience." It will generally refer to newspapers, with the intimation that interest in public speaking is not what it formerly was because of the interest in newspapers.

I will return home as soon after the talk as possible, probably by way of Kansas City. . . . I never know what to say to an audience. There are so many things to say, and I have no great confidence in my ability to edit myself. . . .

I shall be pleased to come to Lawrence during the winter, and spend a day with you. I am full of newspaper notions, of course, and it would be a pleasure to talk informally to your young people.

Sincerely,
E. W. Howe[13]

November 11, 1916.

Dear Mr. Flint:

You were very kind to send me [a] voucher for ten dollars. I did not expect anything at all; and, besides, we had a very pleasant trip to Lawrence. On the way back, we stopped at Tonganoxie, and had a very nice dinner at a very nice place known as the Myers House. As Tonganoxie is only fourteen miles from Lawrence, you might run out there some time. You would find the Myers House thoroughly delightful. The night of the 6th was as warm as June; a bright moon was shining, and the roads excellent.

If you like my address, I am greatly obliged to you.[14]

And so for him there were little interludes in eastern Kansas towns, but he was concerned mainly with *The Monthly*. Except for its attention to events and issues of the times, *The Monthly* maintained a content of almost formula nature. There was an "indignation department," and there was an "information department." Howe provided little items of history, largely factual, with little comment—the life of Voltaire, whom he greatly admired; the story of the *Bounty;* the Black Plague; the affair of Caesar and Cleopatra. He discussed the Colorado coal strike, the Mexican bandits (how he loathed Mexico in those days!), Louis Brandeis (whom he disliked), Billy Sunday (whom he disliked), the *National Geographic Magazine* (the best), *Popular Mechanics* (good), Frontier Days in Cheyenne, Wyoming, the operation of Montgomery Ward & Co., the unfortunate but still contemptible Oscar Wilde, the annual vacations, William Randolph Hearst ("our chief mischief maker"), Upton Sinclair, and books like *The Brass Check* (which, amazingly, Howe liked).

As a newspaperman himself he liked especially to write about the press. Frank Cobb of the *World* was "the best editorial writer in the United States, and my literary hero" (a curious position for the conservative Kansan to announce). In the September, 1915, *Monthly* he wrote that the best writing being done was not in magazines but in newspapers, and not by the rich owners but by the hired help. He never liked to hear of newspapers being "voices of the administration"; they should be only "recorders" of the administration, he thought. Some things that were happening to—and on—newspapers disturbed him, especially the way press agents were seizing space for the likes of the YMCA, the Christian Endeavor, the Boy Scouts of America, Mary Pickford, Douglas Fairbanks, Billie Burke, Billy Sunday, and Leonard Wood. He was stimulated by the *New Republic* and the *Nation,* but he sometimes canceled his subscription to both, or either. The *New Republic* carried the "same old socialistic drivel," praising things like Sinclair's *King Coal.* At one time he gave up the *New Republic* for a weekly called *Commerce and Finance;* the "professors" were writing such silly things in the former magazine. The *Nation* whined too much; its editor was demanding more for the poor than they had a right to. He would try the *Outlook* for a change. But always he had to go back to the *Nation,* for "its excellent if often mistaken writing." For even it could carry something good like Stuart Chase saying that most learning up to that time had been "just so much junk, unworthy of a serious man's attention" (June, 1923).

He took a long trip in October, 1915, to the San Francisco exposition, and he thought maybe it compared favorably with those of so many years before in Chicago and St. Louis. Just strolling about pleased him most. But to a Kansas man the best sights were not the great cities but the farming districts. In California, as he saw it, the farmers wisely took town comforts to their farms instead of going to the city to find them. Go west, you Kansans, and learn how to improve your land! That year he traveled extensively in other parts of the West, going to Glacier National Park, Portland, and New Mexico, and writing about all of these for the readers of his monthly newspaper.

A National Audience

All by himself, Ed Howe was filling eight pages; he observed in January, 1916, that the *Saturday Evening Post* had millions of subscribers to his ten thousand, and also had the world's best writers. He made no effort to rival the *Post,* of course, but his reputation was singular in its own way. He was now being referred to as "The Sage of Potato Hill" by the syndicated writer Dr. Frank Crane, a label that lasted the rest of his life. And he had a few things to say about giving such a title to a man of the soil, one of the plain folks of the world:

> I am neither sage nor philosopher; I know only simple things, and in a long and active life have encountered nothing else. I know nothing that may not be easily explained by simple rules we all have an even chance to learn. I know almost nothing of the wonders of astronomy, but I know others do, and that they have demonstrated their knowledge beyond doubt; we set our clocks, and guide our ships at sea, because of human knowledge that proves itself every hour in the day. The men who tell us a new year begins on the 1st day of January know what they are talking about; proving it was a difficult and long process, but they proved it. . . .
>
> To call a man a Sage sounds impressive; it indicates that he knows many mysterious and hidden things. I know nothing of the kind, so I am not a Sage. I know nothing anyone may not know who keeps his eyes open, and accepts the results of simple experience. [April, 1916]

He saw himself as neither sage nor critic. Someone once sent him a book that seemed to oppose everything in the world; such a book only irritated the angry old editor, even though he knew that he opposed many things himself. Someone else had written a book that was being commended to him, for it seemed to some to be similar to what Edgar Watson Howe, as a troubled young newspaper editor, had written back in the 1880s—a book by a poet named Edgar Lee Masters called *Spoon River Anthology,* and it was a book that had some two hundred characters, as Ed Howe described it, and not half a dozen of them decent people. Ed Howe could not believe in such a book. He had lived in country towns all his life but never in a place like Spoon River. "The real incidents of life are not of the criminal character this author dwells upon so persistently" (August, 1916). He admitted that there were some follies in country towns, such as a failure to take advantage of all sound opportunities, but he felt that the people he knew were generally good and useful citizens.

To make his commentary, he printed in November, 1916, what he called "The Anthology of Potato Hill," the stories that appeared in book form as *An Anthology of Another Town,* in part a takeoff on, in part an imitation of, the popular *Spoon River Anthology.*

In 1921 Jay E. House of the *Philadelphia Public Ledger,* who had known Howe in Kansas, made a trip to Atchison and visited the modest home, overlooking the Missouri River, that Howe called Potato Hill. He saw nothing pretentious about either name or appearance of the home, but "For those who love a rolling panorama of woods and waters banked by distant hills, only the view from Mount Royal back of Montreal and the one from Point Loma across the bay from San Diego approach that from Potato Hill."

House talked and ate with Howe, observed that Howe still grumbled about food, and recalled that the editor used to visit him in Topeka and always returned home with indigestion. "Today he set out to make a modest meal of green bean salad. But before we had finished luncheon, the steak, the 'marshamallowed' sweet potatoes, the Golden Bantam corn, the dessert and the coffee had all tempted him and he had fallen."

To House, Ed Howe was the typical American, "a little careless, sartorially speaking, [who] year after year remains addicted to the same brand of collar and the same style of cravat." He seemed a writer who had more influence with his readers than any other writer House had known. He recalled, in fact, that Bill Bowen, an Atchison druggist, had once said:

"If *The Globe* should come out with a three-line item advising every man, woman and child in town to gather on the vacant lot back of Turner hall at 8 o'clock tonight and stand on their head, two-thirds of the population of the town would be there at the appointed hour and most of them would attempt the acrobatic feat suggested."[15]

In the second decade of the twentieth century the editor was acquiring a truly national audience. And some of that audience probably would do what Howe suggested. *The Monthly,* without great circulation, was widely quoted, as *The Globe* had been, and it was read by persons who possessed influence as shapers of public opinion. Popular magazines, especially, were printing his opinion pieces and his little stories—notably the Curtis publications, the *Saturday Evening Post,* the *Ladies' Home Journal,* and the *Country Gentleman,* but also the *American, Collier's,* the *Independent.*

These printed fiction, essays, diatribes, anecdotes, editorials, reprints. Such writings kept the Howe name alive, for by this time all of his books of the 1880s and 1890s had been forgotten—except for one. That one, *The Story of a Country Town,* was achieving in these years considerable status with some literary critics. Many editions of the book had been published. The historian and critic Carl Van Doren was writing extensively about both Howe and the one book: in *The American Novel* in 1921; in *American and British Literature Since 1890* (written in collaboration with Mark Van Doren) in 1925; in an article, "Prudence Militant: E. W. Howe, Village Sage," in the *Century* in 1923. This critic of a newer generation compared *The Story of a Country Town* with George W. Cable's *The Grandissimes,* which Van Doren termed "allusive, sparkling, felicitous" in its style, and then observed that "By comparison, *The Story of a Country Town* moves with the cold tread and hard diction of a saga."[16] Van Doren was probably his most distinguished promoter at one time. In the *Century* article Van Doren carried his criticism of *The Story of a Country Town* further, marveling that such a book could have appeared at the same time as such cheerful works as those by Mark Twain, the Uncle Remus stories, and James Whitcomb Riley's "The Old Swimmin' Hole."[17] He went beyond the novel to speak of the influence of Ed Howe as a small-town figure, and of how the Kansan put "rural wisdom into speech."

The most controversial literary history of the 1920s, Vernon Louis Parrington's *Main Currents in American Thought,* also made brief comment on *The Story of a Country Town*—"stark, grim, unrelieved, revealing the 'smoldering discontent of an inarticulate frontier.' "[18] Parrington, like later critics, was reading into the novel far more than Ed Howe had intended. Howe's name also appeared in a popular journalistic anthology of the period, several of his "Country Town Sayings" being included in Allan Nevins' *American Press Opinion, Washington to Coolidge,* in which Nevins compared him with his equally famous Kansas neighbor, William Allen White.

The Atchison man was becoming an almost legendary figure. To Gerald Carson, in *Scribner's,* he was "The Village Atheist," yet more than that: "Once a country editor collecting local items on the streets of a country town, Mr. Howe has become a picturesque national figure. His maxims and apologues, as Franklin's were a hundred and fifty years ago, have been repeated and bandied about until they have in many instances quite lost their paternity. . . . If Mr. Howe is an interesting figure—and he is—it is because he has become our most eminent prairie exponent of the American way of thinking."[19]

The Sage of Potato Hill was becoming nationally known as the iconoclast, the critic of society. He resented these terms as he had resented them earlier; they belonged to the rebels, the troublemakers, not to good conservatives like him. Being called a critic definitely did not please him: he was a mere observer, in his opinion, a man writing "in the hope that a few may find in my observations a starting point for better thinking. . . . I do not stop and argue with every foolish man I meet, but keep my ears and eyes open, in the hope of occasionally running into something of value" (March, 1923). A writer in *Vanity Fair* once summed up Howe's way of thinking thus: "Two and two make four. Well, what of it?" Such an estimate satisfied Ed Howe. "A fact is a fact: what of it? Why spend our time in complaining or wondering? Why not accept the facts of life, and make the best of them?" (May, 1923).

He had long been known as a philosopher of common sense. Now his humor and prejudices were being nationally syndicated. He was being carefully read by many editors: Willis J. Abbot, the one-time Hearst editor who later edited the *Christian Science Monitor,* remembered the role that *The Globe* had played for so many people:

"Those of us who had to skim the Kansas exchanges soon learned that the paper bristled with sharp and pungent paragraphs. Howe was more than editor and proprietor; he was the chief, and I fancy for a time the sole reporter. He had a knack of giving a curious twist, or an epigrammatic touch, to his news paragraphs that made his paper readable even to those who had no interest in Atchison."[20]

Another who read Ed Howe and whose own big-city column had some of the folksiness of Atchison was O. O. McIntyre, whom Howe quoted in *The Monthly:*

> It is quite surprising the vogue E. W. Howe, of Potato Hill, Kansas, has in New York. In six afternoon papers of the same day I noted on the editorial pages of all extracts from "E. W. Howe's Monthly," which seems to have its greatest circulation

> down in the White Light district, where it is supposed to be all gloss and glitter, and that domestic life and rural existence are for amiable fat-heads. His human philosophy seems to have just the right kind of punch to whet the appetite of jaded Broadway. When Howe comes to New York, very few know about it until he is way back home. He does not seek the white flame of publicity, but when the reporters and sob sisters do finally corner him here, his life is going to be miserable for a few hours at least. [July, 1919]

Most important in Edgar Watson Howe's growing literary reputation was the encouragement given him by H. L. Mencken. The Howe-Mencken association was an interesting one, lasting from the teen years until Howe's death. It was a curious friendship, too, the unsophisticated man of the provinces seeming so different from the blasé cynic of Baltimore and New York. The two seemed to see in each other people who were trying to cut away sham and hypocrisy and remove them from the American scene. A writer for the *Haldeman-Julius Monthly* saw the two as "meeting on common ground where they view objects alike for a moment, when one, looking through the same instrument as the other, sees something which the other asserts does not exist, and there are remarks about optical illusions." Howe's heroes were the Mellons and the Lorimers and the Rockefellers; Mencken was a scholar. Howe was a kind of "sweaty Orison Swett Marden." He had the great tolerance, being sorry for *some* people, but Mencken held everyone to "strict accountability."[21]

In September, 1915, Ed Howe gave early praise to the brilliant work being done by Mencken, whom he preferred, he said, to Kant and Schopenhauer. He was sure Mencken could have gotten Voltaire's *Philosophical Dictionary* into three hundred pages. ". . . every writer needs a cold, critical Mencken to reduce his words fifty or a hundred to one," Howe said (September, 1915). Mencken reciprocated, according praise to Howe's "success" tracts:

"Here for the first time, is brave, plain speaking. Here is the long-awaited antidote to all the preposterous perunas that bogus reformers ram down our gullets. Here is a counter-blast to the uplift in all its branches. Here are the doctrines, nakedly stated, that lie at the bottom of the American philosophy, the American ethic, the American view of the world; the hard principles that nine-tenths of us cherish in our secret hearts, and that practically all of us put into practice in our daily life."[22]

As for the Kansan, he praised the wit and genius of the man from the East, his ability to dissect, his detachment, his feeling for how preachers and YMCA secretaries and movie actors and lodge members talked. He saw that Mencken cared little for wars and politics and labor disputes and marital problems; these could "never rob Mencken of his sleep nor spoil a dinner for him. . . . What has he to do with the mob except to be diverted by its idiocy" (June, 1921).

In 1928 Mencken visited Howe in Kansas, though Howe did not record what took place (Adelaide remembered Mencken as a "perfectly delightful man"). George Jean Nathan also praised the Kansas editor, particularly in a magazine article in which he recalled how he and Mencken had offered themselves as a presidential ticket, with the stipulation that Ed Howe be their Secretary of State, for Howe "would so raise the percentage of that cabinet post, which currently resembles the batting average of the 1898 Louisville baseball team, at least ninety percent."[23]

In October, 1924, *The Monthly* carried a cartoon by H. T. Webster that revealed how Ed Howe's views were becoming a national staple. Three men were shown talking, one of them saying: "I see where Ed Howe says he knows a man who was married three times and never proposed marriage *once*. That's what I've always said—it's the *woman* who proposes ninety times out of a hundred." Indicating his agreement is Caspar Milquetoast, but a lower panel tells the truth: Caspar timidly listens as his wife tells him how he followed her like a puppy dog and proposed every time he got a chance.

Another friend was Ring Lardner, a quiet man, who smashed at shams the way Howe thought a writer should. Lardner to him was quite different from the stereotyped bohemians of the day, for whom Howe had contempt, with their "bobbed hair, mannish women, highballs, freaky artists and writers, the four-hour day, chafing dish meals, late hours, chefs, head waiters, boot leggers and the like" (April, 1923). Lardner lived in the real world and did not care for such Greenwich Village nonsense.

It seems puzzling that Ed Howe should have proved especially appealing to some of those, like Mencken, Nathan, and Lardner, who tended to damn the conventionalities of American society.

For some of his most representative work published in the decade after he gave up *The Globe* were two tracts called *Success Easier Than Failure* and *The Blessings of Business,* views he had been voicing regularly since the 1880s. They are works quite in the conservative temper that was to dominate America in the 1920s after Wilson and his college professors had been removed from the seats of power.

There is nothing really surprising about what Ed Howe had to say in these little books. His deification of capitalism was entirely in keeping with the Puritan ethic, with the spirit that had marked the settlement of New England, with the cult of free enterprise that became so significant in America that some people almost believed it was provided for in the Constitution. Capitalism was the best of all possible economic systems. A man could succeed if he chose to do so; this was pure Emersonian self-reliance as well as being a basic American attitude. Man could "push himself to the front," as Orison Swett Marden had written in his popular book of the 1890s and in the magazine he called *Success,* which lasted from 1897 to 1912. In his small way Edgar Watson Howe was part of the capitalistic success pattern of the late nineteenth century; he was forming his ideas in those decades when the notion of success through hard work and individual enterprise was a leading concept in American life. His idols had been—and remained—Carnegie, Rockefeller, Edison, and James J. Hill.

He preached in *The Monthly* the gospel of honesty as the best policy, a way of life much preferable to being tricky and making a big gain. This was the best doctrine in the world, and not just a saying of old women. He deplored the fact that Christ had seen fit to bend his message toward the poor, even to give good notice to publicans and prostitutes. "What sort of doctrine is it that condemns the industrious and saving?" he asked (December, 1915). He had never known a man who gave all he possessed to the poor; anyone who did such a foolish thing would nullify all the great gains of history.

Success Easier Than Failure was Ed Howe's attempt to write a good practical philosophy, because he had never found one that suited him. He spoke for the humble folk of the world, they being the ones who had to make an effective and lasting civilization, and not the poet or musician. He stated again the creed of honesty, that one may accumulate money more easily through honesty than without it, that man must practice politeness, fairness, industry, and temperance in order to build himself in society. Education was *not* an important component of success, for the over-educated become as conceited as the lazy children of the rich. "There is something unnatural about anyone who has spent all his life as a student or teacher. . . . our schools teach much that is not real knowledge."[24]

It is obvious that success is easier than failure: failure has less morality about it. Success is the gauge of respectability, and every man has the obligation to make a success of his life. Life is completely understandable, and a program of rewards and punishments for man is part of life. There is rebellion in every unit of life from nation to family because of the conditions of life, but such rebellion does not need to become worse. A man may sit at night and rebel about the world, but if he is wise he arises the next morning and goes about his work and obeys the rules. "The business of life is to Get. This is the law; when the law changes, you will be justified in changing. Give of your store, certainly, but only those who are able to get are able to give."[25]

Don't blame society. Criminals always say someone else was responsible for their errors. And the sociologist who blames society for a family made up of illiterate parents, criminal sons, and daughters who are "scarlet women" is in error. That family itself is responsible for its degradation. Such people have not seized upon their opportunities, but instead have *chosen* to be failures.

Selfishness is a commendable virtue, even though it has its many critics. "I never knew a selfish man who was in the poorhouse or the gutter." Selfish men behave well because it pays to do so, and the rest of society benefits from their selfishness. "The basis of every human thing is selfishness; we do good as incident." And the Puritan spirit had been a great thing for this country:

"When parents insist on their children being brought up according to old-fashioned and respectable rules, that is the Puritan Spirit. The Puritan Spirit gossips about men who drink too much, and women who depart from womanly ways. There is nothing wrong with this sort of Puritanism: it is to be regretted that the Puritan Spirit does not assert itself oftener than it does; we can easily forgive its excesses."[26]

His times were good times in which to be living, he said. The wrongs of the past had been righted; the American people were enjoying the fruits of the revolutions that had taken place. The American people had as much as or more than the reformers had ever said they should have.

It was a hedonistic philosophy that he preached, an approach to life that appealed to many readers. *The Blessings of Business* was similar in approach. Ed Howe was an admirer of the acquisitive instinct; it seemed quite creditable to him that people should be able to make money, and making money was the result of energy and hard work. Rockefeller, as he often said, was a much more useful man than LaFollette; Rockefeller had as much right to his genius in business as Lincoln to his genius in politics. These views were appearing in other articles Ed Howe was writing for the *Country Gentleman,* the *American, Collier's,* and the *Saturday Evening Post:* like the story of the Eglinger brothers of Atchison, for example, a success story that appeared in the *American.* The Eglingers were restaurant operators, and he was sure they would have succeeded no matter what pursuit they chose in life. "Shall we tell the poor man of the Eglinger brothers or of Karl Marx? It seems to me that the Eglinger philosophy is greater than that of Karl Marx, in that it works better."[27]

Business should require no defense, he thought, but if one asked him for a defense this would be his answer:

"The first principle is life; the second, maintenance of life. The thing of greatest human interest and importance, therefore, is the production and distribution of food, the manufacture of necessities;

"Or what we call *Business.*"[28]

John D. Rockefeller had done more for society than the men who criticized him. The true American hero was the man of business, the "man who, in spite of a poor home, poor schooling, and residence in a poor neighborhood, becomes a successful and useful citizen; who somehow acquires politeness, education, and appreciation of the world's important lessons."[29] And the real man to admire is not the accidental rich but the workman who rises by sheer merit. For all but seventeen of four thousand successful American businessmen began their lives as poor boys.

Who are the men who should be honored in our society? We visit public parks and see bronze and marble statues celebrating statesmen, warriors, or poets. Statues—and paper money and postage stamps—should celebrate instead the honest businessmen, much greater men in their communities than the teachers and preachers, writers and orators.

Materialism has been damned as an evil; it should be exalted as a good, for "it is actually the only straight road to the highest civilization possible." Spiritual ideas are worthless; civilization is breaking down not through materialism but through individual faults of the people. And it is useless to fight for inferior men; they must fight for themselves. "The churches and conventions have fought for inferior man since time began, but he is still where he was at the beginning, and always will be, unless he helps himself."[30]

Think of the usefulness of a man like Thomas A. Edison, he said, a man who has made it possible for all of us to live more comfortably and economically. And he is a businessman who won what he has in competition with other men. "Edison has never robbed me; on the contrary, he has benefited me, and I will not hate and misrepresent him."[31]

Then there were the university professors and our editors and our statesmen—specialists all, men who never come into touch with the real problems of life, as do bankers, farmers, and mechanics. Professors are modest, and have every reason to be, but editors and statesmen sit in their ivory towers and smoke and write and try to boss the country.

Morality to him was "demonstrated convenience," a kind of applied materialism. The race had progressed because people had learned the virtue of washing their faces or improving their homes or making things convenient for themselves. The wonderful story in American life, for him, was the tale of J. C. Penney. Here was a businessman who knew the virtue of success and hard work. Every executive of the Penney firm had worked up from the ranks and had been selected because of his honesty and capability and decency.

He described how he felt about heroes:

> I like notable people, but do not give all my admiration to notable men or women; I like notable *things*. How notable "Ivory Soap." I never turn around without hearing of "Carter's Ink" or "Bemis Bags." And "Swift's Bacon:" how much of a hero that is. I went into a store the other day and the grocer told me that when he sold only Swift's bacon, he never has a complaint.
>
> How heroic that statement is!

> Plenty of other men producing bacon, but here is one man so much more careful than others that a grocer away out in the country pays him a tremendous compliment.
>
> I hear of the Parker pens a dozen times a day, and use one. I dropped it the other morning, and until I am able to procure a new one, I will be almost lost. The hero back of the "Parker Pen" is George S. Parker, Zanesville, Wisconsin. I have an affection for him that rivals my affection for Abe Lincoln, and I have never seen Mr. Parker in my life.
>
> Geo. S. Parker is the hero of the seven dollar pen. Chas. H. Ingersoll is the hero of the dollar watch, and I cheer him, too.
>
> I often think of that fine old hero, the *Saturday Evening Post*. For forty years every smart newspaper man has been busily thinking out a plan to do it up, but the *Post* just naturally won't be done up. Somewhere behind this wonderful publication, there is a tremendous amount of ability, character, genius. [April, 1927]

Success Easier Than Failure and *The Blessings of Business* were Ed Howe's attempts to codify his philosophy. There was more time to think about philosophical questions in the quiet of Potato Hill, without the annoyances that had plagued him at *The Globe*. So he philosophized about success and business and the virtues of the small town. Much of his writing was defensive, but it still was the philosophy of this country editor. He did not mind being called "provincial," however. He admitted to the charge of provincialism from some critics; it was of no benefit to be born in a big city, a place of "artificial and vicious ideas . . . ." Vicious ideas originated in big cities; the bad people in the small towns got their ideas from big city publications. Women, especially, were ridiculous in the big cities: there the birth rate was smallest; there the silly fashions originated; there one could see women smoke and drink; there was where women fed their babies from bottles. "It is in the country or in small towns where old-fashioned common sense is most prevalent; it is to the people in the country and small towns that we must look for the regeneration."[32] Of the values and virtues of farm life he was especially convinced:

"What a great number of farm boys become noted men because of early training in industry, a virtue too often neglected in town! Farm homes are the saving grace of the country. When I hear of a city man marrying an actress I always think it a pity he didn't marry one of the better-class farmers' daughters—fine, natural women, as a very general rule."[33]

His politics were becoming increasingly conservative, and again he found it necessary to answer charges: his critics were calling him a reactionary. He wondered if it had occurred to any wise men that only reaction would save Russia, and every other troubled country in the world, including the United States, which was drifting into socialism. "Only reaction will save those men who drink too much, idle too much, lie too much, eat too much" (June, 1918). What is wrong with "reacting," after all? "Suppose we follow a wrong road. Is there anything wrong about going back, and getting on the right road?" He would gladly abandon a false direction in life, just as he would *not* abandon just, economical, and efficient principles. "Conservatism" suited him even more; on Judgment Day we might all arise and find that the conservatives were right and the liberals and progressives wrong. Conservatives were the people to trust; "the best evidence that a man has achieved a little common sense is that he is referred to as an old fogy by fools."[34]

He saw himself as a preacher of common sense; he had never heard any good arguments put forth for intemperance or profanity or idleness or viciousness. He called in 1924 for another Tom Paine, for a man who would issue a call like that issued by Paine in 1776. For Ed Howe was a common man himself, from common stock, a man who had never known a real genius, so far as he knew, but who had known hundreds of common men who had achieved what he considered true distinction.

He continued to maintain the skepticism that had marked his editorial utterances and his novels since the 1880s. Man could not really be happy, he said, and this continuing search people made for happiness was the cause of much of the misery in the world. He was content, but his life was not what he would term happy. Horrible and lasting illness was to be the fate of many, and all people should assume this. He was not morose, merely adjusted. He knew the moral of *King Lear,* and "If his fate should accept me, I should realize that the meanness of his two daughters was very much like human nature everywhere, and that my misfortune was due to my own lack of sense" (June, 1914).

He presented observations and protests on a variety of subjects, all demonstrating how much he was a true man of his age—the age of business enterprise. He was with Cain in saying "I am not my brother's keeper"; poor Cain had been abused for a just and apt remark, he thought. He scoffed at the idea of universal love; there was no such thing. People should beware of sentimentalists, because they would rob them or bore them but never love or benefit them. People are all right as individuals, but not in mass. Yet the voice of the middle class was still, to him, the nearest thing to the voice of God; it came closer to representing the true law than the words of a Moses or a Mohammed. And this man of enormous contradictions believed so strongly in majority rule that it seemed outrageous to him for any one man to control an age (yet soon Ed Howe would be praising the accomplishments of Benito Mussolini).

About politics and reform he was as dubious as he had been in an earlier day. Too many politicians were so busy talking patriotism that they made the taxpayers forget how much government was costing: ". . . the taxes King George imposed were a mere bagatelle compared with the taxes imposed by those who call themselves our Obedient Servants." Congressmen dividing up the pork barrel were really no better than Louis XV was in spending millions on his "House of Pleasure." The "people," too, deserved blame, for they did not understand or care about the importance of fairness in public affairs. "If I had great influence I should exercise it in warning the people that there is something wrong with every big promise."[35] For the *Country Gentleman* he was writing extensively about farmers and country life, and he suggested that farmers might do something to bring about a regeneration of true and lasting values in American life.

In an age of new religions and modifications in the orthodoxy of the past Ed Howe was still a professed disbeliever, once in a great while making the admission, however, that perhaps religion was not too bad. He had praise for the man who reportedly threw a Gideon Bible from his hotel room in Chicago: he had wanted to do the same thing himself. He thought that if he were a preacher he would form his own church, as Brigham Young and Mary Baker Eddy had done, so that he might be a pope instead of a mere pastor.

Though his audience was wider, the wraths he had to brave were fewer than they had been forty years before, for now others were laughing as much at the religious attitudes of Americans as he had done. But still, how dangerous it was for him to speak so in the days of evangelism triumphant! "We have been told many years that Jesus will appear again, and set things right. Why does He delay?" Relief had been promised for thousands of years; it was badly needed in October, 1919. Pictures of Christ amused him: the artists trying to get an expression onto the face that said: "I am *so* anxious to help people"—the same expression, Ed Howe said, that you could see on the faces of politicians (December, 1912).

Christianity was a failure; if we had been no more successful with other things we would still be making fire with flint and hunting game with bow and arrow. "I do not believe there is a devil, but we deserve one," he wrote.[36] And Howe loved to make the popular Billy Sunday the object of his digs. Billy Sunday was quite aware of Howe, too. Speaking in nearby Lawrence, he said: "And there's old Ed. Howe. He's not much on religion, but I'm strong for him, anyway" (May, 1916).

Except for H. L. Mencken it is doubtful that any other figure of the time wrote as disparagingly of religion. Christian Science was a joke to Howe; he said he could write the precepts of Science and Health in twenty lines. A Christian Scientist who really thought things out would have to laugh his religion "out of court." Catholicism, far as it was from his beliefs, made more sense than any other religion, for it came closer to the true representation of Christian dogma. All about him he saw people being hoaxed into religious belief and practice, or at least conventional religious adherence. He wrote about his neighbor Abe King, a godly man who attended church regularly and criticized the sinners of the world: "The trouble with Abe is that when he hears the mighty voice of the Lord, he hears nothing of the eight dollars borrowed money he has owed me three years, and which he forgets in a way that amounts to dishonesty" (April, 1911).

His religion was his personal philosophy. But one kind of sermon could move him: the organ and choir he heard while passing a church. The wrangling inside would drive him away again, he was sure. And how he scorned the man who was proud of his ability to utter a beautiful prayer. "Is not a prayer, however beautiful it may be from a literary standpoint, a ridiculous performance? Is not a prayer directed upward, or downward, or sideways, suggestive of voodooism?" (December, 1912).

Yet in some of his writings, particularly those that were published in pamphlet form in the 1920s, he became almost benign. He did not believe in church dogma, but he was becoming more friendly to the church as he grew older; pastors were at least decent men, trying to do their best. The good done by the church, too, might outweigh the bad; dogmatic religions were dying; many church members no more believed in supernaturalism or superstition than he did.

He seemed to have had his say about sex, love, and women. Sex was still, though, the great unmentionable subject; he agreed with Elbert Hubbard's remark that "Life is a degradation, and man lives in the slime-pits of lust." "Love" was just another four-letter word (October, 1911). He continued to preach that a man—or a woman—embarking upon a love affair knows the pitfalls ahead. He must run the risk of being punished, just as he knows that eating certain foods gives him dyspepsia. And he rejected the view that man had an *urge* to reproduce his own kind: ". . . in his amours man thinks only of reproduction in the hope of avoiding it. Reproduction is nature's design, not man's."[37] Man was a natural polygamist, and he would behave "like a woods bull" were it not for the restraints of society.

For most of his writing days he had been known as a woman-hater, but he did not carry the hatred into private life. His unfortunate marriage kept him from wanting *that* again, but he associated with women, was attracted to them, and often included them in the parties on his trips. The little aphorisms about women continued, however, to be as bitter as those he had written in the past:

> I know what women expect, and give it to them without disagreeable argument; they'll get it, anyway.
>
> I admire women greatly, but I could go before the judge and convict some of them of insanity solely on the evidence of their literary and art clubs.
>
> Our standards are undoubtedly changing: bad women do not go to hell as quickly as formerly; they hang around and make trouble longer.
>
> I will join any movement that will benefit women, as I will join any movement to benefit mankind generally, but I'll march in no Suffragette parade, and hear the men and boys along the sidewalk call me Sister.
>
> The worst luck a woman ever has is her father, unless it's her husband.[38]

In some of his last writings he contended that there was a natural unfriendliness between the sexes. Men and women have always been fighting, and there has been brutality in the battle as well as gallantry in the presence of society. Women generally have won the battle, especially in America, the home of the most henpecked men in history. "We are now in the reconstruction period," he said, "and women are as unwise in victory as were the Northerners after the Civil War."[39]

He was writing voluminously and not very selectively. He appeared to have opinions on almost all subjects (often taking issue with past positions he had stated), and he was as ready to grind out a trivial little anecdote as to write in more philosophical vein. *The Monthly* remained much like the old *Globe* in what it published, and *Globe*-type writings also appeared in the form of "Potato Hill Notes" in the *Country Gentleman:*

"When Potato Hill people say a man is 'peculiar,' it means they don't like him very well.

"Marsh Edson often speaks of that vast fund of information that isn't so.

"Doc Bailey says too many of the tombstones in the graveyard are due to calomel. He says there is excuse occasionally for a little quinine, and at times he uses a little castor oil, but is very bitter against calomel."[40]

These were not written specifically for the magazine in all cases; Ed Howe constantly rewrote himself and copied anecdotes and lifted notes from "Globe Sights," and his writings appeared and reappeared in numerous places. For *Collier's* he wrote philosophical editorials. For the *American* he wrote success pieces and sketches like "The Life, Death and Obsequies of George Coulter" (which also was published in *The Monthly* and found its way into *The Anthology of Another Town*). His minor writings—at least some of them—bore such titles as these:

"A Kin Story" (a simple little family episode).

"The Stubborn Woman—A Story."

"Gee Whiz, What a Farm!" (the gospel of success in Iowa).

"Two Very Substantial Citizens You Probably Never Heard Of."

"Oh, Those Women."

"Hardin the Blacksmith and the Uplift."

"The Confession of a Recreationist."

"Short Sermons from Kansas."

"The Apologies of an Old Fogy."

"Every Man His Own Philosopher."

"Socialism in the Light of Common Sense."

"Our American Habit of Optimistic Drunkenness."

"Confessions of a Common Man."

"The Devil Is a Fool."

"Torch and Powder."

"The Wagon and the West" (his story of the trip from Indiana).

"What Life Has Taught Me."

"The Preaching of a Brother-in-Law of the Church."

Each title tells a little of the philosophies of Ed Howe, the things which he had long preached and was wondering in the 1920s if they would ever impress themselves upon his reluctant readers. For the *Country Gentleman* he wrote a series of semi-humorous pieces on the history of Kansas, hitting on such matters as the Civil War, the great John J. Ingalls of Atchison, the buffalo, the ridiculous notion that there is more wind in Kansas than in other states of the Midwest. He wrote of his pride in the agricultural college at Manhattan, "the University of Applied Practice," which taught really valuable subjects—engineering, blacksmithing, flour milling, and also imparted the kind of learning one received at Harvard or Oxford. And there were commentaries on the things Kansans hold sacred: the small town and the right to take sides on issues and the good life one could enjoy in Kansas.

Some of his magazine articles were nostalgic, semi-inspirational pieces like "The Old Doctor":

"And he drove away with the blessings of every man, woman and child in the community, for here was a good man honored in his day and generation. Large and strong, he could have knocked together the heads of any two of his neighbors, but instead of doing it his life was gentle and helpful. A quiet man, he delivered no sermons except by the uprightness and usefulness of his life."[41]

And some were philosophical, like an article that praised the book, *The Genius of American Business,* by Julius H. Barnes. Businessmen must come to the rescue of literature, which had fallen into bad hands, he said. They must apply their superior knowledge to our education and tell the story of business that should be told.

There was now a mass audience to read the magazine articles. And there were new books from Ed Howe, like *Ventures in Common Sense* (1919), which brought him a reputation not only in the United States but in Great Britain as well, where the work was retitled *Adventures in Common Sense.* In that book he organized his subject matter—more or less—writing about such matters as women, politics, religion, business, literature, newspapers, the people, industry, war, fame, thrift, materialism, provincialism, and the like. For *Ventures* H. L. Mencken wrote an introduction, of which Ed Howe was so proud that he reprinted most of it in *Plain People.* Here are excerpts:

> In his *Monthly,* for the first time, he could throw off the taboos and hesitations that lie upon even the most independent of daily papers, and the results of this new freedom were quickly visible. I doubt that there is another periodical in America which shows so remarkable a subscription list to-day. I scarcely know of the editor of a big daily, indeed, who doesn't glance at it now and then, and the same thing is true of the editors of the principal magazines. What primarily attracts practical men is the extraordinary charm of his naive and confidential manner, his quite exceptional capacity for putting the plain thoughts of a plain man into such English that the professional eye immediately discerns its skillfulness and delights in its disarming persuasiveness. Above all, what his readers recognize in him is the rare quality of honesty—a quality, in fact, so seldom encountered in American writing that it would be stretching the truth but little to say that it is never encountered at all. Our Puritan culture, as every one knows, makes for many laudable virtues: enterprise, industry, philoprogenitiveness, patriotism, the fear of God, a great appetite for brummagem ideals, a high desire to be righteous, a noble gratitude for the fact that we are not as other men are. But one of the things it does not make for is that austere intellectual passion which exalts a bald fact above comfort, security and the revelation of God—one of the things it does not promote is common truthfulness. . . .
>
> A man thoroughly American, a man especially enmeshed in the Puritanism that is the national curse, a Middle Westerner of the Middle Westerners, and by no means disposed to conceal it, he yet manages to get the method of the free spirit into his study of the phenomena that lie about him, and even into his examination of the thing that he is himself. This is the remarkable fact that sets him off from the whole vast herd of other national sages: he is the only one who practices resolutely

a relentless honesty, sacrificing every appearance, however charming, to what he conceives to be the truth. . . .

There is nothing in the doctrine of Howe that is very startling; what joy the man of meditative habit gets out of it, barring occasional delight in its broad, rustic humors, must be mainly the joy of simple recognition. It is all, considering it a moment, obvious enough; some of it is downright platitude. But nevertheless it is platitude of a special sort—the platitude of fact, not of mere maudlin fancy. It stands diametrically opposed to the mush that passes so widely for the national philosophy; it is in direct opposition to all the current presumptions in politics. He has no belief in the bombastic bosh of what is called Public Service, now garbled so raucously and by such palpable frauds. He believes in intelligent self-interest, and guesses, probably correctly, that self-interest is what actually rules even the loudest of the prophets of altruism, in politics, in the professions, in business, in government and in all the large affairs of the world.[42]

Ventures was philosophical observation. Howe's *Anthology of Another Town* (1920) was another kind of book, one that seemed inspired by *Spoon River Anthology,* a little, perhaps, by *Winesburg, Ohio,* though Ed Howe seemed to be reminding people mainly of his own *Story of a Country Town.* In a series of vignettes, some sharp, some pretty dull, he demonstrated narrowness, gossip, limited interests, and unhappy married life as they existed in a village, the whole providing an amusing picture of small-town life. There was, for example, the story of "Uncle Jimmy Haskins":

When there is anything going on in the surrounding country some of the town men drive out. The habit not only brings trade but extends our acquaintance.

Last week I drove out to attend the golden wedding of Uncle Jimmy Haskins. There were a good many children and grandchildren present, and all the neighbours; and after dinner Uncle Jimmy and his wife told reminiscences.

Mrs. Haskins remembered little but hard work. It seemed wonderful to me that a woman should work as hard as she did, even in the early days, and she made out quite a case, I thought, against her daughters, her daughters-in-law and the other women present.

I suppose Uncle Jimmy worked hard too, but he didn't say much about it. I was struck with the fact that the most remarkable event he could recall in his history was that he once killed a squirrel with a rifle after several other men had fired at

> it repeatedly. Here was a man seventy-seven years old, yet he had no other adventure worth recalling. Uncle Jimmy has five sons, who are prosperous farmers, and four daughters, who married good men. He is a man of fair intelligence and ability, yet he has nothing to boast of except one lucky shot at a squirrel!
>
> Uncle Jimmy went to work early. I heard him recall that he did farm work when he was six years old and that his father used to complain bitterly that the boy had been a burden until he passed into his seventh year [Henry Howe's old complaint about the boy Ed]. For seventy-one years therefore he had been going to bed only to be called in the morning to go to work, and nothing remarkable has happened to him except shooting a squirrel.
>
> I have heard it said that every man's life would make a book if candidly written, but probably this is a mistake; certainly Uncle Jimmy's memoirs would be rejected by a publisher. In his day there were bears and deer and buffaloes, but he never killed one. He was once young and rode about looking for adventure, but never found any.
>
> In the early days there were bold and wicked men, but they never disturbed him. For seventy-odd years he has locked his doors and fastened his windows at night, but has never been robbed. In seventy-seven years he has never had an illness worth recalling. The wind and lightning have threatened more than three-quarters of a century without hitting him.
>
> I have been thinking of Uncle Jimmy's humdrum life and am compelled to confess that so far mine has been much like it.[43]

Another of the stories was about John Davis, a fine and polite young man who took a Bible with him on his wedding trip. "It was a praiseworthy thing to do, but many people laughed over the incident. Indeed, some of the young people say they heard the bride herself laugh about it."[44] One was about Mart Towne, who seemed to be ready to fall over at any time because of illness, but who had so many remedies suggested to him that a man offering a new one had to stand in line. Another was about Cleve Hunt, a Baptist, who was going with Mary Harris, a Presbyterian. The two went to each other's churches, but sat there showing their contempt for the proceedings, and church attendance in the town picked up just so folks could watch the private row going on. Or Doc Robinson, the town drunkard, who was believed to have been a noted surgeon, well educated, unhappy in love, and the younger son of a titled family in England. "I looked Doc up and discovered that the only notable thing that ever happened in his life was that he attended a veterinary college in Canada, where he was born on a farm and where he lived until he came to this country to make horse liniment, the basis of which, alcohol, he sweetened and drank, and thus became a drunkard."[45] Or Taylor Ward: "It is generally said certain mean men in this town should be chased out for the general good; and Taylor Ward says that if the meanest men should be voted on all of us would get votes."[46]

Such stories were by no means restricted to the *Anthology;* they appeared in numerous other volumes by Ed Howe—like, for example, the famous Little Blue Books, published by E. Haldeman-Julius in Girard, Kansas, and selling for a dime. *E. W. Howe's Monthly* advertised these for years, carrying comments from critics who had praised the editor for other things he had written. A further indication of Ed Howe's attitudes could be found in the Little Blue Book titles:

Preaching from the Audience (1926).

Notes for My Biographer (1926).

Sinner Sermons (1926)—"short sermons preached by a sinner: a man who is not a professional preacher of religious sermons."[47]

Dying Like a Gentleman and Other Stories (1926).

When a Woman Enjoys Herself, and Other Tales of a Small Town (1928).

Her Fifth Marriage and Other Stories (1928).

The Indignations of E. W. Howe (1933).

"Dying Like a Gentleman," one of his warmest stories, dealt with a man named Oliver K. Steele, a merchant, who died of cirrhosis of the liver:

> One day, at the noon hour, Nathan Knox, the restaurant man, showed a number of customers his account books. For thirty years, Nathan said, he had had orders from Oliver Steele to feed the hungry who couldn't pay, and send the bill to the brick store. The account had been transferred into many books, and the word "paid" appeared twelve times every year. Nathan once told Oliver he was feeding some rather tough men, a few of them thieves, he feared.
>
> "Did they eat what you gave them?" he asked, and on being told that they did, added: "In feeding a hungry man, never ask about his morals. Go ahead."[48]

One of Ed Howe's funniest stories, and one that he liked so much that he told it over and over again, was published in *When a Woman Enjoys Herself.* He called it "A Sensitive Man":

Many years ago a man named Jerry Shackleford lived in a lonely house in the woods south of town. His wife asked him one afternoon to get an armful of oven wood; she was baking and wanted wood to heat the oven of the cook-stove to the best advantage. But he delayed going, and his wife finally spoke to him sharply, as her bread was ready to bake. Jerry was very sensitive, and the reproof made him so mad that he went out of the house, and for fifteen years nothing was heard of him.

His wife continued living in the old house, and the neighbors told the story of the runaway in whispers. They noted that through every night a light burned in the window, as though inviting Jerry to return.

One cold blustery night as Mrs. Shackleford sat with her feet in the oven of the cookstove, to keep them warm, the front door opened and Jerry walked in carrying an armful of oven wood, which he deposited in the wood box behind the cookstove.

Mrs. Shackleford was glad to see her husband and welcomed the chance to make up, but she thought she should in some way indicate that his long absence had been unusual and improper, so she said: "Well, I will say you have been a long time about it!"

That made Jerry mad again, he was so sensitive; so he went out of the house again and has never been heard of since.[49]

When a Woman Enjoys Herself contained some of his better anecdotes and his more biting observations. He told, for example, of an educated man who came home and brought the town the first news of Keats and Shelley. "Some of us had heard of Dante and tried to read the *Divine Comedy,* but in wondering why it was called a comedy gave it up." There was also the tall man who wore a long, shiny coat and came to town, and people wondered what he had come for, and learned: "He was looking for an argument on baptism." Or a little story which may have revealed some of Ed Howe's own frustrations as a parent:

"Frances," Ben Ames said to his fourteen-year-old daughter, "do you want your parents to let you go your own way, and take no interest in your welfare? Do you want us to give up advising you? We are older, and have had more experience. Do you object to our taking an interest in you, and trying to direct your course? Do you want us to accept your judgment in everything, and make no suggestions about anything?"

Ben is a lawyer, and his wife is fond of his ability in an argument. She had been having some trouble with Frances, who belonged to the younger set, and wanted to "go" more than was thought good for her. So Mrs. Ames believed Ben's talk would do the child good.

But Frances answered her father's questions so promptly as to floor both of them:

"Well, yes," she said.[50]

In the comic tales that appeared in the Little Blue Books could be found the flavor of rustic America. His stories must have seemed pretty common to sophisticated readers, with their country smells, screen doors, outdoor water hydrants, fly-swatters, preserved pickles, and fans being fluttered to beat the Kansas heat. For Ed Howe was a primitive, one of the last of his type. He reached many readers in the way they were being reached by Will Rogers, and he did not seem to be trying nearly so hard.

An Aging Man Views His Times

A Kansas historian, examining the career of Edgar Watson Howe, has written:

"His own protests against social injustice were as ruthless as the life he was recording. Howe possessed that fatal gift of being an intimate part of the society in which he lived, yet as one detached or outside it, viewing it in all its inconsistencies, contradictions, and sordidness which seemed to violate needlessly the ideals which he thought it should be capable of achieving."[51]

Well, maybe. But social injustice, unfortunately, was not the central theme of Ed Howe. The reformers opposing social injustice received only his contempt. He wanted to reform society, true, but in a sense quite different from the reformation wanted by other reformers. "Detached" he was; out of the mainstream, yet commenting on it.

Away from *The Globe* he could write about and talk about whatever he chose, often with a vast supply of misinformation. He felt no compulsion to review Atchison or Kansas politics, or even national politics. This was the glory of *The Monthly*. He could pour forth his prejudices without worrying about whether he was giving the readers a balanced picture. Yet had he ever worried about that?

In his early years on *The Monthly* two of his old complaints

—the yellow press and the Muckrakers—were becoming lesser forces in American life. He still wailed about them, especially about the undue power that good conservatives gave to the Hearsts, by patronizing their journals; about the way the Muckrakers had caused people to tire of magazines, reform magazines and otherwise.

In these new times progressivism was becoming pronounced in America; of three presidential candidates in 1912 two were progressive, and the other was far from reactionary. With progressivism came the kind of unrest Ed Howe had deplored back in the 1880s and 1890s, when he had taken on Debs and Coxey. Firmly as always on the side of management, he admitted in the April, 1911, *Monthly* that he once had been a union man himself but that the average strike was "the meanest, the most unfair, the most uncalled for, the most unnecessary, and the most ruinous to the men." He was becoming tired of reading denunciations of the International Harvester Company, which seemed to him to be a worthy and useful organization, quite unlike the image of it usually seen in the press. Industrial violence, like the bombing of the building of the *Los Angeles Times,* shocked him right down to his conservative toes. He was especially angry that Clarence Darrow had enlisted himself on the side of the accused McNamaras. He was sure that Darrow was wrong in saying that some workingmen were as shackled as the Negro slave.

Would the *Outlook* (whose editor was then Theodore Roosevelt, the hunter of lions), which had said brutal acts also had been committed by employers, please tell Ed Howe of a case wherein an employer had blown up a business block and destroyed the lives of twenty-one men? It was labor that had committed outrages in the Northwest, not management. He had never heard of an employer beating an employee in a dispute over wages. "What is the idea of this rush to apologize for idleness and crime, and viciously lie about law-abiding, industrious and useful citizens? What is the magic of the word 'workingman,' since we are all workingmen?" (February, 1912).

He was applying the *Success Easier Than Failure* philosophy to current affairs. Among the generalizations he also was uttering a few truths. So much was big business on the defensive, he said, that it made no effort to answer unfair and lying attacks by press and politicians. The result: millions of people believed the discreditable things being written. Big business should engage in a campaign of education, should purchase advertising in the five hundred biggest newspapers in the land, and tell the truth about itself to counter the lies. But keep big business clean in the meantime (was the old foe of the Muckrakers changing, or was he merely his inconsistent self?), for many of the things said about business twenty years earlier were, unfortunately, quite true.

The Colorado coal strikes distressed him, but not because of the treatment of the miners. The disturbers were "ignorant foreigners," yet the crusading newspapers took their side at the expense of the useful men of America—natives of the United States. Why should these outsiders receive better pay than a good Kansas farmer? Protest seemed to be abroad in the land almost as much as in the days of Coxey's army. History told Ed Howe that in 1381 Parliament had passed a heavy tax and the people arose and marched on London. "Why don't the American people try a march on Washington?" Revolution? Well, the railmen went to Washington and got a law passed in their behalf. Women were picketing the White House and the President was being very attentive to their demands. Why not listen to the people for a change, instead of every troublemaker who seeks something just for himself?

E. W. Howe's Monthly of August, 1912, had much to say about the great Bull Moose campaign. Howe started with a predisposition toward Taft, who had proved to be a good conservative (despite the tariff), had promoted international peace, and was less dangerous generally than his political sponsor. Roosevelt was becoming more and more of a nuisance (though of the potential first ladies Howe best liked Mrs. Roosevelt, a woman who knew her place and had kept out of the newspapers). Taft seemed, all told, the best of the three candidates, a true gentleman, a man who uttered no unkind words about Roosevelt, the latter a person who was talking all the time about morality but behaving in a pretty unfair way toward Taft. Woodrow Wilson had caught Howe's eye by December, 1911, and Howe was writing of him as being one of the most sensible men in the country. He was impressed with Wilson even more during the campaign, and he even said once that he intended to *vote* for Wilson. He didn't, of course; his Republicanism was too ingrained, and Wilson gradually became to Howe a man even more troublesome than Roosevelt. In March, 1914, the editor could not see that Wilson had done much except raise taxes and living expenses and make business dull and put men out of work and get a salary of $75,000 when he used to get only $4,000 as a school teacher.

The most-discussed subject in *The Monthly* soon would be the war in Europe, but Ed Howe meanwhile was occupying himself with other happenings and causes. The sinking of the *Titanic* was mentioned: he commented on how Christian Science had explained that a "Thought Clamor" had sunk the vessel because of hatred of the rich, and he wondered why a "Love Clamor" could not have saved the sixteen hundred persons aboard. Woman suffrage led him to ask why "modest, intelligent, useful women" did not rise and strike down the nonsensical fad. Boys' clubs (he kept up the tirades about the Boy Scouts of America) were a nuisance, designed to send boys to idle vacation when they should be home working. The Leo Frank lynching in Georgia was an example of anarchy at work, a group of men electing to take the law into their own hands. Harry Thaw was still receiving far more newspaper attention than such a wretch deserved: "Theodore Roosevelt himself never had a prouder strut than that which now distinguishes Thaw" (October, 1913). The Mexican revolution: "the most cruel, brutal, unnecessary, uncivilized wrong ever perpetrated," proof to the Kansan that there was more mischief at work than moral awakening, as some people were saying in those days (September, 1911).

When war broke out in Europe in 1914 Ed Howe had a cause that would occupy him as prohibition had done in the old days on *The Globe*—or the Spanish-American War and the activities of William Jennings Bryan. Howe was a pacifist—up to a point. He was an isolationist, too, but again up to a point. He argued that progress was brought not by revolutions and wars but by the experience of many people, that "great leaders" often had acted cowardly and selfishly, that "War has always been an enemy of the human race, and its stoutest accessory has always been foolish strife" (August, 1912). Leaders had always been able to bring on war by talk of bravery and vanquishing the foe, but what was war but a movement designed to destroy men and property, and starve women and children?

His feelings about Germany were mixed, as were those of many Americans. He had always had admiration for the efficiency of the German people, that being one reason why Germany should win the war. For Germany had been devoted to common sense for forty years while the rest of the world had wallowed in stupidity. There were no bad children in Germany, no inefficient women, no Campfire Girls, no Boy Scouts, no Billy Sundays cheating the public, no governments that treated business like an outlaw. But the invasion of Belgium, with the attendant German atrocities (real or imagined), could not be defended: "The Germans had no more right in Belgium than has an armed burglar a right to be in your house between two and three o'clock in the morning" (October, 1914). In Hubbard's *Fra* he wrote about how he had liked the Germans, of the German ships on which he had sailed, about some of his ancestors having been German. He praised German gentleness, bravery, fairness, politeness and ability. But he blamed the German people for being tricked by the Kaiser, the man responsible for the terror taking place in Europe.

He observed that another nation which he had admired, Japan, was becoming a world power, and he suggested that the Japanese would become in their time a problem for the West. "We Yankees are always saying we can whip a stack of wild cats; and we'll have a stack of wild cats to whip if Japan ever gains possession of China" (March, 1915).

The 1916 election campaign led him to believe that Charles Evans Hughes, if elected, would be no better than Wilson, perhaps more extravagant. His disenchantment with Wilson was becoming more pronounced at the same time, but for real laughs he turned to the Ford Peace Ship proposals, which were funnier than Mutt and Jeff (which no one laughed at). Henry Ford took himself too seriously (but the real Ford joke, he decided in a month or so, was the way Ford was running away from all his automotive competitors).

This World War was a war of propaganda, and Ed Howe had always been wary—he thought—of propaganda. But he was doing some loaded propagandizing himself. How could old soldiers sit around and engage in reminiscences of a thing like war? How could a man of decent instincts reflect on the time he had killed another man? Ed Howe would rather kill a neighbor with whom he had argued than a man with whom he had no personal quarrel. He thought it alarming that a person who believed in peace should be called a coward, and as war talk became more common in 1916 he wrote that the only danger of war was that being manufactured by the press and statesmen. Those searching for the cause of the war could gain enlightenment from the man from Kansas: it was all a big fool trick.

"If you say blood is thicker than water, let me remind you that there is a thousand times more German than English blood in the United States" (February, 1917). German immigrants had built America; how many English had fought in the Revolution or the Civil War? "It seems to me, in looking at the hurly-burly from Potato Hill, that the people have gone crazy for war with a people who do not want to fight us," he said. Did the American people as a whole want war? No, but the war spirit was being stirred up by the newspapers and the politicians. Free speech was being placed in danger, and people were afraid to talk, for fear of being called "slacker" or "traitor."

In April, 1917, America entered the European war, and the May issue of *The Monthly* was much preoccupied with the question. As in '98, Ed Howe now was able to commit himself to whatever his country had to do. We would need real soldiers, we would need a supreme commander (Roosevelt?), we would need to remember the great efficiency of the Germans. We must fight, as the Germans fight, because our system was threatened. We must curtail grains in whiskey, and the use of tobacco—strange things for Ed Howe to be advocating, but he was trying to think of ways the nation could conserve itself for battle. Already he was afraid that the United States would commit itself to long occupation and an even worse thing: rebuilding of the devastated lands, an idea already being advocated by "that liberal spender," a man named Herbert C. Hoover. "Who authorized our military men to say the American people must assume the main burden of the stupendous war in Europe? Who authorized Mr. Hoover to say we must habilitate France?" (June, 1917).

He accepted the war but he did not like it—the Council of National Defense, the Liberty Loan campaign, the talk of Hoover, the behavior of the government toward pacifists. He doubted that the American people would submit to the sacrifices necessary to win; he feared that there were not funds sufficient to prosecute a long campaign in Europe. "I also object to Douglas Fairbanks and Mary Pickford traveling around delivering speeches" (May, 1918). There came a homely editorial in which Howe thought about his nephew Arthur, who had gone to war, a boy who had spent many years at Potato Hill, and he noticed how Uncle Bruce often seemed to look off toward Camp Funston, where the boy was stationed.

Howe's tone seemed changed, perhaps, by late 1918. Now it was Germany that seemed the victim of hysteria, as Europe itself had had its inquisitions and tortures and crusades, as America had had religious hysteria and race riots and lynchings. He had little to say when the war came to an end. But he thought "The Peace League" was as big a joke as the Peace Ship, though at least Henry Ford had paid for the expenses of the latter, and not the taxpayers. And what could be less impressive than the simple propositions put before the negotiators at Versailles? Mr. Wilson, with his fourteen points and his idealism, he very much disliked: "because he has caused me more trouble than any other public man who has yet lived. I believe he is responsible for most of the troubles with which my country and the world are now afflicted. And I believe many others as cordially dislike Mr. Wilson as I do. . . . My objection to him is that he is a tremendous sentimentalist, and, occupying a great position, and consequently exercising great power, has tried to put his notions into effect" (November, 1919).

Wilson had come to symbolize the kind of man the Kansan disliked most—the "good man" type, who wanted to pay teachers more, who promoted more education (especially that not of the practical variety), who favored more churches, who tried to spread democracy throughout the world, who believed in literature, study groups, and pensions. "That he has no conception of the real problems of life he has fully demonstrated as president. He will go down in history as the most mischievous public man the world has ever known" (June, 1920).

So the Atchison editor entered the postwar world. He entered it as much a noninterventionist as ever. He was growing even more disgusted with the idea that the United States should occupy itself with the affairs of other people, and he said so in an article in a national magazine:

> I am told it is probable the planet Mars is inhabited. It may have people suffering for food, or for the advice of our active Americans. There may be young people there in need of the services of our expert dentists, missionaries, or specialists

> in hookworm. Therefore it may be desirable to build a railroad to Mars, in order to rush in freight trains carrying supplies and passenger trains bearing welfare workers.
>
> But if a railroad to Mars is plainly impossible, it seems to me we should be willing to let the Martians take care of themselves, as we have long been compelled to do, until such time as we can think up a better plan, and straighten out our own tangled affairs.[52]

Now there was revolution in Russia, and Ed Howe thought one revolutionary was as bad as another, in any country. He remembered a little girl in Atchison who used to hold her breath and kick and scream and excite the whole town. Susie was her name, and she seemed to have a lot of followers, who liked "insurgents" and thought there was much to be said for the likes of Susie. Russia was full of such people—that fellow Kerensky, for example, the "moving spirit of the present wild life in Russia" (June, 1917); that fellow Trotsky, "a disturber since he was old enough to crawl"—and, something that annoyed Ed Howe as much, looking like "a Jew clerk in a clothing store in a country town" (March, 1918). The majority opposed this "wrong idea" that was overtaking and conquering the Russian nation but did nothing about it. In America there was a similar situation, a minority being allowed to run things. Why was "Bolshevikism" allowed to exist? Because of the "proletarians and poets." Anyone with a good business head could see that Bolshevism would abolish all private property and transfer all factories and railways to the proletariat ("the lowest class of society"). Ed Howe hoped that if revolution ever truly came to America that the people would make it a "sensible one," a bloodless one, one that put the troublemakers to work instead of executing them.

The postwar era eventually became for Ed Howe a time when he could be truly at home, when *The Blessings of Business* would become the philosophy of Presidents and Congresses. First he looked at the witch hunts of Attorney General Palmer and compared the gentleman with the boy who cried "Wolf!" Howe suggested, out of his own conviction about socialism in America, that the wolf eventually would come. Socialism was a much greater danger than the influenza epidemic that was occupying the attentions of the American people; he blamed the epidemic on (1) the newspaper excitement about it and (2) the medicine prescribed by the doctors. Like many Americans he was adjusting himself to the idea of prohibition, even though he had long fought it: "Whisky is an evil as certainly as burglary; it will benefit any community, state or nation to get rid of it" (January, 1919). He liked the Ku Klux Klan, and vowed to join as soon as a camp was organized in his neighborhood, for he admired the talk of 100 per cent Americanism and anti-woman suffrage and believed the Klan would do things that were neglected by legislative bodies. He promised to organize a Yankee branch of the Klan and make *The Monthly* its organ. He laughed at the new things being done by advertisers, who made claims so different from the primitive ones made forty years before in *The Globe:*

> I have lately been reading the advertising of a soup manufacturer. His vegetables are picked when the morning dew is on them, by young maidens who have just washed their hands and put on clean frocks; great scientists and great cooks, noted the world over, study formulas for soups, and they are tested by noted epicures, that the people may have something new, something better, something cheaper, something delicious, something that will build up the body along proper lines. I bought a can of the soup for nine cents, and could hardly eat it. I did get it down, but it was so indigestible that I spent a restless night. There are millions of American women who can take a ten cent soup bone, a few vegetables, and make better soup. The cook whose subject I am does it regularly.[53]

All these years he had been following American politics, but never would he feel so comfortable with politicians and their ways as in the 1920s. The nomination of Warren G. Harding seemed quite all right, and the sensible people now were making the selections, too; neither party had consulted "literary men" like Upton Sinclair about the nominations. Early in the year Howe had felt that Harding and James Cox were running on platforms exactly alike, but Harding was still his man. He predicted victory, and he predicted that the people would like their choice. And he hoped that a committee of businessmen would be appointed to manage the President, because the plain people needed representation in Washington. The campaign convinced him that Harding was the best man, especially because of Harding's speech of November 2 ("God knows if I am called to responsibility I am going to be honest with everybody in the world"), which seemed to him far better than the Gettysburg address (a speech "foolishly sentimental, reeking with Lincoln gush"). He liked Harding, thinking he was "just a plain, ordinary fellow, but can be on the square, and that's all there is to it" (November, 1920). Ed Howe kept hearing profound gentlemen saying: "Of course Mr. Harding is not a Lincoln." That was just fine with Howe: we were not in need of great speeches for the history books but plain common sense. "Some day the fact will be admitted that Lincoln was almost a poor President," Ed Howe once wrote; "some day it will be admitted that his conduct of the war was almost weak."[54]

Another Republican, Herbert Hoover, continued to annoy him with talk about using other people's money to feed the Russians; so did what he saw as a continued encroachment by the federal government upon the rights of states; so did the evangelists and boomers and social welfare workers and various grades of Bolsheviki who were assuming too much power. About the only real fear Howe had about Harding was expressed in an editorial about the possibility of a chap named Harry Daugherty becoming Attorney General, and in another which commented on the naming of Daugherty, Albert Fall, and Will Hays to the cabinet. All seemed unfit to Ed Howe, who had more prescience, perhaps, than many others at that time—at least about Harding's Cabinet. He wished Harding would stay home more, instead of going off motoring and making talks "concerning the glow of the rising sun, the scent of the rose, and inventing new forms of the boast that we are the richest nation in the world" (July, 1922). Yet he disagreed with the position of William Allen White, who was concerned about Harding's limited background and disinterest in books (practical affairs were more important to Howe than books any day). And he defended Harding in a *Monthly* editorial:

"I wish to say, in answer to an indignant letter from a subscriber in Ohio, that Mr. Harding is a very good president, as presidents go. He *looks* better than any other occupant the White House has had in many years: possibly we have never had a president who *looked* the part better, or was more dignified. And the literary quality of his Thanksgiving proclamations is high: his state papers generally are written with a skill and polish. . . . I like Mrs. Harding, also: there have been wives of American presidents who embarrassed their husbands, but Mrs. Harding is womanly and modest, and accorded very general respect" (February, 1922).

Such a statement makes one wonder to what extent Ed Howe

was pulling a joke on his readers. Soon after that editorial was written the Teapot Dome scandal broke, and Ed Howe was sympathetic with Albert Fall because of the way he had been deserted by his friends, and he was sure that Fall was not as guilty as the indictments would indicate. Howe tended to write off the affair as a minor matter; no one really got much out of the oil deal, and a lot of fuss was made unnecessarily. When the scandals about Harding and Nan Britton were being discussed, Howe gave the late President sympathy: "I find no more fault with Nan Britton because of her adventure than I find with Warren G. Harding because of his. And I think rather better of him since reading this book than before. He was a gentler, a fairer man in his love affair than in politics."[55]

And if Harding was at least a good man, another man of the age was a fraud—Albert Einstein: "Einstein knows nothing of value to you. His 'theory of relativity' is not important. Einstein is evidently fussing about nothing; even if his theory is true 'in a larger view,' it doesn't amount to anything in the view you are compelled to take. I decide that Professor Einstein is another false alarm" (April, 1921).

How easily Ed Howe could write off the great and the small! He had little respect for Henry Ford, that hero of the 1920s who never received the kind of admiration Howe gave to Rockefeller, for example. Ford was to him a naïve dreamer, a fellow who got involved in foolish causes, like his blaming the Jews for prohibition. Ford's *Dearborn Independent* was a journalistic mistake, published by a man who was "about as mischievous a Socialist as Eugene Debs." As for the idea of Ford being placed in the White House, it was "an indictment of the intelligence of Americans.... If all we demand in a chief executive is that he be widely known, why not Charley Chaplin, with Mary Pickford as vice-president, to please the women?" (August, 1923).

There was something about Margaret Sanger that bothered him, but he thought birth control might not be a bad idea, sometimes, especially if it would "reduce the birth rate to the vanishing point." Discussion of psychoanalysis bored him; it was "merely one of a thousand forms of flub-dub." The new word "jazz" and all it stood for disgusted him: soon we would be having "jazz children" produced by the "jazz young people" of the day. He accepted flappers, as he accepted other living creatures, but he saw no reason why they should be accorded the gallantry given to better women down through the centuries. Talking pictures seemed disagreeable, like the static he kept hearing on the radio. Crime, especially kidnapings, robberies, and murders, offended his soul, and he wondered if maybe the old-time vigilantism of the frontier might not become necessary again to protect the American people. The provincial Kansan was truly in a world he never made. As a newspaperman he had been glad to get one good item a day; now he could read about an airship going around the world, about the government appropriating 500 million dollars, a river to be improved, a plan to lower railroad rates, automobile and airplane accidents, killings by "dry agents" by the dozen, dynamiting of buildings by workmen in wage controversies, famine and war in China, rioters gaining control of a Parliament. "Although engaged in the newspaper business from the time I was twelve until compelled to quit by advancing years, I seem never to have been in it at all, it is so different" (August, 1929).

The Sacco-Vanzetti case, one of the big news stories of the 1920s, would seem to have been the kind of thing Ed Howe would seize onto, yet he wrote little about it in *The Monthly*. His general view was that the convicted men had had every opportunity to prove the wrongness of their conviction, and he thought it shocking that there had been rioting in the world because of the executions: "It is the right of free speech that is guaranteed in the Constitution," he said, "not the right to loot and burn" (August, 1927).

The Scopes trial in Tennessee was another matter; this one, predictably, delighted the old man in Atchison, and gave him an opportunity to knock Bryan and organized religion again. Evolution had disposed absolutely of the idea of Christianity: "If Evolution is true the world was not created as the Bible says it was; the story of Christ, as related in the New Testament, cannot be true" (May, 1925). He anticipated the trial at Dayton with glee and foresaw an entertaining duel between Bryan and Clarence Darrow. But he thought scientists were foolish to take the case for evolution "before a jury in a hill town in Tennessee":

"They have won a verdict in every standard educational institution in the world. Why should they be interested in an opinion from a little town in Tennessee? Men of culture might as well appeal to the barbarous Russians for a verdict against

Communism. Abraham Lincoln might as well have taken his case against slavery before a jury in Georgia."[56]

Bryan died shortly after the celebrated trial was over, and so he passed from Howe's life and his editorial criticisms, though the editor wrote an obituary charitable in tone. Warren G. Harding passed, too, proving, ultimately, to be a disappointment. But Calvin Coolidge satisfied the Kansan right from the beginning. Howe wrote the man who had succeeded to the presidency an open letter, recommending that he not sit on the porch in his stocking feet to prove his status as a common man, or do other similarly ridiculous things, "but be a modest, well-groomed, well-behaved gentleman determined to give the high position you occupy the duties expected by law and common sense; no more, no less" (August, 1923). Coolidge was no statesman, he was better than that, "a plain, honest man with plain ideas: a New England Yankee with considerable Yankee shrewdness," no great writer or great speaker but a man able to handle the critical problems of America (June, 1924). General Dawes, vice-president under Coolidge, was all right, too; what truth there was in Dawes's words: "The time has come when common sense must be crowned king"! Shelley and Whitman could offer nothing better than that. Howe wrote in 1928 that Coolidge was "about the only president I have admired from start to finish" (April, 1928). Coolidge had warned the American people against depending on federal help, and had his advice been followed the people would not have used all their time and energy riding in automobiles and listening to the radio and going to movies and flirting and gossiping and drinking bootleg whiskey.

Ed Howe looked abroad and found someone he admired almost as much—Benito Mussolini. But he feared he was alone in thinking the Fascist movement had been the most important movement in history. Here was an uprising "along honest, decent and correct economic lines," a "powerful protest against the foolish sentimentalism that has become the world's greatest curse." The people of the United States should march on Washington, he said, as the Fascisti had done in Italy. Fascism was a commendable revolution against communism, socialism, and labor unions, a truly reactionary revolution to get rid of reform and return to order and industry, "a revolt of the industrious and worthy against anarchists and disturbers."[57] Mussolini had restored law and order; he had been able to use clubs and pistols more effectively than the mobs that were opposed to him.

It was the business-like methods that pleased him about the Italian dictator. Mussolini was practical, no visionary dreamer. Look at the American scene and ask who were the best people, the real leaders? Well, Phil Armour—a greater man than Schubert, and an Armour ham was a greater accomplishment than the *Unfinished Symphony*. "Suppose a man *is* able to play the piano a little better than the average. Or compose a symphony. What of it? That sort of thing is relaxation after the real day's work" (April, 1918). Howe's heroes were men who had lived as he had lived and had gone ahead and made successes of themselves despite the difficulties of life. Of no value were Shakespeare, Homer, Napoleon, and Buddha. He preferred Darwin, Edison, Nietzsche, Schopenhauer, Henry Wallace (a preacher, farmer, and a sound and helpful man), plus mechanics, scientists, and modest neighbors—and Andrew Mellon, especially Andrew Mellon, a much better man than Hoover, for example, the latter being a fellow who wanted to improve rivers at the expense of the taxpayer. He was a much more valuable man to civilization than, say, a poet, "no mythical saint of the distant past enjoying the favor of tradition and of fanatical followers, but a man of blood and bone living in the greatest of all ages, and who has survived the assaults of the most vicious critics" (March, 1926).

Likewise useless were the conventional heroes of the time. Only a fool could believe that a certain Sergeant York actually had captured one hundred and thirty-five German soldiers during the war and killed twenty-five. "If there is any way of getting at the truth, I will bet he didn't do it" (December, 1921). Only a fool could care about Babe Ruth, who, when a ball was thrown at him, could hit it harder than other men "now striking at balls." Or Billy Mitchell, for it was absurd to believe that this colonel could know things about the air service and airships that other men had not thought of. Or Charles Lindbergh, whose accomplishment in flying the Atlantic could lead only to others trying it and ending up in the water. Or Robert M. LaFollette, who was a trouble-making reformer, no better dead than alive.

Ed Howe started the election campaign of 1928 with strong admiration for that plain man of the people from New York, "a man so common he is called Al," the Al Smith who had attracted his notice in 1925. Smith remained his candidate for some time, and "I shall vote for him," he said, feeling, however, that because of Catholicism Smith could not be elected. The very fact of Smith's being nominated amazed him, but he thought the Know-Nothingism of the nineteenth century was not as bad as the campaign being conducted against Al Smith. When Howe went to the polls election day he behaved, of course, according to his old basic prejudices; he voted for Herbert Hoover, the man he had been condemning since World War relief days: "In spite of myself I have long had a good deal of admiration for Herbert Hoover, although I picked at him. I have never doubted he is a fine gentleman, an honest man, and possessed of unusual intelligence and information. If he will get rid of his disposition to spend too much public money, a fortunate selection for the presidency has been made" (October, 1928).

How the man could rationalize his decisions!

As the disciple of success in his time, Edgar Watson Howe could not understand what happened to the American nation in 1929. He had written that there was no excuse for poverty in a land such as ours, where opportunity was so great, and he had no sympathy for those persons (except the aged and ill) who were stricken by economic difficulty. Farm relief in the summer of 1929 seemed to him "the most disastrous mistake" in American history, because it was sought not by the farmers but by farm politicians. And in the month of the great crash he was writing:

"I have always believed in the Capitalistic System because it seems to be the best actual experience has been able to devise. All evidence supports it, while the system recommended by the dissenters has been tried many times, and always failed. It is being tried now in Russia, under perfect conditions, and has failed again" (October, 1929).

He ended his—and the nation's—decade of optimism with another of his affirmative utterances, that the woes which seemed to be overcoming the American people could be combated only through the idea he had long preached—good habits were better than bad, as well as being easier and more profitable.

The Arts in an Age of Cynicism

Ed Howe would have been the first to scoff at the notion that he was a creative writer. The Missouri River from his window was better than an artistic reproduction. From Potato Hill the view topped anything Raphael had ever painted. Creativity was a joke.

In the 1920s he continued to marvel at the success of certain books and writers and thinkers: Spinoza, *Pilgrim's Progress, Don Quixote, The Divine Comedy.* Emerson he continued to like, seeing him as "our brightest star," even though he did not care for Emerson's kind of man. Parson Weems he liked, too, and he thought the cherry tree fable was much better than a currently praised volume called *The Rubaiyat:* Weems praised truth, Omar Khayyam "sings the glories of drunkenness." So Ed Howe slashed away, repeating prejudices he had been voicing since his first consciousness of himself as a man of editorial influence. Stevenson he still could not abide, especially *Dr. Jekyll and Mr. Hyde.* "There is something lacking" in the style of Conrad. How could you expect the people to buy good books when good books were so rare? But textbooks—these were the really good books, because they were books full of information, simply put down.

The sentimental drew his barbs, and the "filthy" sickened him, including much that he considered filth in the Bible and other great literature, the kind of stories a decent man would not repeat. He had heard of Frank Harris' *My Life and Loves* but would not read it; Harris seemed a man as vile as Oscar Wilde, a writer Harris had praised in two volumes. Contemporary art and literature brought satirical observations—a portrait of Mrs. Harry Payne Whitney, by Robert Henri, for example, in which Mrs. Whitney seemed to be reclining on the lower edge of a huge dish, which was inclined upward at a 35- to 45-degree angle. She was wearing an undershirt and jacket, and her lower limbs were in an ordinary suit of muslin underwear, with a bow and ribbon at the ankles. Was this art? Could Henri be serious? Why did Mrs. Whitney submit to such libel? Or there was that new play-right, Eugene O'Neill, so impudent in asking people to sit five hours at a play. Or a new poet named E. E. Cummings, who did not capitalize his name. Easier to take than Cummings, in his opinion, was a book by Booth Tarkington called *Alice Adams*—no grand passions or exciting stuff, "a wonderful picture of the love affairs of our ordinary nice girls; her humiliation over her home, her parents, her brothers, the slights of her girl friends, her dread of the Business College sign, which is always intruding itself" (July, 1921). *Moby-Dick,* a book he had long wanted to read, was just becoming really popular. The psychology in it was difficult to grasp, but the whaling details were good, taking him back to his favorite sea story, *Two Years Before the Mast.* Upton Sinclair continued to trouble him most among America's writers, an honestly mistaken man who was unable to be anything else.

Good reporting remained for him some of the best reading—the work of Walter Lippmann, for example. Or another example—a reporter for the *Kansas City Star* (his name was unknown to Howe) had covered the Scopes trial and used language that people could understand. These were better than Sherwood Anderson, who might be receiving critical praise but whose *Dark Laughter* was not, for Ed Howe, a "triumph in American literature." Not only that, but the book was vulgar. One who wrote much better books was Kathleen Norris; her work had the quality of Turgenev. Also clever was Fannie Hurst, whose work was like a great oil painting. And people were all talking about a book called *All Quiet on the Western Front,* an unusual book but one filthy enough to be barred from some libraries.

Dreiser he greatly admired; he recommended—in 1926—the reading of *Sister Carrie,* which he had found had a moral and pitiful comment to make about life. And he followed the career of Sinclair Lewis closely, never admitting, if he was aware of it, that many believed that he himself, because of *The Story of a Country Town,* was the forerunner of the Lewis "school." He did not care much for *Main Street.* For there were in every town, Gopher Prairie or Atchison, "characters" such as Lewis had described. There also were good people, industrious and well behaved, but such people did not find their way into literature, except to be called "a hypocrite or hog, or plodder, but how often the town drunkard gets into books!" Literary experts, he said, were trying to prove that *Main Street* towns were as old as the human race. "Now some one should write a book called 'Broadway,' and show that cities have always been centers of ignorance, destitution, crime: a little more culture in spots, but a general average below 'Main Street' " (May, 1925).

Lewis' Babbitt did not seem a bad type to Ed Howe; he observed that people who were calling others "Babbitts" thought themselves quite bright but that really most of us, not just poor old George Babbitt, were pretty dull folks. He liked *Arrowsmith,* and he was interested in the fact that Sinclair Lewis was working on a book about the ministry. He was afraid that Lewis' book would deal too much with love affairs and not enough with the methods and quarrels and doctrines of churches. When he finally read *Elmer Gantry* he found it below *Arrowsmith* in quality, but still an accurate picture of the church: "There is very little exaggeration; indeed, the arguments and incidents are not as smashing as may be heard wherever men or women meet, and discuss the church" (March, 1927). The evangelist Sharon he especially admired as a genuine characterization. *Dodsworth* did not appeal to him. He had lived a long time and had never known anyone like Sam Dodsworth, or any woman like Dodsworth's wife, Fran. "The great genius of Mr. Lewis must be admitted, but what queer notions of life he has" (February, 1929).

Occasionally the editor had an outing at the movies and the theater. He went to see *Rain,* and admired it, not because it was a good play—it wasn't—but because it attacked missionaries and religion. His taste in movies demonstrated his liking for the practical and realistic. The film *Grass,* made in Persia and depicting a tribe seeking food for its livestock, not only was natural and believable but an answer to Rudolph Valentino and the "castles manufactured in a few hours by movie carpenters." Another film called *The Drums of Love* disgusted him; "the kissing of the hero and heroine is the nastiest thing I have seen in many years." The early talking picture called *The Rogue Song* brought laughter, for the hero (who had it coming, because he was a common thief) was caught, stripped, whipped by enemies, and still sang a song while tied to a stake. "Has a common man a right to object to Art?" he asked. "If so, I file protest against 'The Rogue Song;' it robbed me of fifty cents earned in honest material ways" (April, 1930). He also found a film about flying (probably *Hell's Angels*) more laughable than anything else, especially for the way it had drawn in the suckers throughout the country. Chaplin's *City Lights* was enjoyable, and quite frankly it was a relief to see a silent picture again after all the talk in the talkies. But the movies were usually a wasted evening:

"Occasionally I am persuaded to try the movies again; but by the time the Free Advertising is disposed of, my day is ruined. First, the Republican national committee shows the Hoover grandchildren, or Hoover approving another drive. Then come the golf kings, the whist kings, the football kings; next a lot of local advertising, and usually a local speaker to demand that everyone present give until it hurts to the Boy Scouts. Then a play that in concept and execution would disgrace an idiot whose friends hope for at least partial recovery. Then home and to bed, to toss in discouragement" (February, 1932).

Days in Kansas and Florida

In a personal note in *E. W. Howe's Monthly,* the editor both expanded on the life he was living and gave his views on an issue of the times: "I am spending the winter in Miami, and give you my word I have not seen a drunken man here, and scarcely hear the subject of whisky mentioned. Prohibition seems as successful here as in Kansas. Miami has just held a celebration lasting a week. It attracted enormous crowds, and I mingled with them day after day. I assure you upon my honor that I did not see a single drunken man during the week; I have heard no one complain of such a nuisance. . . . Yet literature is clamoring for greater appropriations to overcome the drunken orgy going on (in print) in Miami" (January, 1921).

He was now spending his winters in Florida, twenty-one of them altogether, away from the sometimes harsh winds and snows that came to eastern Kansas. The winter of 1916-17 was the first, spent in Tampa, a city that Ed Howe often said he liked best—fewer tourists, quiet, possessing commercial promise. But Tampa was cold and disagreeable, and after he traveled the state he decided that he liked Miami well enough to live there. And it was there that he and Adelaide spent the rest of their winters in the southland. At one time he had leaned toward Palm Beach as the best place in Florida, a city that resembled Monte Carlo, but a person would be advised to live there only if he cared for hotel life.

The Florida routine was a quite one for the Howes. The old editor spent much of his time reading, visited the farmer's market twice a week, enjoyed his friendships, especially the good businessmen who had made their homes in Miami, and even went to the home of William Jennings Bryan, who gave the Howes a full tour and won the admiration of Adelaide.

The Monthly described in detail his 1918 trip to Florida, which he made by way of New York and Philadelphia. In New York he went to visit H. L. Mencken, who was already one of his heroes. It was their first visit, and Howe liked the way Mencken talked the Kansas language, even though he did have a rather disreputable occupation, that of professional critic. He also met Mencken's crony, George Jean Nathan, a man of prejudices against children, animals, automatic pianos, prayers, authors, actors, prints of *Mona Lisa,* and churches—a person quite different from Mencken. Both were polite to Adelaide, and this he liked. He observed that Nathan was noted for correct dressing, but said Adelaide thought Mencken equally well groomed, if not the better dressed of the two.

Howe also had been invited to visit the great William Dean Howells, who was then in his last years, and he drove to Howells' hotel—the Blackstone—in a busy street, with snow falling. Howells did not seem to be a man as old as he was said to be: "I have never seen another man of eighty equally well preserved mentally and physically." They talked for about an hour, and Howe told Howells that he appreciated him as both man and writer. "O, my dear," Howells responded, "when anyone talks to me like that, I do not know what to say."

He went to Ziegfeld's *Midnight Frolic* and to the Hippodrome, which had been built by Skip Dundy, whom Howe had known in Falls City. He liked the chorus girls, and he liked the pleasant atmosphere of the show. As a man of some substance and already a writer for their publications he was entertained by Roscoe Peacock of Philadelphia, the circulation manager of the Curtis Publishing Company, and by Hamilton Holt, editor of the *Independent.*

How proud he was of the great men with whom he was rubbing shoulders in those days! And how this irritated an old friend back in Kansas, who had been reading about Ed Howe and his associations in Florida:

In a recent number of the *Saturday Evening Post*, E. W. Howe, of Atchison, has a most interesting article on Miami, Florida. It is by far the best article in the *Saturday Evening Post* of that issue, and the *Saturday Evening Post* is the most interesting weekly published in the English language, which fosters the most interesting periodicals in the world. The article describes in simple, understandable language what the great Florida resort is like. Mr. Howe describes a certain club built by millionaires and used exclusively by them. And he says that he was "honored by an invitation to luncheon there."

Which makes us tired.

For there are 18,000 millionaires in America; some of whom have given society value received, some of whom have merely grabbed money off the Stock Exchange. The fact that a man is a millionaire signifies what he has got, but not that he has given. And a man's value in the world depends not on what he has but on what he has given.

For the 18,000 millionaires there is but one Ed Howe. Some millionaires have given more than Ed Howe; Edison has, so has Ford, so have scores of others; but not thousands, not even hundreds. E. W. Howe has given the world wisdom, he has given the world pleasure, he has given the world half a dozen great books. It took more brains, it took more of a man to write "The Story of a Country Town" than it took to make a million—or a dozen of them. And it gives us a pain to read that as smart and self-respecting a man as Ed Howe should feel "honored" to be invited to a club which has no distinction except that it is built by millionaires, operated by millionaires, and owned by them. Personally there is vastly more honor in being entertained at the Century Club in New York, or the National Arts Club, or the Players', or any of a dozen professional men's clubs, than to be entertained at a club that has the low vulgarity to brag about the money of its owners and builders. It is brains and not money that count in this world, and they are by no means synonymous. Ed Howe knows better. He knows that there are a dozen men in Atchison richer than he who have not done half as much for the town as he has done. And that's what makes a man valuable; not his money. And Ed Howe has done so much in this world that he should feel the equal of any one; he should walk into the millionaires' club as a self-respecting equal of the best of them. He should not be pulling a forelock and talking about being "honored" by an invitation anywhere![58]

That was William Allen White talking, and his editorial demonstrated how great the gap was between him and Howe on the subject of deference to the rich and mighty. Howe *was* proud of knowing the millionaires, and he stayed that way. In early 1918 he announced that *The Monthly* would be edited for a time from 1411 Nance Avenue in Tampa, where he had rented a furnished bungalow. The house was on the Bay Shore Drive, with Tampa Bay in the foreground, and Howe could watch the steamers and sailing ships, look at the pine trees and gardens, and amuse himself with the sandy soil in which flowers and vegetables grew so abundantly. He thought that the house was so lovely it might have been furnished out of *House Beautiful.*

Detailed descriptions of the trips to Florida became a commonplace in *The Monthly:* 2,080 miles to Miami; six barrels of gasoline, costing eighty-one dollars; seven miles to the gallon, thanks to mud and rain; no dry roads anywhere from Atchison to Columbia, Missouri; the car a Winston 48; two new tires and tubes on the way; 196 towns passed through. That was the year that he spent the winter at Clyde Court, furnished apartments in Miami.

So the reader, if he cared, could obtain a picture of the editor living the good life in the South. There were fishing stories, conversations with old men met on the streets, anecdotes about people like the head porter at Clyde Court, discussions with a man who was devoted to both Christian Science and prohibition, little occurrences like a brush with the police:

"In Miami, Florida, where we are spending the winter, Adelaide drives the automobile. The other day a crossing policeman yelled at her: I didn't think anyone would dare do it, but this fellow did. Adelaide was in the right of it: I was sitting beside her, and am well trained. After that, when we went by this crossing policeman, Adelaide had a look of scorn on her face that was magnificent. And it seemed to have its effect: one day the policeman called to her: 'Lady, I was wrong; I apologize' " (February, 1921).

"FLORIDA NOTES," the headings read. At Clyde Court, he wrote, there were forty-five male guests, and sixty-seven women. Men love to eat too much, and die; therefore the widows in Florida, Howe said. The head man at a convention knocked the practice of wearing badges; this delighted Ed Howe. Surf bathing? Not up to much; the bathtub was more suited to a man of his figure. Eight steamships one day off Miami Beach, at the same time. A woman's club, with eight members, had been formed; the ladies planned to buy and read *The Sheik,* and then *Jurgen* (he gave them the bad news that the censored *Jurgen* would now cost them twenty-five dollars a copy instead of merely twenty-five cents, the price of *The Sheik*). Two lamb chops: eighteen cents. Churches in Miami had more people in them on Sunday evenings than churches in other cities. In a Miami millinery white clerks were seen waiting on fourteen customers, all of them Negroes. Women everywhere—that was Miami.

At Clyde Court he met subscribers to *The Monthly* who called on him to visit in the agreeable winter climate. Such people as John Golden, the New York theater man; John T. McCutcheon, the cartoonist for the *Chicago Tribune;* H. T. Webster, who drew "The Timid Soul"; Cyrus H. K. Curtis and George H. Lorimer—all visited Ed Howe. Curtis' yacht, the *Lyndonia,* was in Florida, and Howe gave a luncheon for the celebrated publisher. He hired a Cuban army band to play at the Miami casino, and saw many young girls—"otherwise well behaved"—smoking cigarettes. Miami strawberries were served; the weather was pleasant; the sea was inviting. And various celebrities passed by—Will Hays of the Harding cabinet; Fleischmann of the yeast company; Gillette of the safety razors; John Wanamaker, the department store titan; Fritz Kreisler; John Philip Sousa; and George Matthew Adams, whose syndicate carried the writings of Ed Howe to the world.

One wonders at this point about the seemingly austere editor from Atchison, with his usually pious views about partying and drinking and smoking. He was a social drinker, his niece recalled, but he never changed his attitude toward women who smoked. He made, despite his Kansas suspicions about such things, several excursions to Miami night spots; and Ray Long, editor of the Hearst magazines, and Mrs. Long invited him to the Flamingo Hotel, where other guests were the Ring Lardners, the John Goldens, and Neysa McMein, magazine illustrator. ". . . the business of the afternoon seemed to be to smoke cigarettes, visit, dance and listen to the music. . . . It was all tremendously interesting and novel to a member of a country club out West." That evening Oliver H. Bogue of Indiana, a former vice president of the Rock Island Railroad, took Howe to dine at the Royal Palm Hotel. And the next day was spent at the beach:

"Here both men and women wear one-piece suits, and the

exhibition of 'figures' attracted great attention from at least one western man; but he soon became accustomed to it, and paid no more attention to it than he does to a street crowd at home watching a circus parade. Hundreds of fat women go in, and these interested me more than did the young women and girls."

The place seemed full of notables. And the bougainvillaea, hibiscus, poinsettia, sunshine, and grass were all lovely. There was also a luncheon on the *Lyndonia,* as guests of Curtis. "I was inclined to shrivel up in the presence of this man, but he was so modest, genteel and cordial that I was soon able to study him a little."[59]

So now there was a social whirl in Florida, and there were celebrities in his life, though generally Ed Howe saw Florida as a place full of the kind of people you meet most of your life—good, substantial people mainly, fine and wholesome people. And the climate was ideal. Howe visited Palm Beach and St. Petersburg, and the beach at Daytona, and decided he still liked Miami best. One Sunday he heard Bryan conduct his weekly Bible class at the Royal Palm Park, and another time Bryan addressed an excursion of editors and then sat with Ed Howe. "I have long admired him," the forgetful Kansan wrote, "and regretted he is not a useful business man. What a fine banker he would have made, with the sane, safe ideas that distinguish bankers!" (March, 1924).

If he had come to be more charitable toward Bryan he was still annoyed (or pretended to be) by the behavior of certain women, notably two grandmothers and a spinster (probably Adelaide) who were trying to reform him in the nice way women have of trying to improve their men:

"The betterment of the world, they believe, can only come about through the betterment of men. The conversation is not directed to me, but I usually find I am in it. . . . Sometimes Adelaide, my niece, makes a remark that startles me; it indicates that I have been closely associated with her fifteen years, and do not know her. I have long been thinking of her as a good Indian who wouldn't send a man to the stake, but sometimes she has a touch of savagery toward the men that causes me to shiver" (January, 1925).

Life remained mainly simple for Ed Howe, even in great and booming Miami, a city full of men who had accomplished the miracles of an Aladdin, but still a city that was too noisy, too hazardous, the streets being as busy as those in the big cities to the north. He was glad in the spring to return to the country sights of Atchison, which was pretty dull, admittedly, after Florida. Howe was just a country boy, he kept saying, and he tried to be a country boy even in Miami. His chief delight there was the old men, successful people "now looking peacefully toward the sunset," thousands of such men in Miami, men with records of achievement, most of them living with their "original wives," living in and owning the best homes in the city. "The noted actresses, tennis players, prize fighters, and swimmers, may go hang, so far as I am concerned" (January, 1927).

Good friendships were formed in the Florida years. He was interviewed there by Nunnally Johnson, the journalist who became a motion picture producer and writer. He was proud of his friendship with Ray Long, the Hearst editor, and *The Monthly* printed a photograph of Howe, Adelaide, and Mrs. Long at the races in Miami. He was visited by Charles Curtis in March, 1928, shortly before Curtis became the Republican vice presidential candidate, and he referred to Curtis (who used to be the subject of shafts in *The Globe*) as "one of the old fellows I have known in Kansas during a residence of more than fifty years" (January, 1929). Frank B. Shutts, who later became publisher of the *Miami Herald,* spoke fondly of the six months a year that Ed Howe spent in Miami, shopping in the stores and observing what was going on, and he believed that Miami shared Ed Howe with Atchison. Most important, perhaps, was Howe's friendship with the writer Corra Harris, whom he met in Florida, an educated and religious woman but an unusual and entertaining person whom he greatly admired. Once he visited her at her home in the hills of Georgia, a farm of three hundred or four hundred acres. And they sat in front of the fireplace and talked, he mainly listening, and later that night he became ill:

"Rain was falling, and here I was twenty-five miles from Cartersville and an undertaker. My condition was alarming, but I was not specially scared; I was within a few days of my seventy-sixth birthday, and one cannot live forever. . . . I went back to bed, since there was nothing else to do. The pain eased after a time, and I went to sleep. . . . Some day old Nature will fail me, in attending to its big business, but it has been very kind in the past" (March, 1929).

Ed Howe and Corra Harris became correspondents, and Mrs. Harris wrote Howe of how she had observed his pleasure in his children, and of how she had written about him for the "Candlelit Column" of the *Atlanta Journal:*

"The editor wrote back and said he liked it best of all. 'I got a big kick out of your skill and steady hand in cutting open Ed Howe. It is a fine piece of literary surgery, opening up that old boys heart in front of your Candlelit audience.'—Sounds bloody, but I assure you it is the best I can do to praise and honor a great man, with, of course, a beam in my eye to cast a witty light upon your invinciable [sic] humanness."[60]

It was a pleasant life that Ed Howe lived in the 1920s—winters in Florida, the remainder of the year at Potato Hill, trips to other parts of the country. New England in the late summer of 1921—famous sites, monuments, and Harvard (simply a lot of buildings). New York in 1923—meeting Herbert Bayard Swope, executive editor of the *World* (and a highly admirable man, too); an offer to meet Lloyd George, whom Howe disliked, so he declined the offer; an offer to meet John D. Rockefeller, Jr., whom he also disliked, so that meeting also did not take place. But Swope introduced him to Franklin P. Adams, whom Howe had long admired. And the *New York Daily News* carried a photograph of Howe with Adelaide, his daughter Mateel, and Nellie Webb of *The Globe* staff, all talking to a New York patrolman. He met the *Daily News* publisher, Joseph Medill Patterson, who was then riding high with his relatively new tabloid. And Howe was annoyed by the way the press described him, as an outlander:

"The New York newspaper reporters made me say all sorts of things, and I'll stand by them. . . . I am tired of those persons who, anxious to be interviewed, deny what they are quoted as saying. I have myself had disagreeable experiences with them. So I admit saying 'By gosh,' 'tarnation' and everything else western farmers are supposed by city people to say" (November, 1923).

In the fall of 1925 he went on a speaking tour to Chicago and the University of Iowa. He was always uneasy about his speaking engagements, feeling that he was not much of a public speaker. He described a talk he once gave, an incident probably not nearly as painful as he felt called upon to describe it:

> I knew soon after my arrival in the town that everything was going wrong. The citizen who had made the "guarantee"

> was mad, realizing he had been victimized, and had engaged in a violent quarrel with my "manager." My advertising had attracted one man who had heard of me, and he had called at the hotel, from the windows of which I could see the opera house brilliantly lighted, and no one going in. I told him I would return the money guaranteed for my appearance, and redeem the few tickets sold, but he insisted that I go through with it. So I walked with him to the opera house, angry and ashamed, and arrived late. There was no one to introduce me, but I immediately began, introducing myself. I did not go on the stage, but stood among the thirty who had gathered in one spot.
>
> In introducing myself I said I was a fool who had been led to believe there was a demand for his services as a speaker; and then I launched into an assault on lecturing and lectures in general. I dislike both, and know a good many things to say on the subject. I had a few notes of my talk, but never took them from my pocket.
>
> There was one gloomy man present who had made me uncomfortable in the audience the night before, in another town, but I defied him, and soon had him interested. I also noticed that the stage hands came down and sat near me. This encouraged me so much that I began to enjoy myself, noting that for once in my life I was able to say what I wanted to say. There was so much enthusiasm in the audience that a good many were attracted from the street, and came in, as there was no doorkeeper to oppose them: the doorkeeper had joined my thirty friends and the stage hands.
>
> I would give much to be able to talk all the time as well as I did the night I was mad at lecturing, and when I told those present I intended to return their money, and quit the tour; which I did, and this seemed to advance me in their favor.[61]

Though many were coming to recognize him as a humorist, he did not think much of what Americans called humor or of those newspaper writers trying to be funny every day of the year and almost never succeeding. Serious people do not devote themselves to jokes, he wrote; Americans are such poor talkers that they tell jokes hurriedly so that someone else will not break in on them.

His place was more and more the national scene, but Ed Howe was maintaining the Kansas friendships—and whacking away at those whom he disliked in the state. High on the latter list was Arthur Capper, the veteran Republican senator against whom Ed Howe had been warning the voters for many years. Capper was mainly a good hand-shaker, he thought, a dangerous man politically, able to be on every side of every issue, "for high taxes, low taxes, God, the devil, virtue, villainy, whisky, prohibition, and gets away with it!" (May, 1924). Though he never cared much for Capper, the senator usually had good words for Howe, remembering how the editor had been kind to him in his early reportorial days on the *Topeka Daily Capital,* and praising Howe in a special edition of *The Globe* for always saying that work is essential to happiness and prosperity.

Howe went to the little town of Girard to meet the famous E. Haldeman-Julius, publisher of the Little Blue Books, an editor and social thinker who was very different in convictions and positions from Arthur Capper—or even Ed Howe. Mrs. Anna Haldeman-Julius later wrote about meeting Howe and his niece, and she offered a description of what he was like in *The Monthly* days:

"Mr. Howe was delightful. . . . He has the small town man's insatiable, neighborly curiosity, added to the newspaperman's training in thorough, accurate observation. And for all that he had traveled and read widely, it was obvious that Ed Howe, as he is familiarly known in Kansas, was in charming essentials a small town man. He likes to talk and is fluent with anecdotes, which often carry a little sting, not too sharp and yet unmistakable."[62]

He talked with his hosts about his father and the preaching days in Missouri. He gave the impression that everything he saw was potential copy for his publication. The hostess credited Adelaide Howe with much of the success and peace of mind that Howe seemed to have.

Ed Howe continued the association with William Allen White that had begun back in the 1880s when the Kansas University college boy had called on him in Atchison. In 1924 White made a third party gubernatorial effort in opposition to the Ku Klux Klan, and he visited Howe in Atchison October 7. White had entered the race "because the two other candidates are sinful," and one day he telephoned ahead of time to the Atchison editor and told him to get a room ready. Howe recalled that White was "a delight from the time he came lubbering up our front steps until he went lubbering down them." The Emporian told Howe not to bother to come hear him talk, and Howe agreed, sending Adelaide instead. Throughout the visit White was busy at the telephone, receiving words of encouragement, talking with friends:

"William Allen White is a good talker: in his conversation he says nothing of the subjects he writes about; around a dinner table or an evening fire he is natural, human, witty and wise. Perhaps another Boswell in time will accurately present the man from Emporia."

White talked about his son Bill, whom he said would care for him in his old age, "but will do it by building a little house in the yard, and attaching him to a rope, that he may not wander away, and do foolish things." Adelaide served wild ducks for dinner, and White ate two of them ("He is as fat as a seal," said Howe). He also drank coffee, which Mrs. White had on his proscribed list. Adelaide had provided guest towels, and White left them alone, using only a wash cloth. "His wife being away, I don't believe he washed his neck and ears, and won't, until she joins him again. And we had provided a $1.25 bottle of bath salts for him!"

As for White's candidacy, Ed Howe thought that White's quarrel was not with the Klan but with the railroads. "I am glad Mr. White is running for governor. He loves the fuss he has kicked up, and is doing no harm" (October, 1924).

Ed Howe and William Allen White enjoyed each other but really had little in common. White had acquired his national reputation in part from dabbling in politics, from associations with such people as Theodore Roosevelt. He was becoming more liberal all the time, probably offending much of Kansas Republicanism (a common comment in Kansas was that the *Emporia Gazette* was Democratic three years out of four). He was an idealist and a visionary about some things, a literary critic said in comparing him with Ed Howe:

"White holds that altruism is gradually replacing self-interest in social practice; that self-interest leads to demands for special privilege and vicious corporate practices; that these latter are good for neither winners nor losers; that cranks and reformers teach social wisdom; that many of the incapable and irresponsible are more sinned against than sinning. On two points only do the eminent Kansans concur: that the man of talents and industry can make a decent living, and that the voice of the people is anything but the voice of God."[63]

The Emporian had written fondly of Ed Howe in castigating him for bowing to wealth and influence. In 1925 he wrote further: "A gentle, kindly, grouchy old gentleman is Ed Howe, who refuses to love his neighbor as himself because he knows the truth about himself and suspects the same about his neighbor. He had done more good, under protest that he was doing evil and deserved no credit, than any man in the country."[64]

In Florida Ed Howe had come to know William Jennings Bryan and to regret, perhaps, some of the harsh things he had been writing since 1896. One day in 1925 he met the man who would soon be doing battle with Bryan in Dayton, the famous Clarence Darrow, whom Howe had long read about and did not admire much (though he liked the way Darrow said things). It was a strange visit. They did not talk of the Loeb-Leopold case, which had been so much in the news, or of the evolution furor, but of simpler things. Howe told Darrow that the Boy Scouts were his favorite abomination; Darrow nominated the YWCA, and said he also had lost confidence in the suffrage amendment. Howe regarded Darrow as a very tired man, one who would not even rise to the bait when he told him that he was a socialist and that socialism was foolishness. Darrow also told Howe that he had been requested to give a speech "skinning" Bryan; Howe concluded that perhaps a good skinning was what *many* people needed.

The editor was losing his confidence—if he ever had any—that newspapers really cared much about freedom of the press, the freedom he so asserted each month in his own publication. A new magazine of the decade impressed him, however; it was called *Time,* it had clever editors, and he thought that it, and another interesting new monthly called *The Reader's Digest,* would succeed. His own *Monthly* was now costing, since 1923, twenty-five cents a year, or a dollar for five years. Subscribers were still writing him friendly words, some of which he did not care to receive, like praise from a subscriber in West Virginia who thought him one of the great men of the time, but who also thought Eugene Debs a great man. A gentleman in Mountain View, New Jersey, who published a paper called *The Open Road,* had devoted eleven critical columns to Howe: Howe had never given his sympathy to the Russian people, he was not friendly to Communism, he thought success was easier than failure, and he admired Mussolini. "Bruce Calvert and I can never agree," said Howe. "He is a Communist, Idealist, Religionist, and finds his greatest comfort in a sunset, a rose, a walk through the woods. . . . He is foolish to read my publication, and I shall return his money" (October, 1926).

He had been making attacks on higher education for most of his writing days. And in the spring of 1927 he received two honorary degrees. One was from Washburn College in Topeka, and Howe commented: "I have passed all the grades in the World's School, and am now unworthily wearing cap and gown; I regret I did not make better use of my time, but might have done this had my elders used better methods of teaching" (May, 1927). The other degree was from Rollins College in Winter Park, Florida. The citation read: "Edgar Watson Howe, editor, author, sage: For your drab Kansas classic *The Story of a Country Town;* for your incomparable books of travel; for your myriad whimsy paragraphs of common sense, but above all for your mastery of the greatest of all literary arts, the art of being interesting."[65]

He was mainly taking life as it came, and enjoying things he once would have growled about. Baseball, for instance: he offered his help to the Philadelphia Athletics to try to stop the customary climb of the New York Yankees to the top. He still had the capacity to enjoy Kansas, however, especially as fall neared and there was hope for relief from the blistering days:

> I write this late in August, the fat season in my section;
> Melons, grapes, peaches, sweet corn, pears, young chickens and many other tempting things, are at their best;
> I am so tempted to eat too much that I long for the lean season.
> I would do better in a land where nature is stingy;
> I almost long for some of the starvation we hear of in China and Russia;
> America is too generous;
> I have always lived where there is too much to eat too easily procured; I would have been a healthier man had I been the slave of a stingy master. [September, 1929]

The Last Ten Years

He had friends all over the United States, many of them formed in the Florida winters, and on April 29, 1927, some of these friends gave Ed Howe a dinner in New York. For him it was a lavish affair. He felt as though he were going to an execution when he entered the automobile of "two distinguished men at the Waldorf." And the hotel flunky at the door was "appalling in his magnificence."

> I was jammed into the crowd, and ascended to the second floor, where we emerged into a great lobby. Hundreds of people there; men and women gabbling as at an afternoon tea. I had a moment of consciousness here, and recalled a line written by Oliver Wendell Holmes describing such an affair: "Gobble, gabble, get." I dimly recall meeting Irvin Cobb, who was toastmaster, and that he was better looking than I expected to find him: reports as to Mr. Cobb's beauty, as they reached me far in the West, had not been favorable. I also recall that as he sat beside me, he had "the figits," a malady I am familiar with from personal suffering. His feet beat a tattoo under the table, and it seemed to me I was never that bad. I recall Bob Davis, whose speech consisted of taking money out of his pocket, and subscribing to the paper I edit; I recall Rupert Hughes, somehow, and Senator Arthur Capper, of Kansas, but when Irvin Cobb arose, and I knew he was about to introduce me, I think I lost consciousness, for I have no idea what I said. Fannie Hurst was a guest at the dinner, but I did not know it until she confessed it in a letter.[66]

Bruce Barton, then a well-known name for his tract called *The Man Nobody Knows* (which Ed Howe described as a religious book), told Howe that there were as many notable persons at the dinner as he had seen at any such occasion in the city. The New York press estimated the attendance at two hundred. The country editor was overwhelmed. Cyrus H. K. Curtis made the chief address, and a Gruen fiftieth anniversary watch was given Howe, with this inscription: "Presented to E. W. Howe by admiring friends to commemorate his fifty years of inspiring service in American journalism. April 29, 1927."[67]

Howe had hoped to meet Hendrik Van Loon, whose work he had admired for its intelligence and simplicity, and he "believed" that in the confusion and crush they were introduced. "No doubt I was introduced to dozens of famous people I have long wished to meet, but I am conscious at this moment that I have never seen any of them."[68] There was soon another party. On his return from New York the staff of *The Globe* gave the old man a picnic at Jackson Park, near the Missouri River. It was a family-staff party only. And that fall, the Commercial Club of Acthison, assisted by other civic organizations, gave Howe another dinner in honor of his fiftieth anniversary. Three hundred persons attended, and many could not be admitted. William Allen White, who gave a talk at the dinner, said it seemed to him the best compliment ever paid a country editor. Ed Howe believed that no other citizen of Atchison had even been honored in such style. And for the *Emporia Gazette* White wrote an editorial in which he sprinkled praise and presented *his* views of Ed Howe's religious views:

> The *Kansas City Journal* the other day reported the fact that at the dinner given for Ed Howe by the Atchison Chamber of Commerce, at Atchison, every minister in town attended. Ed Howe has been denounced all over the place as an old atheist, as a cantankerous infidel and as a no-God editor. As a matter of fact, Ed Howe is a pretty pious man. He does not care for organized orthodox religion. Lots of good men feel that way. But he is too smart a man not to know that the world just didn't happen; that the rules of good conduct and decent behavior and physical well being were not the result of some purpose and plan. The fact that Ed Howe knows the rules of life makes him know that the rules of life were worked out by some intelligence higher and larger than ours, so infinite that it cannot be personified in human terms. The Atchison preachers know this instinctively. They stand by Ed Howe because he is a force for decency in the community, a force of good living and neighborly conduct and friendly consideration and community teamwork. Conduct is 90 per cent of religion. Ed Howe's philosophy though it denies much orthodox dogma, creates the same kind of men and women that the best religionists would create if they could, and sometimes do. [October, 1927]

Howe reprinted the editorial, though he denied some of White's assertions, such as that business about the higher intelligence, for example. One thing is sure: he gobbled up all the attention he had received in just one year. Notices of the dinners would be placed in his grave, he said, as evidence "that I lived among my fellow men with reasonable uprightness. I have blundered, and have been humiliated for many minor discrepancies, but in the higher walks of misconduct, I am proud and grateful that such witnesses testify my average has been reasonably good."[69]

On December 8, 1927, *The Atchison Globe* published its fiftieth anniversary edition, one of those interesting yet overdone matters in which business organizations love to indulge. A lead story congratulated itself and accepted the praise of being the "foremost 'country daily' in the United States." It gave credit for the paper's long success to the people of Atchison and northeast Kansas. It promised to do as well in the future as it had done in the past. It promised to promote progress, preach sobriety and industry, be the mouthpiece of all points of view, and fight for integrity at all times. And it carried a long and generally moving editorial about its founder:

> Fifty Candles Glow
>
> Fifty candles serenely shed light in the southwest room of the Editorial Department of *The Atchison Daily Globe* today.
>
> In the southwest room, because there Mr. Edgar Watson Howe, founder of *The Globe,* conducted this newspaper before his retirement.
>
> Those fifty candles glow in token of *The Globe's* Fiftieth anniversary and Mr. Howe's advent into the newspaper field of this city.
>
> Each candle bespeaks a tribute to the founder, E. W. Howe, who in that room daily toiled at a wheezy old typewriter, from whence came pert and scintillating paragraphs, wholesome and helpful editorials, and community comment, all of which interested a whole world as well as the small province which the editor claimed as his "field of endeavor."
>
> *The Atchison Daily Globe* during Mr. Howe's years at the helm was, of course, as now, a "country newspaper."
>
> But because of the genius and originality of E. W. Howe, *The Globe* attained to a prestige envied by scores of big, powerful, metropolitan newspapers.
>
> During the early years of *The Globe* it was small—in fact, tiny.
>
> But due to the unique and sound philosophy of its first editor, *The Globe,* while little, was as bright as any American publication; and its rays penetrated to the uttermost parts of the earth.
>
> One could go to Egypt, and there find a "Globe Sight."
>
> One could loll around in a settlement of torrid Africa, and "stumble" onto a weird foreign journal and in it find a quotation from *The Globe.*
>
> In far away Russia, the land of snow and ice, one could pick up a funny looking newspaper, and there read a bit of humor, or a paragraph of philosophy, or a clever comment, translated to the Russian tongue from "Ed. Howe's Little Old Atchison Globe."
>
> In every land, in every clime, on this, the Lord's foot-stool, one could read "the unique slant" of E. W. Howe, the man who created *The Atchison Daily Globe* a half century ago today,

and made it the most widely quoted country newspaper in the world.

E. W. Howe having founded and established *The Globe,* and having trained the "old heads" who today publish and edit *The Globe,* it is fitting and right that this Anniversary Edition be dedicated to him, and that much of the subject matter relate to his history, his work, his personality, his philosophy, his style and diction, his mental keenness and uniqueness of character.

Fifty years!

That's a long time. [Dec. 8, 1927]

Much earlier in the century *The Globe,* when Ed Howe was still the editor, had gone through such an occasion, but it was pleasant to be doing it again. Into the newspaper office came the expected words of praise. Henry Haskell, editorial writer for the *Kansas City Star,* commented on how the reputation of Edgar Watson Howe had spread far beyond Atchison (as a man of literary interests Haskell wrote more about *The Story of a Country Town* than about *The Globe).* Victor Murdock of the *Wichita Eagle,* one of Howe's Kansas contemporaries, praised him. Ewing Herbert of the *Hiawatha World,* who had once tried to compete with Ed Howe in Atchison, a "big league" editor, as *The Globe* described him in its headline, George Horace Lorimer of the *Saturday Evening Post,* and J. E. House of the *Philadelphia Public Ledger* were quoted.

So these were years of pride for Ed Howe—and years of disappointment, too, and perhaps of tragedy. The editor had mellowed, but the family wounds of early in the century had never entirely healed. Adelaide had become his chief solace in life, though he also was close to his son Gene. With his brother Bruce he lived a simple life, working with him nearly every afternoon in the field or garden at Potato Hill. Ed Howe knew he was not a good man, but he thought his brother was:

"He is always patient, whereas I am sometimes irritable when it does me no good; I often declare my rights when I might better have been quiet. . . . But my brother is so even-tempered, so fair, that he has long been a wonder to me, and as he lives next door, I often go over to marvel at so unusual a man" (May, 1929).

For his son Jim he retained pride. Jim had been with the Associated Press for many years—at sea, and covering battlefronts in Germany, Russia, and Poland. He had become an almost legendary figure in his press association, and in 1929 *The Monthly* carried a picture of the Jim Howe residence in Peking, with the Howes on their balcony, and their eight servants.

He had pride in his daughter, Mateel, too, who had been married in 1910 to Dwight T. Farnham and had become well known for her writing, her work appearing largely in women's magazines. She was living in Connecticut, and was pretty much out of touch with the life of her father. It was commonly believed that he had always tried to dominate her; there reportedly had been a quarrel over wedding invitations at the time Mateel was planning her marriage, for Ed Howe wanted to style them in his way and Mateel wanted to be more orthodox. She reportedly came to the wedding still crying—but that obviously could have been due to a variety of reasons.

In 1927 Mateel Howe Farnham received the $10,000 *Pictorial Review* prize for a book, *Rebellion,* which first was serialized in the magazine and then published by Dodd, Mead. It was her first novel, and the father was proud. In *The Monthly* he wrote about visiting her in New York, and said she had invited him to write an introduction to the book:

> The title of her novel is *Rebellion,* and I shudder when I realize what it means. All women go on the war-path around fourteen, and fight the men until they die. I long for an armistice, but do not expect one.
>
> I have not read *Rebellion,* I do not know what it is about, but am willing to wager it does not contain the admiration for at least one man she displayed at twelve. No doubt its comments on my sex will be just and accurate. . . .
>
> If *Rebellion* criticizes me I shall not object.
>
> I long for the success of *Rebellion,* as I longed for her success when she read her first piece at school. I am wondering if there is anything I can do to help her with the great audience to which her work is now submitted. . . . I hope the verdict on her latest writing may be as favorable as was my verdict on her first. It was an essay delivered as a little schoolgirl, and her subject was "My Father."[70]

Mateel's dedication to the novel read: "To my mother, Clara Frank Howe, whom I have never known to do a selfish or an unkind thing, this, my first book, is gratefully and affectionately dedicated."

It is easy to describe the plot of *Rebellion:* a daughter in conflict with her father. Mateel's heroine is named Jacqueline

Burrell, the daughter of John Taliaferro and Emily Burrell, who live in the town of New Concord, Kansas. The town has a newspaper called *The Daily Globe,* edited by a man named Ed Howard. The girl's father is autocratic and domineering; he especially objects to his daughter going to the stable to associate with the old Negro, Simon, whom she loves and with whom she frequently talks. Jacqueline is an extremely outspoken young woman, and she has opinions that conflict with those of her old-fashioned father. She advocates woman suffrage, for example, and woman agitators disgust John Burrell:

> "They're the curse of this generation," cried Mr. Burrell one morning at breakfast. "Brazen, short haired, harsh voiced creatures who think it's smart to kick up a perpetual rumpus because the Creator did not see fit to make them men. For myself I think it is an insult to decent womanhood to pay any attention to those snarling, unsexed creatures, but they seem to have intimidated every body of nincompoops in this country that dares call itself a legislature. Rome was dominated by just such another lot of harridans two thousand years ago and any student of history will back me up in my assertion that the fall of Rome can be directly traced to giving woman the vote. When I was a young man women respected themselves and were in consequence respected, revered, looked up to, as my mother was."[71]

The heroine is a late child, and her mother, Emily, dies when the girl is only sixteen. To protest her father's attitudes she refuses to go to the funeral, and there follows a series of arguments, father and daughter always making up, at least briefly. Something that particularly annoys Jacqueline is the terms of her mother's will, which she believes had been enforced upon the timid woman by her domineering husband: the money is to be maintained in trust for the daughter until she is thirty unless she makes a marriage that will satisfy her father. Jacqueline soon goes away to Bryn Mawr; but while she is at home she tries to solve a mystery about her grandfather and one Martin, a puzzle that has arisen from an old letter she has found in the attic. While at home she has a date with a young man, and her father goes into a tirade on seeing her kiss the boy. He threatens to send Jacqueline to a convent, but she refuses, says her mother would not have approved of it, and fires back at her father her opinion that men who feel as he does about women are "beasts—pigs." Men want to go out and have a good time with other women but leave the ones they plan to marry at home piously waiting until they are ready to settle down. "Talk about revolting things! I never heard of anything so revolting in my life! If all men feel that way, I would not marry one of them for anything on earth."[72]

Away at school, living in another part of the country, Jacqueline Burrell, a little girl from the country, finds there are things to learn besides lessons. She learns that being from a prominent family in eastern Kansas is of no significance in a selective eastern school, "where the very word Kansas, for some unaccountable reason, seemed to be cause for laughter." Despite the clashes with her father, clashes which occur frequently, she always has a deep affection for him, and he for her, but he is jealous, and he appears to want her to be an old maid. He visits her in the East, and usually sees her wearing hats; he is completely unprepared when she comes home for Christmas and reveals that she has bobbed her hair.

Jacqueline is never again happy at home: a domineering Negro servant named Sheeby, whom her father has hired, virtually takes over the household. The girl and her father achieve a partial rapprochement, but the daughter wants to leave New Concord, to get a job and not be a mere Junior Leaguer. But she promises to stay at home for two years. One day on an afternoon walk she meets a young man named Kent Allen, who had been a Signal Corps officer in the World War, and she goes to meet him on weekends in a house by the river, where they paint and drink tea and smoke cigarettes: "I haven't had one of these since I don't know when," said Jacqueline. "If my father knew I had ever soiled my lips with tobacco, he would explode into a thousand pieces."[73] Though ostensibly a carpenter Kent is also an architect, who had gone to Columbia University and hopes to study at the Beaux Arts in Paris. The servant Sheeby learns about the affair, and tells Mr. Burrell, who goes into a rage. He had permitted his daughter to have callers, though he had tried to discourage them by opening wide the library door and sitting where he could watch what was going on, and glaring at the young men. And at ten he would walk into the hall, wind the tall clock as noisily as possible, pace back and forth, and remind the caller in that way that it was time to go home.

Jacqueline, not surprisingly, realizes that what she feels for

Kent is love. She and Kent confront her father, but he is very rude, and Kent's mother, for that matter, is afraid that a marriage would delay her ambitions for her son. Other complications enter. Jacqueline nags her father: will she inherit her rightful money? And the old man Simon, long ill, tells John Burrell something which gives him a great shock, a story about the grandmother having married one Martin Richards before she married the grandfather—but Simon dies without completing the story. Jacqueline hears the story from Simon, and keeps looking for evidence, which (shades of *The Purloined Letter*) she finally finds in the frame of a picture. She confronts her father with the shocking story, demands her money, her bluff wins, she is miserable, she breaks with her father, she gets the money, and she marries Kent. Burrell refuses to attend the wedding, and the family break seems complete. But as the story ends the servant Sheeby—of all people—is getting the father to relent, and he is making plans to fix up the house for his daughter's return from Paris.

Thus ends the novel, which is scarcely a work of art. Yet with all its soapiness it has valid touches, a good feeling for the language, and perceptions about the Ed Howe-Mateel relationship that are almost painful in their penetration. Ed Howe's prejudices are found throughout the book, and it is obvious that the work is at least partly autobiographical: New Concord easily could be Atchison; there is a character named "Mize," a familiar Atchison name; there is talk of driving "up to St. Joe." The romantic touches are as flagrant as the tolling bells and storms in Ed Howe's own novels:

"He had named her Jacqueline not only because there had been for many generations in Virginia a Jacqueline Burrell, 'the toast of the county,' but because the very liquid sound of it connoted moonlight and the scent of jasmine, candlelight on polished mahogany, the songs of mocking-birds . . . and lovely timid ladies who walked in old-fashioned mignonette-scented gardens, with blush roses in their hair, and shy sweet lips and shyer glances."[74]

Ed Howe had written the introduction for his daughter's prize novel, but it did not appear in the published version. Both Howe and Mateel denied that the fictional John Burrell could be identified with Howe, and Howe wrote a magazine article telling about his affectionate relationship with his daughter. Mateel and her husband attended the New York dinner for Howe, and she wrote a letter to the *Kansas City Star* denying that the father was "even an approximate likeness" of her own father. Howe had often commented in his writings that Mateel as a girl had been something like queen of the house, and he of course would deny that any father in Mateel's life had made her unhappy or had denied her an inheritance—that being quite unlikely, of course, in the Howe family.

Mateel wrote that her father was, of course, "forceful, vivid and picturesque. . . . If I tried to picture him and could produce nothing better than a Mr. John Taliaferro Burrell, I never would try to write again" (August, 1928). It is unreasonable to charge that the parallels run deep between life and novel: Ed Howe, unlike John Burrell, could not care less about his ancestry; he was apparently lavish with his money, taking his daughter on expensive trips; he wrote lovingly of her in many telling editorial comments. He denied, then, that *Rebellion* angered him, but the question arose ten years later when his will was read, and there *were* those touches that revealed at least minor similarities between Howe and Burrell.

Mateel Howe Farnham, meanwhile, continued her writing career—a group of romantic and undistinguished novels: *Marsh Fire* (1928), *Wild Beauty* (1930), *Battle Royal* (1931), *Lost Laughter* (1933), *Great Riches* (1934), *Ex-Love* (1937), and *The Tollivers* (1945).

Her father was getting another of *his* books into print. This would be his testament, the story that he, at least, wanted to give the world, his best writing since *The Story of a Country Town.*

He had long thought about writing an autobiography, which "is what a man dares tell about his life. He doesn't tell it all, or half. But his readers can imagine the rest, from the things they themselves can't tell."[75] That is an honest and revealing statement: what one cannot learn about Ed Howe remains the intriguing part of the story. He wanted to write his autobiography; he also had been encouraged by William Allen White to write what might be the true story of his life and of his times as well.

Howe announced in early 1928 that the autobiography had been accepted for both serial and book publication, that he was at work on the revision, and that it would soon be out of his hands. The work first appeared in the *Saturday Evening Post,* which had carried so many of Howe's stories and published prejudices. For six weeks he was bared before the world, and he received hundreds of letters of praise, only one unfriendly letter coming to the editor of the *Post,* only three to him personally. In 1929 Dodd, Mead & Company, which had published Mateel's *Rebellion,* also published the autobiography, which Ed Howe called *Plain People*—a theme he had been pounding into his readers since the 1870s.

Plain People is a moving, prejudiced, funny, and infuriatingly un-thorough book. Ed Howe told only what he wanted to tell. He left out names, he had almost no record of dates (he kept no diaries, he kept few documents, he kept only the important letters, like those from Howells and Mark Twain). The book will observe that such and such happened "thirty or forty years ago, as I recall," or it will say that "it seems to me" that such and such was the case. Howe tells of his boyhood in Indiana and Missouri, of the country towns, of the preacher-printer-father, of the love affairs, the tramp printer days throughout the prairie and Rocky Mountain country, the founding of *The Globe,* the lonely years, the one great novel (little is said about the other books), the children, his leaving *The Globe* and establishing *The Monthly,* the national reputation he attained. He put into the book whatever seemed apt to him—Mencken's long introduction to *Ventures in Common Sense;* a concluding section of some of the best from the *Country Town Sayings.* His marriage is discussed, but not in detail, and a reader leaves the book with countless questions unanswered, even though he has been greatly entertained along the way.

For it is a charming story of provincial life in America from the 1850s to the late 1920s that Ed Howe tells. It has the feel of the small town and the countryside that distinguishes almost everything he wrote. It has his philosophy of success, his justification of the decision to stay in the country town, even though an offer apparently never came from a big paper. It has his considered contempt for politics, for "Long ago I was impressed with the declaration of a statesman that one-half our public expenditures might be saved and the service improved."[76] Religion and sentiment get brand new lumps. And the good old days are not the good old days in his view; he prefers the present.

For democracy he had more praise than he had offered in his editorials and "Globe Sights":

> I rarely read without finding a fresh and more vigorous attack on Democracy: the gloomy Dean Inge said lately it is becoming plain that democracy has done its work—that it is a most wasteful and unstable form of government, and a luxury we cannot afford. Are we so worthless we cannot govern ourselves? I believe so much in human rights that I cannot imagine myself submitting willingly to king or dictator; I so much admire the people I cannot quite admit they must have a master. Slavery has been found objectionable; slaves rebel so often that an intelligent system of liberty has been found to work better. There are many evidences that the people are not doing well with democracy: the great excesses in human history have been due to too much of it. The old Romans wrecked a democratic government: a dictator rescued them. The Russians are murdering themselves and democracy; the reign of terror in France ended only because of the iron hand of a dictator. There is reason back of this general fear of democracy. If I long for anything with patriotic fervor it is that the people of the United States may learn to govern themselves so well they will never be disgraced by a dictator. And if we do this, we must behave better. We are grossly offending nature. The only remedy is for the people themselves to better appreciate the blessings of democracy, which always fails in the hands of shiftless, idle, unfair people.[77]

Among the more interesting of his published stories in the book were those about his youthful romances; already, before the book appeared, they had occasioned comment from the *Post* serialization. Letters had expressed amusement and wonder at his statement that he was engaged to be married when only fifteen. One of those interested in this story was Bruce, who calculated that his brother would have been not fifteen but only fourteen. Now that was too much for many people to accept, but Ed Howe stuck to his story:

> It is true I was engaged to be married while living there, to a girl at least twenty years old; judging as best I can from my present knowledge of the ages of men and women (and I am rather accurate) she was older than twenty. And I recall distinctly of the absurd affair that she was a nice girl;
>
> What is more, I "set up" with her night after night, with the consent of her sister, a married woman. It is also true that another girl named "Maidie" often "set up" with us. I think her idea was to see what such an affair was like, having no lover of her own. I frequently went to sleep when courting and, if the weather was warm, the girls fanned me, that I might sleep

peacefully, and awaken refreshed to new appreciation of their sex. [September, 1928]

Reviewers were kind to *Plain People,* and the book was added to the list of those which Howe regularly advertised for sale in *E. W. Howe's Monthly.* The *New Republic,* which he had often called a foolishly socialistic publication, wrote: "We get a God's plenty of the pragmatic middle-western philosopher who sees what a man can see, earns his daily bread, and is nobody's fool—many simple, acute observations on life. . . ." The *Chicago Daily News* said: "a remarkable document for its sustained interest, its honesty, its philosophy, its authentic picture of American life of its period, and above all remarkable for the directness, dignity and force of its style." The *Saturday Review of Literature* said: "Such a book as Ben Franklin might have written; E. W. Howe is Franklin's spiritual legatee." Heywood Broun wrote in the *New York Telegram:* ". . . prose of a sort to make every other journalist bite his nails in envy. . . ." Harry Hansen said in the New York *World:* "He has been hailed by H. L. Mencken, praised by George Jean Nathan, applauded by Ray Long, introduced by Irvin Cobb, and handed a watch by Cyrus H. K. Curtis, but his sayings have not been cackled over as much as they deserve."[78]

Carl Van Doren reviewed the book in the *Nation,* seeing Howe as a sensitive man, one moved by music, wanting to be buried with newspaper notices in his grave: "Before we know it we shall be making out of Mr. Howe a wildly romantic figure, with regrets and deep hurts and dark repressions."[79]

Ed Howe was going into advanced old age, and he knew it. More and more he was conscious of heredity (he had blamed the Howes and the Irwins for his being an ordinary man). He heard himself described as an iconoclast, but he did not like the word; he was "only an old man begging people not to go crazy" (January, 1932). His friends kept expecting him to come to terms with religion, but he never did:

"I have long believed that when a man rejects any religious system, he rejects all of them. The question at issue is spirituality and materialism; God and nature. If there is any good for honest unbelievers to accomplish, they must agree on the reason of their opposition, which is that religion is not only baseless, but harmful" (June, 1930).

Yet he was more tolerant as he grew older, he wrote in one

of the most low-keyed editorials on religion he ever published: "As I grow older I become more tolerant; I do not like irreverence, or untruthful and vicious attacks on anything. Occasionally I criticise the church, but mean no offense to any worthy man. Millions of such preach or sit patiently in pews. With all our religious hypocrisy we continue to starve preachers, who say occasionally the people fight religion. It isn't true. The attitude of men toward the subject is naturally friendly; men not only think favorably about religion, but millions of them think it a sin not to become hypocrites, and pretend to believe when they do not" (December, 1932).

He continued to write about women, doing an article called "These Women" for the *Forum* in 1930, and about the question of sex, in general. He was sure he would have known the meaning and importance of decency earlier, "and with less mud on my conscience, had my father frankly taught me." He assumed that the old Methodist preacher father thought his son was innocent and had not heard of wicked things. "Heard of them! I was born with them" (July, 1932). He was astonished at the way birth control was being discussed so glibly, a subject that at one time was equated with murder. Newspapers of the early 1930s puzzled him: why was Clara Bow in the papers oftener than Andrew Mellon? Why was so much attention given to news from Hollywood, and to sports and politics? As he grew older there was no doubt in his mind about the people he liked best:

"In my seventy-sixth year I know a good many old people, but rarely like one. Since experience is the greatest teacher, the old may be able to preach sounder sermons than the young, but it is a failing in all of us that our preaching is better than our practice. . . . Nor do I like young people any better; they annoy me with blemishes as numerous as I find in the old. Foreigners unite in astonishment at the behavior of our young people, and in this we pretty generally join them at all ages above forty. . . . I believe the age at which men and women are most agreeable to me now is between forty-five and sixty, with occasional exceptions above and below both lines" (May, 1929).

He was a prejudiced old man, and he knew it. *The Monthly* in the later 1920s was little more than a collection of his complaints, and it never changed. Reform was nonsense. Sex was overdone in the movies. American schools were full of poor teachers. Public libraries were futile. Why cannot man avoid war? He wrote editorials about success. About women. How no one reads Shakespeare any longer, if anyone ever did read him. Or Shelley. What a bad force William Randolph Hearst continued to be in public life. What a fine magazine the *Atlantic Monthly!* Jazz—did people really *like* such a thing? What a great man Thomas Edison was, and what a fraud John Dewey. And musical tastes: Liszt's "Second Hungarian Rhapsody" should be kept off concerts.

The central fact for Ed Howe in considering public affairs became the great depression. It was the central fact for anyone in the 1930s. It all troubled him, because it came into conflict with his central belief that man could pull himself up by his own bootstraps and succeed—if he only wanted to. Emersonian self-reliance was his creed, yet here were all these people out of work, and starving, even in Atchison. An editorial early in March, 1930, seemed to show he was unaware that the euphoria of the 1920s was giving way to despair, though it did show that he knew something had happened that he neither liked nor understood:

> The dominating note concerning the United States, both at home and abroad, is our enormous prosperity.
>
> Still, I know thousands of poor.
>
> Are we not at present wasting public money extravagantly and foolishly to relieve farmers, comprising possibly one-half the population?
>
> There is widespread rioting among workingmen because of lack of employment;
>
> And in the cities and towns there are millions of very poor who are not organized, and therefore never get their grievances on the wires, in the newspapers, or in the halls of Congress or legislatures.
>
> In my town in the west, I know hundreds who are regularly helped by the county commissioners or city councilmen; and there can be no doubt as to their names or numbers since both are printed regularly in the local papers. . . .
>
> Yet the big noise that goes up from the United States is "Prosperity," with more than half the people demanding and receiving charity. . . .
>
> I am not one of those who say the rich are robbing the poor; what I say is all of us, poor and rich alike, are indulging in an extravagant drunk, and calling our spree prosperity.

There followed four years of *Monthly* observations on the

economic situation in America. When the American Legion asked for an increase of 35 million dollars in pension money, and the Senate granted double that amount in a near-unanimous vote, Ed Howe thought it all insanity, and he asked why President Hoover did not realize what an opportunity lay before him to take his case to the nation, by radio, and tell the American people how to be sane—even if it meant sacrificing a second term in office.

There had always been poor people, but the old man seemed to be seeing more of them. He saw old people in his neighborhood on the edge of want, but making out with economy and hard work. Under such circumstances was government extravagance not utterly inexcusable? Economy was the answer; why didn't the President, in talks before the Legion and the American Federation of Labor, urge the curbing of these extravagant demands? He could not believe that the reasonable men in those organizations would object to economy during hard times. Yet talk of "confidence" also was stupid:

"A Prominent Man declares in a newspaper interview that the present business depression is due to a State of Mind; that if we all thought there was no panic, there would be good times again.

"There ought to be a law against that sort of nonsense being printed. The present is especially a time when the fools should be hammered with common sense clubs" (October, 1930).

He blamed the Republican party, and especially Senators Norris, Borah, Capper, and LaFollette, and announced that he would quit the party until it acted more intelligently than the Bryan Democrats had acted in the days of free silver. There *were* hard times, and Ed Howe was admitting it with considerably more readiness than back in the 1880s and 1890s when such talk seemed Populist troublemaking. He read in the newspapers that when the government asked for scrubwomen to work in public buildings five thousand women appeared and spent a whole night waiting for the employment office to open. Did those congressmen who were spending money for river improvements and Boulder Dam and excursions to Europe and pensions for strong young men read that story in the papers?

He believed himself to be in a lonely position. He kept reading about the new economic philosophy of America: that the more people waste, the more prosperous they would become. The reverse is the truth, he said. *The Monthly* declared against the dole, which had failed in England. Old age pensions had failed in New Zealand. Farm relief had failed in the United States, but still people said they favored it. What was wrong with a country where sixteen hundred farmers could march and demand relief at the grocery stores, where hundreds of members of the American Legion could march on the nation's capital demanding relief, where congressmen could meet such men on the steps of the capitol and deliver speeches endorsing their proposals? The most disastrous period in American history would prove to be the spring of 1931, when the United States abandoned civilized ideas and took the ideas of the fanatic Karl Marx for its own. Communism was joining hands with fiscal irresponsibility. America was as silly as in Bryan's time, and we had no Mark Hanna to fight the spendthrift politicians. Radicalism was triumphing; there could be no good in a reign of terror—we would see Borah turn on Brookhart and Capper and LaFollette and send them to the guillotine or gallows or firing squad.

In editorial after editorial Ed Howe was showing how he was disturbed by what was happening in America: the ascendancy of the radicals and the decline of the conservatives, the talk and actual possibility of revolution, the moving away from common sense, the spending of funds for unnecessary projects. Our great American tragedy was "our present poverty in the midst of plenty," our evidence that we had become a "dissipated, extravagant, stupid" people. The gold standard had been departed from not only in government but in morals, in business, in writing, in preaching, in family life. The Red philosophy was winning out.

Some of his compassion began to go to Herbert Hoover: a vastly unpopular man in office at the wrong time, a man who had to be a candidate for re-election at a time when no one should be thinking about politics. Hoover was a poor politician, too clean for politics. Neither candidate satisfied Ed Howe in 1932; he announced that he would vote for the radical whose running mate was a Negro (though of course he did not). "If the Radical should be elected, and an avenging God strike him dead for his sins, a Negro in the White House would be no more humiliation than the American people deserve for their amazing cowardice and carelessness in politics" (August, 1932). The Democratic ticket was a joke: Franklin D. Roosevelt did not improve upon acquaintance, and John Nance Garner was funny-looking. Howe's serious —and obvious—declaration came in October: He would vote again for Hoover.

Events of the summer of 1932, and trends in American life, had roused him. He had always liked Will Rogers but thought Rogers' praising the bonus marchers as being as orderly and as fair as bankers was pretty bad. A drive to obtain funds for the Boy Scouts the preceding winter had caused him to call on "the name of the Great Jehovah" (an unusual request) in protest: "We are unusually poor this winter, and confronted with the necessary work of feeding hungry men, women and children. Why should we be asked in addition to promote hikes, weinie roasts, troublesome parades in the streets, and encourage boys to neglect their natural duties at home?" (December, 1931).

Maybe Paul Whiteman, the jazz king who made jazz popular, was the man responsible for all this trouble. This was jazz:

"It is Night Club silliness; debauchery, drinking bootleg whisky at high prices; making rounders out of reasonably respectable men and women. In 1929 I heard Whiteman's orchestra of thirty-three players. It wasn't very good; I refused several invitations to hear it again. . . . Paul Whiteman innocently had much to do with the present depression, dishonesty, and campaigns for relief. In 1929 he led all others in free newspaper space. His popularity and earnings were so great he had bad imitators: everything else was jazzed" (April, 1932).

Most of Ed Howe's solutions to the economic crisis were not quite so simple or so simple-minded; most of them stemmed, however, from his basic belief that common sense could solve all problems. The editor had only a year as public spokesman in which to contend with Franklin D. Roosevelt. Hoover he had never really liked, his opinions going back to the war relief period. Hoover had played politics as President, and the public had been annoyed by his constantly being before them in the press and the films. The editor did not like prospects from Democrats, either, on the eve of Roosevelt's inauguration:

"Herbert Hoover was a weak man in his best days as president; he is a weak man now that he is preparing to leave the White House.

"In his last public appearance he advised Republicans to stand by the new administration, which will be Democratic. . . .

"And note what the Democrats, recommended so highly by Mr. Hoover, are doing. They have agreed that Mr. Roosevelt, the new president, shall have more power than any other president ever had: power to override congress and the supreme court: power to still further insult the old and sound doctrine of state's rights" (February, 1933).

He feared Roosevelt's politics and he feared his policies. He anticipated governmental extravagance even worse than that under Hoover, and, worst of all, Roosevelt seemed a "reform president." Another prominent Democrat frightened Ed Howe, a noisy man from the South named Huey Long—impudent, always talking, contemptuous of good rules of life, so much all of these things "that I look for him to become the next Democratic president, or explode with a loud report" (March, 1933). The wife of the new President also was too much in evidence, showing up in three newspaper photographs on one day, and winning an entire column from *Time* magazine. ". . . as a citizen who has been jarred enormously already, I modestly suggest that such helpfulness as a wife may exercise on a husband, be exercised by Elinor [sic] in a more dignified and helpful way" (June, 1933). General Hugh Johnson, the NRA administrator, looked like our "first consul," a dictator, with the nerve of Napoleon but probably not the sense. Johnson had far too much power for one man to be able to exercise.

When the prohibition amendment was passed Howe had accepted it, despite his years of fighting the "temperance" folks. Now, in 1933, he seemed ready to do away with the amendment. He crossed the river into Missouri, where saloons had been set up, and he found such places as orderly and clean as a church picnic. "Let me record that never before have I seen men and women I knew to be respectable mingling freely in an open saloon. It is another of the new things now so common in the United States" (August, 1933).

The New Deal seemed fantastic in its extravagance: talk about improving the Missouri River above Kansas City, money to repair battleships, experiments in farming and finance that had been tried before and cast aside as nonsensical, more bridges, money loaned without security or excuse.

"Nothing like it in folly was ever known in the history of men; even Woodrow Wilson and Herbert Hoover were not so reckless in their noble and foolish experiments. Yet the people everywhere are clamoring for new appropriations, new thefts, new extravagances and new experiments. They say: 'Others are getting it; we are entitled to our share' " (July, 1933).

Ed Howe looked on depression times with eyes of sorrow and wonder. History had known human sensuality, cruelty, religious fanaticism, famine, meanness, rioting, destruction, poverty, and plagues. The ancients had made records, but it looked to him as though mankind had been on a binge from 1929 to 1933 that would rival anything in the past: ". . . every citizen put a fool's cap on his head, and widely proclaimed himself an ass."[80]

So, as the New Deal proceeded, Edgar Watson Howe, for a year at least, was the loyal opposition, opposing demands for handouts, opposing any kind of governmental paternalism, observing that the Biblical injunction for the well-to-do to give all they had to the poor was "foolish and unnatural." He told his son Gene that voting for Roosevelt in 1936 would be one of the worst things Gene could do; a Kansas City newspaper quoted him as saying: "If Roosevelt is reelected it won't signify a vindication of his first term policies but rather that Americans are a bunch of imbeciles and supine drones. I think we have all been cowards not to have locked the barn long before now."[81]

Other issues of the time brought expressions as bitter or as controversial. Crime was abroad in the land, it seemed; within a brief period forty-seven innocent persons had been killed by stray bullets in a gang shooting. The remedy? Well, San Francisco citizens had once tried something called the vigilantes. And the Black Shirts had found a solution in Italy. India's Gandhi was a reformer so bad that his disturbances had brought death to hundreds of his followers. "I have never heard of him except as a disturber" (June, 1930). Gandhi was quite unlike an Englishman named Winston Churchill, who had been harmed by fanatics like Gandhi: "If he should appear at a street meeting in London, and talk common sense as freely as Gandhi is permitted to talk nonsense, probably he would be mobbed by his own countrymen who so warmly welcomed the half dressed, half insane fanatic from India" (October, 1931). The Lindbergh kidnaping? A "pitiful" thing. Howe suggested making a careful check of "suspicious characters who have no visible means of support. . . . The cost of crime to the worthy majority is enormous and burdensome"

(May, 1932). He compared a celebrated local girl named Amelia Earhart with the great Lindbergh. She emerged a poor second, because she was a publicity seeker and wasn't even as good-looking as the Lone Eagle. A new religious sect called the Holy Rollers was a troublesome minority to his way of thinking: "Their decent neighbors must deal with them, not only about religion, but about their sore eyes, their hook worms, their bad hygiene, bad farming, bad whisky, and bad habits generally" (June, 1933). And there was a woman named Texan Guinan, who had just died, a disreputable person at whose funeral dozens of stupid people were injured.

For the *Rotarian* Howe wrote an article about his home town, praising the success of the city despite the nearby opposition of Kansas City. For the *Post* he wrote "As I Grow Older." A bronze bust was made of him by Mrs. Sheila Burlingame of St. Louis, a native of the Kansas town of Lyons, and it was exhibited in New York City in 1931. Ed Howe was thinking about and reflecting on old age, on how good people are to the old, in theory, at least, but how most of us really want the old "to wander off like old dogs, die without bothering us, and bury themselves."[82] Sons of thirty think they can improve on the conduct of their fathers, but in the end find "insurmountable difficulties, as their fathers did," and then become old and receive scoldings from their sons "in a manner almost as humiliating as whipping." He looked again at his book, *The Story of a Country Town,* and admitted that there was more of himself in the despondent Jo Erring than in any other character of the book. He revised the novel for a special edition and, forty years older than when he first wrote it, found he had conflicting emotions. The book seemed all right in the first eleven chapters, but it then seemed to get worse, about the time Jo's love affair began.

His winters were still being spent in Florida, and his name appeared in the 1936 Society Register of Miami. The Florida winters helped him, for life would have been boring in Atchison. In the later years he moved in from Potato Hill and lived in the house on Third Street, where Adelaide was his constant companion. The old letter from Mark Twain was a prized possession, and Adelaide had to hide it or he would get it out and show it to visitors. He was a solid citizen of the town now, a director of two banks.

His son Gene had gone to Amarillo, Texas, in 1924, and was regionally celebrated as editor of the *Amarillo Globe;* Jim was in India, and from him he received a letter about an article Howe's friend A. B. Macdonald had written in the *Kansas City Star,* which he thought "a splendid write up," and Jim also sent a description of a dinner with friends, "Malabar hill and Bombay in the distance."

Hints of retirement began to be dropped, as they had been dropped in *The Globe* prior to his departure late in 1910. He was expressing dissatisfaction with some of his work; the October, 1932, issue of *The Monthly,* in particular, displeased him, and he solicited comments on the matter from his subscribers. "There are a great number of old writers in the country who should quit, as they do not improve and are steadily losing such vigor as they once had. I am willing to submit to a straw vote, and abide by its decision, as Mr. Hoover did" (November, 1932).

In the *Emporia Gazette* there appeared an editorial on the occasion of a visit by Jim Howe, "the most famous reporter Kansas ever has developed—one of the world-famous reporters," telling how the son of Ed Howe had been on the German line with the AP when surrender came; in Russia when revolution struck; in Warsaw when the Poles drove off their Russian invaders; in the fighting around Shanghai; in the Ruhr during the French occupation; in the Japanese war zone of Manchuria; in India covering the rise of Gandhi. And William Allen White had loving words for the father and all his children:

"Ed Howe was in revolt before H. L. Mencken went to kindergarten. He was a realist in the days of W. D. Howells. He wrote mercilessly but beautifully in Atchison when the great Russians were his contemporaries in the latter quarter of the last century.

"But that isn't the point. The point is that the old bull has begot his kind: Jim, Gene and Mateel. He has put his mark on them. He has given them his brains and his distinction. He has proved the worth of heredity" (October, 1932).

Ed Howe thought of himself as a comfortable and active man despite his eighty years. He had never been an athlete but he could still do physical labor when necessary. He had no weighing machine, and did not diet, though he did eat less. One meal a day was his recommendation. He knew that he smoked too much, but that did not seem to him as harmful as over-eating. "Maybe some of my machinery is nearer worn out than I know, but it is operating better now than I ever expected" (November, 1933).

His Atchison friends gave him another dinner in 1933, this one marking the fifty-sixth anniversary of his arrival in the city. The speakers were Henry J. Allen, former Governor and United States Senator, and, not surprisingly, William Allen White. There were flowers, an orchestra of forty persons, Swiss yodelers, distinguished guests, policemen handling traffic, messenger boys bringing in telegrams, and Ed Howe reporting the event himself. He especially liked the speech by Allen, but he did not report its contents. White's speech was no better, in Howe's opinion, than one he might give himself. White said, in part:

"Years ago a man came to Atchison and fell into White Clay Creek. The man cried, 'Help! Help!' Two distinguished citizens of Atchison passed and, hearing him, crossed to the other side of the street. He sank into the water again. Almost drowned, he came to the surface and screamed, 'To hell with Ed Howe.' So Ed Howe and the sheriff, two constables and the chief of the Atchison police leaped into the water, dragged him forth, beat him, and threw him into jail. That's what Atchison thinks of Ed Howe."[83]

One of his good friends in the late years was Will T. Beck, the editor of the *Recorder* in Holton, who recalled that in the mid-1930s Howe owned farm land near Holton and would make Sunday visits there and then come to the Becks' for dinner. "At all of our dinners, Howe was talkative and delightfully expansive, and naturally we gave him the floor." And the editor would tell about life in Florida and retell anecdotes that had appeared in his books in the 1920s.

Ed Howe's eyesight had begun to fail, and he had been feeling that *The Monthly* was not going well. With no prior announcement he suspended operation of the monthly magazine with the November, 1933, issue. Once again, as on other occasions, there appeared newspaper and magazine commentaries on the editor: in the *Literary Digest;* in a new weekly magazine called *Newsweek;* and the best of these, in the *Nation,* which said:

> He has his high place among those American writers who have chosen the footpath to fame. This is the path of common sense, and it is so seldom taken in our practical land that one who follows it to the end is set down as an eccentric. Mr. Howe

> as the Sage of Potato Hill (Kansas) has been one of our eccentrics. Without the mockery of Artemus Ward, without the rage of Mark Twain, without the boisterous brogue of Mr. Dooley, he has yet managed to strike us as something of a crank; and all because he has refused to surrender his rustic illusion not only that the world is a very simple place to those who can see it simply but that those who do not so see it are deliberately perverse. To every problem he has turned the cold shoulder of a sage who knows that "millions of people have lived millions of years and tried everything," the best of them finding in the end that there are no problems beyond the primeval ones connected with the practice of "fairness, politeness, industry, and thrift."[84]

It was curious, in a sense, that Edgar Watson Howe had become so well known. He had ignored the traditional routes of editors to fame, and he had deliberately chosen to move against the tide in his last years on *The Monthly*. He could have been a political power in Kansas, but political activity by editors disgusted him, as it fascinated White and most other editors of the state. He called himself a reactionary; he was without doubt a conservative Republican. And he loathed the New Deal.

He must have begun to get almost tired of honor and recognition. A dinner was given for him in Topeka on June 30, 1934, sponsored by the Topeka Chamber of Commerce. The menu was published on one sheet, which showed the front page of the first *Globe* and the last issue of *The Monthly*, along with a picture of the unsmiling old editor. Frank A. Ripley, president of the Topeka chamber, presided; the ubiquitous Will White was toastmaster; Governor Alfred M. Landon and Howe were on the program, and the speakers were Colonel Robert R. McCormick of the *Chicago Tribune* and Samuel Thomas Bledso of Chicago, president of the Santa Fe Railway. There was a souvenir booklet, "in recognition of his genius as reporter, publisher, philosopher and humorist."

> To Edgar Watson Howe,
> Dear Friend:
>
> This evening, your friends, including a noble band of your compeers from your own high calling, from all parts of the country, express our sincere appreciation for the inspiration you have given to us as a great reporter, an interesting stylist, a keen humorist and a philosopher of the cardinal virtues of character. We take pleasure in attesting our confidence in and

friendship for you and offer our salutations, praise and good wishes with a full chorus of respect and affection.

You have passed through the fiery conflicts that grow out of the ambitions of others and preserved a personal consistency with yourself and an unswerving and unselfish fidelity to your convictions.

It is our sincere wish that you may have a long continued life, crowned with health and prosperity, happiness and honor.

We ask that you preserve this token as an evidence that your friends have paused for an evening to do honor to a man who has been honest and industrious and has done his best. Pass it on that it may show that men do appreciate honesty and sincerity, genius, enterprise and the ability to do.

The mark that points to greatness,
That shows the thoughtful trend,
Is the hand that grasps you fondly
And gladly calls you friend.[85]

Platitudes were overwhelming the old cynic. The newspapers reported three hundred fifty in attendance, "handpicked notables," as the Associated Press phrased it. McCormick talked about Ed Howe's courage and common sense and used the occasion to charge that there were "malignant and persistent efforts to curb the liberty of the press," that a Massachusetts merchant had lost his NRA "blue eagle" because he was outspoken in an advertisement. The Santa Fe executive talked more about the editor from Atchison, the town whose name was part of that of the railway.

Ed Howe had been known in many quarters as the foe of small-town and country values. As people looked at his career in retrospect he seemed almost the George Babbitt type that some people thought he had criticized way back in *The Story of a Country Town.* There were kind words about Ed Howe in the first year of his final retirement, and there were scathing ones. In the *Nation,* Ernest Boyd wrote of Howe as a small-town philistine who had attracted attention outside the Kansas scene: "In the light of the past five years some quotations which I shall make from Mr. Howe's works take on an added idiocy, but their fundamental falsity has been obvious to every thinking person since the beginning of the Industrial Revolution, at least." Boyd said such expressions had been repeated *ad nauseam* in *The Monthly* and in the little pamphlets and books—notably in *Success Easier Than Failure* and *The Blessings of Business.* Howe had been endorsed by many, he wrote, including those who would "revolt at such piffle if uttered by a Congressman, a popular preacher, or a public-relations counsel."

> When he is not denying the existence of almost every fine character in history by asserting that profiteering is the only motive for human action, when he is not sneering at altruism and idealism as forms of lying trickery, when he is not defying the palpable evidence of history by denying moral and intellectual progress, his statements take on a particularly ludicrous form of ignorant egomania. He will dismiss Goethe on the ground that he, E. W. Howe, never heard of him until lately and has not read him. . . . "Did Shakespeare," he asks, "or Goethe, or Whitman, or Buddha, or Tolstoy, or Confucius, or Rousseau ever teach you as important lessons as you learned from your parents, from your worthy and intelligent neighbors, from the leading men of practical affairs in your own country and age? *They did not,* and you know it." . . .
>
> It would seem on reflection, that we have met E. W. Howe before, in line rather than in print. He is Caspar Milquetoast, propped up by a country newspaper until he has acquired in print the courage of a *mouton enragé*.[86]

This attack received no published response from Ed Howe, who may never have seen the article. On May 2, 1935, Howe spoke for publication in Miami, and announced that he soon would be undergoing an operation for removal of cataracts from both eyes. The operation would take place in Baltimore at the Wilmer Clinic:

"My hope is to go to bed one night after a hard day's work and never awaken. That would be the absolute triumph. . . . After all, a man must die some day. He ought to do it as amicably and as decently as possible.

"The doctors tell me that my physical condition is surprisingly good for a man of my age, but common sense doesn't indicate I'll live to be a hundred."[87]

He spoke again from Baltimore two weeks later, when he told the press that America needed a "big butter and egg man" to turn it from destruction. "If we found one, we'd make him dictator so quick it would make your head swim."[88] His butter and egg man would be a good businessman—and not Franklin D. Roosevelt.

At the hospital he was visited by H. L. Mencken. Gene left Amarillo to be in Baltimore. The operation was successful, and the editor announced that he was "on borrowed time," that he was "ready to die like a gentleman," but that he needed two years to complete his book, *Final Conclusions,* "the greatest book in the world." He also planned to resume publication of *The Monthly*. There would be problems, he realized:

"I can't read, which is an annoyance. And do you know, it's the hardest thing in the world to find someone to read to me without mispronouncing a lot of words? But I can see well enough to get around and to recognize people when they are close to me.

"After all, I've had the use of my eyes longer than most people."[89]

Various persons were making journalistic pilgrimages to Atchison. Gene Sullivan, who started his newspaper career on *The Globe* and later became managing editor of the *Coffeyville Journal* in southern Kansas, recalled the annual Associated Press interviews upon Ed Howe's return from Florida each spring. He wrote of one interview: "He impressed me as a lonely old man playing out his string and wishing he could trade everything he had for another look at his 21st birthday." Sullivan got the impression that there were two Ed Howes—the one the reading public knew; the other a shy and lonesome man "who drives himself with an ambition that didn't permit him personal peace or rest" (Oct. 19, 1952).

Mary Angell Webster interviewed him in early 1935 for "I Cover the Bookfront." "Well, I'm eighty years old and I'm not much good," he told her. "Sit down." He observed that he was not a typical Kansan, that he never had been.

"Kansans are exemplary people, but they're extremists. I don't believe in extremes of any kind. I'm not much of a churchgoer, for example; but I'm a moral man. I'm not a teetotaller; but I'm temperate in drink, as I am temperate in all things. I've been criticized. I've had my share of it."[90]

For "Progress in Kansas," a publication of the Kansas Chamber of Commerce, he was interviewed in early 1937 by Harold C. Place. Ed Howe gave his philosophy of old age: up to the age of forty an individual jumps to hasty conclusions. Between that time and seventy he tempers his opinions and undergoes a cooling-off. Then he becomes fixed in ideas and viewpoint. The world was getting better, he thought, but not more moral. There was not enough good behavior. At the Topeka dinner of 1934 he had received an autograph book, and he brought it out for Place to sign, as he did for other visitors. Another of the visitors was Adele Mehl

Burnett, who interviewed him for the *Kansas Teacher*. Once again the autograph book was brought forth, and the diplomas from Washburn and Rollins, and the manuscript of *The Story of a Country Town*. "I am an old, crotchety, ill-tempered man," he told the visitor. "The hardest work I have is to control my temper."[91]

He had told Harold Place that his son Gene was violating every idea and opinion he had ever held. Still Gene felt extremely close to his father in those last years, he later recalled: ". . . after he gave me *The Atchison Globe* and later, when I came to Texas, he became more tolerant of me than of any other person. We took trips together. I got so I could express my own opinions somewhat, though cautiously. I told him of attending church occasionally, and most anything I did was all right. He offered, at one time, to hand over to me a substantial part of his life's savings in an enterprise in which I was interested, but I told him frankly I didn't care to have the responsibility. He never invested money with me because I didn't want it, and he understood it perfectly."[92]

For the most part Ed Howe had become a man living in seclusion. One Atchison woman said her daughter of fifteen, born and raised in the city, had never seen Howe. A one-time Atchison resident recalled that he lived half a block from the Howe home, from 1926 until 1937, and that he had seen Ed Howe often.

"He rented a garage from us for his big black car and I would occasionally be sent to his house to collect the five dollar monthly rent. One of his family or servants would usually give me the check, but I would see him in his home and he was not a frightening man. He just seemed very old and very tired. He was usually sitting down. When he did stand, he was stooped over. He carried a cane, and moved slowly when he walked. I cannot remember the sound of his voice, but I had the impression that he was rather soft-spoken. He did not smile often. His eyes were sad."[93]

Of some significance, perhaps, was the fact that the boy had expected Howe to be "a frightening man." It was local legend; the newspaper and *Monthly* comments and gossip, and the long attacks on religion and women, had made him out a kind of ogre, which he really was not.

He had mainly given up his forceful opinions. Once in a while he commented on politics; he admired Alf Landon, and had been sure that Landon would defeat Roosevelt, and he and Landon and the *Literary Digest* all lost. He returned in May, 1937, from a winter in Miami, liked the looks of the crops in eastern Kansas, and was interviewed by the *Kansas City Star:*

> "I feel fine," he said. "I have lived in Kansas sixty years and I think that one forms a strong affection for a state after that long, particularly if its people are kind to you as Kansas people have been to me.
>
> "This morning on the train I arose early as we neared Fort Scott and was pleased with the general green appearance of the crops and the landscape along the railroad. It was good to hear the people on the train talking about the wonderful crop prospects in that section of Kansas and for the state as a whole.
>
> "I have been particularly humiliated by the weather in Kansas in the last three years.
>
> "At 84 I have had more favors from nature than one can expect. I cannot see very well but above everything else I try to remain in good humor, try to be polite and practice the ordinary virtues. A man must regulate his personal habits as well as his principles. After all, personal habits form a man's principles.
>
> "As usual the *Kansas City Star* and *Times* followed me to Florida again this year as they have every year for the last twenty. I think they are the best newspapers in the United States. I have made some pretty big publishers mad because of my attitude in this respect, but when I want to know the facts about some particular item of current interest I can always find them in the *Star* and *Times*.
>
> "I am growing fonder of the railroads every year. On the way home every train we rode on arrived at its destination a little ahead of time."[94]

On July 17, 1937, he suffered a slight stroke of paralysis and his condition was reported as "fairly serious." He had been under a doctor's care but had been able to move about the home. On October 1, the wire services carried the news that Ed Howe's former wife, Mrs. Clara Howe, was dead and that funeral services were to be conducted for her October 2 at Falls City. She was ninety, and had died at the home of Mateel, at Westport, Connecticut.

It was the next day, October 3, that Edgar Watson Howe died in his sleep, at 2:20 a.m., in the family home. Cause of death was given as gradual paralysis and infirmities of age, with complications of pneumonia. He was eighty-four, and he had achieved the "absolute triumph" he had talked about.

The funeral services were held at 2 o'clock the afternoon of October 5, Episcopal burial services read by the Reverend B. H. Smith of Trinity Episcopal Church. Burial was in Mt. Vernon Cemetery. Ed Howe had condemned churches much of his life, yet the final ceremony surrounding his memory was a religious one. His son, James, had been on the way to Atchison and to Falls City from his home in California. Eugene was in Falls City for the funeral of his mother. Both managed to attend their father's funeral, but Mateel was ill in Connecticut and attended neither service.

And the tributes followed. H. L. Mencken described both his distress and his sympathy. George H. Lorimer, Nunnally Johnson, H. T. Webster, Henry Haskell, Arthur Capper—all paid tributes. Eleanor "Cissy" Patterson of the *Washington Times-Herald* commented, and Roosevelt's cabinet sent an official expression of sympathy. Kansas editors, that interesting breed of journalists so proud of their craft, and always congratulating each other about it, wrote editorials: the *Lawrence Journal-World,* the *Leavenworth Times,* the *Wichita Eagle,* the *El Dorado Times.* The *Kansas City Star* printed a eulogy; so did the *Journal-Post* of that city. The *Salina Journal* suggested, with more perceptiveness than some of the sugary utterances that were made: "Possibly he felt out of place in a world where so many experiments are under way, and so many of them in conflict with the theories that he regarded as essential in life and government."[95] Into Atchison came the telegrams and the newspaper editorials. The *Nation* saw Howe as a man "often right, just as he was often outrageously wrong; though it took time to tell, as he said it would."[96] The *New York Times* said he had seen the world as "an amazing spectacle," one that he had been constrained to comment upon.

The most meaningful were the tributes in *The Globe* itself. One was labeled "The Printer's Tribute":

"Now that the hour glass has been turned for the last time for Edgar Watson Howe, may we of the printing fraternity, from whose ranks Mr. Howe climbed to the highest pinnacle of success, add our tribute.

"We loved and admired Mr. Howe for his forcefulness through simplicity, for the inspiration his life gave us. We shall carry on while he enters the portals into the Great Unknown, where he is only a cub again.

"THE PRINTERS OF THE GLOBE."

The other was the editorial from "The Globe Family":

> If Edgar Watson Howe, founder of *The Atchison Globe* and its editor and publisher for 34 years, were at our elbow today, to give counsel, he would say something like this:
>
> "In all you write, strive for brevity."
>
> And if we were to ask him what tribute from us to him would please him most, he no doubt would say:
>
> "If you insist on writing something nice about me, say that I always longed to be known as a great country reporter."
>
> We will comply with Mr. Howe's wishes, will make this editorial brief, and do declare that his ambition to become known as a great country reporter was realized.
>
> Mr. Howe's fame rested largely on his ability to be concise. As a newspaper man, magazine writer and novelist he constantly strove for brevity in expression, and that manner of expression did much to establish him in the world of letters. He was uncanny in his capacity to condense an opinion to a few lines, and thus get his idea over to his public. No one had to read many and sundry lines to arrive at Mr. Howe's salient idea.
>
> As a country reporter, Mr. Howe was without peer. While gathering news he worked on the principle that every man or woman was interesting or knew something interesting, and for that reason was a source of news or community lore. We marveled at the way Mr. Howe used to go along Commercial street and contact people. He managed to get news from every type of person—from laborer and banker alive. We remember the days of blizzards. The temperature would be 15 degrees below zero, the wind would be howling around the corners and beating snow and sleet against the store fronts, and a glance up and down Commercial street would meet with no human being. Yet Mr. Howe, nothing daunted, would make his regular rounds, and find small groups of men huddled around the stoves in stores, and would on his return to his desk pound out three columns of intensely interesting news and comment. He got news where there wasn't any news, and is well entitled to the appelation, "the world's greatest country reporter."
>
> But we must bring this editorial to a close, else we violate the counsel of Mr. Howe, "Strive for brevity." Our only "add" is that he distinguished his town and country as well as himself by having contributed to the thought of the world, and by having been most lovable in conversation and as an advisor to those of us who stood in need of counsel. [Oct. 4, 1937]

A decision had to be made by the sons about publication of the unfinished book, *Final Conclusions*. The book never appeared. On October 8 the will was opened, and many conjectured that Mateel's *Rebellion* had borne fruit, for Ed Howe left his only daughter one dollar. The estate consisted of $200,000: Miss Adelaide received $50,000; Miss Nellie Webb, *The Globe* writer, $1,500; the remainder of the estate to be divided between James P. Howe and Eugene A. Howe, "the latter being charged for $35,000, the amount advanced to him by his father when he, Eugene A. Howe, bought the controlling interest in *The Atchison Globe* in 1911."

The brothers announced that they would divide equally with Mateel, for they believed their father had planned to change the will.

Emergence of a Legend and a Myth

All his writing days Edgar Watson Howe had been conscious of himself as both a journalistic and literary figure. Frequently he had commented on the propensity of human beings to pose a bit in their photographs, so that the world would look at them and see them in the image *they* wanted to project. And he was such a story-teller and anecdote-builder that even in his own time it was difficult to separate myth from reality.

His friend, William Allen White, in an editorial eulogy, called Ed Howe "a plain man who lived a plain life among plain people."[97] That was probably Howe's own view of himself, but his associations had been, much of the time, with the high and the mighty, and he was proud of the start William Dean Howells and Mark Twain had given him in American letters and of his latter-day friendships with Elbert Hubbard, H. L. Mencken, the executives of the *Saturday Evening Post,* and the wealthy people he met in Miami.

His reputation seemed secure in 1937, even though his latter years had been lived in a time unfriendly to some of his philosophical persuasions. Even a magazine like the *Nation,* which was far to the left of Ed Howe, had praised him oftener than it had criticized him. Mencken, in somewhat overblown words, called

Howe "the most adept master of language ever heard in America."[98] That view possibly was held by many who had been reading the books and the editorials and "Globe Sights" and the magazine articles and pamphlets for so long. The impression of Howe as a Kansas editor was maintained as a sharp and vital one; Rolla Clymer, that familiar journalistic spokesman of the state, in his Kansas Historical Society presidential remarks years later, said of Howe: "He was doubtless the best straight-away reporter that this state ever had, and he built up the prestige of his paper on the power of the personal item. He was also an able business man; in the period around 1912 when purse-proud editors were scarce, Mr. Howe was netting $20,000 a year from his newspaper without a job printing office."[99]

Ed Howe seemed, in 1937, a bigger man even than William Allen White. Time had not yet made of the Emporia editor an almost mythical figure in Kansas, a name to speak in reverent tones, a figure before which one must genuflect.

Some balance in the Howe story was provided only four months after the funeral and the tributes of October. A college professor (later a journalism professor, too, but at that time in the English department at the University of Iowa) named Wilbur L. Schramm wrote about Ed Howe for the *Saturday Review of Literature*. He saw Howe as a man who might have been known as another Benjamin Franklin in more fortunate times but who had to be known in his day as "merely a five-cent Carnegie." Howe had been "ensaged" at a time when bankers and politicians were being installed as the reigning lights of the land. His *Story of a Country Town* had led a literary movement thirty years before the movement really started, and he was out of sympathy with the movement by the time it was in full swing. By the winter of 1937-38, Schramm thought, things were taking place that would have brought wry smiles to the face of Ed Howe: "Henry Wallace making love to the small business man," "the regionalists preaching individual initiative as opposed to mass action and urban collectivism," "Sinclair Lewis advising the Middle West, from a Cedar Rapids lecture platform, to hold on to its Babbitts."

Ed Howe, he said, had been the preacher of go-getterism, speaking the platitudes of the Gilded Age: "Keep your feet on the ground, your hand on your purse, your eye on a bargain."

"The same things have become familiar to us more recently

through the satire of Sinclair Lewis. It is the 'Pep, Punch, Go, Vigor, Enterprise' of Honest Jim Baussler in *Main Street.* It is the young people of Gopher Prairie speaking: 'There would be no more trouble or discontent in the world if everybody worked as hard as Pa did when he cleared our first farm.' It is George F. Babbitt defining the Ideal Citizen for the Zenith Real Estate Board in terms of zip and Regular Guys and four to ten thousand a year and adding machines and bathtubs and automobiles per hundred people and distrust of professors and 'intelligentsia.' "[100] Schramm was mainly right about Ed Howe, with one exception: *Howe never had preached anything else.* He was a boomer in the days of *The Story of a Country Town.* He may have been part of a literary movement, but he was never aware of being part of it. His point in *Country Town* was that man is a mess and the human race is a mess and both blunder and foul up things no matter where they are—even, or maybe especially, in the cities.

For Schramm was one of many already making a minor literary cult out of Ed Howe's writings. Percy H. Boynton, in *Literature and American Life,* was saying that Howe, like Mencken, was a belittler of ideas and convictions and institutions. Ludwig Lewisohn, in *The Story of American Literature,* was crediting *The Story of a Country Town* with sounding "the first strong note of that long and bitter revolt from the American village, wholly stripped of its pseudo-pastoral and sentimental trimmings. . ." Ima Honaker Herron in *The Small Town in American Literature* was singling out Ed Howe as the man who had dared, in the day of Mississippi River reminiscence, romanticism of the southern gentry, and sentimental verse from the Hoosier countryside, to present "an unflattering picture of a bleak, cramped Kansas town." Bleak, surely, but not Kansas. Alfred Kazin, in *On Native Grounds,* was writing of Howe's "dour, lean savage book" (but wisely pointing, too, to the romantic trappings of the work). *The Reader's Encyclopedia* was coupling Howe with Joseph Kirkland as a leader of literary naturalism. Van Wyck Brooks in *The Confident Years* would see *The Story of a Country Town* as the only notable work of the Midwest area being written as Hamlin Garland was starting his career. Arthur Hobson Quinn, in *The Literature of the American People,* would write of the book's pessimism and conscious bitterness (but also of its stilted dialogue and unmotivated melodrama). Henry Steele

Commager, in *The American Mind,* would refer to Howe's town as "a Kansas Sodom." Max Lerner, in *America as a Civilization,* would note that Ed Howe's novel "laid bare the meanness and sterility of small-town life."

A generation, then, of students through courses in modern American literature (if they ever heard about the book, that is) would be coached in the stereotyped impression of Ed Howe's one great book. It remained for American Studies, with all its symbolism and near-mysticism, to give the great recent impetus to the literary reputation of Edgar Watson Howe.

The impetus came, most importantly, from Henry Nash Smith's *Virgin Land: The American West As Symbol and Myth,* a remarkable and meaningful intellectual history. Smith's theme was that there had been a pronounced separation between myth and reality in our perceptions of the American land. The agrarian dream had gone sour, he said; the "noble husbandman" of Thomas Jefferson had become a figment of eighteenth-century imagination. There never was a noble husbandman, and Ed Howe pioneered in telling us so. He expressed in *The Story of a Country Town* his disillusionment at the fading of the agrarian utopia, and through his character Lytle Biggs he attacked the cult of the "yeoman," telling us that there is no particular merit in farmers or such. His world "is a world of grim, savage religion, of silent endurance, of families held together by no tenderness, of communities whose only amusement is malicious gossip."[101] Each writer who has dealt with the American soil has been dissected and almost psychoanalyzed to determine the extent of his adherence to the old stereotype from Thomas Jefferson: the farmer in a state of nature whom he described in *Notes on Virginia.*

The latest of the critics who have read carefully through *The Story of a Country Town* but who have not read Ed Howe's editorials is John William Ward. He has provided the "afterword" for a paperback edition of *The Story of a Country Town,* and he says that the novel "marks the moment when the myth of the garden in America gave way to the wasteland of broken dreams."

". . . it is the earliest expression in our fiction of disenchantment with the agrarian ideal of the simplicity and virtues of rural life and the noble farmer, living in pastoral harmony with a fructifying and beneficent Nature. Second, and closely related to the first, *The Story of a Country Town* stands at the beginning of the literary movement called 'realism' in American literature, with its programmatic acceptance of the daily life of ordinary people as the proper subject for fiction. If not a total success as a novel, *The Story of a Country Town* remains important because it marks important new directions in our cultural history."[102]

Isolate the book, remove it from the author and his life, link it to a literary movement, and all of this is so. Ed Howe, however, always believed in the "myth of the garden." His Kansas *was* the garden, even on those hot August days when the corn was burning before his eyes. His small town *was* the repository of the virtues supposedly confined in the bosom of the noble husbandman. Man *did* live a finer and truer and cleaner life when he was close to nature. That message ran through the works of Ed Howe—with the possible exception of the one important novel, the one that all the literary critics apparently have read.

But coupled with this naïve admiration for the virtues of the pastoral life was Ed Howe's misanthropy, which sometimes has been ignored by those more fascinated by his misogyny and his attacks on organized religion. He was essentially pessimistic about human nature under *any* circumstances, despite all the Puritan ethic success talk. That was much more to the point in *The Story of a Country Town* than a dislike—if not contempt—for small-town living and small-town attitudes, which has been read into Ed Howe's philosophy by so many literary critics.

By the early 1960s Edgar Watson Howe had come to be a legendary name in American literature circles. And it was ironic that it was in the colleges, particularly in the "impractical" departments he had long deprecated, that his name was so important. *The Story of a Country Town* was issued in a new quality hardback edition in 1961. By mid-1965 three paperback editions were available, making it fairly certain that *The Story of a Country Town* would be laid upon the operating table of seminar rooms all over the country. The name of Ed Howe was becoming bigger in schools of journalism, too. Frank Luther Mott had written about Howe as an important journalistic figure; so had most of the other gentlemen writing survey histories of journalism. John Tebbel in *The Compact History of the American Newspaper* (1963) gave Ed Howe even more attention than he gave William Allen White.

In Atchison, the public library has twelve of Howe's books. Most of the pamphlets are not listed there. Nor is *Success Easier Than Failure,* which is perhaps his most representative work.

In 1941 an article appeared in the *Saturday Evening Post* that is likely to perpetuate the Howe legend more than even the writings of the literary critics—Gene Howe's "My Father Was the Most Wretchedly Unhappy Man I Ever Knew." The editors of the *Post,* for which Ed Howe had written so much, had been trying to get the son to write his impressions, and an article he had written for the *Amarillo Globe* was sent to the *Post*—apparently not by Gene but by staff members of the paper. Gene wrote about the terror he had felt toward his father, of the then soaring reputation of Ed Howe that seemed so impressive, of the miseries of Howe's marriage and of life at home. He wrote about his father as a man who knew no middle ground, whose moods were either up or down. He believed his father had failed, in a sense, that he could have been an even greater man than he was: "Probably it is ill becoming his son, one to whom he has been more than generous, to say that in my opinion he made but little of his opportunities and possibilities; but I believe that for every yard of success he hewed out for himself so painfully he should have made miles. I know of no one endowed as he was who accomplished so little. He should have been almost another Will Rogers. I am convinced he had the soundest, rarest sense of humor of any man of his time. He was a master of English, a pioneer in literary style, and he had a great wealth of fire and force and enthusiasm."[103]

The article is not the whole truth, in the opinion of Adelaide Howe, who lived so long with Ed Howe. And one wonders how, if Ed Howe was entirely what was represented in the article, his niece was able to live with him, in apparent happiness and comfort, for so many years. One also wonders why staff members at *The Globe* believe the article was over-harsh. Why had Mateel Howe, who had clashed so with her father, wanted to write *her* impressions of her father after the article by her brother appeared? Jim Howe writes that Mateel had an inkling of the story before it appeared, that she made "frantic efforts" to get in touch with a *Post* executive to try to stop the story. Jim also blames both *Amarillo Globe* and *Post* for "jazzing up" the story, including the somewhat extravagant title placed upon it.

It was reported that twelve thousand letters, many of them

in protest, were sent to the *Post* after publication of the article. The article, in any case, has provided the most lasting impressions of Ed Howe. What Gene Howe wrote seems to have become dogma, even though a paper like the *Kansas City Star,* in an editorial published shortly after the article appeared, questioned some of what Gene Howe had said:

"In his last years, after he had retired from his combats, Ed Howe's unhappiness seemed to fade. At least that is the impression outsiders got. Howe became a general pet. At Miami, Fla., where he spent his winters, the *Saturday Evening Post* crowd and other distinguished people took him up. And how he loved their attention! Doubtless he had unhappy interludes. But in general he gave the feeling to those who visited him that he was having a swell time, basking in the sunshine of those who appreciated his unusual qualities."[104]

Gene Howe's appraisal of his father became, then, a major item in creating the legend—if that's what it is—of Ed Howe. Gene himself remained in Amarillo. He became a local celebrity, a very popular figure in the Panhandle country, especially because of his column called "The Tactless Texan." His own end was far more tragic than his father's. He committed suicide in 1952. The cause was not determined. There may have been business troubles; he may have been having problems with his vision.

Mateel Howe continued to write fiction. She died in May, 1957, in Westport, Connecticut.

Jim Howe retired to Walnut Creek, California, where he became known as a raconteur, a gourmet, and a wine-fancier. He is the only living child. His zest for living seems unhampered by the tragic gloom that afflicted, on occasion, the other children.

Miss Adelaide Howe, as she was familiarly known in Atchison, lived in the old Howe home on Third Street. Until her death in the fall of 1967 she remained the chief tie to the Ed Howe past.

In May, 1951, Gene Howe sold his controlling interest in *The Atchison Globe* to Paul Allingham of Amarillo, who had known Ed Howe when Allingham was a young reporter years before, and Al Bennett of Atchison. Allingham, as of 1968, was the publisher of the paper. *The Globe* is a conservative Republican newspaper, still a booster, a journal, printed by the offset process, that played a key role in rebuilding part of the business district of the city into a beautiful mall area after two disastrous flash floods in the late 1950s.

Ed Howe's "Globe Sights" are still quoted throughout the world. One appears as an overline every day on the front page of the newspaper he founded. His portrait hangs in the Newspaper Hall of Fame of the University of Kansas School of Journalism, which bears the name of his old friend William Allen White. The people of Atchison and the people of the entire state are forgetting him. But the name of Edgar Watson Howe still rings bells with many old-timers throughout the country, and *The Story of a Country Town* is read in classes in literature, and the "Country Town Sayings" occasionally are quoted. An Ed Howe would be an anachronism in the Kansas of the late 1960s. But from 1877 until 1937—a sixty-year span— Howe was rivaled by only one other Kansas editor, and in those years he came to represent country-town journalism, and country-town philosophy, to much of America.

Notes

(In the notes I have tried to avoid the monotonous inclusion of such Latin terms as *"op. cit.,"* especially in making many references to such works as *Plain People*. However, *"op. cit."* seemed necessary for occasional clarification, and I have stayed with our old friend *"Ibid."* References to *The Atchison Globe* normally are by date only (as February 4, 1879), except where it seemed advisable to give the name of the newspaper for clarification. Similarly, references to *E. W. Howe's Monthly* normally are by date also (as April, 1923). In giving names of newspapers and magazines in the work itself I generally used the style of the source itself, rather than converting everything to the italic form.)

I. THE HERITAGE OF AN EDITOR

1. Most of the biographical facts—or fragments—are provided by Howe himself in his autobiographical *Plain People* (New York: Dodd, Mead & Company, 1929), and are used by permission of the publishers.
2. E. W. Howe, "The Wagon and the West," *Saturday Evening Post,* CXCVII, No. 20 (November 15, 1924), pp. 13 and 120-125.
3. Reminiscences are in *Plain People.*
4. Historical edition of *The Globe,* July 20, 1954.
5. Most of the tramp printing recollections are in *Plain People,* pp. 55-130.
6. Frank C. Grable, secretary of a fruit society in Florida in 1927, quoted in *Plain People,* p. 107.
7. D. J. Wood, "Recollections of Ed W. Howe," *Nebraska History Magazine,* XVIII, No. 2 (April-June, 1937), p. 144.
8. In addition to *Plain People,* details of the Golden venture are in Ruth E. Brune, "Ed Howe in the *Golden Globe,*" *Western Humanities Review,* VIII, No. 4 (Autumn, 1954), pp. 365-368.
9. *Golden Globe,* March 7, 1874; February 7, 1874; June 27, 1874; October 24, 1874; and May 16, 1874, all quoted in Ruth E. Brune's article in *Western Humanities Review.*

II. *THE ATCHISON GLOBE:* FIRST YEARS

1. *Globe,* December 8, 1927. Hereafter dates of specific issues of the *Globe* are placed in parentheses in the text.
2. *Plain People,* p. 135.
3. *Ibid.,* p. 195.
4. Everett Dick, *The Sod-House Frontier, 1854-1890* (Lincoln, Neb.: Johnsen Publishing Co.), p. 202.
5. Factual details of early days on *The Globe* are abundant in *Plain People,* Howe's many other writings, secondary book and magazine articles, and files of *The Globe* itself. Many of these appeared in special editions of *The Globe* and in articles written in 1911, when Ed Howe retired from the paper, and in 1937, after his death.
6. Many of Howe's reminiscences were carried in the December 8, 1927, special edition of *The Globe.*
7. *Plain People,* p. 132.
8. Gene Howe, "My Father Was the Most Wretchedly Unhappy Man I Ever Knew," *Saturday Evening Post,* October 25, 1941, in John E. Drewry (ed.), *Post Biographies of Famous Journalists* (Athens, Ga.: University of Georgia Press, 1942), p. 190.
9. *Plain People,* p. 267.
10. *Ibid.,* pp. 265-266.
11. Sheffield Ingalls, *History of Atchison County, Kansas* (Lawrence, Kan.: Standard Publishing Co., 1916), pp. 213-215.
12. *Plain People,* pp. 275-276.
13. Ethel Ingalls interview in *Kansas City Star,* October 4, 1937.

III. THE BUILDING OF A REPUTATION

1. James D. Hart, *The Popular Book* (New York: Oxford University Press, 1950), p. 161.
2. Much of the data on popular

literary tastes is from Frank Luther Mott, *Golden Multitudes* (New York: Macmillan, 1947), pp. 145-167.

3. Ralph Barton Perry, *Characteristically American* (New York: Knopf, 1949), p. 30.
4. See, especially, Henry Nash Smith, *Virgin Land: The American West As Symbol and Myth* (New York: Vintage, 1957).
5. *Plain People,* pp. 102-103.
6. "The Story of a Story," *Kansas City Star Magazine,* February 22, 1925.
7. *E. W. Howe's Monthly,* March, 1911.
8. *Plain People,* p. 214.
9. *The Story of a Country Town* (Boston: James R. Osgood & Co., 1882), v.
10. *Ibid.,* p. 12.
11. *Ibid.,* p. 128.
12. *Ibid.,* p. 165.
13. *Ibid.,* p. 129.
14. *Ibid.,* p. 144.
15. *Ibid.,* pp. 252-253.
16. *Ibid.,* p. 325.
17. *Ibid.,* p. 379.
18. *Ibid.,* p. 265.
19. *Ibid.,* p. 88.
20. *Ibid.,* p. 45.
21. *Plain People,* pp. 214-215.
22. Henry Clay McDougal, *Recollections, 1844-1909* (Kansas City, Mo.: Franklin Hudson Publishing Co., 1919), pp. 345-356.
23. The Howells review appeared in *The Century,* but some writers assume it was in *The Atlantic Monthly*. This note was in the "Miscellaneous" column of *The Kansas Magazine,* VIII, No. 6 (November, 1887), p. 367.
24. Howells, "Two Notable Novels," *The Century,* XXVIII (August, 1884), p. 632.
25. James B. Stronks, "William Dean Howells, Ed Howe, and *The Story of a Country Town,*" *American Literature,* XXIX, No. 4 (January, 1958), pp. 474-475.
26. The Mark Twain letter, like the Howells, is found in several books.
27. "Recent American Fiction," *Atlantic Monthly,* LV (January, 1885), pp. 121-132.
28. These evaluations appeared in (1) an advertisement in *The Globe;* (2) the *Topeka Daily Capital,* September 28, 1883; and (3) the *Hiawatha World,* September 27, 1883.
29. *Washington Post,* January 26, 1902.
30. Carl Van Doren, "Prudence Militant: E. W. Howe, Village Sage," *Century, LXXXIV* (May, 1923), p. 153.
31. *The Mystery of the Locks* (Boston: James R. Osgood and Company, 1885), p. 1.
32. *Ibid.,* p. 26.
33. *Ibid.,* p. 161.
34. *Ibid.,* pp. 258-259.
35. Dorothy Anne Dondore, *The Prairie and the Making of Middle America: Four Centuries of Description* (Cedar Rapids, Iowa: Torch Press, 1926), p. 14.
36. *A Moonlight Boy* (Boston: Ticknor and Company, 1886), p. 120.
37. *Ibid.,* p. 186.
38. *Ibid.,* p. 200.
39. Hamlin Garland, *Roadside Meetings* (New York: Macmillan, 1930), pp. 94-96.
40. *Ibid.*
41. *A Man Story* (Boston: Ticknor and Company, 1888), p. 42.
42. *Ibid.,* p. 83.
43. *Ibid.,* p. 352.
44. *Ibid.,* p. 372.
45. William Allen White, "Mr. Howe's New Novel," *The University Review,* X, No. 4 (December, 1888), pp. 111-113.
46. *The Confession of John Whitlock, Late Preacher of the Gospel* (Atchison: Globe Publishing Co., 1891), p. 31.
47. *Ibid.,* pp. 12-13.
48. *Ibid.,* pp. 18-19.
49. *Ibid.,* pp. 20-21.
50. *Ibid.,* p. 57.
51. *Ibid.,* p. 91.
52. William Lloyd Woodhouse, "The Writings and Philosophy of E. W. Howe," unpublished master's thesis, University of Kansas, 1941, p. 77.
53. *An Ante-Mortem Statement* (Atchison: Globe Publishing Co., 1891), p. 23.
54. *Ibid.,* pp. 38-39.
55. *Ibid.,* pp. 44-45.
56. *Ibid.,* p. 51.
57. *Ibid.,* p. 138.
58. *Ibid.,* p. 173.
59. *Ibid.,* p. 176.
60. *Ibid.,* pp. 176-177.
61. *Plain People,* pp. 216-217.

62. *Ibid.*, pp. 157-160.
63. *Ibid.*, pp. 160-161.
64. Ingalls, *History of Atchison County, op. cit.*, p. 228.
65. *Plain People*, p. 164.
66. *Ibid.*, p. 153.
67. *Ibid.*, p. 221, and "Kansas Newspaperdom," in *The Journalist*, XVII, No. 17, July 8, 1893.
68. E. W. Howe, *Notes for My Biographer* (Girard, Kan.: Haldeman-Julius Co., 1926), p. 14.
69. Rolla A. Clymer, "A Golden Era of Kansas Journalism," *Kansas Historical Quarterly*, XXIV, (Spring, 1958), p. 100.
70. *Plain People*, pp. 218-219.
71. Gene Howe, *Saturday Evening Post* article, *op. cit.*, p. 198.
72. *Plain People*, p. 268.
73. William Allen White, *Autobiography* (New York: Macmillan, 1946), p. 147.
74. Quoted in Ingalls, *History of Atchison County, op. cit.*, p. 844.
75. *Ibid.*, p. 846.
76. Noble L. Prentis, *A History of Kansas* (Winfield, Kan.: E. P. Greer, 1899), p. 299.
77. Hill P. Wilson (ed.), *Eminent Men of the State of Kansas* (Topeka: Hall Lithographing Co., 1901), p. 125.
78. *Plain People*, p. 165.
79. *Ibid.*, pp. 172-173.
80. Mary Elizabeth Lease, Populist agitator often referred to as Mary Ellen Lease, became a familiar name in *Globe* columns in her years of Kansas notoriety.
81. Much of the foregoing was recalled in a special edition of *The Globe*, October 3, 1937.

IV. THE EDITOR'S VIEWS IN THE *GLOBE* YEARS

1. *Monthly*, September, 1912.
2. *Plain People*, pp. 197-198.
3. The Murdock family was a prominent name in Kansas journalism with its influential *Wichita Eagle*.
4. White, *Autobiography*, p. 274.
5. E. W. Howe, "Provincial Peculiarities of Western Life," *The Forum*, XIV (September, 1892), p. 91.
6. Robert Rienow and Leona Train Rienow, *Of Snuff, Sin and the Senate* (Chicago: Follett, 1965), p. 111.
7. Ingalls, *History of Atchison County, op. cit.*, pp. 392-393.
8. *Plain People*, p. 196.
9. James C. Carey, "People, Problems, Prohibition, Politicos and Politics—1870-1890," in John D. Bright (ed.), *Kansas, the First Century* (New York: Lewis Historical Publishing Co., 1956), pp. 384-391.
10. Gene Howe, *Saturday Evening Post* article, *op. cit.*, pp. 193-194.
11. *Ibid.*
12. Arthur M. Schlesinger, *The Rise of the City, 1878-1898* (New York: Macmillan, 1933), p. 121.
13. *Plain People*, p. 185.
14. U.S. Ninth Census, 1870, quoted in Allan Nevins, *The Emergence of Modern America*, 1865-1878 (New York: Macmillan, 1927), p. 343.
15. *Topeka State Journal*, March 13, 1900.
16. *Ibid.*, March 18, 1900.
17. Howe, "Country Newspapers," *Century*, XX (September, 1891), pp. 777-780.
18. Howe, *The Trip to the West Indies* (Topeka: Crane & Co., 1910), pp. 15-16.
19. *Ibid.*, pp. 39-40.
20. *Ibid.*, pp. 40-41.
21. *Monthly*, March, 1911.
22. Howe, *Ventures in Common Sense* (New York: Knopf, 1919), pp. 134-136.
23. *Ibid.*, p. 211.
24. Henry J. Haskell, "Houn' Dawg vs. Art," in Duncan Aikman (ed.), *The Taming of the Frontier* (New York: Minton, Balch & Co., 1925), p. 229.
25. *Ventures*, p. 219.
26. *Monthly*, April, 1912.
27. *Monthly*, February, 1912.
28. *Ibid.*, October, 1918.

V. LAST YEARS ON *THE GLOBE*

1. Ethel Ingalls interview in *Kansas City Star*, *op. cit.*, October 4, 1937.
2. Interview with T. E. Snowden, in William Irvin McReynolds, "Gene A. Howe: The Tactless Texan," unpublished master's thesis, University of Texas, 1962, p. 39.
3. Gene Howe article in *Saturday Evening Post*, *op. cit.*, p. 195.
4. Letter from James Howe, February 24, 1964.
5. Gene Howe article in *Saturday Evening Post*, *op. cit.*, pp. 196-199.
6. Clipping from *Globe*, June 21,

1907 (probably an error, as divorce took place in 1901).
7. *Plain People,* pp. 280-281.
8. Article by Wes Izzard in *Globe,* February 4, 1951.
9. *Monthly,* April, 1927.
10. Undated clipping from *Kansas City Star,* summer of 1903.
11. This trip is reported in Howe's two-volume work, *Daily Notes of a Trip Around the World* (Topeka: Crane & Co., 1907). Hereafter references to this work appear in parentheses in the text, citing vollume and page numbers.
12. Advertisement in *Globe,* January 3, 1908.
13. *Philadelphia North American,* March 3, 1907.
20. *The Trip to the West Indies, op. cit.,* p. 5.
23. Walt Mason, "Interesting People: Edgar W. Howe," *The American Magazine,* LXXI (March, 1911), pp. 609-610.
24. Ingalls, *History of Atchison County, op. cit.,* p. 222.
25. *Monthly,* March, 1911. Hereafter issues of the *Monthly* are indicated in parentheses in the text.
26. Howe, "The Old Dog in the Sun," *The Independent,* LXX (June 1, 1911), pp. 1205-1206.
27. All in January 4, 1911.
28. "The Quitting of 'Ed' Howe," *The Independent,* LXX (February 2, 1911), pp. 271-272.

VI. *E. W. HOWE'S MONTHLY*

1. All in January 11, 1911.
2. *Plain People,* p. 271.
3. *Topeka State Journal,* January 31, 1911.
4. *Topeka Daily Capital,* January 31, 1911.
5. Interview with Miss Adelaide Howe.
6. *Travel Letters from New Zealand, Australia and Africa* (Topeka: Crane & Co., 1913), pp. 31-32.
7. *Ibid.,* p. 184.
8. *Ibid.,* p. 242.
9. *Ibid.,* pp. 274-275.
10. *Ibid.,* p. 342.
11. *Ibid.,* p. 372.
12. Letter of May 10, 1916.
13. Letter of October 26, 1916.
14. Letter of November 11, 1916.
15. *Philadelphia Public Ledger,* in *Topeka State Journal,* October 20, 1921.
16. Carl Van Doren, *The American Novel* (New York: Macmillan, 1921), p. 229.
17. Van Doren, "Prudence Militant," *Century, op. cit.,* p. 152.
18. Vernon Louis Parrington, *Main Currents in American Thought* (New York: Harcourt, Brace and Company, 1927), III, p. 377.
19. Gerald Carson, "The Village Atheist," *Scribner's Magazine,* LXXXIV (December, 1928), p. 733.
20. Willis J. Abbot, *Watching the World Go By* (Boston: Little, Brown & Co., 1934), p. 54.
21. Grover C. Hall, "E. W. Howe and H. L. Mencken," *Haldeman-Julius Monthly,* II, No. 2 (July, 1925), pp. 163-167.
22. *New York Evening Mail,* October 3, 1917, in December, 1917, *Monthly.*
23. George Jean Nathan, "E. W. Howe: Unbuncombed, Unsentimental, Clear Thinking and Practical," *Haldeman-Julius Quarterly,* I, No. 2 (January, 1927), pp. 195-197.
24. *Success Easier Than Failure* (Topeka: Crane & Co., 1917), pp. 19-20.
25. *Ibid.,* pp. 37-38.
26. *Ibid.,* p. 63.
27. Howe, "Two Very Substantial Citizens You Probably Never Heard Of," *American Magazine,* LXXXVIII (July, 1919), p. 65.
28. *The Blessings of Business* (Topeka: Crane & Co., 1918), p. 5.
29. *Ibid.,* pp. 11-12.
30. *Ibid.,* pp. 35-36.
31. *Ibid.,* p. 48.
32. *Ventures, op. cit.,* pp. 244-245.
33. Howe, "Better Farmers," *Country Gentleman,* LXXXIV, No. 2 (January 11, 1919), pp. 15-16.
34. *The Indignations of E. W. Howe* (Girard, Kan.: Haldeman-Julius Publications, 1933), p. 43.
35. "Hardin the Blacksmith and the Uplift," *Saturday Evening Post,* CXCII, No. 30 (January 24, 1920), p. 29.
36. *Indignations, op. cit.,* p. 14.
37. *Ibid.,* p. 11.
38. *Ventures, op. cit.,* pp. 35-44.
39. "These Women," *Forum,* LXXXIII (April, 1930), p. 244.
40. "Potato Hill Notes," *Country*

Gentleman, LXXXV, No. 37 (September, 1911), p. 26.
41. "The Old Doctor," *Saturday Evening Post,* CXCVII, No. 32 (February 7, 1925), p. 36.
42. *Plain People,* pp. 244-250.
43. *The Anthology of Another Town* (New York: Knopf, 1920), pp. 60-61. Permission of the publishers.
44. *Ibid.,* p. 74.
45. *Ibid.,* p. 106.
46. *Ibid.,* p. 142.
47. *Sinner Sermons* (Girard, Kan.: Haldeman-Julius Co., 1926), p. 4.
48. *Dying Like a Gentleman and Other Stories* (Girard, Kan.: Haldeman-Julius Co., 1926), pp. 22-23.
49. *When a Woman Enjoys Herself, and Other Tales of a Small Town* (Girard, Kan.: Haldeman-Julius Co., 1928), p. 10.
50. *Ibid.,* pp. 18-19.
51. James C. Malin, "The Democratic Party and Atchison: A Case Study, 1880," *Kansas Historical Quarterly,* XXVIII (Summer, 1962), p. 157.
52. "A Good Word with a Bad Reputation," *Collier's,* LXXIV, No. 7 (August 16, 1924), p. 21.
53. *Ventures, op. cit.,* p. 254.
54. *The Trip to the West Indies, op. cit.,* p. 8.
55. "The Nan Britton-President Harding Affair," *Haldeman-Julius Monthly,* VII, No. 6 (May, 1928), p. 39.
56. *Notes for My Biographer, op. cit.,* pp. 22-23.
57. *Ibid.,* p. 13.
58. Helen Ogden Mahin (ed.), *The Editor and His People* (New York: Macmillan, 1924), pp. 202-204.
59. "In Miami with the Sage of Potato Hill," *Kansas City Star,* March 3, 1932, reprinted from letter to *Globe.*
60. Letter, August 6, 1932.
61. *Plain People,* pp. 226-227.
62. Mrs. Anna Haldeman-Julius, *Famous and Interesting Guests at a Kansas Farm* (Girard, Kan.: Haldeman-Julius Co., 1936), p. 24.
63. Percy H. Boynton, *Literature and American Life* (Boston: Ginn and Company, 1936), p. 835.
64. *Chicago Tribune,* October 4, 1937.
65. *New York Times* obituary, October 4, 1937.
66. *Plain People,* pp. 227-228.
67. *Ibid.,* p. 206.
68. *Ibid.,* pp. 228-229.
69. *Ibid.,* p. 207.
70. Pamphlet in Kansas State Historical Library; introduction written for *Rebellion.*
71. Mateel Howe Farnham, *Rebellion* (New York: Dodd, Mead and Company, 1927), p. 12.
72. *Ibid.,* p. 69.
73. *Ibid.,* p. 147.
74. *Ibid.,* p. 17.
75. *Notes for My Biographer, op. cit.,* p. 3.
76. *Plain People,* p. 254.
77. *Ibid.,* pp. 292-293.
78. Quotations from an advertisement in April, 1929, *Monthly.*
79. Mark Van Doren, "The Sage of Sensibility," *The Nation,* CXXVIII (April 17, 1929), p. 480.
80. *Indignations, op. cit.,* p. 52.
81. *Kansas City Journal-Post,* October 4, 1937.
82. *Ventures, op. cit.,* p. 203.
83. Bracke, *Wheat Country, op. cit.,* p. 187.
84. "E. W. Howe Retires," *The Nation,* CXXXVIII (January 10, 1934), p. 35.
85. "Edgar Watson Howe, Venerable Editor, Is Honored in Topeka," *Santa Fe Magazine,* XXVIII, No. 9 (Chicago: Railway Exchange, August, 1934), p. 8.
86. Ernest Boyd, "The Sage of Potato Hill," *The Nation,* CXXXIX (August 29, 1934), pp. 247-248.
87. *Kansas City Star,* May 2, 1935.
88. *Lawrence Daily Journal-World,* May 16, 1935.
89. *Kansas City Times,* June 10, 1935.
90. Mary Angell Webster, "An Interview with Ed Howe," *I Cover the Bookfront,* II, No. 9 (May, 1935, Topeka), p. 11.
91. Adele Mehl Burnett, "Little Journeys to the Homes of Kansas Authors: E. W. Howe," *Kansas Teacher,* XLIV, No. 4 (February, 1937), pp. 28-29.
92. Gene Howe article in *Saturday Evening Post, op. cit.,* p. 201.
93. Robert C. Harwi, "The Two Atchison Daily Globes," a paper written at the University of Kansas, 1959, p. 9.
94. *Kansas City Times,* May 10, 1937.
95. *Salina Journal,* October 7, 1937.
96. Editorial obituary, *The Nation,* CXLV (October 16, 1937), p. 391.

97. Quoted in Ima Honaker Herron, *The Small Town in American Literature* (Durham, N. C.: Duke University Press, 1939), p. 209.

98. Quoted in *Kansas City Journal-Post,* October 4, 1937.

99. Clymer, "A Golden Era of Kansas Journalism," *op. cit.,* p. 100.

100. Wilbur L. Schramm, "Ed Howe Versus Time," *Saturday Review of Literature,* XVII (February 5, 1938), pp. 10-11.

101. Smith, *Virgin Land, op. cit.,* pp. 285-286.

102. John William Ward, "Afterword," in Howe, *The Story of a Country Town* (New York: Signet, 1964), pp. 302-304.

103. Gene Howe article in *Saturday Evening Post, op. cit.,* p. 187.

104. *Kansas City Star,* October 24, 1941.

Bibliography

Because this work is so largely concerned with the *writings* of Edgar Watson Howe it is obvious that those writings constitute the primary sources. These were, first, *The Atchison Globe* from December 1877 through December 1910, and *E. W. Howe's Monthly* from 1911 through most of 1933. A considerable amount of selection clearly became necessary, but I am satisfied that I read about as much of Ed Howe as was physically—and psychologically—possible at the time of research.

Howe was not only a journalist; the writing he did for audiences beyond Atchison was easily as interesting, and as significant, as that which he did for the people in Kansas. So there were his books. The most important, because the first of these was part autobiography cast in the form of fiction and the second because it truly was autobiography (with the unusual limitations of autobiography), were *The Story of a Country Town* (Boston: James R. Osgood and Company, 1882, and in subsequent editions which included introductions, afterwords, and the like) and *Plain People* (New York: Dodd, Mead & Company, 1929). The other Howe books I used, and discussed were:

An Ante-Mortem Statement (Atchison: Globe Publishing Co., 1891).

The Confessions of John Whitlock, Late Preacher of the Gospel (Atchison: Globe Publishing Co., 1891).

A Man Story (Boston: Ticknor and Company, 1888).

A Moonlight Boy (Boston: Ticknor and Company, 1886).

The Mystery of the Locks (Boston: James R. Osgood and Company, 1885).

In a special category are the two tracts which say so much about the editor's philosophy—*The Blessings of Business* (Topeka: Crane & Co., 1918) and *Success Easier Than Failure* (Topeka: Crane & Co., 1917).

Then there were the travel books, from which I drew heavily:

Daily Notes of a Trip Around the World (Topeka: Crane & Co., 1907), I and II.

Travel Letters from New Zealand, Australia and Africa (Topeka: Crane & Co., 1913).

The Trip to the West Indies (Topeka: Crane & Co., 1910).

The 1920s brought a great many collections of Howe's work. In this category are *The Anthology of Another Town* (New York: Knopf, 1920) and *Ventures in Common Sense* (New York: Knopf, 1919). There also are those slight volumes known as "Little Blue Books," all published in Girard, Kansas, by Haldeman-Julius Co. These titles from Howe (some of the work showed up in previous—and subsequent—writings) include the following:

Dying Like a Gentleman and Other Stories, 1926.

Her Fifth Marriage and Other Stories, 1928.

The Indignations of E. W. Howe, 1933.

Notes for My Biographer, 1926.

Preaching from the Audience, 1926.

Sinner Sermons, 1926.

When a Woman Enjoys Herself, and Other Tales of a Small Town, 1928.

Ed Howe wrote many other articles, of course, some of which are discussed in the text. These, mainly from magazines of national circulation, are:

"The Apologies of an Old Fogy," *Saturday Evening Post,* CXCIII, No. 24 (December 11, 1920), pp. 27 and 161-162.

"As I Grow Older," *Saturday Evening Post,* CCVII, No. 46 (May 18, 1935), p. 81.

"Atchison Globe Knocks," *The Kansas Knocker,* I (October, 1900), pp. 23-24.

"Before I End My Life," *Ladies' Home Journal,* XXIX, Nos. 5 and 6 (May, 1912, and June, 1912), pp. 13-14 and 9-10, respectively. (This is *An Ante-Mortem Statement,* first published in 1891).

"Better Farmers," *Country Gentle-*

man, LXXXIV, No. 2 (January 11, 1919), pp. 15-16.

"A Bit of Weston, Missouri, History," *Missouri Historical Review,* XLVII (October, 1952), pp. 29-36.

"The Boy and the Man," in "Playtime on the Prairie," *Wallace Winner* (Wallace, Nebraska, October, 1919), p. 6.

"The Confession of a Recreationist," *Saturday Evening Post,* CXCIII, No. 16 (October 16, 1920), pp. 19 and 169-170.

"Confessions of a Common Man," *American Magazine,* XCV, No. 6 (June, 1923), pp. 34 and 92-100.

"Country Newspapers," *Century,* XX (September, 1891), pp. 776-783.

"Country Town Sayings," *Independent,* LXX (April 13, 1911), pp. 770-775.

"The Devil Is a Fool," *Collier's,* LXXIV, No. 10 (September 6, 1924), p. 19.

"Ed Howe's Religious Confessions," *Literary Digest,* LXIII (December 6, 1919), pp. 35-36.

"Every Man His Own Philosopher," *Saturday Evening Post,* CIII, No. 44 (April 30, 1921), pp. 33-34.

"Every Man Knows Better Than He Does," *Fra,* XVIII, No. 2 (November, 1916), pp. 50-51.

"False Lights," *Fra,* XIV (September, 1915), p. 186.

"Found Something to Go On," *American Magazine,* LXXIII (February, 1912), p. 464.

"Gee Whiz, What a Farm!," *Country Gentleman,* LXXXIII, No. 29 (July 20, 1918), pp. 1 and 16.

"A Good Word with a Bad Reputation," *Collier's,* LXXIV, No. 7 (August 16, 1924), p. 21.

"Hardin the Blacksmith and the Uplift," *Saturday Evening Post,* CXCII, No. 30 (January 24, 1920), pp. 29 and 40-46.

"In Miami with the Sage of Potato Hill," *Kansas City Star,* March 3, 1923, reprinted from letter to *The Globe.*

"'Jug' McChesney, Dean of Traveling Men," *American Magazine,* XCV (February, 1923), pp. 62-63.

"Kansas—Past and Present," *Country Gentleman,* LXXXIV, No. 41 (October 11, October 25, November 15, 1919), pp. 17, 12 and 30, respectively.

"A Kin Story," *American Magazine,* LXXV (December, 1912), pp. 153-156.

"The Life, Death and Obsequies of George Coulter," *American Magazine,* LXXII (October, 1911), pp. 700-703.

"Listening In," *Country Gentleman,* LXXXIV, No. 24 (June 14, 1919), p. 25.

"Loafing Round in Florida," *Country Gentleman,* LXXXV, No. 9 (February 28, 1920), pp. 30 and 100.

"Loyalty," *Fra,* XIV, No. 4 (January, 1915), pp. 126-127.

"My Home Town, Atchison," *Rotarian,* XLIII, No. 3 (September, 1933), pp. 21-23 and 55.

"My Only Daughter," introduction written for *Rebellion;* pamphlet in Kansas State Historical Society Library.

"The Nan Britton-President Harding Affair," *Haldeman-Julius Monthly,* VII, No. 6 (May, 1928), pp. 37-39.

"A New Travel over an Old Road," *Saturday Evening Post,* CXCIII, No. 15 (October 9, 1920), pp. 11 and 54.

"Oh, Those Women," *Independent,* XCIX (August 2, 1919), p. 158.

"The Old Doctor," *Saturday Evening Post,* CXCVII, No. 32 (February 7, 1925), pp. 36 and 127.

"The Old Dog in the Sun," *Independent,* LXX (June 1, 1911), pp. 1204-1206.

"The Old Visiters," *Saturday Evening Post,* CXCIII, No. 35 (February 26, 1921), pp. 24, 36 and 38.

"Our American Habit of Optimistic Drunkenness," *Current Opinion,* LXXIII, No. 5 (November, 1922), pp. 637-638.

"Paragraphs from the Provinces," *Saturday Evening Post,* CXCIV, No. 7 (August 13, 1921), pp. 16 and 86.

"The Preaching of a Brother-in-Law of the Church," *Saturday Evening Post,* CXCIX, No. 29 (January 15, 1927), pp. 27 and 143-144.

"Provincial Pecularities of Western Life," *Forum,* XIV (September, 1892), pp. 91-102.

"The Real Palm Beach," *Saturday Evening Post,* CXCII, No. 42 (April 17, 1920), pp. 42-49.

"Reflecting the Ideals of Industry," *Nation's Business,* XII, No. 8 (July, 1924), pp. 36 and 38.

"Selections from E. W. Howe," *Kansas Magazine,* 1935, pp. 94-96.

"Short Sermons from Kansas," *Sat-*

urday Evening Post, CXCIII, No. 23 (December 4, 1920), pp. 25 and 105.

"Socialism in the Light of Common Sense," *Current Opinion,* LXXIII (September, 1922), pp. 368-369.

"The Story the Ship's Captain Told to Me," *Kansas City Star Magazine,* October 19, 1924, pp. 3-5.

"The Stubborn Woman—A Story," *Current Opinion,* LXII (March, 1917), pp. 214 and 228.

"The Submerged Majority," *Saturday Evening Post,* CXCII, No. 21 (November 22, 1919), pp. 31 and 86.

"The Tale of Two Countries," *Saturday Evening Post,* CXCV, No. 16 (October 14, 1922), p. 88.

"These Women," *Forum,* LXXXIII (April, 1930), pp. 244-246.

"Torch and Powder," *Collier's,* LXXIV, No. 17 (October 25, 1924), p. 29.

"Two Very Substantial Citizens You Probably Never Heard Of," *American Magazine,* LXXXVIII (July, 1919), pp. 64-65.

"The Wagon and the West," *Saturday Evening Post,* CXCVII, No. 20 (November 15, 1924), pp. 13 and 120-125.

"What Life Has Taught Me," *Collier's,* LXXV, No. 2 (January 10, 1925), p. 25.

"Why Is Io-way!," *Country Gentleman,* LXXXIII, No. 45 (November 9, 1918), pp. 3-4 and 24.

The article by Gene Howe, which appeared October 25, 1941, in the *Saturday Evening Post,* was a key source. Entitled "My Father Was the Most Wretchedly Unhappy Man I Ever Knew," it was reprinted in John E. Drewry (ed.), *Post Biographies of Famous Journalists* (Athens, Ga.: University of Georgia Press, 1942), pp. 187-201. I also used the novel by Mateel Howe Farnham, *Rebellion* (New York: Dodd, Mead and Company, 1927).

Three theses offered both facts and insights. These were William Irvin McReynolds' "Gene A. Howe: The Tactless Texan," University of Texas, 1962; Robert S. Shannon's "A Study of the Diction and Phraseology in Ed Howe's 'The Story of a Country Town,'" University of Kansas, 1929; and William Lloyd Woodhouse's "The Writings and Philosophy of E. W. Howe," University of Kansas, 1941.

Many articles have been written about Ed Howe, mostly in his lifetime. A good many of these were mentioned in the text. These—articles in magazines, in scholarly publications, in books, in newspapers—follow, listed alphabetically and with no comment:

"Accidents of Authors," in "Miscellaneous," *Kansas Magazine,* VII, No. 6 (November, 1887), pp. 367-368.

Boyd, Ernest, "The Sage of Potato Hill," *Nation,* CXXXIX (August 29, 1934), pp. 247-248.

Brune, Ruth E., "Ed Howe in the *Golden Globe,*" *Western Humanities Review,* VIII, No. 4 (Autumn, 1954), pp. 365-368.

Brune, Ruth E., "Found: Ed Howe's *Golden Globe,*" *Western Humanities Review,* VI, No. 1 (Winter, 1951-52), pp. 99-102.

Burnett, Adele Mehl, "Little Journeys to the Homes of Kansas Authors: E. W. Howe," *Kansas Teacher,* XLIV, No. 4 (February, 1937), pp. 28-29.

Carson, Gerald, "The Village Atheist," *Scribner's Magazine,* LXXXIV (December, 1928), pp. 733-739.

Chase, Frank M., "Get Back to Lessons Our Mothers Taught Us," *Dearborn Independent,* XXIV, No. 6 (December 1, 1923), p. 9.

Clymer, Rolla A., "A Golden Era of Kansas Journalism," *Kansas Historical Quarterly,* XXIV (Spring, 1958), pp. 97-111.

Cooper, Kenneth S., "E. W. Howe —A Self-Educated Educator," *Educational Forum,* January, 1962, pp. 233-237.

"Daily Notes of a Trip Around the World" (review), *Independent,* LXIV (January 2, 1908), p. 320.

Dick, Everett, "Ed Howe, a Notable Figure on the Sod-House Frontier," *Nebraska History Magazine,* XVIII, No. 2 (April-June, 1937), pp. 138-143.

"Edgar Watson Howe, Venerable Editor, Is Honored in Topeka," *Santa Fe Magazine,* XXVIII, No. 9 (August, 1934), pp. 6-11.

"Ed Howe: Sage of Potato Hill Ends Long Publishing Career," *News-Week,* III (January 6, 1934), p. 34.

Editorial obituary, *Nation,* CXLV (October 16, 1937), pp. 390-391.

"E. W. Howe Retires," *Nation,* CXXXVIII (January 10, 1934), p. 35.

Haldeman-Julius, Mrs. Anna, "Famous and Interesting Guests at a Kan-

sas Farm," Haldeman-Julius, Co., 1936, No. 8.

Hall, Grover C., "E. W. Howe and H. L. Mencken," *Haldeman-Julius Monthly,* II, No. 2 (July, 1925), pp. 163-167.

Hammers, Clyde C., "Edgar Watson Howe, Born One Hundred Years Ago," *Kansas Magazine,* XXII (1954), pp. 6-11.

Harger, Charles Moreau, "Those Kansas Editors," *Independent,* LXVIII (February 24, 1910), pp. 395-398.

Haskell, Henry J., "The Frankensteins of Kansas," *Independent,* LXXXII (April 12, 1915), pp. 68-69.

———, "Houn Dawg vs. Art," in Duncan Aidman (ed.), *The Taming of the Frontier* (New York: Minton, Balch & Co., 1925), p. 229.

"Honor Paid to E. W. Howe, Founder of the Atchison Globe," *The Earth,* XXXI, No. 8 (August, 1934), pp. 6-7.

Howells, William Dean, "Two Notable Novels," *Century,* XXVIII (August, 1884), pp. 632-633.

Hull, Myra E., "Edgar Watson Howe," radio talk given over KFKU, University of Kansas, January 25, 1934.

"Kansas Editor Breaks into Society," *Newspaperdom,* XIV, No. 13 (June 11, 1903), p. 11.

McDougal, Henry Clay, *Recollections, 1844-1909* (Kansas City, Mo.: Franklin Hudson Publishing Co., 1919).

Mason, Walt, "Interesting People: Edgar W. Howe," *American Magazine,* LXXI (March, 1911), pp. 608-611.

Nathan, George Jean, "E. W. Howe: Unbuncombed, Unsentimental, Clear Thinking and Practical," *Haldeman-Julius Quarterly,* I, No. 2 (January, 1927), pp. 195-197.

National Cyclopedia of American Biography (New York: James T. White and Company, 1900), X, p. 138.

Nevins, Allan (ed.), *American Press Opinion, Washington to Coolidge* (Boston: D. C. Heath and Company, 1928).

Place, Harold C., "A Visit with the Sage of Potato Hill," *Progress in Kansas,* III, No. 4 (Kansas Chamber of Commerce: March, 1937), pp. 3-4.

"The Quitting of 'Ed' Howe," *Independent,* LXX (February 2, 1911), pp. 271-272.

"Recent American Fiction," *Atlantic Monthly,* LV (January, 1885), pp. 121-132.

Ripley, John W., "Another Look at the Rev. Mr. Charles M. Sheldon's Christian Daily Newspaper," *Kansas Historical Quarterly,* XXXI, No. 1 (Spring, 1965), pp. 1-40.

Schramm, Wilbur L., "Ed Howe versus Time," *Saturday Review of Literature,* XVII (February 5, 1938), pp. 10-11.

Stronks, James B., "William Dean Howells, Ed Howe, and *The Story of a Country Town,*" *American Literature,* XXIX, No. 4 (January, 1958), pp. 473-478.

"Tearing the Mask of Hypocrisy from American Morals," *Current Opinion,* LXIII (December, 1917), pp. 403-404.

"They Stand Out from the Crowd," *Literary Digest,* CXVII (January 20, 1934), p. 9.

Van Doren, Carl, "Prudence Militant: E. W. Howe, Village Sage," *Century,* LXXXIV (May, 1923), pp. 151-156.

Van Doren, Mark, "The Sage of Sensibility," *Nation,* CXXVIII (April 17, 1929), p. 480.

Ward, John William, "Afterword," in E. W. Howe, *The Story of a Country Town* (New York: Signet, 1964), pp. 299-309.

Webster, Mary Angell, "An Interview with Ed Howe," *I Cover the Bookfront,* II, No. 9 (May, 1935).

White, William Allen, "Mr. Howe's New Novel," *University Review,* X, No. 4 (University of Kansas: December, 1888), pp. 111-113.

Wilson, Hill P. (ed.), "Edgar Watson Howe," *Eminent Men of the State of Kansas* (Topeka: Hall Lithographing Co., 1901), p. 125.

Wood, D. J., "Recollections of Ed W. Howe," *Nebraska History Magazine,* XVIII, No. 2 (April-June, 1937), p. 144.

So much has been written about Kansas that it is difficult to select what is most appropriate. However, it seemed advisable to obtain some pictures of what the state and the town of Atchison were like in the late nineteenth century. Always worth another look is Carl Becker's essay "Kansas," reprinted from *Turner Essays in American History* (New York: Henry Holt and Company, 1910), pp. 85-111. John Ise's *Sod and Stubble* (New York: Wilson-Erickson, 1936) is a moving portrayal of pioneer days. The American

Folkways Series contributed William B. Bracke's *Wheat Country* (New York: Duell, Sloan & Pearce, 1950), and the Rivers of America Series Floyd Benjamin Streeter's *The Kaw* (New York: Farrar & Rinehart, 1941). These are perceptive studies of the state. Other works I consulted:

Atchison Centennial, 1854-1954, A Historic Album of Atchison, Kansas (Atchison: Lockwood Company, 1954).

Bright, John D. (ed.), *Kansas, the First Century* (New York: Lewis Historical Publishing Co., 1956).

Clugston, W. G., *Facts You Should Know About Kansas* (Girard, Kan.: Haldeman-Julius Publishing Co., 1945).

Connelley, William E., *History of Kansas Newspapers* (Topeka: Kansas State Historical Society, 1916).

Directory of the City of Atchison, Atchison County, Kansas, for 1884 (Atchison: Haskell & Son., 1884).

Federal Writers Project, *Kansas: A Guide to the Sunflower State,* American Guide Series (New York: Viking Press, 1939).

Fourteenth City Directory of the City of Atchison for 1893-4 (Atchison: Home Printing Co., 1894).

Genealogical and Biographical Record of North-Eastern Kansas (Chicago: Lewis Publishing Co., 1900).

How and Where to Get a Living: A Sketch of "The Garden of the West" (Boston: Atchison, Topeka & Santa Fe, 1876).

Howes, Charles C., *This Place Called Kansas* (Norman: University of Oklahoma Press, 1952).

Ingalls, Sheffield, *History of Atchison County, Kansas* (Lawrence: Standard Publishing Co., 1916).

Isely, Elise Dubach, as told to Bliss Isely, *Sunbonnet Days* (Caldwell, Idaho: Caxton Printers, 1935).

Kansas in 1875: Strong and Impartial Testimony to the Wonderful Productiveness of the Cottonwood and Arkansas Valleys (Topeka: Atchison, Topeka & Santa Fe, 1875).

McNeal, T. A., *When Kansas Was Young* (New York: Macmillan, 1922).

Malin, James C., "The Democratic Party and Atchison: A Case Study, 1880," *Kansas Historical Quarterly,* XXVIII (Summer, 1962), pp. 154-166.

Prentis, Noble L., *A History of Kansas* (Winfield, Kan.: E. P. Greer, 1899).

Whittemore, Margaret, *Historic Kansas: A Centenary Sketchbook* (Lawrence: University of Kansas Press, 1954).

The last category is those books which told me things about Edgar Watson Howe, about the America in which he lived, and about the journalistic and literary worlds in which he achieved, at least in his time, considerable recognition. It is almost a platitude even to list some of these books, some of which I have leaned on for almost all historical research I have ever attempted. So I merely list them, placing the significant alongside the relatively trivial, but recognizing that those most valuable in this book on Ed Howe have been mentioned in the text or have been cited in the footnotes.

The other works:

Abbot, Willis J., *Watching the World Go By* (Boston: Little, Brown, 1934).

Allen, Frederick Lewis, *Only Yesterday* (New York: Bantam, 1959).

Atherton, Lewis, *Main Street on the Middle Border* (Bloomington: Indiana University Press, 1954).

Banta, R. E. (ed.), *Indiana Authors and Their Books 1816-1916* (Crawfordsville, Ind.: Wabash College, 1949).

Bartow, Edith Merwin, *News and These United States* (New York: Funk & Wagnalls, 1952).

Beard, Charles A. and Mary R., *The American Spirit* (New York: Macmillan, 1942).

————, *A Basic History of the United States* (New York: New Home Library, 1944).

————, *The Rise of American Civilization* (New York: Macmillan, 1937, rev. ed.).

Beer, Thomas, *The Mauve Decade* (New York: Vintage, 1960).

Bird, George L., and Merwin, Frederic E. (eds.), *The Press and Society* (New York: Prentice-Hall, 1951).

Blake, Nelson Manfred, *A Short History of American Life* (New York: McGraw-Hill, 1952).

Bleyer, Willard G., *Main Currents in the History of American Journalism* (Boston: Houghton Mifflin Company, 1927).

Boynton, Percy H., *Literature and American Life* (Boston: Ginn and Company, 1936).

————, *The Rediscovery of the Frontier* (Chicago: University of Chicago Press, 1931).

Brooks, Van Wyck, *The Confident Years: 1885-1915* (New York: E. P. Dutton, 1952).

Bryce, James, *The American Commonwealth* (New York: Macmillan, 1914), II.

Buck, Solon J., *The Agrarian Crusade* (New Haven: Yale University Press, 1920).

Burlingame, Roger, *The American Conscience* (New York: Knopf, 1957).

Callahan, James D., *Jayhawk Editor* (Los Angeles: Sterling Press, 1955).

Cargill, Oscar, *Intellectual America: Ideas on the March* (New York: Macmillan, 1941).

Clugston, W. G., *Rascals in Democracy* (New York: Richard R. Smith, 1940).

Cochran, Thomas C., and Miller, William, *The Age of Enterprise* (New York: Harper Torchbooks, 1961, rev. ed.).

Commager, Henry Steele, *The American Mind: An Interpretation of American Thought and Character Since the 1880's* (New Haven: Yale University Press, 1950).

Curti, Merle, *The Growth of American Thought* (New York: Harper, 1951, 2nd ed.).

Dick, Everett, *The Sod-House Frontier, 1854-1890* (Lincoln: Johnsen Publishing Co., 1954).

Dondore, Dorothy Anne, *The Prairie and the Making of Middle America: Four Centuries of Description* (Cedar Rapids, Iowa: Torch Press, 1926).

Emery, Edwin, *The Press and America* (Englewood Cliffs, N. J.: Prentice-Hall, 1962, 2nd ed.).

Flanagan, John T. (ed.), *America Is West* (Minneapolis: University of Minnesota Press, 1945).

Ford, Edwin H., and Emery, Edwin (eds.), *Highlights in the History of the American Press* (Minneapolis: University of Minnesota Press, 1945).

Furnas, J. C., *The Life and Times of the Late Demon Rum* (New York: G. P. Putnam's Sons, 1965).

Gabriel, Ralph Henry, *The Course of American Democratic Thought* (New York: Ronald Press, 1940).

Garland, Hamlin, *Crumbling Idols* (Gainesville, Fla.: Scholars' Facsimiles and Reprints, 1952 ed.).

————, *Roadside Meetings* (New York: Macmillan, 1930).

Ginger, Ray, *Age of Excess* (New York: Macmillan, 1965).

Goldman, Eric F., *Rendezvous with Destiny* (New York: Vintage, 1956).

Greene, Theodore P. (ed.), *American Imperialism in 1898,* Problems in American Civilization (Boston: D. C. Heath, 1955).

Greenway, John, *The Inevitable Americans* (New York: Knopf, 1964).

Hacker, Louis M., *The Triumph of American Capitalism* (New York: Columbia University Press, 1940).

Hart, James D., *The Popular Book* (New York: Oxford University Press, 1950).

Hazard, Lucy Lockwood, *The Frontier in American Literature* (New York: Thomas Y. Crowell Company, 1927).

Hendrick, Burton J., *The Age of Big Business* (New Haven: Yale University Press, 1919).

Herron, Ima Honaker, *The Small Town in American Literature* (Durham, N.C.: Duke University Press, 1939).

Hicks, John D., *The American Nation* (Boston: Houghton Mifflin, 1945).

Hofstadter, Richard, *The Age of Reform* (New York: Vintage, 1960).

————, *The American Political Tradition* (New York: Vintage, 1948).

———— (ed.), *Great Issues in American History* (New York: Vintage, 1958), II.

————, *Social Darwinism in American Thought* (Boston: Beacon Press, rev. ed., 1955).

Howard, Leon, *Literature and the American Tradition* (Garden City, N.Y.; Doubleday and Company, 1960).

Howells, William Dean, *Criticism and Fiction* (New York: Harper, 1891).

————, *Imaginary Interviews* (New York: Harper, 1910).

————, *Literature and Life* (New York: Harper, 1902).

Hughes, Helen MacGill, *News and the Human Interest Story* (Chicago: University of Chicago Press, 1940).

Hutton, Graham, *Midwest at Noon* (Chicago: University of Chicago Press, 1946).

Ingalls, John James, *The Writings*

of John James Ingalls (Kansas City, Mo.: Hudson-Kimberly Publishing Co., 1902).

Kazin, Alfred, *On Native Grounds* (New York: Reynal & Hitchcock, 1942).

Kennedy, Gail (ed.), *Democracy and the Gospel of Wealth,* Problems in American Civilization (Boston: D. C. Heath, 1949).

————, *Evolution and Religion,* Problems in American Civilization (Boston: D. C. Heath, 1957).

————, *Pragmatism and American Culture,* Problems in American Civilization (Boston: D. C. Heath, 1950).

Koch, Adrienne, and Peden, William (eds.), *The Life and Selected Writings of Thomas Jefferson* (New York: Modern Library, 1944).

Lee, Alfred McClung, *The Daily Newspaper in America* (New York: Macmillan, 1937).

Lerner, Max, *America as a Civilization* (New York: Simon and Schuster, 1957).

Lewisohn, Ludwig, *The Story of American Literature* (New York: Harper, 1937).

Macy, John (ed.), *American Writers on American Literature* (New York: Horace Liveright, 1931).

Mahin, Helen Ogden (ed.), *The Editor and His People* (New York: Macmillan, 1924).

Mathiessen, F. O., *American Renaissance* (New York: Oxford University Press, 1941).

Miller, Perry (ed.), *American Thought: Civil War to World War I* (New York: Rinehart & Co., 1954).

Morison, Samuel Eliot, *The Oxford History of the American People* (New York: Oxford University Press, 1965).

Mott, Frank Luther, *American Journalism, a History: 1690-1960* (New York: Macmillan, 1962, 3rd ed.).

————, *Golden Multitudes* (New York: Macmillan, 1947).

Mott, Frank Luther, and Casey, Ralph D. (eds.), *Interpretations of Journalism* (New York: F. S. Crofts & Co., 1937).

Nevins, Allan, *The Emergence of Modern America, 1865-1878* (New York: Macmillan, 1927).

Nugent, Walter T. K., *The Tolerant Populists* (Chicago: University of Chicago Press, 1963).

Parrington, Vernon Louis, *Main Currents in American Thought* (New York: Harcourt, Brace and Company, 1927), III.

Perry, Ralph Barton, *Characteristically American* (New York: Knopf, 1949).

Quinn, Arthur Hobson, *American Fiction: An Historical and Critical Survey* (New York: D. Appleton-Century, 1936).

———— (ed.), *The Literature of the American People* (New York: Appleton-Century-Crofts, 1951).

Rienow, Robert and Leona Train, *Of Snuff, Sin and the Senate* (Chicago: Follett, 1965).

Saveth, Edward N., *Understanding the American Past* (Boston: Little, Brown, 1954).

Schlesinger, Arthur M., *The Rise of the City, 1878-1898* (New York: Macmillan, 1933).

Shannon, Fred A., *The Farmer's Last Frontier* (New York: Farrar & Rinehart, 1945).

Smith, Henry Nash, *Virgin Land: The American West As Symbol and Myth* (New York: Vintage, 1957).

————, "The Western Farmer in Imaginative Literature, 1818-1891," *Mississippi Valley Historical Review,* XXXVI (December, 1949), pp. 479-490.

Spiller, Robert E., *et al., Literary History of the United States* (New York: Macmillan, 1948), II.

Steffens, Lincoln, *The Autobiography of Lincoln Steffens* (New York: Grosset & Dunlap, 1931).

Tarbell, Ida M., *The Nationalizing of Business, 1878-1898* (New York: Macmillan, 1936).

Taylor, George Rogers, *The Turner Thesis,* Problems in American Civilization (Boston: D. C. Heath, 1949).

Tebbel, John, *The Compact History of the American Newspaper* (New York: Hawthorn, 1963).

Van Doren, Carl, *The American Novel* (New York: Macmillan, 1921).

Van Doren, Carl and Mark, *American and British Literature Since 1890* (New York: Century Co., 1925).

Villard, Oswald Garrison, *The Disappearing Daily* (New York: Knopf, 1944).

Wagenknecht, Edward, *Cavalcade of the American Novel* (New York: Henry Holt and Company, 1952).

Webb, Walter Prescott, *The Great Plains* (New York: Grossett & Dunlap, 1931).

Weinberg, Arthur and Lila (eds.), *The Muckrakers* (New York: Capricorn, 1964).

Weisberger, Bernard A., *The American Newspaperman* (Chicago: University of Chicago Press, 1961).

Whicher, George F., *William Jennings Bryan and the Campaign of 1896*, Problems in American Civilization (Boston: D. C. Heath, 1953).

White, William Allen, *Autobiography* (New York: Macmillan, 1946).

Wish, Harvey, *Society and Thought in Modern America* (New York: Longmans, Green and Co., 1952).

Woodward, W. E., *A New American History* (New York: Farrar & Rinehart, 1936).

Index

This book was designed by Fritz Reiber. The text was set in 10 pt. Linotype Baskerville, headings in 30 pt. Monotype Figaro. It was printed by the University of Kansas Printing Service and bound by the State Printer.